THE
NORTHWEST FLORIDA
EXPEDITIONS
of Clarence Bloomfield Moore

Classics in Southeastern Archaeology

Stephen Williams, Series Editor

Publication of this work has been supported in part by grants
and donations from the following agencies and institutions.

Southeastern Archaeological Conference
The Florida Anthropological Society
The Florida Archaeological Council
The Seminole Tribe of Florida
Panamerican Consultants, Inc.
Dan Josselyn Memorial Fund

THE
NORTHWEST FLORIDA
EXPEDITIONS

of Clarence Bloomfield Moore

Edited and with an Introduction by
DAVID S. BROSE and NANCY MARIE WHITE

The University of Alabama Press
Tuscaloosa and London

Copyright © 1999
The University of Alabama Press
Tuscaloosa, Alabama 35487-0380
All rights reserved
Manufactured in the United States of America
1 2 3 4 5 • 03 02 01 00 99

The works by Clarence B. Moore reproduced in this volume were published
originally in 1901, 1902, 1903, 1907, and 1918.

∞

The paper on which this book is printed meets the minimum requirements of
American National Standard for Information Science-Permanence of Paper
for Printed Library Materials, ANSI Z39.48-1984.

Library of Congress Cataloging-in-Publication Data

Moore, Clarence Bloomfield.
    The northwest Florida expeditions of Clarence Bloomfield Moore /
edited and with an introduction by David S. Brose and Nancy Marie
White.
        p.   cm. — (Classics in southeastern archaeology)
    Includes bibliographical references and index.
    ISBN 0-8173-0992-6 (pbk. : alk. paper)
    1. Indians of North America—Florida—Gulf Coast—Antiquities. 2.
Indians of North America—Florida—Apalachicola River Valley—Antiqui-
ties. 3. Moore, Clarence Bloomfield—Journeys—Florida—Gulf Coast. 4.
Moore, Clarence Bloomfield—Journeys—Florida—Apalachicola River
Valley. 5. Archaeological expeditions—Florida—Gulf Coast. 6. Archaeo-
logical expeditions—Florida—Apalachicola River Valley. 7. Excavations
(Archaeology)—Florida—Gulf Coast. 8. Excavations (Archaeology)—
Florida—Apalachicola River Valley. 9. Gulf Coast (Fla.)—Antiquities. 10.
Apalachicola River Valley (Fla.)—Antiquities. I. Brose, David S. II. White,
Nancy Marie. III. Series.
E78.F6 N67 1999
975.9'01—dc21   99-6364

British Library Cataloguing-in-Publication Data available

Contents

Preface and Acknowledgments

All southeastern archaeologists know the great value of the archaeological reports of Clarence Bloomfield Moore. Moore's work in the region of northwest Florida was written up between 1901 and 1918 and was the first widely disseminated report of the artifacts and mortuary patterns of what are today recognized as the Deptford, Santa Rosa–Swift Creek, Weeden Island, and Fort Walton–Pensacola complexes. His papers were thus of great interest to those curious about the arts or culture of Florida's early inhabitants. Moore's papers have been long out of print, however, and their detailed contents and interpretative insights are seldom fully recaptured in many overviews of Florida archaeology now available. In our own work across portions of this region, we carried dirt-stained, dog-eared copies of these indispensable papers into the field. Here, reprinted in facsimile for the first time, are all five of Moore's papers on the archaeology of the northwest Florida region. We know they will be welcomed.

With our own experience as guide, we have cautiously tried to add to this reprinting some of the broader concepts that we would have found valuable. We hope that our introduction will offer the reader a critical context in which Moore's reports might be more usefully read. We have tried to avoid becoming mired in interesting but relatively less important details such as the *Gopher*'s sailing characteristics or Moore's personal relationships, choosing rather to illuminate his archaeology in terms of what he was trying to do and the degree to which he succeeded. We have also tried to provide for the reader a sense of what the archaeologists who followed him have made of Moore's work and of the sites he visited.

Moore's reports on his five seasons of work in northwest Florida (Figure 1) span nearly a generation and are separated by, and occasionally incorporate references to, reports he wrote on other regions of the South. Indeed, some of his summary comments can be fully understood only by reference to expeditions Moore undertook outside the region during the years that separate the explorations. The five papers reprinted here are as Moore prepared them for publication. Because these *Classics in Southeastern Archaeology* will be reprinted by the University of Alabama Press on a regional basis, there will be overlaps where Moore recorded a few sites in larger reports of other regions or states.

Materials that Moore reported on in *Certain Aboriginal Remains of the Northwest Florida Coast, Part I* that concern Alabama sites (1901:423–433) are also included and critically discussed in *The South and Central Alabama Expeditions of Clarence Bloomfield Moore,* edited and with an introduction by Craig T. Sheldon

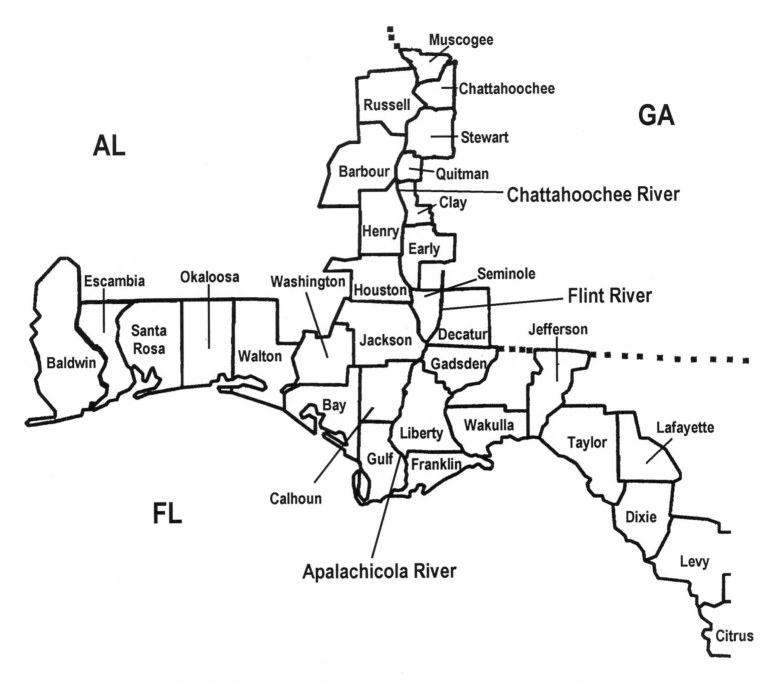

Figure 1. Counties of northwest Florida, south Georgia, and south Alabama where Moore's sites are located.

(2000). Nonetheless, that material is also included here, reflecting Moore's disregard for state boundaries. In *Certain Aboriginal Remains of the Northwest Florida Coast, Part II* are Moore's reports (1902:348ff) of sites farther south along Florida's west coast, especially the Crystal River site. These are also included and critically discussed in *The West and Central Florida Expeditions of Clarence Bloomfield Moore*, edited and with an introduction by Jeffrey M. Mitchem (1999), but we include them here because in those sections Moore integrates the discussion into his conclusions, and we thought it would be too confusing if we deleted it. *Certain Aboriginal Mounds of the Apalachicola River* (Moore 1903:439–492), concerning only northwest Florida sites and materials, is reprinted only in this volume. *Mounds of the Lower Chattahoochee and Lower Flint Rivers* (Moore 1907) reports on Moore's excavations along both sides of both rivers at once, including sites in Florida, Georgia, and Alabama. The Alabama site data (1907:438ff) also appear in the Sheldon volume. Finally, in Moore's *The Northwestern Florida Coast Revisited* (1918), both we and Sheldon reprint the Alabama site data (1918:528–530), and the Florida data from Levy and Citrus Counties (1918:568–574) also appear, with critical comment, in Mitchem's volume. The Arkansas and Louisiana materials (1918:574–577) were reprinted and discussed in *The Lower Mississippi Valley Expeditions of Clarence Bloomfield Moore,* edited and with an introduction by Dan F. Morse and Phyllis A. Morse (1998), and covered the balance of Moore's investigations in that area.

As editors for these papers, we are grateful to our many colleagues across the country whose knowledge and understanding have been made so unstintingly available to both of us. For assistance in assembling modern site information we thank many, especially the Florida Site File and archaeologist Charly Branham; Terry Simpson, who compiled a database of more than one thousand sites for the Apalachicola/Lower Chattahoochee Valley (Simpson 1996); Frank Schnell of the Columbus Museum in Georgia; archaeologists at the University of West Florida; and colleagues in agencies, companies, universities, and the site files in Georgia, Alabama, Louisiana, and Arkansas. Special thanks are due to Gordon Willey, Stephen Williams, David Phelps, George Percy, and Jim Miller for sharing much insight and many personal reminiscences, only some of which could be used here. Of course, we alone are responsible for the opinions expressed here, and we regret any errors we may have made in presenting the data so freely made available to us.

Our gratitude must also be noted for three institutions whose willingness to respond to our many inquiries was truly selfless: the Huntington Library in New York, the National Anthropological Archives of the Smithsonian Institution, and the Florida Division of Historical Resources (formerly the Division of Archives, History and Records Management) in Tallahassee. Both of us (Brose in 1978 and White in 1986) visited Moore's collections and are grateful to those in the Collections Department at the Museum of the American Indian and at the library in New York (especially Mary Davis). Finally, we wish to acknowledge the encouragement, guidance, and patience exhibited by Judith Knight of the University of Alabama Press. Her vision and dedication exceed a diligence and scope that even Moore would have envied.

Introduction
Clarence B. Moore's
Work in Northwest Florida, 1901–1918

David S. Brose and Nancy Marie White

With the cessation of the Seminole wars of the 1840s, antiquarian curiosity drew various naturalists, military, and civil officials to west Florida, including Henry Schoolcraft, who used the early Jesuit reports of Native American ritual to interpret materials dug from mounds at Apalachicola (1854). For the later nineteenth century, the best overview of the semiprofessional archaeology of northwest Florida before Moore is presented by Willey (1949:15–21).

Stage Setting for a History of Regional Archaeology

Willey lists the various government ethnologists, such as Daniel Brinton, Charles Rau, and S. T. Walker, who wrote occasional reports on their mound excavations in the 1870s and 1880s. In the late 1880s, John Rogan, sometime Smithsonian Institution field investigator, dug two mounds at the mouth of the Aucilla River and probed into the Mercier Place [Kolomoki] Mound group well up the Chattahoochee River. The former of these projects received brief notice in Thomas's massive mound exploration report, which accompanied the *Twelfth Annual Report of the Bureau of Ethnology* (Thomas 1894).

Just as the senior author was starting in Florida archaeology, James B. Griffin gave him useful introductions, seemingly simple questions (some of which we cannot yet answer), and offprints of Moore's *American Naturalist* articles on Tick Island and Mulberry mound (Moore 1893a, 1893b) bearing Cyrus Thomas's penciled autograph. Thomas was aware of Moore's work, however little it may have influenced his own larger project (for Florida, Thomas discusses only the mollusks the prehistoric builders of two small mounds used and/or ate [1894:327, 333]). Nevertheless, we believe that what Thomas tried and succeeded in doing would have a profound impact on what Moore would try and would do.

In his introduction to the Smithsonian reprint of Thomas's volume, Bruce Smith (1985:14–16) approvingly noted that for him, as for other modern academic synthesizers, Thomas's work represented both the end to nineteenth-century antiquarianism and the beginning of large-scale, systematic, problem-oriented "20th century" archaeological research. More germane, however, as Thomas himself noted (1894:20), was the mound exploration project's demonstration that questions relating to prehistoric America were not to be answered by the study of its ancient monuments alone but also would need to involve study of the languages, customs, arts, beliefs, traditions, and folklore of the Native Americans. And yet, by Thomas's own admission, should his vast project demonstrate that the builders of the mounds were indeed "Indians" (1894:21), future archaeological investigations would be bound within more narrow and less speculative horizons than it had hitherto enjoyed.

Willey and Sabloff noted the success of Thomas's enterprise as systematic research pointing to an integration of ethnography, physical anthropology, and archaeology, which made American anthropology renowned. Yet, ironically, they asserted that Thomas's success was responsible for "helping to retard certain developments in the archaeology of the Eastern United States and in North American archaeology in general" (1974:49). Their only explanation (Willey and Sabloff 1974:86) was the complaint that for too long twentieth-century American archaeology failed to study cultural evolution in all time periods due to its reluctance to take the entire world as its subject and its refusal to abandon the study of historical linkages such as Thomas had demonstrated. Willey and Sabloff also chided Thomas for failing to change popular nineteenth-century attitudes about living American Indians, a charge few archaeologists could escape today.

Enter C. B. Moore: Stage Left

Introducing Moore's Moundville reports, understandably the first of these University of Alabama Press reissues, Jim Knight (1996) provided a précis of Moore's life, work, and archaeological influence. Born to enough wealth to do whatever he wished, Moore had no wife or heirs and had the position, education, and inclination for self-direction. After journeying the world for six years, during many of which he was not well, he found his avocation exploring the coasts and rivers of the southern United States to illuminate the aesthetics of the past.

We can answer few of the questions that might interest those who see today's world as postmodern. We know Moore traveled with a companion, Dr. Milo Miller, who did skeletal identifications, and with Captain J. S. Raybon, who piloted the *Gopher* and often scouted ahead to locate sites (Wardle 1956). Moore did some digging himself and took extensive notes and recopied and edited them for rapid publication. (In the Huntington Free Library there are, however, notes in the handwriting of at least two different people.) Whether there were any women on his boat or in his life we do not know, nor do we know the crew size. Newspaper accounts of the day (Mitchem 1999) indicate that Moore did hire local help, including African-American laborers, to do most of the heavy work. It is unknown who supervised them and whether any of his field crew accompanied him from place to place or from year to year. Nonetheless, we do know that, in those ways we can reconstruct, Moore's behavior mirrored that of other ardent amateurs in the arts and sciences who would certainly have considered themselves members of the same established ("affluent") and properly educated class. These ad libitum scholars would have been equally reluctant to introduce details of their personal lives into the contributions they made to their adopted professions. Yet, like all art and science, archaeology is a product of its intellectual climate, and the hopeful tone of Moore's early and highly productive expeditions to northwest Florida corresponds with those years when enlightened and progressive Anglo-American empires seemed poised to rule the world for the good of all. Equally worth consideration is the sense of loss and the ennui characterizing the views of many educated "gentlemen" following the Great War for Civilization and the epidemics of 1917–1918, a sense of futility that seems reflected in Moore's report of his last archaeological return to northwest Florida.

Although Moore may have visited Florida as early as 1873 (Mitchem 1999), it was not until 1891 when, following lightly in the footsteps of other Harvard scholars, he plunged into the careful excavation of sand mounds and shell middens along the coast and the lower rivers flowing to the bays and estuaries of northern Florida, Georgia, and South Carolina (Stoltman 1973). Milanich and Fairbanks (1980:3) referred to Moore as "this energetic man," adding that although it was easy to be critical in hindsight, Moore did dig carefully, kept respectable notes, and observed astutely. They also noted that he showed a decided preference for burial mounds containing elaborate grave goods. As early as 1894, W. H. Holmes had reviewed the materials from Moore's eastern Florida excavations, and his slightly negative comments seem to have set a direction for Moore that would endure for nearly a quarter century:

> Exploration has not yet gone far enough on the peninsula of Florida to give archaeologists a firm grasp on the problems of its prehistoric art. The general nature and range of the remains are pretty well understood, as they form no marked exception to the rule in this latitude, but *little has been done in the study of those details that must be relied upon to assist in assigning the art remains to particular tribes and stocks of people, in correlating them with culture features of neighboring regions and determining questions of chronology* [Holmes 1894:105; emphasis added].

Willey (1949:22) was almost certainly correct in recognizing the major stimulus toward Gulf Coast Florida mounds that F. H. Cushing's excavations around Tarpon Springs and then at Key Marco in 1895 and 1896 may have represented to Moore. Also, Brose (1980) has drawn attention to Captain C. C. Riggs, a contemporary of Moore's, who as early as 1892 had promoted a life of seasonal riverboat mound exploration and prehistoric pottery collecting, free from academic constraint. With Riggs's widely publicized exhibition and sale of artifacts at Wanamaker's New York store in the fall of 1896, Moore could hardly fail to have been aware of Riggs's program of archaeology as capitalist [ad]venture, just when Moore's own work was attracting slightly negative academic attention. Following the 1893 Columbian Exposition, both Moore and Riggs were corresponding with W. H. Holmes, whose knowledge of aboriginal ceramics grew with their interest. Riggs sought and received premarket authentication from the Smithsonian's emerging expert. And both Riggs and Moore were sending ceramics to the Buffalo Historical Society, which was, at the same time, debating whether or not to purchase Riggs's collection; the debate was resolved by purchase in 1908 (Brose 1980). Quite unlike Riggs, Moore is not known ever to have sold artifacts, though he certainly gave many away. His extensive correspondence and widespread gifts to public education institutions were generous contributions in the spirit of the dedicated amateur he consciously exemplified. Nevertheless, as has been noted (Stoltman 1973; Brose 1980), with northwest Florida, Moore's technical and descriptive quality seems to decline in rather direct relationship to the number of mounds excavated and the quantity of pottery recovered each season.

As befitted a gentleman scholar, Moore was eminently well read. His citations reveal knowledge of most current archaeological work in the areas to which he would travel. That makes even more curious his failure to acknowledge even the existence of Cyrus Thomas's (1894) report of the mound exploration program as the paper accompanying the *Twelfth Annual Report of the Bureau of Ethnology*. Judging from Moore's subsequent reports, this publication of what was perhaps the most significant archaeological document prior to his own Florida sojourns seems to have been a significant event in Moore's intellectual development, closing forever that speculative door that had once opened wide on vistas of lost tribes and sunken continents (as Robert Wauchope put it in 1957). So, too, the very thoroughness of Holmes's 1903 report on prehistoric pottery of the eastern United States may well have closed for Moore that other door that Holmes had opened a decade earlier in his 1894 review of Moore, which had perhaps offered to Moore the chance to illuminate all hidden mysteries of the past that could be elucidated by study of the craft of aboriginal southeastern potters.

Moore's Northwest Florida Itineraries

In 1900, having turned his attention to the west coast of peninsular Florida and after sailing the waters of Mobile Bay (Sheldon 2000), Moore began the first of what would be five expeditions to the northwest Florida region. As in the past, Captain Raybon of the *Gopher* had spent the prior season surveying likely sites and searching out local owners' names so that Moore himself could secure permission to dig. Dr. Miller again accompanied Moore to provide what we today call basic skeletal demography.

Moore began his exploration of the west Florida coast in a season lasting over four months and stretching from the Bear Point site, jutting into Perdido Bay at the Alabama border (Sheldon 2000), to a point just west of St. Andrews Bay in Florida, a distance along the coast of about 115 miles. His proclaimed strategy was to use pottery to trace prehistoric cultural influences and connections across the South (Moore 1901:421), much as W. H. Holmes had suggested in 1894. Through his contacts with Holmes, Moore (1901:422) had seen Sternberg's materials, and he believed that Sternberg and Walker had missed the great caches of human and animal ceramic effigies that were likely to be still within the mounds at Bear Point and Walton's Camp (Fort Walton temple mound; see Figure 2), which Moore sensed to be a significant research consideration. Moore related the history of the 1528 Narvaez expedition chronicled by Cabeza de Vaca. He used it when his excavations at Bear Point yielded burnished black Pensacola wares decorated with Southern Cult (Southeastern Ceremonial Complex) motifs and associated with sixteenth-century Spanish material; this pottery was to be one of Moore's more certain horizon markers to which he referred much of the region's materials.

At the Fort Walton temple mound Moore depicted the stratigraphic evidence for multiphased constructions, only the latest of which resembled the aboriginal pottery from Bear Point. He also commented on the differential distributions of ceramic techniques (1901:439), which would later lead Sears (1954, 1977) to rediscover a "sacred-secular dichotomy." At Hogtown Bayou and the Point Washington Cemetery, Moore first documented the late Fort Walton urn burial complex (1901:469ff) and placed it as pre-European. His first foray into the region concluded

Figure 2. Summit of Fort Walton Temple Mound, 8Ok6, showing reconstructed temple with imitation thatched roof (of textured concrete) and carved wooden birds on poles extending up from roof. Inside the structure are exhibits connected with the adjacent Indian Temple Mound Museum run by the City of Fort Walton Beach, Florida. (Photo by Nancy White)

by speculating on the south Appalachian origins of complicated stamping, the prevalence of small check-stamping, and the likely Florida origin of "killed" pottery (1901:496). He had also recognized more westerly (Mississippian) forms and decorative styles made on pastes that were not shell-tempered. The cultural significance of this Fort Walton ceramic characteristic is still being explored, and Moore's consideration of a northern, rather than southern, cultural relationship remains moot (Brose and Percy 1978).

Moore complained, with no trace of irony, about those who had first dug into many of the mounds to sell the artifacts they could recover. Although never a merchant of recovered artifacts, Moore was a distributor of them. Perhaps the more admirable differences between him and those less affluent looters he castigated should be sought in his level of record keeping, his interest in physical analyses, and his rapid publication in the scientifically respected journal published by the Philadelphia Academy of Natural Sciences, one of many eastern U.S. institutions with wealthy benefactors of culture and natural history (Patterson 1995:44).

In 1902 Moore returned to complete his planned explorations of the northwest Florida coast, spending four months traveling eastward from St. Andrews Bay around the Apalachicola delta, then east to Cedar Keys and south to Tampa Bay. By comparison with the western panhandle, Moore knew of no previous scientific work in these more easterly areas. Among the more important of the sixty-eight mounds and aboriginal cemeteries he excavated were the mounds at Alligator Bayou, Sowell,

Hare Hammock, Pierce, Huckleberry Landing, Porter's Bar, Green Point, Yent, and the Tucker and Mound Field sites.

In his 1901 paper Moore had assiduously noted to which institution he had given the ceramics excavated from each northwest Florida site. In 1902 and thereafter, he did not do so. Although his notes show he gave away many items to landowners and friends, most of his collection would be given to the Philadelphia Academy (later to be purchased by the Heye Foundation) or to one of several other highly reputable public institutions. There are probably many Moore items undocumented in various collections. Research by University of South Florida archaeologists has located materials from Apalachicola in the British Museum; these may be from the large Pierce mounds group that Moore dug.

At the West Bay Post Office and Burnt Mill Creek mounds (1902:142ff) Moore first encountered the Middle Woodland early Weeden Island cutout pedestal and effigy vessels that he initially called "freak vessels" (1902:353) but later consistently described as "openwork." These were to enthrall him. At Alligator Bayou he described the first of what would be several caches of exotic materials as mound deposits (1902:150). He noted many others along this stretch of the coast, culminating at the Pierce mounds, where he discussed the Ohio Hopewell-like nature of these materials (1902:224) and related some specific items to similar materials from the Crystal River site, farther down the Florida Gulf Coast. (Moore later was to point out items from other northwest Florida sites, such as Huckleberry Landing, Yent, Green Point, Bird Hammock, Hall Mound, and Warrior River mounds, that connected them with Pierce and Crystal River.) He even employed geochemical analyses to determine the origin of the fireclay platform pipe he excavated from the mound at Green Point (1902:256).

From Cedar Key south to Tampa, the large mounds with grave goods played out, and Moore speculated on the inverse relationship they seemed to have with shell middens. He concluded by remarking that northeast and northwest Florida had similar ceramics but very different mortuary customs (1902:349–353). In all, Moore's second-year report completed what was a real pioneering venture, opening new vistas on different and distinctive ceramic traditions for anthropology to study (cf. Holmes 1902).

In the 1903 season, investigation of the largest river transecting northwest Florida took Moore more than 107 miles up the Apalachicola to its origin in the confluence of the Flint and Chattahoochee rivers. Moore had been told that this valley was rich in archaeological remains. Among the more interesting sites he dug were the multicomponent mound at the Chipola Cut-off (1903:446–466), which was later apparently destroyed by riverbank erosion; the Davis Field, Bristol, and Yon mounds; and the mound near Blountstown, which Moore mentioned he could not secure permission to dig (1903:468), thus sparing it to be noted as the Cayson Site (where the editors of this volume first practiced their Florida archaeology [Brose et al. 1976]). At the mound at Aspalaga Landing, nearly a kilometer from the river and on high bluffs, Moore (1903:480ff) noted the scattered cultural debris in the plowed fields surrounding it. Overall, Moore found the quality and diversity of artifacts from the interior river sites inferior to those from sites along the coast (1903:492).

Moore spent the 1904–1906 seasons at Moundville and in the Mobile Bay drainage basin (Knight 1996; Sheldon 2000) before returning to the Crystal River site (Mitchem 1999). He finished the 1906 field season by investigating the lower Chattahoochee and lower Flint rivers, publishing his results in 1907. This work took him more than another one hundred miles upriver from the confluence of the Chattahoochee and Flint, where the Apalachicola is created, into Georgia and Alabama. The Chattahoochee forms part of the Florida-Georgia border, then the Georgia-Alabama border for about 150 miles. As in former years, agents sent in advance gained him permission to dig at mound sites. There were few along the smaller Flint River (Moore 1907:427), but on the Chattahoochee he worked at Kemp's Landing, Shoemake's Landing, and near Fullmore's Upper Landing. He missed the Kolomoki mounds at what was then called the Mercier Place, and at the interesting Rood's Landing mound group, which Moore compared to Moundville (1907:448), the owners ran him off.

Moore noted that the (Weeden Island) openwork vessels, perforated or "killed" vessel bases, animal effigy forms, and pottery caches deposited on the east side of these inland mounds were similar to those of the coast. He wrote no conclusions, however, and unfortunately his documentation of many small mound sites where Weeden Island ceramics are associated with complicated-stamped Swift Creek ceramics has been generally ignored in most broader syntheses.

From 1907 to 1916 Moore was a freshwater sailor, roving the Mississippi River and its tributaries and investigating not only mounds but, increasingly, domestic sites, which he had disparaged throughout these west Florida volumes as mere domiciliary mounds or worse. By 1918, he had explored all the navigable rivers in the Southeast not likely to be iced up in winter (Moore 1918:515). Then, after an absence of a decade, he revisited the coast of northwest Florida to seek again the elusive openwork ceramic vessels that he first encountered at Burnt Mill Creek in 1901 and that he so frequently had found on the Apalachicola-Chattahoochee River system. Dredging had opened the mouth of the Choctawhatchee River to boats the size of the *Gopher,* and Moore looked for especial success because he believed that land clearing due to population growth would have exposed many more small mounds (he was sure he had gotten all the large ones!). He investigated the Choctawhatchee River and Bay for two months and then from autumn 1917 to spring 1918 retraced his earlier expedition to the Apalachicola, the Flint, and down the west coast to Crystal River. He was disappointed in the Choctawhatchee, with its low banks, low visibility, and unspectacular mounds, acknowledging that late winter floods had prevented investigation of many "low mounds and rises" (Moore 1981:517).

In the 1918 work Moore repeated his earlier observations on the consistency of east-side pottery deposits in northwest Florida mounds, as well as ceremonial "killing" of vessels before interment, to the extent that some had holes made in the bottom before firing (1918:516). Almost gleefully, he noted that general treasure seekers did not know about the east-side deposits and dug in the center of mounds, getting no benefit beyond outdoor exercise!

An unfortunate aspect of his 1918 work is the lack of a good map showing where the sites are. Judged by the earlier works, Moore's reporting standards had dropped considerably, for unknown reasons. He barely described most sites and did not give precise locations, an enormous handicap for all later work. A few sites he had visited and described earlier were revisited (and some of these [see Table 1] were given a different name in 1918!), but most were newly recorded sites. Although it is possible to relocate these sites with descriptions of boat landings and tax records showing 1918 landowners' names, this has seldom been done, and there is little modern information for many sites Moore reported in 1918.

Moore's conclusions to this paper (1918:496) are the most inconclusive of any he wrote. He noted the novelty of Fort Walton urn burials, that they were pre-European, and that their pottery displayed what we should today call Mississippian modes and motifs but that it was not shell-tempered. He stated that these ceramics co-occurred with complicated-stamped types (today called Lamar) similar to those in Georgia and South Carolina, although the Florida ceramics were never grog-tempered (one of Moore's few observational mistakes). Moore again noted that in northwest Florida small check-stamped ceramics were ubiquitous, and again he speculated that the practice of killing pottery had originated in Florida and had then spread across much of the Southeast. He had come full circle (cf. Moore 1918:496; Moore 1901:421).

Exit C. B. Moore: Stage Right

Although relatively little academic attention to the region's prehistory followed Moore's publications, the elaborate openwork pottery in the northwest Florida mounds, which drew him to the region several times, continued to attract archaeologists of every type. Moore's remained nearly the only archaeological information most people had for the region for two generations. W. H. Holmes (1914) repackaged his 1903 ceramic overview, transforming his ceramic style zones into culture areas everywhere but in Florida. Holmes's monumental study of aboriginal American pottery largely superseded all previous studies, thus somewhat isolating Florida archaeology, as represented by Moore's recovered ceramics, from significant involvement in the anthropological integration in the pre–World War II era of American prehistory.

During the 1920s a few southeastern states, such as Arkansas and Texas, initiated major archaeological surveys. A few federal archaeologists, such as Henry Collins and Matthew Stirling, worked their hometown mounds during vacations. J. W. Fewkes spent a dreary Washington winter excavating Weeden Island on Tampa Bay (Stoltman 1973). The depression era did bring WPA archaeologists back to some of Moore's Florida sites (Milanich 1994:9–11), but none visited the northwestern panhandle. As Midwestern anthropology began drawing the profession into a critical review of archaeological taxonomy, Emerson Greenman (1938), fresh from work on Hopewell mounds, looked at Moore's mounds to list traits they shared with those of Ohio (Brose 1979). Then, just before federal archaeology closed for the duration of World War II, Moore's sites in northwest Florida were revisited, and Moore's importance for southeastern archaeology was revived by Gordon Willey.

Gordon R. Willey and Clarence B. Moore Redux

In a personal reminiscence for Harvard's Peabody Museum, Gordon Willey described his 1936 introduction to eastern United States "mound area" prehistory. His

1940 Columbia graduate work with Richard Woodbury in Florida (Willey and Woodbury 1942), "a successful season of digging, classifying pottery and chronology building in a region where this had never been done before" (Willey 1998a:11) is given only half a paragraph, perhaps reflecting his later estimation of it as an initiation fee to be paid to be allowed to accompany Duncan Strong to Peru, where more important(?) archaeological issues could be addressed.

In his Peabody recollection, Willey (1998a:17) argued that the best American archaeologists of his generation really had been quite like those who later would call themselves processual and critical. He made no mention of the rest of his work through the 1940s, which resulted in his 1949 Smithsonian publication *Archaeology of the Florida Gulf Coast*. That major work remains one of the few instances in which many of Moore's sites in a particular region were systematically reexamined. In that work, Willey proposed to create a synthesis, integrating his cultural/chronological ceramic taxonomy with a smattering of physical anthropology and a critical review of earlier archaeology and ethnohistory in order to reconstruct the prehistory of Florida's Gulf Coast—a task he (and others) clearly felt he had accomplished (Willey 1949:1, 577–585). Perhaps Willey later saw his northwest Florida chronology-building field and laboratory work as a final graduate student project, an academic rite de passage of somewhat less intrinsic archaeological value (and cf. Willey 1989). For Willey (Ford and Willey 1941), the less exciting post-Pleistocene woodlands were filled with burial or temple mounds probably derivative of more complex cultures and containing pottery useful for tracing relationships in space and time (Brose 1985). That the prehistory of the eastern United States involved archaeological issues perceived to be of less critical importance seems a view Willey himself still politely reflects in his short prefatory contribution to the reprint of that 1949 volume (Willey 1998b). Thus in a profound way, the archaeology of northwest Florida may have been for Gordon R. Willey little more than what it was for Clarence B. Moore.

Clarence Bloomfield Moore Today

Clarence B. Moore was a contributing member of the American Anthropological Association, a corresponding reader of nearly all of the Smithsonian Institution's anthropologists and many of its zoologists and geologists, and even the employer of the highly respected Aleš Hrdlička as a physical anthropologist. In 1903 he published in the foremost professional journal a reasoned argument bolstered with ethnohistorical observations and chemical analyses on the native origin of some of the copper artifacts that he had encountered. In addition to his reports of mound or cemetery ceramics, Moore (1902:177) was among the first to describe other archaeological phenomena. He was aware of site formation processes, noting the effects of palmetto roots on pottery, and he included an occasional stratigraphic or plan drawing.

At the end of the nineteenth century, the academic milestones of eastern American archaeology were the works of Frederic Ward Putnam and Cyrus Thomas. Like those of another contemporary, Warren K. Moorehead, Moore's efforts could have been seen by some of his colleagues as following the great and comprehensive interpretive tradition (cf. Putnam 1886). However, we believe that, as with Moorehead, Moore's legacy rests predominantly on the descriptive side of field archaeology. In many cases, his notes on northwest Florida's culturally deformed human skulls, bison bone tools, and exotic raw materials provide, across a wide region, documentation impossible to acquire today.

As with many other areas where Moore worked, the sites he investigated in northwest Florida provided the only available knowledge when the first regional syntheses came to be written. For that reason, many ceramic types or archaeological complexes or cultures have been named after these sites. Later work has sometimes demonstrated that these "classic" expressions of a type or complex at the sites Moore investigated were rather poor or aberrant examples of their class. Yet any discussion of regional sociopolitical dynamics or economy or ceremonialism in northwest Florida must begin with Moore's data, for Moore visited among the more sensational sites in the region, and, despite his claims to have leveled mounds, there is often a lot left in them. Also, at many mound sites he reported, Moore did not note associated domestic deposits. Now located and tested at many sites, these deposits yield data on site function, subsistence, regional settlement, and ritual activities (though modern scholars seldom recover large numbers of whole pots).

Following Willey's (1949) work, such Florida archaeologists as John Goggin at Yale and the University of Florida and John Griffin, Charles Fairbanks, and Hale Smith at the Florida and National Park Services and Florida State University sought out and excavated at sites Moore had noted. Since the rekindling of processual or anthropological archaeology, many state and regional works have come to incorporate Moore's sites in their general models of prehistoric settlement, subsistence, and social patterns (Brose 1985; Milanich 1994; Milanich and Fairbanks 1980; Sears 1962; Walthall 1980; White 1985).

Opportunities to investigate further some sites from Moore's work came in the 1950s with the U.S. Army Corps of Engineers' creation of the Jim Woodruff Reservoir (later Lake Seminole) at the confluence of the Flint and Chattahoochee rivers. As the corps inundated thirty-three thousand acres and produced more than one hundred miles of new shoreline, the Smithsonian's River Basin Survey program paid Florida and Georgia archaeologists Ripley Bullen (1950, 1958), Carl Miller (n.d.), Joseph Caldwell (1978), and A. R. Kelly (1950) to relocate sites noted by Moore. Bullen (1958:331–332) could not find Moore's mound at Kemp's Landing in 1950 but easily found it in 1958 when the forest within the planned reservoir was cleared by bulldozers. Whereas Moore had noted only a few skull fragments, Bullen encountered a great deal of human bone scattered by machine clearing.

Farther upstream, survey and salvage by Hurt (1975), Huscher (1959a, 1959b), and DeJarnette (1975), in advance of construction of the Walter F. George and the Columbia (George W. Andrews) dams and reservoirs, relocated some of Moore's sites as well. Recent shoreline surveys have reevaluated these reservoir studies (Belovich et al. 1982; Knight and Mistovich 1984; White 1981), demonstrating that Moore and other archaeologists could indeed miss some big ones. The Cemochechobee mounds (Schnell, Knight, and Schnell 1981), just below the Walter F. George Dam, were not located until the 1970s.

On the Apalachicola River, some of Moore's sites were identified by Florida State University and Case Western Reserve University projects in the early 1970s (e.g., Brose et al. n.d., 1976; Percy and Jones 1976), and many of Moore's sites have been investigated by University of South Florida archaeological projects supported by historic preservation grants from the Florida Division of Historical Resources (Henefield and White 1986; White 1996a, 1996b, 1999). The University of West Florida has researched sites Moore reported in the Pensacola area. Numerous references to Moore's investigations and conclusions in Alabama, Georgia, and Florida occur in academic works and unpublished survey reports. (Table 1 lists references for individual sites Moore recorded.)

From the outset, studies attempting to interpret mound ritual and cultural interactions in northwest Florida refer to sites Moore first explored (Greenman 1938; Sears 1954, 1962, 1977; Willey 1945). Middle Woodland burial mound ceremonialism and settlement cannot be discussed without reference to Moore's work (Brose 1979; Brose and Percy 1974; Percy and Brose 1974; Smith 1979), and Moore's site data figure largely in interpretations of Fort Walton culture as well (Brose 1984; Brose and Percy 1978; Brose et al. 1976; Scarry 1984; White 1982).

The artifacts Moore unearthed are also a source of continuing research. Any careful reader of these papers will notice that materials Moore recovered were widely distributed. The major collection, deposited at the Academy of Natural Sciences in Philadelphia, was later bought by George Heye for his Museum of the American Indian in New York and is now in the Smithsonian's new Museum of the American Indian. Many of these artifacts need documentation; no thorough list or typological classifications, initiated long ago by Goggin, have been completed, and there have been few raw material or stylistic analyses since those by Moore himself.

The field notes and other documents Moore made while he was in northwest Florida remain full of promise, carefully curated in the archives of the Huntington Free Library in the Bronx, New York (Davis 1987). Anyone reading these archives learns to recognize Moore's handwriting, shorthand, and recording systems (in keeping with the role of well-traveled scholar Moore occasionally even scrawled a word or two in French) and to compare his initial notes with the published accounts of each site. There are only tiny discrepancies (for example, the mound in the Magnolia Cemetery in Apalachicola is described as 4 feet 9 inches high, whereas the published account says 5 feet) and a small amount of additional information in the notes, such as some unpublished burial descriptions or mentions of gifts of artifacts to landowners, friends, and colleagues. In sum, the northwest Florida legacy of Clarence B. Moore remains rich for further exploration. How long it will do so is debatable.

The sites listed in Table 1 should be examined and evaluated before they are all gone. Many sites Moore explored have remained unseen or unreported for nearly a century, for much of northwest Florida remains forested and underpopulated. With the pace of twenty-first-century development, this situation will not last. Moore had noted that the treasure hunting on the northwest coast was the worst he had seen in any part of Florida, but he thought the size of northwest Florida mounds partially protected them from the single digger (Moore 1902:128). Now many of these sites have been looted recently by well-organized groups with waterscreens and night-vision goggles. Other mounds, where regulations required professional investigation before construction, have received limited attention by investigators not familiar enough with the area's archaeology. Furthermore, nearly all of Florida's roads and developments are built on some fill "borrowed" from prehistoric sand mounds or shell middens. On the other hand, some contract project reports give details of Moore's previously lost sites, and many local residents have collected artifacts and graciously shared data with professionals, assisting both fieldwork and site preservation.

Chronology for Moore's Northwest Florida Sites

Although it is beyond the scope of this introduction to present a complete overview of the culture history of the northwest Florida region, Table 2 offers a brief chronology. Because Moore was interested in elaborate and beautiful artifacts, often of exotic raw materials, he quickly came to concentrate his investigations in northwest Florida on the mounds and cemeteries where such remains were interred with the dead. Some archaeological explanations of the Woodland and Mississippian ceramics and other items from these sites and how they fit into regional chronological syntheses may be helpful.

In northwest Florida Early and Middle Woodland Swift Creek complicated-stamped ceramics usually co-occur with either incised and punctated Santa Rosa ceramic types or with Weeden Island incised, punctated, cutout, and/or red-painted vessels, or with both (Brose 1979; Willey 1949). These co-occur in burial mounds and, as has been increasingly clear, also in domestic contexts, sometimes with plain and check-stamped ceramics. In the western panhandle, Santa Rosa rocker-stamped and other types similar to the Middle Woodland Porter types of Mobile Bay are more common than complicated-stamped types. From northern Louisiana across the Gulf Coastal Plain, Weeden Island–like incised, punctated, cutout, excised, and red-painted types occur farther east than do the complicated-stamped Swift Creek wares. This is also true moving southeast along the west Florida coast (e.g., Hutchinson et al. 1991; Milanich et al. 1997). Yet we do not know if the complicated-stamped types now showing up in dated pre-Weeden Island contexts along the Florida Gulf Coast are simply earlier or are also different in cultural attribution, as they are in Georgia. Later, elaborate Weeden Island Incised and Punctated ceramic types and the most intricate geometric complicated-stamped ceramic types decline in frequency, leaving check-stamped and simple incised types and fewer or no burial mounds by Late Woodland (late Weeden Island).

Spatial/temporal overlaps also exist in Mississippian adaptations in northwest Florida. Fort Walton, the regional Mississippian variant, is characterized by grit-tempered or sand-and-grit-tempered ceramics. Yet increasingly west of St. Andrews Bay, Pensacola series ceramics resembling many Fort Walton types are shell-tempered, similar to most Mississippian ceramics in the Southeast. There is evidence that this is a clinal shift with both geographic and temporal components in the southwest Alabama/northwest Florida area (Brose 1984; Brose and Percy 1978; White 1982). As Moore recognized, stylistically late Fort Walton ceramic assemblages adopt Lamar complicated-stamped wares similar to ancestral Lower Creek types from Georgia (Boyd, Smith and Griffin 1951; Scarry 1984; White 1982, 1996b). Nevertheless, Moore's Chipola Cutoff mound contained only Fort Walton pottery with Spanish metal and other European items, demonstrating how little is known of Florida west of Tallahassee during the protohistoric or the Mission period . . . and much of what is known begins (and some of what is known ends) with what Moore recorded.

Explanations for Site Names and Numbers

All of Moore's sites in these five papers are listed in Table 1, along with site numbers, current summary data, cultural components given in order of prominence in the deposits (not chronological order), and references. Blank spaces mean no data exist; question marks mean the characterization is uncertain. Other important site names are given below Moore's names, and less important names are provided in the comments column. Problems abound in trying to tabulate all Moore's sites today. We discuss below common inconsistencies in naming and numbering the sites.

Occasionally Moore had no separate entry or name for a site. For example, at the end of the discussion of three sites in Alabama that begins the 1901 volume, he notes extensive shell mounds at Inerarity Point on the Florida side of the bay, but describes them no further. Several counties where Moore worked split later into smaller counties with new names, as reflected in the site number prefixes. Numbers were first assigned to Moore's sites in Willey's 1949 synthesis or were provided later by lab workers who did no field checking. These numbers do not necessarily refer to the same site. For example, a midden near a mound Moore found would be given Moore's site name; thus the number would refer to both. As site numbering systems evolved, new county prefixes were used, but not always with the same numbers. Thus when Jackson County changed from J- to Ja, the number Ja1 was reserved for the most important site in the county, and the site originally given the number J-1 was assigned a new Ja number.

Sometimes a new number was assigned to just a part of the original Moore site or to any site in the general vicinity thought to have been visited by him. Sometimes Moore's description noted several mounds that were miles apart under the heading of a single name. For example, Mound near Graveyard Point (Moore 1901:435) was referred to by Willey (1949:205) as Graveyard Point and numbered Sa3. When the Florida Site File later came up with a new county abbreviation for Santa Rosa County and assigned the number SR3, they gave it the name Graveyard Point. In the same section of Moore's report on the site, he mentions in the second paragraph another mound two and one-half miles west of the first one. This second mound was assigned the number SR44 and named Graveyard Point Mound. Later investigators of this latter site (Thomas and Campbell 1993:369–372) give no name for it, classify it as a preceramic shell mound, and do not note the inconsistencies with Moore's report, which mentions nothing being recovered. There is not enough evidence to be sure this is the same mound that Moore investigated. Other problems arise when several of Moore's sites are seen to be part of one large site. For example, recent University of South Florida investigations suggest his Pierce mounds, as well as the Cemetery, Cool Spring, and Jackson mounds and the mound near Apalachicola, are all part of a single ceremonial complex of extensive duration (Figure 3).

Site names can be confusing; Moore might name a site after a river landing where he stopped his boat, but the site might have been quite a distance from the landing. Later archaeologists, finding prehistoric materials on the riverbank at that landing, may have used the same name for a different site. In other cases the name used for Moore's original site was also applied to a habitation area for those who

Figure 3. Small mound at farthest western end of the Pierce Mounds group, relocated by University of South Florida field school students after partial clearing in 1995; this may be Moore's Jackson Mound, numbered 8Fr15. (Photo by Nancy White)

built the mound or those who inhabited it a millennium later. Some sites have separate numbers for individual mounds and village areas of what may be a single complex site, further confusing the picture. Sometimes slight changes were made in Moore's site names when they were incorporated into site files and given numbers. Often the apostrophe and/or letter "s" are left off somebody's landing or bayou, or the words "mound near" are deleted by the later tabulators.

Problems similar to those in Florida are encountered in Alabama and Georgia, where succeeding investigators renumbered earlier sites (even some of their own for which numbers were already published) in inconsistent fashion (White 1981:23–29 passim). One site in Georgia near county borders was given six site numbers at different times, with three different county prefixes! State site files are improving, but none are perfect. Because few current site file managers were even born when official numbers were assigned and reassigned to Moore's sites, they cannot provide much clarifying information. Moreover, the typical investigator, hired to do a specific project, seldom has the opportunity to sort out the confusing historiography and meta-archaeology of a particular site.

Perhaps these caveats are overly precise; many of Moore's sites in Florida were originally plotted on USGS topographic quadrangle sheets with a large circle and the notation "GV," meaning general vicinity. In addition, sometimes Moore was way off in direction, estimated distance, mound content, and the degree of damage he or others had done to the various sites. Having gone on many wild mound chases in northwest Florida, we can say that many of these sites remain to be relocated, whereas some are undoubtedly gone forever: inundated, eroded into the river, or thoroughly leveled. Reviewing the Florida Site File information revealed discrepancies beyond this introduction to correct. Like future workers, readers should be aware that a great deal of field and archival checking is needed.

Unless a recent published reference exists (and even if it does in some cases), the state site files still have the most comprehensive data on the sites and are to be understood as the final arbiter for Table 1 data. Further investigations of any site should begin at the state site files where information is being compiled in electronic database and GIS formats. In the last column of Table 1, references given are the most important and/or latest source of data for investigations at the site. No attempt was made to find every article in which the site is discussed, though for some sites additional references clear up confused names or numbers.

Sites to Visit

With much of Florida's northern panhandle still forested, and few museums or universities in the region, archaeology education has only moderately affected the area. Looting continues as "Indian trading post" stores advertise artifact purchases and as sleepy fishing villages on the shores and barrier islands are bulldozed and transformed into copies of Miami Beach. Most coastal sites have been damaged or lost to development or storms (Figure 4), though many inland sites remain to be relocated. Upriver in the interior, one can still find something close to the nineteenth-century Florida Moore visited (see Figure 5, for example).

Only a few of Moore's sites are well preserved and also easily accessible to the interested traveler, but they are worth noting. More intrepid explorers can get landowners' permission and trek up waterways or through forests on logging or hunting roads, but for easy visiting on public lands, there are the following:

• Fort Walton temple mound, 8Ok6 (Figure 2), and adjacent museum run by the city of Fort Walton Beach, on U.S. Highway 98, forty miles east of Pensacola.

• Chattahoochee Landing mounds, 8Gd4 (Figure 6), on the west side of the town of Chattahoochee, Florida, in the park on the east bank of the Apalachicola River. From U.S. Highway 90 the road turns south just before the bridge over the river and leads right to Moore's temple mound next to the boat ramp, passing by another small mound that it has cut in half.

• Mound below Columbia, 1Ho27, at the Omussee Creek public use area on the Chattahoochee River not far from Columbia, Alabama.

• Fort Gaines Mound, 9Cla48, in a historic cemetery close to the Chattahoochee River in Fort Gaines, Georgia (the mound has a gazebo on top).

• Crystal River mounds, 8Ci1, state archaeological site and museum, north of the town of Crystal River, Florida, on road running west from U.S Highway 19, about one and one-half hours north of Tampa.

Figure 4. Eleven Mile Point site, 8Fr10, shell midden on shore of St. George Sound right after destruction suffered in fall of 1995 from Hurricane Opal (note risen sea level indicated by stumps in water). (Photo by Nancy White)

Figure 5. Yon Mound, 8Li2, view facing east-northeast, showing logging road cutting into northwest edge of mound; rectangular white sign on tree in right center of photo is Army Corps of Engineers marker notice. (Photo by Nancy White)

Figure 6. Chattahoochee Landing Mounds, 8Gd4, view facing east of the large temple mound close to the river, next to the boat ramp, photographed in the 1980s. The mound suffered both massive erosion, evidenced by the large old tree roots now hanging in midair, and looting, shown by the cut into the side and pothunter's small tunnel (dark horizontal opening in right center of photo). By the 1990s the city of Chattahoochee had dumped riprap on this side of the mound, cleaned up the park, and put a picnic table on top of the mound. (Photo by Nancy White.)

Table 1. Sites in C. B. Moore's Volumes on Northwest Florida

Name	No.*	Affiliation*	Cultural/Temporal Description	Later Work, References, Comments

Certain Aboriginal Remains of the Northwest Florida Coast, Part I [1901]

Name	No.*	Affiliation*	Cultural/Temporal Description	Later Work, References, Comments
Bear Point	1Ba1	Pens	protohistoric sand burial mound, shell midden	Willey 1949:197–200; Fuller 1985
Near Bear Point		MWdld?	sand burial mound, shell midden	apparently never given site number in Baldwin County, AL
Josephine P. O.		?	small sand mound	apparently never given site number in Baldwin County, AL
Inerarity Point	8Es18	Wdld, FW	shell mounds and middens	U West Florida records; site number uncertain
Maester Creek	8SR780	WI	sand burial mound	Willey 1949:204–205
Graveyard Point	8SR3	late(?) WI	sand mound	Willey 1949:205–206
2.5 mi W of Graveyard Point	8SR44?	preceramic, LArch?	small shell? mound	Thomas and Campbell 1993:369–372 (?)
Near Santa Rosa Sound	8SR1	SR-SwCr-eWi, late WI, FW-Pens	2 mounds, shell midden	Willey 1949:203–204; Bense and Wilson 1997
Walton's Camp (Fort Walton Temple Mound)	8Ok6	Pens-FW, Dept, SwCr	temple mound, shell midden (FW type site), other mounds	Willey 1949:72–88, 213–214; Lazarus and Fornaro 1975; Lazarus n.d.
Don's Bayou	8Ok9	?	sand mound	
Black Point	8Ok4	SwCr-WI	sand mound, shell midden	Willey 1949:212–213
Rocky Bayou (east) (west)	8Ok2 8Ok3	late WI? eWI?	sand mound, shell midden sand mound	Willey 1949:211 Willey 1949:211–212
Basin Bayou (west)	8Wl14	SwCr-eWI	burial mound	Willey 1949:223
Near Jolly Bay	8Wl15	late FW	burial (flat-topped?) mound	White, Steube, and Ward 1987:4
Near Black Creek	8Wl67	WI?	3 mounds, midden?	
Near Point Washington	?	SwCr-eWI	sand burial mound, shell midden	Willey 1949:221–222; apparently no new site no. though Willey gave it Wl-11

*See pages 30–31 for explanation of abbreviations.

Name	No.	Affiliation	Cultural/Temporal Description	Later Work, References, Comments
Cemetery Near Point Washington	8Wl16 8Wl33?	late FW	protohistoric cemetery	Willey 1949:225–226
Near Hogtown Bayou	?	?	small mound	no data; 1 line in 1901; not mentioned when cemetery 8Wl19 dug in 1918 (see below)

Certain Aboriginal Remains of the Northwest Florida Coast, Part II [1902]

Name	No.	Affiliation	Cultural/Temporal Description	Later Work, References, Comments
West Bay Post Office	8By11	SwCr-eWI	burial mound	Willey 1949:238
Near West Bay Creek	?	?	mound	apparently never mentioned again though Moore dug another mound nearby with exactly the same name (see 1918 list below, 8By12); possibly went unnoticed when site numbers assigned?
Brock Hammock	8By14	SwCr-eWI	burial? mound	Willey 1949:239; Moore later returned to 2 other mounds nearby (see 1918 list below)
Larger Mound near Burnt Mill Creek	8By15	eWI	burial mound	Willey 1949:239–240
Smaller Mound near Burnt Mill Creek	8By16	SwCr-eWI	mound	Willey 1949:240
Alligator Bayou	8By18	SR-SwCr-eWI	mound	Willey 1949:241
Fanning's Bayou	8By19 8By95	SwCr-eWI	burial mound, associated shell midden (?)	Willey 1949:241–242
Near Head of North Bay	8By20	eWI	burial mound	Willey 1949:242
Anderson's Bayou	8By21	SR-SwCr eWI?	burial mound	Willey 1949:243
Near Large Bayou	8By22	SwCr-eWI	burial mound	Willey 1949:243
Holley Mound	8By1	SwCr-eWI Dept?	sand burial mound, shell midden	Willey 1949:228–230

Name	No.	Affiliation	Cultural/Temporal Description	Later Work, References, Comments
Sowell Mound	8By3	SwCr-eWI, FW	burial mound, shell midden	Willey 1949:64–71, 231; Percy et al. 1971
Near Bear Point	8By5	FW, SWCr-eWI, Span?	sand burial mound, shell midden, circular shell enclosure, 3 platform (?) mounds	Willey 1949:233; Moore returned in 1918 (see below)
St. Andrew's Cemetery	8By23	late? FW	cemetery within shell enclosure (?)	Willey 1949:244
St. Andrew's Mound	8By2	SwCr-eWI, FW	3 shell mounds, shell midden	Willey 1949:230; now called West St. Andrews
Davis Point (West)	8By7 8By9	SR-SwCr-eWI, late WI?	burial mound, shell midden	Willey 1949:234–235; now Davis Pt West, to distinguish from another in Moore 1918 (see list below)
Pearl Bayou	8By25	SwCr-eWI	burial mound	Willey 1949:244–245; nearby midden By24
Laughton's Bayou A	8By27	SwCr-eWI	sand burial mound, shell midden, circular shell enclosure	Willey 1949:246
Laughton's Bayou B	8By28	eWI	burial mound with shells	Willey 1949:247
Strange's Landing	8By26	eWI	burial mound with shells	Willey 1949:245–246; nearby historic and prehistoric middens: By117, 118, 120, 121
Baker's Landing	8By29	SwCr	burial mound, shell midden, circular shell enclosure	Willey 1949:247
Hare Hammock Larger Mound	8By30	SwCr-eWI	burial mound, with shells, shell midden	Willey 1949:248
Hare Hammock Smaller Mound	8By31	SwCr-eWI	sand burial mound, sand and shell midden	Willey 1949:248–249; revisited 1918, when Moore called it Crooked Island (see below)
Gotier Hammock	8Gu2	SwCr-eWI	burial mound	Willey 1949:253–254
Indian Pass Point	8Gu1	eWI	sand burial mound	Willey 1949:252–253; White 1999

Name	No.	Affiliation	Cultural/Temporal Description	Later Work, References, Comments
Eleven Mile Point	8Fr10	SwCr-eWI, Dept, FW	burial mound, shell midden	Willey 1949:273–276 White 1996a:39–40
Cool Spring Md	8Fr19	SwCr-eWI	burial mound	Willey 1949:284; probably part of Pierce; Carr 1975, White 1996a:38–39
Mounds Near Apalachicola (2)	8Fr20, 8Fr21?	? ?	a sand and a shell mound, shell midden	probably part of Pierce; White 1996a:38–39
Cemetery Mound	8Fr21	MWdld	shell and sand burial mound, shell midden	mound gone; probably was part of Pierce; Carr 1975, White 1996a:38–39
Pierce Mounds	8Fr14	SwCr-eWI, FW	burial mounds, shell platform mound, sand platform mound? shell midden	Willey 1949:278–282; unclear how many mounds (5?); Carr 1975, White 1996a:38–39
Singer Mound	8Fr16	?	sand mound with shells	probably part of Pierce (see above)
Jackson Mound	8Fr15	SR-SwCr-eWI	sand burial mound	Willey 1949:282–283; possibly part of Pierce (see above); White 1996a:38–39
Huckleberry Landing	8Fr12	SwCr (EWdld)?	sand burial mound with shell, shell midden/mounds	Willey 1949:277–278
Porter's Bar	8Fr1	SwCr-eWI, LArch, FW	sand burial mound, shell midden	Willey 1949:265–267; Site File; USF lab
Green Point	8Fr11	SwCr-eWI	sand and shell burial mound, probably shell midden too	Willey 1949:276–277; probably part of Porter's Bar
On Carrabelle River (also Near Carrabelle)	8Fr23	?	burial mound	Site File lists it as Carrabelle River Mound
Tucker Mound	8Fr4	SR-SwCr-eWI, Dept	burial mound, shell midden	Willey 1949:269–271, Sears 1963; probably continuous site with Yent
Yent Mound	8Fr5	SR-SwCr-eWI	burial mound, shell midden	Willey 1949:271–272, Sears 1963; probably continuous site with Tucker

Name	No.	Affiliation	Cultural/Temporal Description	Later Work, References, Comments
Marsh Island	8Wa1	late FW, SwCr-eWI	burial mound with stratified MWdld and FW components	Willey 1949:286–288
Nichols Mound	8Wa3	WI? FW?	3 mounds, shell midden	Willey 1949:288–289
Mound Near Ocklocknee Bay	?	?	burial mound?	apparently never given site no.; Site File lists Ochlockonee Bay Midden, 8Fr6, nearby
Hall Mound	8Wa4	SwCr-eWI	sand burial mound and causeway with shell, shell midden	Willey 1949:290–292
Mound at Panacea Springs	8Wa84?	?	mound	Willey 1949:291
Near Spring Creek	8Wa5	SwCr-eWI	burial mound, causeway?	Willey 1949:292
Near the Mound Field	8Wa8	SwCr-eWI	burial mound, shell midden	Willey 1949:55–64, 294
Mound near St. Mark's	8Wa12	eWI	burial mound, shell midden	Willey 1949:296
Aucilla River Mound	8Ta1	SwCr-eWI	burial mound of clay with limestone slabs	Willey 1949:301–302; revisited by Moore 1918 (Lewis Place, below)
Mounds Near the Econfenee River	8Ta4 8Ta5	MWdld?	2 mounds, 1 sand with burial, 1 with limerock in center	Willey 1949:304; Site File lists them as A & B, Econfina River
Warrior River Mound A	8Ta2	SwCr-eWI	sand burial mound with limestone slabs, other mounds	Willey 1949:302–303
Warrior River Mound B	8Ta3	SwCr-eWI	burial mound with limestone slabs and shell, shell midden	Willey 1949:303–304; also called Spring Warrior Creek; Site File has extensive data
Mound Near Steinhatchee River	8Di8	?	sand burial (?) mound	Willey 1949:306
Goodson's Fish Camp	8Di9	?	sand burial mound	Willey 1949:306
Bear Hammock	8Di10	eWI?	sand burial mound	Willey 1949:306; M. Tallant called it Smith mound

Name	No.	Affiliation	Cultural/Temporal Description	Later Work, References, Comments
Murphy Landing	8Di12	MWdld?	sand burial mound with shells	Willey 1949:306
Horseshoe Point	8Di1, 8Di2, 8Di3	SwCr-eWI	sand burial mound, shell midden, 2 other mounds	Willey 1949:304–306; Kohler and Johnson 1986
Hog Island	8Lv26, 8Lv27	MWdld	a shell mound, a shell and sand burial mound, a third mound with limerock, and a shell midden	Willey 1949:315; Moore returned there in 1918 (below); sometimes confused with other sites; Mitchem 1999
Pine Key	8Lv40 8Lv2? 8Lv4?	SwCr-eWI	burial mound or cemetery	Willey 1949:308; may be recorded under Graveyard Island, Seven Miles North of Cedar Keys, Palmetto Island; Borremans and Moseley 1990:32; Borremans n.d.; Mitchem 1999
Mound Near the Shell Heap	8Lv41	?	a (burial?) mound of shell and sand, a large shell mound	Willey 1949:315; Mitchem 1999

Certain Aboriginal Mounds of the Apalachicola River [1903]

Name	No.	Affiliation	Cultural/Temporal Description	Later Work, References, Comments
Brickyard Creek	8Fr8	SwCr-eWI	burial mound	Willey 1949:273; White 1999
Burgess Landing	8Gu3	SwCr-eWI, Dept	sand burial mound	Willey 1949:254; USF lab
Isabel Landing	8Gu4	SwCr-eWI	burial mound	Willey 1949:254; White 1999
Chipola Cutoff	8Gu5	late FW, SwCr-eWI	burial mound with protohistoric materials	Willey 1949:254–256; Henefield and White 1986:125; White 1999
Estiffanulga	8Li7	SwCr-eWI?	sand burial mound	Willey 1949:264–265
Near Blountstown (Cayson)	8Ca3	FW, Lam	temple mound, burial mound, village	Brose et al. 1976, n.d.; White 1982:153–154
Davis Field	8Ca1	SwCr-eWI	clay burial mound	Willey 1949:251–252

Name	No.	Affiliation	Cultural/Temporal Description	Later Work, References, Comments
Yon Mound	8Li2	FW, Lam	temple (?) mound and village	Willey 1949:262; Brose et al. n.d.; White 1996b
Mound Below Bristol	8Li3	SwCr	sand burial mound	Willey 1949:263
Mound at Bristol	8Li4	SwCr-eWI	burial mound	Willey 1949: 263–264
Atkins Landing	8Ca5	FW, LC	mound	White 1996a:28
Mounds Near Aspalaga	8Gd1	SwCr-eWI	3 mounds (1?=burial mound) and freshwater shell midden	Milanich 1974; White 1996a:24–25
Sampson's Landing	8Ja1	SwCr-eWI	sand and gravel burial mound	Willey 1949:249–250, Percy 1976:127–130
Chattahoochee Landing	8Gd4	FW, Dept, Arch?	7 (?) mounds including platform, midden	Bullen 1958:350–352 White 1982:137–142, 1996a:21; some sources also call it Gd2; Bullen called it G-4

Mounds of the Lower Chattahoochee and Lower Flint Rivers [1907]

Chattahoochee River:

Name	No.	Affiliation	Cultural/Temporal Description	Later Work, References, Comments
Kemp's Landing	8Ja2	SwCr-eWI	burial mound of clay and limerock (?)	Bullen 1958:331–333; White 1981:30–44; Bullen had originally called it J-51; now inundated
Hare's Landing	9Se33	SwCr-eWI	sandy clay burial mound	Willey (1949:259) called it Dr1; Caldwell 1978; White 1981:44; site now inundated
Old Rambo Landing	9Se15	FW, late? WI	sandy clay mound	White 1981:490–493
Steammill Landing	9Se103	late WI	low clay mound, small freshwater shell midden	White 1981:559–560 (called it Stubble Field)
Shoemake Landing	9Er1	SwCr-eWI	sand burial mound	Willey 1949:261 (called it Ey1); apparently never relocated, though Er6 and Er142 are close (Belovich et al. 1982: 304–307, 348–350)

Name	No.	Affiliation	Cultural/Temporal Description	Later Work, References, Comments
Fullmore's Upper Landing	1Ho6	eWI	burial mound	Hurt 1947:35
Mound Below Columbia (Seaborn Mound)	1Ho27	FW, Lam, late WI	temple mound, village	also called Omussee Creek mound, Ho1, 2, 3 (Hurt 1947:55), Crawford Mound (Huscher 1959a); Neuman 1961; Belovich et al. 1982: 165–168
Purcell's Landing	1He3	FW, Lam, LC, Arch	4 mounds within .5 square mile	Hurt 1947; Neuman 1959; Belovich et al. 1982:179–183; associated with He103
Paulk's Landing	9Er110	LC, Arch	mound	Belovich et al. 1982: 323–324
Howard's Landing	?	?	flat circular clay mound	apparently not assigned site number or relocated; 9Er97 through 9Er104 are close (Belovich et al. 1982: 126–135)
Colomokee Landing or Colomokee Creek	9Cla87	FW, Lam	low clay mound, habitation	Belovich et al. 1982: 298–303; data in Columbus Museum
Fort Gaines	9Cla48	?	conical mound	no later investigations; mound still sits in cemetery under gazebo
Starke's Clay Landing (Mandeville)	9Cla1	Dept, SwCr, FW, Lam, LC	a platform mound and a conical mound	Kellar, Kelly, and McMichael 1962; Smith 1975
Georgetown	9Qu1	FW, Lam Arch, WI?	mound, village	Huscher 1959b; Knight and Mistovich 1984:27; also called Gary's Fishpond Mound
Above Eufaula	1Br14	FW, Lam	mound and village	Hurt 1947:57; later called Lampley Mound; Huscher 1959b; Knight and Mistovich 1984:27

Name	No.	Affiliation	Cultural/Temporal Description	Later Work, References, Comments
Upper Francis Landing	1Br15, 1Br2	FW, SwCr-eWI, Dept, LArch, LC	red clay platform mound, village	Hurt 1947:57; later called Reeves Mound, Shorter site; Huscher 1959b; Knight and Mistovich 1984:27
Rood's Landing	9Sw1	FW, Lam	8 mounds	Caldwell 1955; data at Columbus Museum
Hall's Upper Landing (Lawson Fields or Kasita Site)	9Ce1	LC	historic aboriginal town	Willey and Sears 1952; O'Steen et al. 1997
Woolfolk's Landing	9Ce3	FW, LC	2 mounds	Brannon 1909; Huscher 1959b; Elliott et al. 1995:50
Abercrombie Landing	1Ru61 1Ru10, 1Ru1	late FW, Lam	historic aboriginal mound and cemetery	also called Fitzgerald Mound site or Kendrick Mound site; Brannon 1909; Fairbanks 1955; Huscher 1959b; DeJarnette 1975
Mound Landing	9Me2, 9Me3	Lam	mound, village	Brannon 1909; Hurt 1947:17; Huscher 1959b; Schnell 1973; Ledbetter 1994; also called Kyle Mound; also called Me34, Me35
Flint River:				
Log Landing	9Dr27	late WI or Dept	sandy clay mound, fresh-water shell midden	White 1981:39, 61–62; now inundated; erroneously numbered Dr48 on some early maps
Munnerlyn's Landing	9Dr2	eWI, LArch?	sand burial mound	Willey 1949:259–260; White 1981:37, 48–49; the number Dr2 was erroneously given to up to 2 other sites in the 1940s–1950s
Kerr's Landing	9Dr14	eWI	sand burial mound	Willey 1949:260 (called it Dr3); Kelly 1960:31–34 (called it Dr2, Bower Plantation); White 1981:38, 52–53

Name	No.	Affiliation	Cultural/Temporal Description	Later Work, References, Comments
Chason Plantation	9Dr3 9Dr4	SwCr, late? WI, LArch, LC	cemetery or burial mound, associated multicomponent occupation	White 1981:37, 333–339; other names are Chason's Blue Springs, Chason Springs, Oklafunee, Coxpur, DeSoto's White Springs (Kerr's landing given this number earlier)

The Northwestern Florida Coast Revisited [1918]

Choctawhatchee River :

Name	No.	Affiliation	Cultural/Temporal Description	Later Work, References, Comments
Bunker Cut-off	8Wl21	FW	circular burial mound	Willey 1949:227
Otter Creek	8By35, 8By38, 8By39	FW, WI(?)	mound and shell midden	Moore says little; Site File lists 3 sites with this name
Wise Bluff	8Wl17	SwCr-eWI	burial mound	Willey 1949:226
Spring Hill Landing	8Ws2	eWI	burial mound	Willey 1949:228
Dead River (north and south mounds)	8Wl18 8Wl1	eWI SwCr-eWI	burial mound burial mound	Willey 1949:226
Miller Field Landing	8Ws3	SwCr-eWI	burial mound	Willey 1949:228
Douglas Bluff	8Wl20	SwCr-eWI	burial mound	Willey 1949:226
McLaney Place		eWI	burial mound	never assigned site number; Willey (1949: 258) called it Ho1, which is now assigned to another site on the Chattahoochee
Pate Place		?	mound	never assigned site number; apparently never relocated in Houston County, AL

Northwestern Florida Coast and Rivers:

Name	No.	Affiliation	Cultural/Temporal Description	Later Work, References, Comments
Pippen's Lake	8Ok8	eWI	mound	Willey 1949:222–223; he calls it Wl-12
Big Hammock	8Wl3	WI, FW	4 sand mounds (1 with burials) and shell midden	Willey 1949:216–217
Basin Bayou (east)	8Wl14	SR-SwCr	burial mound	Willey 1949:223–224

Name	No.	Affiliation	Cultural/Temporal Description	Later Work, References, Comments
Hogtown Bayou Cemetery	8Wl9	late FW	protohistoric cemetery	Willey 1949:220; Site File name includes the word "Pickens"
Mack Bayou	8Wl10 8Wl8	? FW, late? WI	mound, shell midden	Willey 1949:219–221; 2 site numbers for mound and midden; mound age/function unknown
Philip's Inlet	8By13	SwCr-eWI	sand burial mound	Willey 1949:239
West Bay Creek	8By12	SwCr-eWI	burial? mound	Willey 1949:238–239; Moore says other low indeterminate mounds nearby; he dug another nearby (see 1902 list above) with same name
Brock Hammock	8By14?	?	2 low rises; midden heaps? (1 had a skeleton)	near 1902 mound of same name (see list above); unclear how related or if ever relocated or given site numbers
West of Burnt Mill Creek	8By17	eWI	burial mound	Willey 1949:240–241; Site File calls it Burnt Mill Creek West
Bear Point	8By5			revisited same site as in 1902 (see list above)
Davis Point (East)	8By8 8By164	SwCr-eWI	burial mound, shell midden	Willey 1949:235; shell midden numbered much later
Farmdale	8By32	eWI	burial mound	Willey 1949:249; many sites later recorded in vicinity are probably related (By110-115)
Crooked Island	8By31			Same as Hare Hammock smaller mound visited 1902; see above
Michaux Log Landing	8Li6	SwCr-eWI	burial mound	Willey 1949:264; may be related to Li186; Henefield and White 1986:11–13, 79–80
Ok Landing	8Ca2	SwCr-eWI	burial mound	Willey 1949:252

Name	No.	Affiliation	Cultural/Temporal Description	Later Work, References, Comments
Rock Bluff Landing	8Li5	SwCr-eWI	burial mound	Willey 1949:264; Percy and Jones 1976:108, 119–120
Hardnut Landing	9Dr18	SwCr-eWI	burial mound	White 1981:53–54; now inundated; numbered Dr4 in Willey 1949:260 and Miller n.d., but that number is now for another site
Cemetery near Carrabelle	8Fr2	Dept, SwCr-eWI	cemetery in sand ridge (?)	Willey 1949:38–55, 267–268; could have Early Woodland burials related to Alexander
Old Creek	8Wa28	SwCr-eWI? FW?	sand mound	Willey 1949:299
Bird Hammock A Bird Hammock B	8Wa9 8Wa10 8Wa30	SwCr-eWI SwCr-eWI	burial mound burial mound with ramps, shell midden (ring?) between the 2 mounds	Willey 1949:294–295; Penton 1970; Wa30 is number for whole site
Lewis Place	8Ta1			Same as Aucilla River Mound visited 1902 (see above list)
Warrior River	8Ta6	eWI, Dept?	burial mound	Willey 1949:304; Site File
Hog Island	8Lv26, 8Lv27			originally visited in 1902 (see above list); in 1918 dug 2 of the 3 mounds
Cedar Keys	8Lv43 8Lv279?	eWI?	sand and shell burial mound, shell midden (?)	Willey 1949:314; Borremans and Moseley 1990:25; Borremans n.d.; Mitchem 1999
Cedar Keys Cemetery	8Lv4	eWI, Arch, Mississippian	cemetery (once a mound?) of sand with shell, habitation areas	Willey 1949:309; Borremans 1991, 1993, n.d.; Mitchem 1999
Crystal River	8Ci1	MWdld	multi–mound complex	major discussions in 2 other of Moore's reports from 1903 and 1907 (see Mitchem 1999); Weisman 1995

Name	No.	Affiliation	Cultural/Temporal Description	Later Work, References, Comments
Greenleaf Place	8Ci11	?	sand burial mound	Willey 1949:324–325
Arkansas and Louisiana:				
Site near Golden Lake, Evadale, Mississippi County, AR (Notgrass)	3Ms15	Mississippian	habitation site with burials	Arkansas Site File; Morse and Morse 1998:8, 15
Site near Bassett, Mississippi County, AR (Bell)	3Ms8	Mississippian	habitation site with burials	Arkansas Site file; Morse and Morse 1998:8,15
Mounds near Transylvania, East Carroll Parish, LA	16EC8	Mississippian	4 platform mounds, 2 clay conical mounds, some burials	Hally 1967, 1972; Hartfield et al. 1977; Morse and Morse 1998:6,15 Hally found 12 mounds; Lower Mississippi Valley Survey site number was 22-L-3

Abbreviations:

Florida (8)
By   Bay
Ca   Calhoun
Ci   Citrus
Di   Dixie
Es   Escambia
Fr   Franklin
Gd   Gadsden
Gu   Gulf
Ja   Jackson
La   Lafayette
Li   Liberty
Lv   Levy
Ok   Okaloosa
SR   Santa Rosa
Ta   Taylor
Wa   Wakulla
Wl   Walton
Ws   Washington

Georgia (9)
Ce   Chattahoochee
Cla Clay
Dr   Decatur
Er   Early
Me   Muscogee
Qu   Quitman
Se   Seminole
Sw   Stewart

Arkansas (3)
Ms   Mississippi

Alabama (1)
Ba   Baldwin
Br   Barbour
He   Henry
Ho   Houston
Ru   Russell

Louisiana (16)
EC   East Carroll Parish

Archaeological Cultures (including diagnostic items):

Arch   Archaic (diagnostic points); 8000–1000 B.C.

Dept   (Deptford, Early Woodland, linear check-stamped and simple-stamped ceramics); 1000 B.C.–A.D. 100?

EWdld   Early Woodland (Deptford and/or Swift Creek ceramics only); 1000 B.C.– A.D. 200?

eWI   early Weeden Island (Middle Woodland, elaborate incised, punctate, cutout vessels); A.D. 300–700?

FW   Fort Walton (Mississippian with grit-tempered ceramics); A.D. 1000– 1500

Lam   Lamar (late? Mississippian with complicated-stamped, proto-Creek? ceramics); A.D.1200–1400??

LArch   Late Archaic (fiber-tempered ceramics, steatite bowls); 2500?–800? B.C.

late WI   Late Woodland, late Weeden Island (Willey's Weeden Island II; check-stamped, other WI types but missing elaborate Weeden Island Incised and Punctated or cutout vessels); A.D. 700–1000?

LC   Lower Creek (historic aboriginal; very early Seminole); A.D. 1650?–1850?

MWdld   Middle Woodland (burial mound with exotics; uncertain as to ceramic characterization); A.D. 200–700?

Pens   Pensacola (shell-tempered Fort Walton–type Mississippian ceramics); A.D. 1000?–1500?

Span   protohistoric or early historic Spanish (olive jar sherds, glass, metal); after A.D. 1492

SR   Santa Rosa (Middle Woodland rocker-stamped ceramics); A.D. 1?–500?

SwCr   Swift Creek (Middle, sometimes Early Woodland complicated-stamped ceramics); A.D. 1–700?

Wdld   indeterminate Woodland; 1000 B.C.–A.D. 1000

WI   Weeden Island (Weeden Island ceramics, uncertain as to more diagnostic types); A.D. 300?–1000

Table 2. Cultural Chronology for Northwest Florida

Dates	Cultural Stage	Cultural Adaptation	Diagnostic Artifacts
A.D. 1500–1850	Historic	missionization, disappearance of natives; emergence of Seminoles from Lower Creeks moving in	European metal, glass; later Chattahoochee Brushed ceramics
A.D. 1000–1500	Mississippian	Fort Walton: temple mounds, intensive maize agriculture, but still hunting, gathering, fishing, shellfish collecting on coast	Fort Walton, Lamar, (grit-tempered) and Pensacola ceramics; triangular chert points
A.D. 700–1000	Late Woodland	adoption of maize cultivation, habitation in all environments, decreasing mound ritual	late Weeden Island ceramics (check-stamped, Keith Incised, and Carrabelle types)
A.D. 200–700	Middle Woodland	height of burial mound ceremonialism, possible cultivation of local plants, hunting, gathering, fishing, shellfish collecting	Swift Creek complicated-stamped, Santa Rosa, and early Weeden Island Incised, Punctated, and cutout ceramics, other burial items of exotic raw materials, small stemmed points
1000 B.C.– A.D. 200	Early Woodland	earliest burial mounds, hunting, fishing, gathering, shellfish collecting	Deptford check- and simple-stamped, fabric-marked, some early Swift Creek ceramics, tetrapodal vessels
3500–1000 B.C.	Late Archaic (or "Gulf Formational")	earliest known shell mounds, hunting, gathering, fishing	fiber-tempered ceramics by 2000 B.C., steatite bowls, chert microtools
6000–3500 B.C.	Middle Archaic	hunting, gathering, probably fishing and shellfish collecting too	many stemmed and notched points, probably shell mounds
8000–6000 B.C.	Early Archaic/ Late Paleo-Indian	hunting, gathering, probably fishing	Bolen points, a few Dalton points
12,500–8000 B.C.	Paleo-Indian	hunting Pleistocene big game, gathering and probably fishing too	Clovis, Suwanee, unfluted lanceolate points, pre-Clovis?

References Cited

Belovich, Stephanie J., David S. Brose, Russell M. Weisman, and Nancy Marie
White
  1982 *Archaeological Survey at George W. Andrews Lake and Chattahoochee
        River, Alabama and Georgia.* Cleveland Museum of Natural History
        Archaeological Research Report No. 37.
Bense, Judith A., and Harry J. Wilson
  1997 *8SR0001 Santa Rosa Sound Site Survey Update.* University of West
        Florida Archaeological Institute Report of Investigations No. 63,
        Pensacola.
Borremans, Nina Thanz
  1991 *The Aboriginal Cemetery at Cedar Key.* Management Report to the
        Cedar Key Special Water and Sewerage District and the Florida Divi-
        sion of Historical Resources, Tallahassee.
  1993 *The Archaic Period Component at 8Lv4 Cedar Key.* Report to the Cedar
        Key Special Water and Sewerage District and the Florida Division of
        Historical Resources, Tallahassee.
  n.d. Archaeology of the Cedar Keys, Levy County, Florida. Ph.D. disserta-
        tion, in progress, Department of Anthropology, University of Florida,
        Gainesville.
Borremans, Nina Thanz, and Michael E. Moseley
  1990 *A Prehistoric Site Survey of the Cedar Keys Region, Levy and Citrus
        Counties, Florida.* Report from the University of Florida to the Florida
        Division of Historical Resources, Tallahassee.
Boyd, Mark F., Hale G. Smith, and John W. Griffin
  1951 *Here They Once Stood: The Tragic End of the Apalachee Missions.*
        University of Florida Press, Gainesville.
Brannon, Peter A.
  1909 Aboriginal Remains in the Middle Chattahoochee Valley of Alabama
        and Georgia. *American Anthropologist* 9(2):186–198.
Brose, David S.
  1979 An Interpretation of the Hopewellian Traits in Florida. In *Hopewell
        Archaeology: The Chillicothe Conference,* edited by David S. Brose and
        N'omi Greber, pp. 141–149. Kent State University Press, Kent, Ohio.

1980 How Captain Riggs Hunts for Mound Builders' Relics: An Historical Investigation of Some Influences on C. B. Moore. *Southeastern Archaeological Conference Bulletin* 22:145–152.

1984 Mississippian Period Cultures in Northwest Florida. In *Perspectives on Gulf Coast Prehistory,* edited by Dave D. Davis, pp. 165–197. University Presses of Florida, Gainesville.

1985 "Willey-Nilly" or the Archaeology of Northwest Florida and Adjacent Borderlands, Revisited. In *Archaeology of Northwest Florida and Adjacent Borderlands,* edited by N. White, pp. 156–162. Florida Anthropological Society Publications No. 11. (*The Florida Anthropologist* 38 [1–2 Pt. 2].)

Brose, David S., Patricia S. Essenpreis, John F. Scarry, Helga M. Bluestone, and Anne E. Forsythe

1976 Case Western Reserve University Contributions to the Archaeology of Northwest Florida: Investigation of Two Early Fort Walton Sites in the Middle Apalachicola River Valley: 1973. Ms. on file, Cleveland Museum of Natural History, Cleveland, and Florida Division of Historical Resources, Tallahassee.

Brose, David S., and George W. Percy

1974 An Outline of Weeden Island Ceremonial Activity in Northwest Florida. Paper presented at the 39th Annual Meeting of the Society for American Archaeology, Washington, D.C.

1978 Fort Walton Settlement Patterns. In *Mississippian Settlement Patterns,* edited by Bruce D. Smith, pp. 81–114. Academic Press, New York.

Brose, David S., George W. Percy, Patricia S. Essenpreis, and Frances Clark

n.d. Field notes, photographs, laboratory analyses, and correspondence concerning archaeological excavations at the Cayson Site, Calhoun County, Florida, 1972–76. On file, Department of Archaeology, Cleveland Museum of Natural History.

Bullen, Ripley P.

1950 An Archaeological Survey of the Chattahoochee River Valley in Florida. *Journal of the Washington Academy of Sciences* 40(4):101–125.

1958 Six Sites Near the Chattahoochee River in the Jim Woodruff Reservoir Area, Florida. River Basin Surveys Papers No. 14. *Bureau of American Ethnology Bulletin* 169:315–358.

Caldwell, Joseph R.

1955 Investigations at Rood's Landing, Stewart County, Georgia. *Early Georgia* 2(1):22–49.

1978 *Report of Excavations at Fairchild's Landing and Hare's Landing, Seminole County, Georgia,* edited by Betty A. Smith. Report to the National Park Service, Tallahassee.

Carr, Robert S.

1975 *An Archaeological Survey of the City of Apalachicola.* Florida Division of Archives, History, and Records Management (now Division of Historical Resources), Tallahassee.

Davis, Mary B. (compiler)

    1987   *Field Notes of Clarence B. Moore's Southeastern Archaeological Expeditions, 1891–1918: A Guide to the Microfilm Edition.* Huntington Free Library, Bronx, New York.

DeJarnette, David L. (editor)

    1975   *Archaeological Salvage in the Walter F. George Basin of the Chattahoochee River in Alabama.* University of Alabama Press, University, Alabama.

Elliott, Daniel, J. L. Holland, P. Thomason, M. Emrick, and R. W. Stoops, Jr.

    1995   *Historic Preservation Plan for the Cultural Resources on U.S. Army Installations at Fort Benning Military Reservation, Chattahoochee and Muscogee Counties, Georgia, and Russell County, Alabama. Volume 2: Technical Synthesis.* Report to the National Park Service Southeast Regional Office, Atlanta. Garrow and Associates, Inc., Atlanta.

Fairbanks, Charles H.

    1955   The Abercrombie Mound, Russell County, Alabama. *Early Georgia* 2(1):13–19.

Ford, James A., and Gordon R. Willey

    1941   An Interpretation of the Prehistory of the Eastern United States. *American Anthropologist* 43(3):325–363.

Fuller, Richard S.

    1985   The Bear Point Phase of the Pensacola Variant: The Protohistoric Period in Southwest Alabama. In *Archaeology of Northwest Florida and Adjacent Borderlands,* edited by N. White, pp. 150–155. Florida Anthropological Society Publications No. 11. (*The Florida Anthropologist* 38 [1–2 Pt. 2].)

Greenman, Emerson F.

    1938   Some Hopewellian Traits in Florida. *American Antiquity* 4:327–333.

Hally, David J.

    1967   Post-Coles Creek Cultural Development in the Upper Tensas Basin of Louisiana. *Southeastern Archaeological Conference Bulletin* 6:35–40

    1972   The Plaquemine and Mississippian Occupations of the Upper Tensas Basin, Louisiana. Unpublished Ph.D. dissertation, Department of Anthropology, Harvard University.

Hartfield, Lorraine, G. R. Price, J. Lewis, K. G. Hudson, and G. S. Green

    1977   *Archaeological Assessment of the Ouachita River Basin, Arkansas and Louisiana.* Report to the Division of Archaeology and Historic Preservation, Department of Culture, Recreation, and Tourism. Report No. 22-126. Baton Rouge.

Henefield, Susan M., and Nancy Marie White

    1986   *Archaeological Survey in the Middle and Lower Apalachicola Valley, 1985.* Report to the Florida Department of State, Bureau of Archives, History, and Records Management (now Division of Historical Resources), Tallahassee.

Holmes, William H.

1894 *Earthenware of Florida: Collections of Clarence B. Moore.* Levytype Co., Philadelphia.

1902 Review of *Certain Aboriginal Remains of the Northwest Florida Coast, Part I,* by Clarence B. Moore. *American Anthropologist* 4:521–523.

1903 Aboriginal Pottery of the Eastern United States. *Twentieth Annual Report of the Bureau of American Ethnology, 1898–1899,* pp. 1–237. Smithsonian Institution, Washington, D.C.

1914 Areas of American Culture Characterization Tentatively Outlined as an Aid in the Study of the Antiquities. *American Anthropologist* 18:413–446.

Hurt, Wesley R.

1975 The Preliminary Archaeological Survey of the Chattahoochee Valley Area in Alabama [written in 1947]. In *Archaeological Salvage in the Walter F. George Basin of the Chattahoochee River in Alabama,* edited by D. L. DeJarnette, pp. 6–86. University of Alabama Press, University, Alabama.

Huscher, Harold A.

1959a *Appraisal of the Archaeological Resources of the Columbia Dam and Lock Area, Chattahoochee River, Alabama and Georgia.* River Basin Surveys, Smithsonian Institution, Washington, D.C.

1959b *Appraisal of the Archaeological Resources of the Walter F. George Reservoir Area, Chattahoochee River, Alabama and Georgia.* River Basin Surveys, Smithsonian Institution, Washington, D.C.

Hutchinson, Lee, Terrance Simpson, Nancy White, and Michael McDaniel

1991 Public Archaeology and Middle Woodland Research in the Middle Apalachicola Valley, Northwest Florida. Paper presented at the Annual Meeting of the Florida Anthropological Society, Pensacola.

Kellar, James H., A. R. Kelly, and Edward McMichael

1962 The Mandeville Site in Southwest Georgia. *American Antiquity* 27:336–355.

Kelly, Arthur R.

1950 Survey of the Lower Flint and Chattahoochee Rivers. *Early Georgia* 1(1):27–34.

1960 *A Weeden Island Burial Mound in Decatur County, Georgia: The Lake Douglas Mound, 9Dr21.* University of Georgia Laboratory of Archaeology Series Report No. 1, Athens.

Knight, Vernon James, Jr.

1996 Introduction. *The Moundville Expeditions of Clarence Bloomfield Moore,* edited by Vernon James Knight, Jr., pp. 1–20. University of Alabama Press, Tuscaloosa.

Knight, Vernon James, Jr., and Tim S. Mistovich

1984 *Walter F. George Lake: Archaeological Survey of Fee-Owned Lands, Alabama and Georgia.* University of Alabama Office of Archaeological Research Report of Investigations 32.

Kohler, Timothy A., and G. Michael Johnson

    1986   *Dixie County Archaeological Reconnaissance, Winter 1985–86*. Report to the Bureau of Historic Preservation, Division of Archives, History, and Records Management (now Division of Historical Resources), Florida Department of State, Tallahassee.

Lazarus, Yulee W.

    n.d.   *The Fort Walton Temple Mound and Museum*. Temple Mound Museum, Fort Walton Beach, Florida.

Lazarus, Yulee W., and Robert J. Fornaro

    1975   Fort Walton Temple Mound: Further Test Excavations, DePauw University, 1973. *The Florida Anthropologist* 28:159–177.

Ledbetter, R. Jerald

    1994   Archaeological Survey of Riverwalk South Rotary Park to Fort Benning, Columbus, Georgia. Southeastern Archaeological Services, Inc. Athens.

Milanich, Jerald T.

    1974   *Life in a Ninth Century Indian Household, a Weeden Island Fall-Winter Site on the Upper Apalachicola River, Florida*. Bureau of Historic Sites and Properties, Division of Archives, History and Records Management Bulletin 4:1–44. Tallahasee.

    1994   *Archaeology of Precolumbian Florida*. University Press of Florida, Gainesville.

Milanich, Jerald T., Ann S. Cordell, Vernon J. Knight, Jr., Timothy A. Kohler, and
Brenda J. Sigler-Lavelle

    1997   *Archaeology of Northern Florida A.D. 200–900: The McKeithen Weeden Island Culture*. Reprinted. University Press of Florida, Gainesville. Originally published 1984.

Milanich, Jerald T., and Charles H. Fairbanks

    1980   *Florida Archaeology*. Academic Press, New York.

Miller, Carl

    n.d.   Collected notes and correspondence concerning archaeological survey and excavations in the Jim Woodruff Reservoir, 1953. On file, National Anthropological Archives, Smithsonian Institution, Washington, D.C.

Mitchem, Jeffrey M. (editor)

    1999   *The West and Central Florida Expeditions of Clarence Bloomfield Moore*. University of Alabama Press, Tuscaloosa.

Moore, Clarence B.

    1893a Certain Shell Heaps of the St. John's River, Florida, Hitherto Unexplored (Third Paper). *The American Naturalist* 27:605–624.

    1893b Certain Shell Heaps of the St. John's River, Florida, Hitherto Unexplored (Fourth Paper). *The American Naturalist* 27:708–723.

    1901   Certain Aboriginal Remains of the Northwest Florida Coast. Part I. *Journal of the Academy of Natural Sciences of Philadelphia* 11:421–497.

    1902   Certain Aboriginal Remains of the Northwest Florida Coast. Part II. *Journal of the Academy of Natural Sciences of Philadelphia* 12:127–358.

    1903   Certain Aboriginal Mounds of the Apalachicola River. *Journal of the Academy of Natural Sciences of Philadelphia* 12:441–492.

1907   Mounds of the Lower Chattahoochee and Lower Flint Rivers. *Journal of the Academy of Natural Sciences of Philadelphia* 13:427–456.

1918   The Northwestern Florida Coast Revisited. *Journal of the Academy of Natural Sciences of Philadelphia* 16:514–580.

Morse, Dan F., and Phyllis A. Morse (editors)

1998   *The Lower Mississippi Valley Expeditions of Clarence Bloomfield Moore.* University of Alabama Press, Tuscaloosa.

Neuman, Robert W.

1959   Two Unrecorded Pottery Vessels from the Purcell Landing Site in Houston County, Alabama. *The Florida Anthropologist* 12:101–104.

1961   Domesticated Corn from a Fort Walton Mound Site in Houston County, Alabama. *The Florida Anthropologist* 14:75–80.

O'Steen, Lisa D., John S. Cable, Mary Beth Reed, and J. W. Joseph

1997   *Cultural Resources Survey, Lawson Army Airfield, Fort Benning, Georgia and Alabama.* New South Associates Report No. 447, Stone Mountain, Georgia.

Patterson, Thomas C.

1995   *Toward a Social History of Archaeology in the United States.* Harcourt Brace, Fort Worth, Texas.

Penton, Daniel Troy

1970   Excavations in the Early Swift Creek Component at Bird Hammock (8Wa30). Unpublished Master's thesis, Department of Anthropology, Florida State University, Tallahassee.

Percy, George W.

1976   *Salvage Investigations at the Scholz Steam Plant Site, A Middle Weeden Island Habitation Site in Jackson County, Florida.* Florida Bureau of Historic Sites and Properties Miscellaneous Report Series No. 35. Florida Division of Historical Resources, Tallahassee.

Percy, George W., and David S. Brose

1974   Weeden Island Ecology, Subsistence, and Village Life in Northwest Florida. Paper presented at the 39th Annual Meeting of the Society for American Archaeology, Washington, D.C.

Percy, George W., Calvin Jamison, Katherine Gagel, Robin Heath, and Mark Gottlob

1971   Preliminary Report on Recent Excavations at the Sowell Mound (8By3), Bay County, Florida. Paper presented at the 23rd Annual Meeting of the Florida Anthropological Society, St. Petersburg.

Percy, George W., and M. Katherine Jones

1976   *An Archaeological Survey of Upland Locales in Gadsden and Liberty Counties, Florida.* Report from Florida State University to the Florida Division of Historical Resources, Tallahasee.

Putnam, Frederic W.

1886   *On Methods of Archaeological Research in America.* Johns Hopkins University, Baltimore.

Scarry, John F.

1984 *Fort Walton Development: Mississippian Chiefdoms in the Lower Southeast.* Ph.D. dissertation, Department of Anthropology, Case Western Reserve University, Cleveland. University Microfilms International, Ann Arbor.

Schnell, Frank T.

1973 A Preliminary Assessment of Archaeological Resources Remaining in the Walter F. George Lake Area. Ms. no. 108 on file, University of Georgia Laboratory of Archaeology, Athens.

Schnell, Frank T., Vernon J. Knight, Jr., and Gail S. Schnell

1981 *Cemochechobee: Archaeology of a Mississippian Ceremonial Center on the Chattahoochee River.* University Presses of Florida, Gainesville.

Schoolcraft, Henry R.

1854 Antique pottery from the minor mounds occupied by the Indians in feasts of the dead, on the sea coasts of Florida and Georgia. *Information Respecting the History, Condition and Prospects of the Indian Tribes of the United States* 3:75–82. Collected and prepared under the direction of the Bureau of Indian Affairs. Lippincott, Philadelphia.

Sears, William H.

1954 The Sociopolitical Organization of Pre-Colombian Cultures on the Gulf Coastal Plain. *The American Anthropologist* 56:339–346.

1962 The Hopewellian Affiliations of Certain Sites on the Gulf Coast of Florida. *American Antiquity* 28:5–18.

1963 *The Tucker Site on Alligator Harbor, Franklin County, Florida.* Contributions of the Florida State Museum, Social Sciences No. 9, Gainesville.

1977 Prehistoric Culture Areas and Culture Change on the Gulf Coastal Plain. In *For the Director: Research Essays in Honor of James B. Griffin,* edited by Charles Cleland, pp. 152–185. Anthropological Papers of the University of Michigan Museum of Anthropology No. 61, Ann Arbor.

Sheldon, Craig (editor)

2000 *The South and Central Alabama Expeditions of Clarence Bloomfield Moore.* University of Alabama Press, Tuscaloosa.

Simpson, Terrance L.

1996 Prehistoric Settlement Patterns in the Apalachicola River Valley: A GIS Approach. Unpublished Master's thesis, Department of Anthropology, University of South Florida, Tampa.

Smith, Betty A.

1975 The Relationship between Deptford and Swift Creek Ceramics as Evidenced at the Mandeville Site, 9Cla1. *Southeastern Archaeological Conference Bulletin* 18:195–200.

1979 The Hopewell Connection in Southwest Georgia. In *Hopewell Archaeology: The Chillicothe Conference,* edited by David S. Brose and N'omi Greber, pp. 181–187. Kent State University Press, Kent, Ohio.

Smith, Bruce D.
  1985   Introduction. In *Report on the Mound Explorations of the Bureau of Ethnology,* by Cyrus Thomas, pp. 1–16. Reprinted. Smithsonian Institution, Washington D.C.

Stoltman, James B.
  1973   The Southeast. In *The Development of North American Archaeology,* edited by James E. Fitting, pp. 116–150. Anchor Books, Garden City, New York.

Thomas, Cyrus
  1894   Report on the Mound Explorations of the Bureau of Ethnology. *Twelfth Annual Report of the Bureau of Ethnology, 1890–1891,* pp. 17–742. Smithsonian Institution, Washington, D.C.

Thomas, Prentice M., and L. Janice Campbell (editors)
  1993   *Eglin Air Force Base Historic Preservation Plan: Technical Synthesis of Cultural Resources Investigations at Eglin.* New World Research, Inc., Report of Investigations No. 192. Report to the National Park Service, Southeast Region, Tallahassee.

Walthall, John A.
  1980   *Prehistoric Indians of the Southeast: Archaeology of Alabama and the Middle South.* University of Alabama Press, University, Alabama.

Wardle, H[arriet] Newell
  1956   Clarence Bloomfield Moore (1852–1936). *Bulletin of the Philadelphia Anthropological Society* 9(2):9–11.

Wauchope, Robert
  1957   *Lost Tribes and Sunken Continents.* University of Chicago Press, Chicago.

Weisman, Brent R.
  1995   *Crystal River. A Ceremonial Mound Center on the Florida Gulf Coast.* Florida Archaeology No. 8. Florida Bureau of Archaeological Research, Department of State, Division of Historical Resources, Tallahassee.

White, Nancy Marie
  1981   *Archaeological Survey at Lake Seminole, Jackson and Gadsden Counties, Florida, Seminole and Decatur Counties, Georgia.* Cleveland Museum of Natural History Archaeological Research Report No. 29.
  1982   *The Curlee Site (8Ja7) and Fort Walton Development in the Upper Apalachicola-Lower Chattahoochee Valley.* Ph.D. dissertation, Department of Anthropology, Case Western Reserve University, Cleveland. University Microfilms International, Ann Arbor.
  1985   Nomenclature and Interpretation in Borderland Chronology: A Critical Overview of Northwest Florida Prehistory. In *Archaeology of Northwest Florida and Adjacent Borderlands,* edited by N. White, pp. 163–174. Florida Anthropological Society Publications No 11. (*The Florida Anthropologist* 38 [1–2 Pt. 2]).
  1996a *Archaeological Investigations of the 1994 Record Flood Impacts in the Apalachicola Valley, Northwest Florida.* Report to the Florida Division of Historical Resources, Tallahassee. University of South Florida, Tampa.

1996b *Test Excavations at the Yon Mound and Village Site (8Li2), Middle Apalachicola Valley, Northwest Florida.* Report to the Florida Division of Historical Resources, Tallahassee. Department of Anthropology, University of South Florida, Tampa.

1999 *Apalachicola Delta Remote Areas Archaeological Survey.* Report to the Florida Division of Historical Resources, Tallahassee. Department of Anthropology, University of South Florida, Tampa.

White, Nancy Marie, Fred Steube, and Dorothy J. Ward

1987 *Archaeological and Historical Survey of the Walton Development Property, Walton County, Florida, Preliminary Report.* Report to Baskerville-Donovan Engineers, Inc., Pensacola, Florida. Department of Anthropology, University of South Florida, Tampa.

Willey, Gordon R.

1945 The Weeden Island Culture: A Preliminary Definition. *American Antiquity* 10:225–254.

1949 *Archeology of the Florida Gulf Coast.* Smithsonian Miscellaneous Collections Vol. 113. Washington, D.C. Reprinted 1998, University Press of Florida, Gainesville.

1989 Gordon R. Willey. In *The Pastmasters,* edited by G. Daniel and C. Chippindale, pp. 100–113. Thames and Hudson, New York.

1998a American Archaeology, 1931–1996: A Personal Perspective. *Symbols* (Spring 1998):11–18. The Peabody Museum and the Department of Anthropology, Harvard University, Cambridge, Massachusetts.

1998b Preface. In *Archeology of the Florida Gulf Coast,* University Press of Florida, Gainesville.

Willey, Gordon R., and Jeremy A. Sabloff

1974 *A History of American Archaeology.* 1st ed. W. H. Freeman and Company, San Francisco.

Willey, Gordon R., and William H. Sears

1952 The Kasita Site. *Southern Indian Studies* 4:3–18.

Willey, Gordon R., and Richard B. Woodbury

1942 A Chronological Outline for the Northwest Florida Coast. *American Antiquity* 7:232–254.

Certain Aboriginal Remains of the Northwest Florida Coast, Part I

BY

CLARENCE B. MOORE

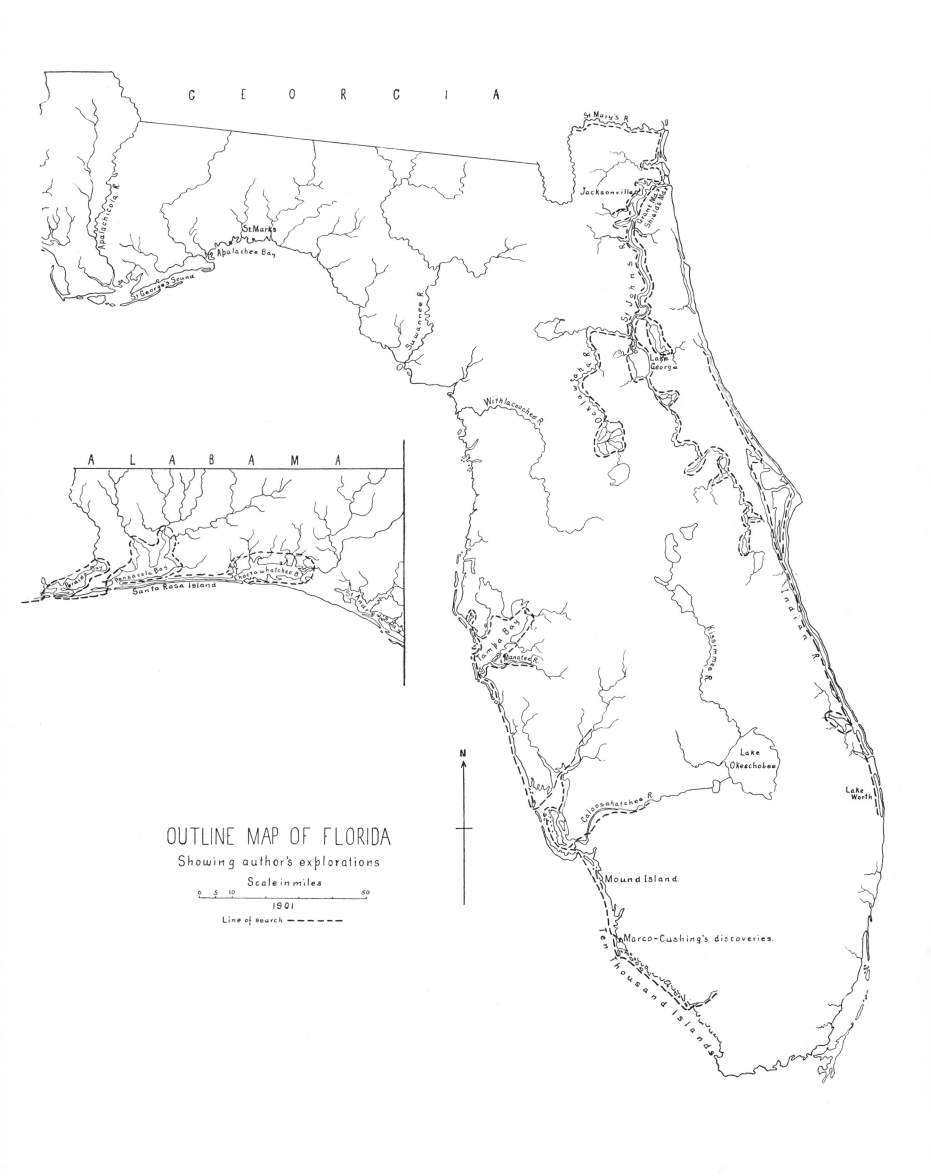

G E O R G I A

ALABAMA

Apalachicola R.

St Marks
Apalachee Bay
St George's Sound

Pensacola Bay
Perdido Bay
Santa Rosa Island
Choctawhatchee B.
St An...

Suwannee R.

St Mary's R.

Jacksonville

Grant Ma.
Shields Ma.

St Johns R.

Lake George

Ocklawaha R.

Withlacoochee R.

Tampa Bay
Manatee R.

Kissimmee R.

Indian R.

Lake Okeechobee

Lake Worth

Caloosahatchee R.

Mound Island

Marco – Cushing's discoveries.

Ten Thousand Islands

N

OUTLINE MAP OF FLORIDA

Showing author's explorations

Scale in miles

0 5 10   50

1901

Line of search ‑ ‑ ‑ ‑ ‑

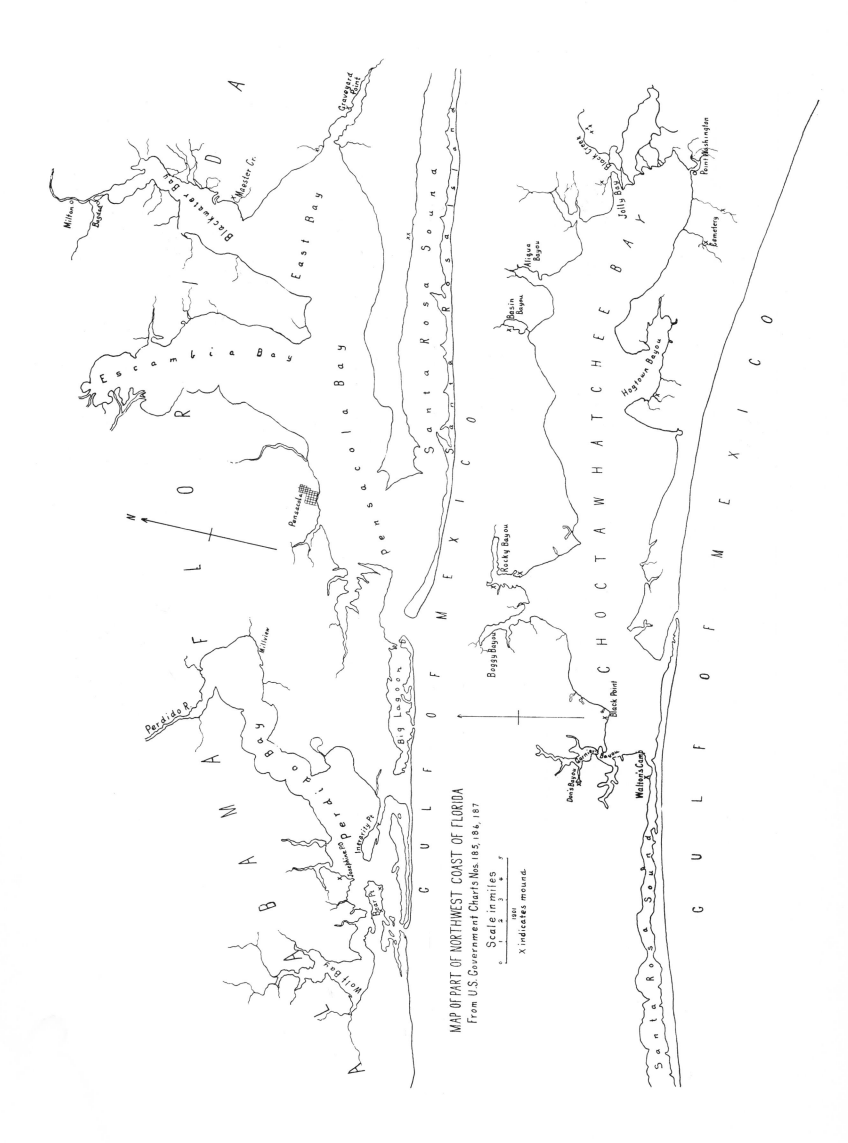

MAP OF PART OF NORTHWEST COAST OF FLORIDA

From U.S. Government Charts Nos. 185, 186, 187

Scale in miles

0   1   2   3   4   5

1901

X indicates mound.

CERTAIN ABORIGINAL REMAINS OF THE NORTHWEST FLORIDA COAST.

PART I.

BY CLARENCE B. MOORE.

During the past ten seasons we have investigated aboriginal remains in the southern United States and have devoted most of that period to Florida and to the States that border it, Alabama and Georgia. By the outline map of Florida which we give, showing the territory covered by our work in that State, it will be seen that nearly all the waterways had been investigated by us, except the northwest coast. Now, this portion of Florida should be of great interest archæologically, bordering, as it does, a section stretching across much of southern Georgia and most of southern Alabama, and an investigation by us looking to the tracing of possible influence from States where we have done so much work, on peninsular Florida, which we know so well, through the coast-territory, seemed to be worth our while.

Beginning, then, in the winter of 1901, at Perdido bay, the coast-boundary between Alabama and Florida (see map), we explored carefully eastward, including Pensacola bay, Santa Rosa sound and Choctawhatchee bay. Our results, which are largely based on the discovery of earthenware, are given in this part of our Report.

It is our hope, next year, if all goes well, carefully to cover St. Andrew's, and St. Joseph's, bay, Apalachicola bay, St. George's sound, Apalachee bay and all the lower northwest coast to Tampa, including, perhaps, parts of some of the rivers that enter the Gulf along our route.

The mounds of the section we have explored, we know from experience, and of the territory we hope to visit, from reliable accounts, have been exposed to relentless attack by seekers for buried treasure. In no part of Florida is the pursuit of this *ignis fatuus* so intense, and persons, otherwise sane, seemingly, spend considerable portions of their time with spade and divining rod in fruitless search. Fortunately, the mounds, though injured, have not been destroyed.

In the way of legitimate research, Mr. S. T. Walker in the Smithsonian Report for 1883,[1] gives an account of his explorations along Pensacola bay, Santa Rosa sound and Choctawhatchee bay, with maps and with figures of human and animal

[1] Pg. 854, *et seq.*

heads which have served as handles for earthenware. Mr. Walker failed to find the deposit of earthenware in the great mound at Walton's Camp.

Professor Holmes informs us that an interesting collection of earthenware was taken from the mound at Bear Point, Perdido bay, by Mr. Parsons, then of the Coast Survey, and we are indebted to Professor Holmes for a series of illustrations of these vessels which resemble those found by us, and which will form a plate in Professor Holmes' forthcoming report on aboriginal earthenware of the United States, to be published by the Bureau of Ethnology.[1]

In the Proceedings of the American Association for the Advancement of Science, 1875, page 282, *et seq.*, G. M. Sternberg, Surgeon, U. S. A., publishes an account of "Indian Burial Mounds and Shellheaps near Pensacola, Florida, Bay." The author describes his explorations in the Bear Point Mound and in the mound at Walton's Camp, Santa Rosa sound, where he, also, we note, missed the great deposit of earthenware.

The student of the archæology of this part of the Florida coast is doubtless familiar with "The Narrative of Alvar Nuñez Cabeça de Vaca," [2] who landed at Tampa in 1527 with part of an ill-fated expedition, and who spent six years (1528–1533) as a prisoner among the aborigines of the northwest Florida coast, living at places where explorations treated of in this volume were carried on, on Santa Rosa Island (Malhado Island) and near Pensacola bay. The inhabitants of this section are described as poor. We are told (p. 50) "for three months in the year they eat nothing else than these [oysters] and drink very bad water. There is great want of wood, and mosquitoes are in very great numbers. The houses are of mats, set up on masses of oyster shells, which they sleep upon, and in skins, should they accidentally possess them." Nevertheless, these coast aborigines were possessed of earthenware. "Before their houses were many clay pitchers of water," we are told (page 35).

Dr. M. G. Miller, who has accompanied us in all our mound work, determined, as to human remains, this season, as before, and aided in our work generally and in putting this Report through the press.

---

[1] We would call the attention of any reader wishing a more thorough acquaintance with the aboriginal ware of this country to:
"Pottery of the Ancient Pueblos."
"Ancient Pottery of the Mississippi Valley."
"Origin and Development of Form and Ornament in Ceramic Art."
All by Professor Holmes and all in the Fourth Annual Report of the Bureau of Ethnology, 1882–1883; and in the same volume "A Study of Pueblo Pottery as Illustrative of Zuñi Culture Growth," by Frank Hamilton Cushing.
"Archæological Expedition to Arizona in 1895," by Jesse Walter Fewkes. Seventeenth Annual Report of the Bureau of American Ethnology, 1895–1896.
"Illustrated Catalogue," etc., by William H. Holmes. Third Annual Report of the Bureau of Ethnology, 1881–1882.
"Contributions to the Archæology of Missouri, Part I, Pottery," by the Archæological Section of the St. Louis Academy of Sciences.
"Antiquities of Tennessee," by Gates P. Thruston.
Various Reports on Antiquities of Florida, Georgia, South Carolina and Alabama, by Clarence B. Moore. Journal of the Academy of Natural Sciences of Philadelphia, Volumes X and XI.
[2] English translation by Buckingham Smith. Privately printed, Washington, 1851.

List of Mounds Investigated.

(See Map)

Bear Point, Perdido bay.
Near Bear Point, Perdido bay.
Josephine P. O., Perdido bay.
Maester Creek, Blackwater bay.
Graveyard Point, East bay.
Santa Rosa sound (2).
Walton's Camp, Santa Rosa sound.
Don's Bayou, Choctawhatchee bay.
Black Point, Choctawhatchee bay.
Rocky Bayou, Choctawhatchee bay (2).
Basin Bayou, Choctawhatchee bay.
Jolly Bay, Choctawhatchee bay.
Black Creek, Choctawhatchee bay (3).
Near Point Washington, Choctawhatchee bay.
Cemetery near Point Washington, Choctawhatchee bay.
Hogtown Bayou, Choctawhatchee bay.

MOUND AT BEAR POINT, PERDIDO BAY, BALDWIN COUNTY, ALA.[1]

This mound was in woods about 150 yards in a N. W. direction from Bear Point, on land belonging to Mr. Arthur B. Jones, of Chicago, Ill.

The mound, which had been fairly riddled by previous digging, was roughly circular in outline, with a diameter at base of 80 feet. The summit plateau, also circular, was 63 feet across. As the mound was partly surrounded by depressions, whence sand for its making had come, its southern portion, built up against a natural slope, was somewhat difficult to determine as to height. On the northwest side the mound was 7 feet 2 inches above the general level and 8 feet on the northeast side. Measured from the south, it was but 1 foot 8 inches above the adjoining territory. Forest trees were on the plateau, including a fallen live oak 10 feet in circumference, 4 feet from the base.

The mound was dug through by us beginning at the extreme margin of the northern portion with a line of men extending about 50 feet. As no interments were met with until the summit plateau was reached, portions of the remaining marginal parts were omitted.

The mound was of yellowish sand, unstratified. A dark band marked the base, which was the original surface of the surrounding country. From the surface of the summit plateau in the northerly portions of the mound, to the base, was 5 feet 4 inches, and this depth was maintained until the slope of the ridge to the south was reached, where the mound and the slope merged.

[1] As Perdido bay is the coast boundary between Alabama and Florida, we have included this mound.

Some distance in from the margin, a second dark band began from 2 to 2.5 feet above the base. This band, which contained bits of charcoal and debris, marked a period of occupation, making it evident that the aborigines, after living for a while on a low mound, had heightened it and used it for burial purposes. Few burials were found below the upper band, and when they were met with, the band had been cut through. Two good examples of the domiciliary mound heightened and then used for burials have been described by us in preceding Reports; namely, the great Shields' Mound, near the mouth of the St. John's river, Florida, and the mound at Matthew's Landing, Alabama river.

In all, human remains were met with in forty-four places, counting only such burials as were seemingly undisturbed by previous digging.

Unless otherwise stated, burials were above the upper dark line in the mound.

Burial No. 1.—Two femurs and part of a radius.

Burial No. 2.—Two skulls with a conch-shell in association. These skulls, like all others in this mound, were badly decayed and are spoken of as skulls because enough of them remained to show that two crania, or the better part of two crania, had been interred.

Burials Nos. 3, 4, 5, 7, 8, 9, 12, 16, 17, consisted each of a single skull, unassociated with other bones. With Burial No. 12 were two shell beads.

Burial No. 6.—A lone skull covered by a circular dish inverted, unfortunately badly crushed. This dish, without basal perforation, of rather coarse, black ware, has incised decoration on the inner surface and a row of notches around the rim. Its diameter is 15.75 inches; its depth, 4 inches. A former cracked portion had been held together by cords or sinews running through perforations on either side of the crack. Incidentally, it is of interest to note that this method of repair was in use in Egypt probably 5000 years ago.[1] This dish has been sent to the Museum at Memorial Hall, Fairmount Park, Philadelphia.

Burial No. 10.—Part of a femur, possibly a late disturbance.

Burial No. 11.—A few decayed fragments of one or two long-bones with a chert lancehead over 4 inches in length.

Burial No. 13.—A grave or a late disturbance. A pit running from, or from near, the surface, cutting through the upper dark band and extending almost to the base of the mound. On the bottom was a bit of a skull and a humerus.

Burial No. 14.—Fragments of decaying long-bones lying in sand unquestionably undisturbed.

Burial No. 15.—A bunch of badly decayed bones, principally long-bones, without a skull.

Burials Nos. 18, 26, 27, 33, 44.—Each a skull with a few other bones.

Burial No. 19.—A few bones without a skull.

Burial No. 20.—Bones falling in caved sand. With them was a quadrilateral

[1] "Naquada and Ballas," by W. M. Flinders Petrie, D. C. L., L. L. D., and J. E. Quibell, B. A., London, 1896.

vessel with four rudimentary feet. The decoration is an incised representation of animal paws. Diameter at opening 3.6 inches; height, 2 inches (Fig. 1).

FIG. 1.—Vessel with Burial No. 20. Mound at Bear Point. (Two-thirds size.)

Burial No. 21.—Over the skull of a child, with which were four large shell beads, was an inverted bowl broken into many pieces. This bowl, since put together, is 11.25 inches in maximum diameter and 4.25 inches in depth. It has no basal perforation. The decoration, incised, Professor Holmes tells us, consists of a conventionalized animal head showing the eye and teeth. On either side are other parts of the animal's body highly conventionalized (Fig. 2). This symbolism on earthenware, which reached its greatest extent along the Gulf coast, will be treated exhaustively by Professor Holmes in his forthcoming work, to which we have already referred.

FIG. 2.—Vessel with Burial No. 21. Mound at Bear Point. (Half size.)

Burial No. 22.—A skull with a few long-bones. With the bones was a beautiful bottle of smooth black ware, with a globular body incised in an interesting way over every portion. A white substance, placed in the lines, greatly emphasizes them. The neck of this bottle is missing through an early fracture. Maximum diameter, 3.25 inches. Near the vessel lay an iron nail.

Burial No. 23.—Part of a dish of smooth black ware with the remainder probably cut away by recent digging. Beneath were disturbed bones.

Burial No. 24.—Certain long-bones without a skull. An arrowpoint lay with them.

Burial No. 25.—Part of a dish of black ware well smoothed, with an incised line encircling the interior below the margin. Recent digging had removed a considerable part of this plate and possibly some bones, as a single molar only was present.

Burial No. 28.—At the base of a pit beginning at or near the surface, which extended through the upper dark band and a short distance below the base, were remains of what had been a wooden box about 2 feet square. Little more than dust remained. Badly rusted nails and small clamps of iron were present. Within the remains of the box, packed together, were: two skulls; four femurs; four tibiæ; two scapulæ; one clavicle; certain ribs and vertebræ; also glass beads.

Burial No. 29.—Skull and certain bones of an adult with some bones of a child, without the skull. With these were thirty large shell beads and three shell hairpins, the shanks partly decayed.

Burial No. 30.—Under an inverted bowl in fragments were: a small bit of shell and certain milk teeth; bitumen; twelve silver buttons; glass beads; an undated silver coin of Spanish-Mexico, which, we were informed at the United States Mint, was struck by Charles and Joanna between 1521 and 1550 A.D.; an iron spike; a small piece of sheet brass or copper with stamped decoration, evidently European. The bowl, which has been pieced together, is of black ware; has a maximum diameter of 15.4 inches, a depth of 6.75 inches. This bowl, whose decoration is much like that of Vessel No. 53 (Fig. 109) from the Cemetery near Point Washington, has been sent to the Museum of Natural History, New York City. We could not determine as to perforation through the absence of a part of the base.

Bitumen, as the reader is doubtless aware, was used by the aborigines as a sort of cement to hold in place in their sockets knives and the like. We shall have occasion again to speak of bitumen in describing the mound near Maester creek, East bay, which is not far from the ancient settlement of Charruco, where Cabeça de Vaca went to live after leaving the aborigines on Santa Rosa Island.

Burial No. 31.—Over the skull of an adult lay a circular dish of black ware in fragments. The rim is notched and a single incised line runs around the inside about 3 inches below the margin. This dish, imperforate as to its base, was sent to the Peabody Museum, Cambridge, Mass., where it has been carefully pieced together. We are indebted to Professor Putnam for photographs of this dish and of all vessels which, sent to the Museum from time to time in a fragmentary condition have there been put together.

FIG. 3.—Vessel with Burial No. 31. Mound at Bear Point. (Half size.)

Below the dish, lying on its side, was an imperforate vase, having a semi-globular body and slightly expanding neck with a diameter at aperture of 5.6 inches, a height of 4.25 inches (Fig. 3). This vessel contained a number of marine bivalves which Mr. H. A. Pilsbry, of the Academy of Natural Sciences, has identified as *Callista gigantea.*

Burial No. 32.—Certain bones of an infant and twenty-two large shell beads.

Burial No. 34.—Inverted and covering an adult skull with a few vertebræ, was a badly crushed bowl of black ware having incised decoration much similar to that on Vessel No. 31 (Fig. 28) from the mound at Walton's Camp. This bowl, which has been sent to the Museum of Natural History, New York City, is 17 inches in maximum diameter and 7 inches deep. A perforation had been made through the base.

In preceding Reports we have described the custom obtaining, mainly in peninsular Florida, to perforate the base of vessels put with the dead in order to "kill" the pot, it is believed, to free its soul to accompany that of the departed. We have described also, how, to a limited extent, this custom was noticed by us in the case of burial urns up the Alabama river and along the Georgia coast. We shall see in this Report how largely this basal perforation was practised along the northwest coast of Florida.

Burial No. 35.—The skull of an adult with part of a bowl lying to one side. A former digging had seemingly carried away the other part.

Burial No. 36.—Inverted and lying over a child's skull crushed flat, was a small, circular dish of black ware very badly broken. There is a certain amount of incised decoration on the inner surface. The base has a perforation. This bowl was sent to the Peabody Museum.

Burial No. 37.—The skull of a young adult was covered by an inverted bowl badly crushed, having an incised decoration much like the design shown on Vessel No. 41 (Fig. 35) from the mound at Walton's Camp. This bowl has been sent to the Peabody Museum, Cambridge, Mass.

With the skull were: two shell ear-plugs; two iron nails; a section of shell somewhat worked; a quartz pebble; three bits of chert; an imperforate vase of black ware with incised decoration, lying on its side, 5.5 inches in maximum diameter of body and 4.25 inches in height (Fig. 4).

Burial No. 38.—Over the skull of an adolescent lay a bowl of brown ware having the body encircled by two incised lines below the margin. One handle which had stood upright above the rim, and was probably the head of a bird or of a quadruped, is missing. The other handle, semi-oval in shape, extends at right angles from the opposite side of the bowl. There is a basal perforation. This bowl has been sent to the Museum of Natural History, New York City.

Burial No. 39.—Two skulls, one of an adult, the other of a child, and a bit of femur were covered by a bowl with base-perforation, 13.25 inches in maximum diameter, 6.5 inches in height (Fig. 5). The decoration, incised, consists of a series of the figures shown in the half-tone reproduction. Professor Holmes believes the central one to be a conventional animal head with conventionalized parts of the body on either side.

Burial No. 40.—A pit running from the surface to the base of the mound,

FIG. 4.—Vessel with Burial No. 37. Mound at Bear Point. (Full size.)

FIG. 5.—Vessel with Burial No. 39. Mound at Bear Point. (Half size.)

which at this point was about 4 feet down. Toward the bottom of this pit had been thrown two skulls and some other bones not in contact, but separated by a certain amount of sand. Above all these more sand had been placed, and then a small pile of bones consisting of certain long-bones, a clavicle and a skull which was badly crushed. Immediately above these, forming an apex to the pile was the skull of an adult capped by an inverted bowl broken but since pieced together.

FIG. 6.—Vessel with Burial No. 40. Mound at Bear Point. (Half size.)

This bowl, 11.75 inches in maximum diameter and 5.5 inches high, has a small basal perforation. The decoration consists of two animal paws between a design made up of parallel curved lines surmounted by a punctate line. The small addition to this design shown in the half-tone occurs but once, and was probably inserted to fill space (Fig. 6). Beneath one of the skulls was a piece of iron.

Burial No. 41.—An inverted bowl of black ware, parts of which were not found, lay over what had perhaps been a burial of which practically nothing remained.

Burial No. 42.—A skull with some long-bones, having in association a discoidal stone of volcanic rock, 3.5 inches in diameter, and an object of iron, probably the handle of a cutlass.

FIG. 7.—Vessel of earthenware. Mound at Bear Point. (Half size.)

Burial No. 43.—In a broad pit reaching almost to the base of the mound were scattered five skulls and a great mixture of other bones, mostly long-bones.

Several small vessels were found unassociated. A vase of black ware (Fig. 7), imperforate, has incised decoration. Its maximum diameter is 5.1 inches; its height, 3 inches. This vase lay inverted, but unassociated with human remains. Probably recent digging had removed them.

In form and style of decoration the vessels surmounting burials in the Bear Point mound resemble somewhat those found by us capping urns on the Alabama river, but while the earthenware on the Alabama usually contains a large admixture of pounded shell, that of Bear Point, as a rule, has no shell, and where it is present, it is finely powdered and appears here and there in the vessel sparsely.

Sherds came from the mound in great numbers and in considerable variety. Some had been dropped singly during the making of the mound, while others lay together in undisturbed sand. On the surface, where diggers had thrown it, was much broken ware, and quantities lay in their refilled excavations. Among the sherds, loose in the sand, were several with complicated stamp decoration.

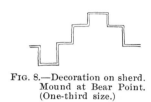

FIG. 8.—Decoration on sherd. Mound at Bear Point. (One-third size.)

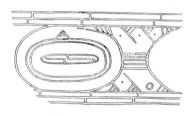

FIG. 9.—Decoration on sherd. Mound at Bear Point. (One-third size.)

Others had the loop-shaped handle so common in the middle Mississippi district and which we found along the Alabama river. Fig. 8 shows a "wall of Troy" decoration from a sherd in the Bear Point mound. Another sherd has a complicated and very neatly incised decoration as shown in Fig. 9. Various animal heads, handles of vessels, were met with, several together beneath the roots of a large tree.

In Fig. 10 we show a number of these handles of vessels: *a*, probably the head of a deer; *b*, a human head with the ears pierced, a duplicate to one found near by, doubtless from the same vessel; *c*, a quail's head; *d*, undetermined; *e*, head of a duck; *f*, a rabbit's head.

Throughout the mound, with human remains at times and again loose in the sand, where perhaps they had been thrown by recent digging, were many pieces of red oxide of iron of a bright crimson color, some showing where parts had been chipped off, probably for grinding, and others having a concave surface where material had been rubbed out for use as paint. With the red oxide, at places, was limonite for yellow paint. When Cabeça de Vaca was living with the aborigines of Charruco he made little trading trips to the westward going to the same Perdido bay where we found this paint in such abundance. He tells us (page 54), "such were what I carried into the interior * * * [conches that are used for cutting, etc.], and in barter for them I brought back skins, ochre with which they rub and color their faces, and flint for arrowpoints, cement and hard canes of which to make arrows, and tassels that are made of the hair of deer, ornamented and dyed red."

Five hammer-stones lay together.

Loose in the sand, but probably in many cases disassociated from human remains by the constant digging to which the mound had been subjected, were: many hammer-stones; pebble-hammers; hones deeply grooved by sharpening of

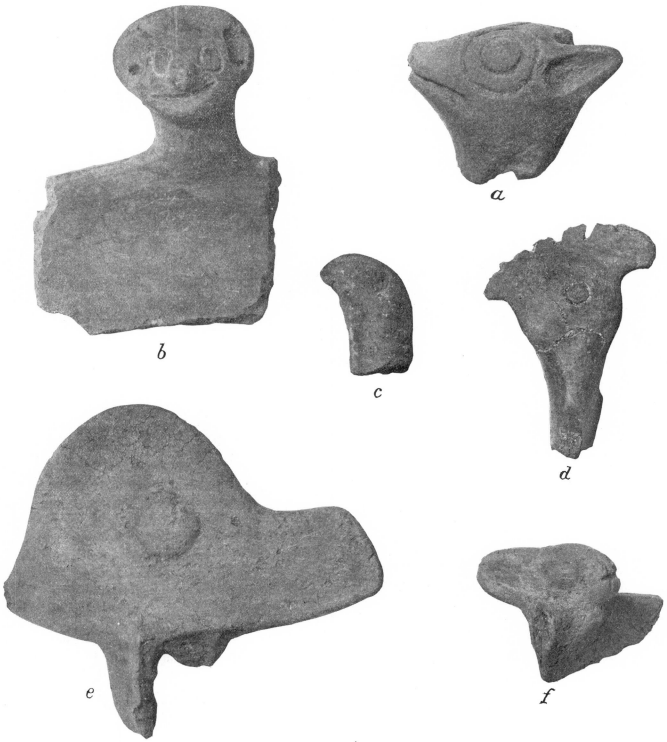

FIG. 10.—Handles of vessels. Mound at Bear Point. (Full size.)

tools; over one dozen arrowheads or knives; two "celts" apparently of sedimentary rock, each over five inches in length; two small chisels, seven discoidal stones of various rocks, including porphyry [1] and shaly ferruginous sandstone, 1.1 to 2.75 inches in diameter.

In this mound, for the first time in our experience, we met with a form of burial where a solitary skull, or a skull with a few bones, is covered by an inverted bowl. In peninsular Florida we have not found vessels used to cover interments. In Georgia, urns containing single skeletons and capped by inverted bowls are found, also cremated remains similarly treated or placed upon the ground with a bowl turned over them. On the Alabama river, where we met with cremation but once, we found large vessels, capped by others inverted, sometimes containing remains of several individuals. The reader will see that the form of burial noticed at the Bear Point mound continues along the upper part of the Florida coast.

In the Bear Point mound were many objects of European provenance, showing some of the burials at least to be of post-Columbian date. This mound clearly adds to the force of what we have always maintained, that when articles were valued by the aborigines, they were interred with the dead, and that it is unlikely that a mound of any size containing no objects showing white contact, was made after intercourse with whites was begun.

Mound near Bear Point, Perdido Bay, Baldwin County, Ala.

About one mile W. S. W. from Bear Point, in a garden belonging to Mr. Bill, resident on the place, is a mound with shell-fields adjoining. The mound, much spread by continual ploughing, has a present height of 30 inches, a base diameter of 48 feet. It is impossible to estimate the original dimensions and inadvisable to give them from hearsay. The entire southern half of the mound, from the margin and central parts of the northern portion, were dug through by us showing the mound to be of unstratified sand. There had been some comparatively recent disturbance.

Burials were first encountered 19 feet from the center. Seven in all were met with, consisting of bunches of bones badly decayed, rather loosely deposited, sometimes with, and sometimes without, the skull.

Two arrowheads, one of quartz, were with the burials, also numerous sherds, the small check-stamp predominating. Others were undecorated or had incised lines or punctate markings, or a larger check-stamp. Several bits of fine, smooth ware bore bright crimson paint. None of the sherds, so far as noticed, had intermixture of pounded shell, though ware of this kind lay on the surface of adjacent shell-heaps.

In the mound, also, were hammer-stones, hones and bitumen which, as we have said, was used as cement.

---

[1] Theodore D. Rand, Esq., of the Academy of Natural Sciences, has kindly determined for us the rocks mentioned in this Report, as accurately as possible without mutilation of specimens.

MOUND NEAR JOSEPHINE POSTOFFICE, PERDIDO BAY, BALDWIN COUNTY, ALA.

A small sand mound about three-quarters of a mile in a northerly direction from the landing at Josephine Postoffice, in pine-woods, was dug through by us without result. The mound was doubtless the former site of a tepee.

At Inerarity Point, on the Florida side of the bay (see map), are numerous shell-fields and small shell-heaps. In addition to extended inquiries, careful search failed to locate a burial mound at this place.

MOUND NEAR MAESTER CREEK, BLACKWATER BAY, SANTA ROSA COUNTY, FLA.

Blackwater bay is an extension of East bay, which is a part of Pensacola bay. The mound, in sight of where Maester creek enters Blackwater bay, was dug through by us by permission of Mr. Frank Berrian, agent, who resides nearby. The mound, of sand, circular in outline, 3 feet high, 30 feet across the base, unstratified, had been dug into in two places by treasure hunters.

In addition to bones disturbed by former digging, and to burials of which almost no trace was left, human remains were met with by us at sixteen points. The form of burial included the bunch, the lone skull, and, in one place, a bunch of long-bones without a skull.

Beneath a cranium, together, were six cannon bones of the deer. Five were broken or partly decayed. One showed an end cut off squarely and seemingly had served as a handle of some sort. A lancepoint of chalcedony, 5.5 inches long, lay loose in the sand, also an arrowpoint of the same material and one of quartzite. In addition were a grooved hone and a small slab of red oxide of iron, showing a concavity through use. A number of masses of bitumen, one about the size of a cocoanut lay together. We have before referred to how Cabeça de Vaca made trading excursions from Charruco, an aboriginal settlement which cannot have been far from this mound, over to the head of Perdido bay, and brought back, among other things, ochre to be used as paint and cement which we know to have been bitumen, in all probability.

The earthenware in the mound consisted of five vessels, all deposited singly in the extreme marginal western part of the mound between south and northwest. They were unassociated.

Vessel No. 1.—A perforate vase with semi-globular body, constricted neck and rim slightly flaring. The decoration consists of roughly incised perpendicular lines around the neck starting from a punctate circle about one-half inch below the rim. Maximum diameter, 6.25 inches; height, 5 inches; diameter of opening, 4.5 inches.

Vessel No. 2.—A bowl of excellent ware, semi-globular body, incurving toward the aperture, and perforate base. The decoration consists of incised and punctate markings (Fig. 11). Maximum diameter, 9 inches; depth, 5 inches; diameter of opening, 6.2 inches.

FIG. 11.—Vessel No. 2. Mound near Maester creek. (About seven-ninths size.)

Vessel No. 3.—A bowl found inverted, oblate spheroid in shape, imperforate. The ware is fairly good. The decoration consists of incised lines and punctate markings around the rim as shown in Fig. 12.

Vessel No. 4.—A bowl badly broken, with faint check stamp markings.

Vessel No. 5.—An undecorated bowl of about three quarts capacity. The base has a perforation.

FIG. 12.—Vessel No. 3. Mound near Maester creek. (Half size.)

MOUND NEAR GRAVEYARD POINT, EAST BAY, SANTA ROSA COUNTY, FLA.

The locality takes its name from a modern graveyard adjoining a small church. The church, which faces the water, is in full sight of the mound, which has been under cultivation and seems greatly extended by it. The mound is roughly circular in outline. Its present diameter is about 75 feet; its height, 2.5 feet. Careful trenching convinced us that the mound was domiciliary in character.

Two and one-half miles in a westerly direction from the mound at Graveyard Point we dug through, without result, a small mound in woods, where treasure seekers had left a considerable excavation.

Other small mounds located during a careful search of bays around Pensacola had been too badly cut to pieces by seekers after treasure to invite investigation.

MOUNDS NEAR SANTA ROSA SOUND, SANTA ROSA COUNTY, FLA. (2).

About twelve miles from the western extremity of Santa Rosa sound, northern side, on ground formerly cultivated, and in full view of the water, were undergrowth removed, are two mounds but a few yards apart, surrounded by a considerable shell deposit. Each has been much spread by the plough.

The larger mound, circular in outline, has a base diameter of 81 feet. The summit plateau is 52 feet across. The height of the mound is 3.5 feet. To the northwest is an excavation 80 feet across and 5 feet 9 inches deep in the center, whence sand was taken for the building of the mound. Careful trenching indicated the mound to be domiciliary in character.

The smaller mound, 26 feet across the base and 2 feet 9 inches high, had been built after the thin shell deposit which covered the field was made, since this deposit extended beneath the mound. Above this shell was from 1 to 1.5 feet of sand in which were numbers of burials. Such as were met with by us in digging part of the mound lay flexed on the right side or showed disturbance, probably aboriginal. There were no artifacts with the remains, and such sherds as were met with had evidently been gathered with the material for the mound. These sherds showed variously the check-stamp, the complicated stamp, incised decoration and crimson paint.

MOUNDS AT WALTON'S CAMP, SANTA ROSA SOUND, SANTA ROSA COUNTY, FLA.

Walton's Camp, which got its name during the Civil War, is near the eastern extremity of Santa Rosa sound, northern side, on property belonging to Mr. J. T. Brooks, resident on the place.

At the water's edge is a shell-heap of considerable size. About 150 yards in a N. E. by N. direction, across a cultivated field, on the edge of woods, is a mound roughly oblong with rounded corners, having a major diameter of base of 223 feet east and west, parallel to the sound. The minor base-diameter is 178 feet. The summit plateau is 179 feet by 135 feet.

A graded way, 78 feet from its beginning to the edge of the summit plateau, joins the mound on the southern side, somewhat east of the center.

The mound is so surrounded by depressions, whence material for its construction was taken, that its exact height above the general level is difficult to get from the exterior. From a point on the southern side the altitude is 10 feet, 7 inches; from the northern side, 12 feet. In the digging it was found that the depth of the mound from the surface of the summit plateau to the base was probably about 12 feet on an average.

There had been much previous digging, the entire central portion of the mound being fairly riddled with excavations.

During our investigation eleven men on an average dug for seven days. This digging consisted of trenching at various points to determine the construction of the

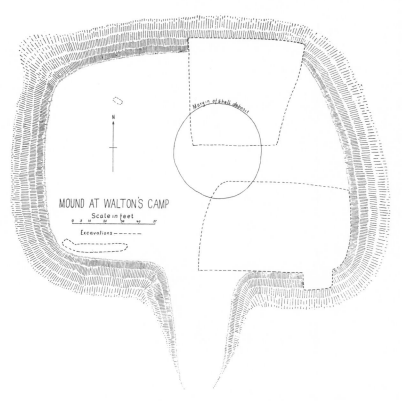

MOUND AT WALTON'S CAMP
Scale in feet
Excavations ------

FIG. 13.—Plan of mound at Walton's Camp, showing excavations.

mound; the removal of a large part of the summit plateau to a depth of from 3 to 5 feet; the investigation of much of the marginal portion on the northern side of the mound (see diagram, Fig. 13, on which our principal work is shown).

Not far from the base, on the northern side, a trench 67 feet across at the start was continued in about 75 feet, converging to 45 feet at the end. This trench did not follow the base after sufficient work had been done to show we were dealing with a mound originally used for domiciliary purposes and later heightened and broadened much in the manner of the mound at Bear Point, and of others of this class found elsewhere by us. Since writing our conclusions on this subject we have, on our return, read Mr. Walker's account of his visit to this mound, and find he, also, realized the fact of its enlargement at various periods.

Not far from the margin on the northern side, a black band about 7 inches thick was met with 4 feet from the surface of the mound, approximately. This band, like the one in the mound at Bear Point, colored by charcoal and organic matter, was the ordinary layer of occupation. The band did not continue through the mound, and was not found at the extremities or in the southern portion.

The central part of the summit plateau, say about 55 feet in diameter, had been heightened about 2 feet by a layer of shell covered with sand. Where this layer began, on the northern side, it was from 6 to 8 inches in thickness. This deposit of shell and sand was not taken into account in our measurement of the height of the mound.

No burials were met with in the northern part of the mound until 35 feet in from the margin of the summit plateau, and then only disturbed fragments left by former digging, no intact burials being found prior to the abandonment of the trench almost at the center of the mound. The western end and the northeastern portion of the mound showed no trace of use as places of interment.

Beginning almost exactly at the southeastern corner of the plateau and extending a little down the slope were burials, many of which were capped by inverted vessels of earthenware. The area where burials with earthenware were most numerous extended 39 feet to the westward and 32 feet to the northward of this southeastern corner. But one large vessel was found farther in and a few small ones which accompanied, but did not lie over, burials. Interments uncovered by bowls extended considerably farther into the mound and to the westward from where the covered burials lay. Burials, then, in the mound were about as follows: in the area to the southeast, as described by us, were various forms of burial, including some of the variety met with by us at the Bear Point mound, where lone skulls, or skulls with a few bones, were capped by inverted bowls. In the extreme southern portion of the central part of the mound were burials without the down-turned bowl, and in the northern part of the center, presumably the same form of burial had existed, as parts of large bowls were not found with the disturbed remains, but all this area, except the comparatively small portion to the south, which was excavated by us, had been so thoroughly dug into by others that exact determination as to form of burial was impossible. Still, judging from the absence of fragments of large vessels, to which we have referred, and that there is no history of the finding of vessels there, we believe all the burials in this central area were similar in form to those met with by us in its southern margin. Roughly speaking, that part of the mound where all burials were without earthenware corresponded with the central shell deposit of which we have spoken, and which is shown on the plan, and we believe this shell deposit was placed in the mound in connection with these burials.

It has seldom been our fortune to investigate a mound where exact determination of burials was so difficult, for, in addition to the great amount of later disturbance, aboriginal burials were so spread that it was difficult to say where one burial ended and another began. According to our account, kept with the strictest attention, 66 burials were met with, none, we believe, over 3 feet in depth. Such of these as were accompanied by vessels of earthenware will be described, particularly, later. Other burials were some at full length, some bunched. In addition, there were solitary skulls and fragmentary parts of the skeleton. Cremation was absent.

Few artifacts, save earthenware, were met with, either loose in the sand or with the dead. There were: pebble-hammers; three large, flat hones of fine-grained ferruginous sandstone; shell beads with a number of burials; two shell hair-pins; three discoidal stones, one of granitoid rock; two rude cutting implements of quartzite; two hatchets, one, 9 inches long, of indurated slate; a flat chisel of the same material, 7 inches long; a bead of bone, 2 inches in length; several masses of red oxide of iron, hollowed out by use as paint; a bead of red jasper, 1 inch in length; many arrow and spear points, some loose in the sand, others with interments. In addition, was a lancehead 3.6 inches in length and 2.6 inches broad, of most unusual form, being heart-shaped as to outline. Mr. Rand is unable to identify the rock of which this lancepoint was made, without mutilating the specimen. Upon the material is a deposit which at first was supposed to be calcareous, but which failed to react with acid (Fig. 14). This interesting specimen lay with two arrow-points near an adult skull.

FIG. 14.—Lancepoint. Mound at Walton's Camp.
(Full size.)

The earthenware in the mound at Walton's Camp was its especial feature. Forty-nine vessels, more or less complete, were taken out by us in addition to some small ones badly broken, which, showing no feature of particular interest, and not in association with burials, will not be described by us.

Many vessels among those taken out, we regret to say, were broken by our men since, lying superficially beneath masses of roots, they were, of necessity, exposed to blows from spades or axes. Many more were found crushed to pieces by roots or by weight of sand, aided, no doubt, by the effect of frost.

In the mound, with whole vessels, were great numbers of fragments in undisturbed sand. Sometimes parts of vessels had been interred, and often parts, broken to pieces, lay in a little pile. Again, numbers of fragments were heaped together.

These often came from many vessels, being a few parts of each so that it seemed as though fragments, usually decorated, had been saved for burial in the mound. These heaps were not found immediately with human remains and were probably buried in a general way. We shall have occasion again to speak of this custom in describing the cemetery near Point Washington.

All through the mound were single fragments of vessels which had got in during the period of occupation or with sand from neighboring fields during construction. These sherds bore, as a rule, the check-stamp as decoration and also various combinations of the complicated stamp. We found no stamped earthenware in conjunction with burials, though there was abundance of it in fragments on the surface of surrounding fields where the aborigines had lived. It would seem, then, that the stamped decoration was in use on vessels intended for domestic purposes and not on mortuary ware.

There is a wide range in the quality of the ware from the mound at Walton's Camp. Some is excellent, much is inferior. As in the ware in the Bear Point mound, small quantities of finely pounded shell are present in places, that is to say locally and not in even mixture throughout the vessel. There is one exception, however, a small vessel where shell coarsely pounded shows on the surface even, as is often the case on vessels of the middle Mississippi district and from the Alabama river. The loop-shaped handle, so often found in the districts we have just named, was present in the mound at Walton's Camp.

A number of heads of earthenware, which had served as handles on vessels, were loose in the sand.

The predominating forms of ware in this mound were the bowl and the dish, and it is interesting to note that a form of dish entirely new, we believe, was discovered by us, namely, a six-pointed, or star-shaped style.

Perforation of the base of vessels was almost universal in this mound, not only in the case of those buried directly with dead, but fragments which included the base had also the perforation, though the remainder of the vessels was not present. We are unable to decide whether parts of vessels were "killed" before interment in the heaps of ware we have described, or whether vessels, having undergone perforation, were broken and then scattered here and there in the mound.

In peninsular Florida we noted, and were first to describe, a curious custom, an account of which we take from one of our preceding publications. "This was the only occurrence in the mound of ready-made mortuary ware. For the benefit of those not familiar with our previous Reports on the Florida mounds, we may say that it was the custom in that State often to knock out the bottom, or to make a hole through the bottom, of earthenware vessels, previous to inhumation with the dead, and that this custom is believed to have been practised with the idea that the mutilation 'killed' the vessel, freeing its soul to accompany that of its owner into the next world. Apparently, however, it entered the minds of the more thrifty among the aborigines that vessels of value might serve a better purpose, and hence there arose a class of ceremonial ware, usually small in size, often of fantastic design and always of flimsy material, with bases perforated during the process of manufacture. This cheap ware was probably kept on hand and did duty for vessels more valuable and less readily spared."

In the mound at Walton's Camp we met with this ready-made mortuary ware in one case only, the most westwardly occurrence in our experience. It is interesting to note this fact since perforation of the base made after completion of the vessel occurs to the westward and up the Alabama river, though sparingly.

We shall now give a description of the various vessels taken from the mound by us and of their finding.

Vessel No. 1.—A vase, perforate as to base, found lying on its side near human remains. The body, oblate spheroid, is decora-

FIG. 15.—Vessel No. 1. Mound at Walton's Camp. (Half size.)

ted with the current scroll. The neck, slightly flaring, has incised and punctate decoration as shown in Fig. 15. Height, 6 inches; maximum diameter, 5.5 inches. This vessel, when found, had parts missing, and, in addition, was struck by a spade.

FIG. 16.—Vessel No. 2. Mound at Walton's Camp. (One-third size.)

Vessel No. 2.—An imperforate bowl found inverted over the skull and some bones of a child, with which were two shell hair-pins and an arrowpoint or knife. This bowl is 15.4 inches in maximum diameter and 7 inches in depth. It has an interesting incised symbolical decoration. The design, which is repeated around the vessel, is shown in Fig. 16.

Vessel No. 3.—This bowl was found in four pieces with fragments of other vessels. Cemented together, it measures 6.5 inches in maximum diameter and 2.8 inches in depth. There is a basal perforation. The decoration, incised and punctate, is shown in Fig. 17.

FIG. 17.—Vessel No. 3. Mound at Walton's Camp. (Half size.)

Vessel No. 4.—This vessel, of inferior ware and without decoration save a scalloped margin, lay crushed to fragments near a single skull with which were four arrowpoints or knives and the curious lancepoint we have figured.

Vessel No. 5.—A circular dish of inferior black ware inverted over a few phalanges. The decoration, rather rudely done, is incised. The basal perforation is to one side of the center. Diameter, 13 inches; depth, 2.5 inches (Fig. 18).

FIG. 18.—Vessel No. 5. Mound at Walton's Camp. (One-third size.)

Vessel No. 6.—A bowl found crushed to pieces, inverted over a solitary skull. The base has a perforation. The decoration, a species of scroll, is incised. The fragments were sent to Peabody Museum, Cambridge, Mass., whence the photograph used in the half-tone was furnished us with the measurements: maximum diameter, 17.25 inches; depth, 5.75 inches (Fig. 19).

Vessel No. 7.—The larger part of a six-pointed dish of black ware, found in fragments and sent to the Davenport Academy of Natural Science, Davenport, Iowa. We shall have occasion, later, to refer to this type.

FIG. 19.—Vessel No. 6. Mound at Walton's Camp. (Two-sevenths size.)

Vessel No. 8.—A bowl, broken, with base perforation, found lying about 2 feet from a bunched burial, at an angle of about forty-five degrees, aperture up. It has been pieced together and sent to the Museum at Memorial Hall, Fairmount Park, Philadelphia. The decoration, incised, is much like that on Vessel No. 40 (Fig. 102) from the cemetery near Point Washington. Maximum diameter, 10.2 inches; depth, 4.1 inches.

Vessel No. 9.—This vessel, much resembling a cap in shape with visor before and behind, is said to belong to a class modelled after trays of wood. It is unbroken

FIG. 20.—Vessel No. 9. Mound at Walton's Camp. (Half size.)

save for a basal perforation. It is of yellow ware, and is notched around the margin except at the handles. There is an incised meander decoration. Major diameter, 10.5 inches; minor diameter, 8.25 inches; depth, 3.6 inches (Fig. 20). It lay, inverted, over a single fragment of bone, though others had probably disappeared through decay.

Vessel No. 10.—A small bowl found with many fragments of earthenware just below the surface.

Vessel No. 11.—This interesting bowl of excellent red ware is intact with the exception of a mortuary perforation. It lay, inverted, over the skull of an adult, the skull of an adolescent, a few vertebræ and the clavicle of a child. The decoration, incised, uniform all around, consists of a series of conventionalized heads in which the eye and teeth are prominent. Maximum diameter, 15.25 inches; depth, 6 inches (Fig. 21).

FIG. 21.—Vessel No. 11. Mound at Walton's Camp. (About half size.)

Vessels Nos. 12 and 13.—Small bowls from the same deposit as Vessel No. 10. One has three small handles. A fourth handle is missing. The other, with incised and punctate decoration much resembling that on Vessel No. 24, this mound, has been sent to Memorial Hall, Fairmount Park, Philadelphia. Both vessels are perforate as to the base.

Vessels Nos. 14, 15, 16.—Vessel No. 14, a counterpart of Vessel No. 9, this mound, lay inverted, in fragments, on a dish of black ware also inverted. This dish, with incised and punctate decoration, is six pointed, or star-shaped. There is a base-perforation. Maximum diameter, 14.75 inches; depth, 3 inches (Fig. 22). This interesting type, as we have stated, we believe to be new. Professor Putnam and Professor Holmes had not seen it previously. Partly between Vessels Nos. 14 and 15 lay a portion of a vessel in fragments. All this ware lay above an infant's skull. Vessel No. 14, pieced together, has been sent to Memorial Hall, Fairmount Park, Philadelphia.

Vessels Nos. 17 and 18.—Small bowls found together just below the surface apart from human remains.

Vessels Nos. 19 and 20.—Vessel No. 19, a circular dish of crude black ware,

8.5 inches in diameter and 1.5 inches in depth, having incised decoration on the inner surface, lay face down on Vessel No. 20, which, inverted, was over a few fragments of the bones of a child. These bones lay upon a large portion of another dish. Vessel No. 20, a bowl of brown ware, intact with the exception of a basal

FIG. 22.—Vessel No. 15. Mound at Walton's Camp. (About half size.)

perforation, has an admirably executed incised and punctate decoration as shown in Fig. 23. Maximum diameter, 13.8 inches; depth, 6.5 inches. Vessel No. 19, also, is perforate.

Vessel No. 21.—A small, rude, imperforate bowl, undecorated with the exception of four knobs on the margin, lay about 1 foot from human remains.

FIG. 23.—Vessel No. 20. Mound at Walton's Camp. (Half size.)

Vessel No. 22.—A large fragment with much of the rim missing lay, inverted, over a skull with a few other bones.

Vessel No. 23.—A star-shaped dish of black ware, found crushed, with a small portion missing, has been sent to the Peabody Museum. No human bones were found in association.

Vessel No. 24.—An imperforate bowl found inverted over the skull of an infant. The decoration is a series of partially interlocked scrolls with punctate and lined work in addition. Maximum diameter, 12.5 inches; depth, 5.3 inches (Fig. 24).

FIG. 24.—Vessel No. 24. Mound at Walton's Camp. (Half size.)

Vessel No. 25.—A bowl 6.8 inches in diameter and 2.9 inches in depth, with perforate base and incised and punctate decoration. This bowl came from just below the surface (Fig. 25).

Vessel No. 26.—A bowl of black ware, perforate, having a notched rim, incised and punctate decoration, lay near Vessel No. 24. Maximum diameter, 6 inches; depth, 3.2 inches. This bowl, with small protuberances, is, doubtless, a life-form somewhat resembling Vessel No. 49, this mound, which, however, is more clearly defined, distinctly representing a fish.

FIG. 25.—Vessel No. 25. Mound at Walton's Camp. (Half size.)

Vessel No. 27.—A perforate bowl found lying on its side near human remains. The decoration is similar to that of Vessel No. 40 (Fig. 102) from the Cemetery near Point Washington. Maximum diameter, 5.1 inches; depth, 2.8 inches.

Vessel No. 28.—Found, badly crushed, inverted over a few fragments of bone. The decoration, which Professor Holmes believes to be a highly conventionalized head with the eye above and parts of the body on either side, is shown in Fig. 26.

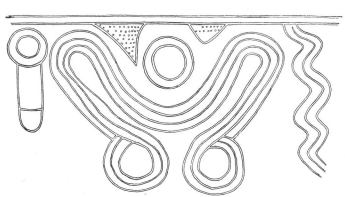

FIG. 26.—Decoration. Vessel No. 28. Mound at Walton's Camp. (One-third size.)

Vessel No. 29.—A perforate bowl in fragments found inverted over a skull and some bones of an infant and certain bones of a child with which were a considerable number of shells of *Marginella*, pierced to use as beads. The decoration consists of a repetition of three upright wavy lines. This bowl is now at the Peabody Museum.

Vessel No. 30.—A perforate vessel 5.5 inches by 4.6 inches and 2.8 inches in depth, representing a frog much after the manner of the ware of the middle Mississippi district. The legs, fashioned separately and pressed upon the body, have fallen off in part (Fig. 27).

Vessel No. 31.—A bowl found, badly crushed, inverted over the skull of an adult. This bowl, which has been pieced together, and sent to the Museum of Natural History, New York, is imperforate. The decoration, incised and punctate, consists of a series of designs as shown in Fig. 28, which doubtless represents jaws with teeth and possibly an eye in the center. Maximum diameter, 16 inches; depth, 5 inches.

Vessels Nos. 32 and 33.—A bowl with a single handle almost upright and the current scroll decoration. The base is perforate. The dimensions are 5.5 inches long by 5 inches across; the height, 2.5 inches (Fig. 29). This bowl lay inverted just below the surface with no bones in association. Beside it lay Vessel No. 33, also inverted, in fragments.

Vessel No. 34.—A small, perforate bowl with incised and punctate decoration (Fig. 30).

FIG. 27.—Vessel No. 30. Mound at Walton's Camp. (Full size.)

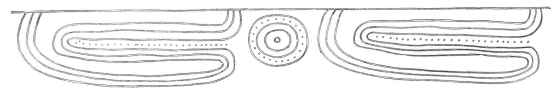

FIG. 28.—Decoration; Vessel No. 31. Mound at Walton's Camp. (One-fourth size.)

FIG. 30.—Vessel No. 34. Mound at Walton's Camp. (Half size.)

FIG. 29.—Vessel No. 32. Mound at Walton's Camp. (Two-thirds size.)

Vessel No. 35.—Small bowl badly broken.

Vessels Nos. 36 and 37.—Both perforate as to the base. Vessel No. 36 (Fig. 31), 7.8 inches maximum diameter, 2.5 inches in depth, with the favorite partially interlocked scroll decoration, was found inverted over Vessel No. 37 standing upright.

FIG. 31.—Vessel No. 36. Mound at Walton's Camp. (Three-quarters size.)

The base of Vessel No. 37 rested upon a number of fragments of pottery piled one upon another in such relation to each other that it was evident the breakage occurred before the fragments were placed together. These pieces, when put together, formed part of a dish, only. Vessel No. 37, a pot, has four loop-shaped handles and incised and punctate decoration. Its maximum diameter is 5 inches; its height,

FIG. 32.—Vessel No. 37. Mound at Walton's Camp. (Half size.)

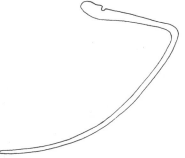

FIG. 33.—Section of Vessel No. 38. (Half size.)

3.2 inches (Fig. 32). There is a deposit of soot showing domestic use, a rare occurrence among mortuary vessels in this part of Florida.

Vessel No. 38.—This vessel with incurved rim and incised decoration on the upper portion, rather rudely executed, has a basal perforation. The vessel lay near the four preceding ones, apart from human remains. Diameter, 9 inches; diameter of aperture, 5 inches; height, 2.75 inches (Figs. 33, 34).

Vessel No. 39.—Certain fragments of a dish piled one on the other over a few decaying fragments of the bones of an infant, with which were shell beads.

FIG. 34.—Vessel No. 38. Top view. Mound at Walton's Camp. (About seven-ninths size.)

Vessel No. 40.—This bowl of about 3 pints' capacity, with perforate base, though inverted, was not associated with human remains. The decoration consists of notches at the rim and a single incised line with five small knobs.

Vessel No. 41.—Parts of a bowl lying over a few remnants of long-bones of a young person. The decoration consists of a series of designs similar to the one shown in Fig. 35.

Vessel No. 42.—A double cup found by the side of the skull of a child.

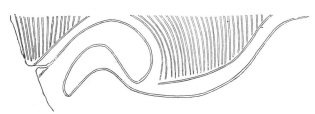

FIG. 35.—Decoration; Vessel No. 41. Mound at Walton's Camp. (One-third size.)

Diameters, 4 inches by 2.5 inches; height, 2.6 inches. There is a scroll decoration incised on the rather inferior ware (Fig. 36). Each base is perforate but not through the knocking out of fragments as in the other cases noted by us, but by means of careful cutting while the clay was soft. We have referred to this custom, so often met with in peninsular Florida, at the beginning of the description of this mound.

FIG. 36.—Vessel No. 42. Mound at Walton's Camp. (Full size.)

Vessel No. 43.—A bowl of poor material with incised decoration, having on one side, as handles, two upright effigies of the human head. At the other side, a flat handle such as usually represents the tail in bird-effigy vessels of the middle Mississippi district, projects horizontally. A considerable part of the base is missing. Maximum diameter, 9 inches; depth, 4 inches (Fig. 37).

FIG. 37.—Vessel No. 43. Mound at Walton's Camp. (One-third size.)

Vessel No. 44.—A small vessel shattered by a blow from a spade. Infant bones were in association.

Vessel No. 45.—A bowl, crushed to pieces, inverted over fragments of the skull of an infant or of a young child. With the exception of a few missing parts, this bowl has been pieced together, showing a perforation of the base. Maximum diameter, 16 inches; height, 5.5 inches. The decoration, shown in Fig. 38, may be divided into three parts, the two to the right of the reader are repeated around the bowl. The part to the left appears but once. This bowl has been sent to the American Museum of Natural History, New York City.

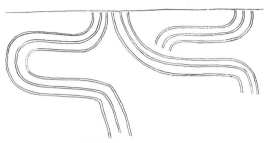

FIG. 38.—Decoration, Vessel No. 45. Mound at Walton's Camp. (One-third size.)

Vessel No. 46.—An imperforate bowl of about one pint capacity, of excellent ware highly smoothed, having five encircling, incised lines below the rim (Fig. 39). It lay near the skull of a child.

Vessel No. 47.—A small, imperforate pot with two loop-shaped handles, found inverted, by the side of an infant's skull with which were three mussel shells.

Vessel No. 48.—A flat-bottomed perforate cup of inferior ware, with rude, symbolical decoration, found near the surface. This cup, struck by a spade, has been pieced together. Diameter of aperture, 4.5 inches; of base, 2.8 inches; depth, 3 inches (Fig. 40).

FIG. 39.—Vessel No. 46. Mound at Walton's Camp. (Half size.)

FIG. 40.—Vessel No. 48. Mound at Walton's Camp. (Two-thirds size.)

Vessel No. 49.—Part of a bowl of about two quarts' capacity, in fragments, found with other ware, apart from human remains. This interesting bowl, showing the influence of the middle Mississippi district, is a life-form representing a fish. On one side a clearly defined head projects. Half way around, on either side, projections doubtless represent fins. That part of the bowl which included the

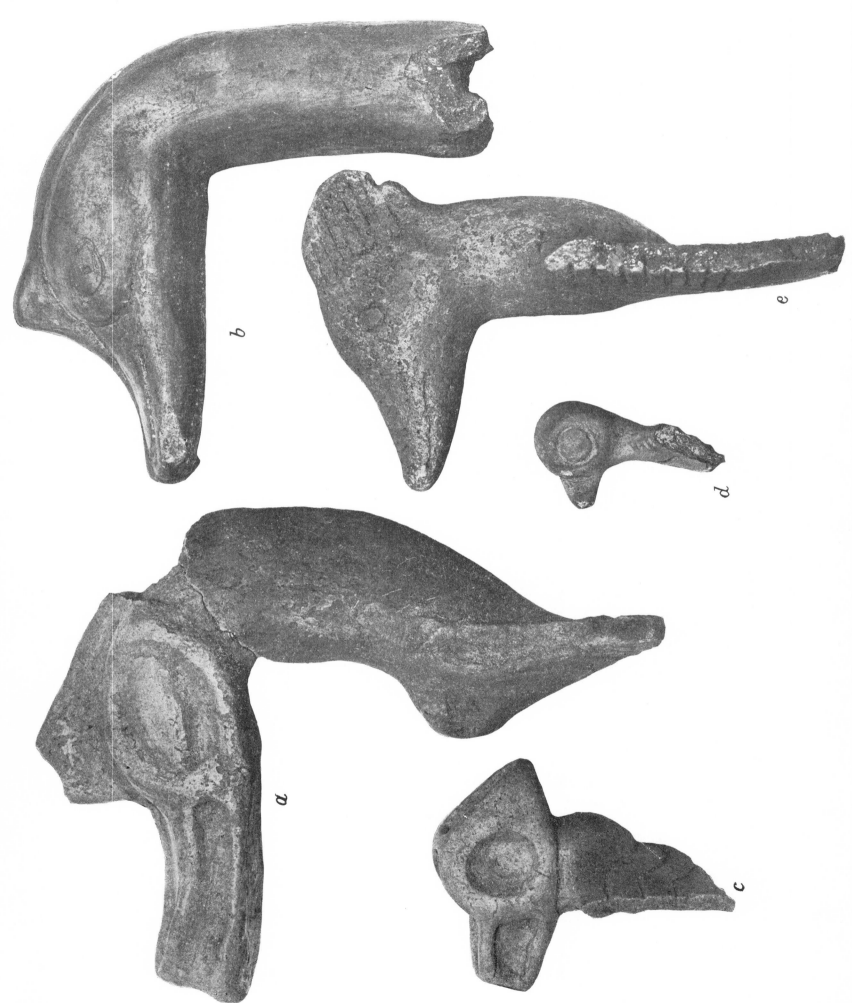

Fig. 42.—Handles of earthenware vessels. Mound at Walton's Camp. (Full size.)

tail is missing.   The decoration, found on various vessels representing fish, perhaps symbolizes fins (Fig. 41).

FIG. 41.—Vessel No. 49.   Mound at Walton's Camp.   (Half size.)

Fig. 42 shows five handles of bowls, representing heads of birds, from the mound at Walton's Camp.

Four interesting sherds have been selected from those found at the Walton's

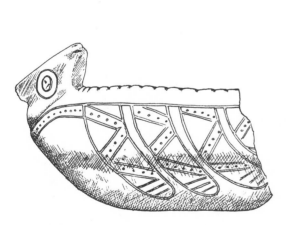

FIG. 43.—Sherd. Mound at Walton's Camp.
(Half size.)

FIG. 44.—Sherd.   Mound at Walton's Camp.
(Half size.)

Camp mound.   Fig. 43 shows the head of an owl with conventionalized wing.   Fig. 44 gives the complicated stamp decoration already described as coming from the midden refuse in the mound. Fig. 45 represents a head, a series of which evidently ran around the vessel. The drawing is made from two fragments, one of which shows one portion of the head; the other, the remainder. Fig. 46, when turned on end, shows a head with eye, mouth and teeth.

FIG. 45.—Sherd. Mound at Walton's Camp. (Half size.)

In the cultivated field to the west of Mr. Brooks' house and about one-quarter of a mile in a westerly direction from the great mound, in full view from the Sound, is a sand mound at present 7.5 feet in height. It had been much dug into before our visit. Careful investigation on our part met with no success and confirmed our belief that the mound had been erected for domiciliary purposes.

Various small mounds are in the neighborhood of the great one investigated by us. Careful digging convinced us that all were of a domiciliary character. In one containing midden refuse with much shell was a piercing implement of bone and a buck-horn handle with a socket to receive an implement.

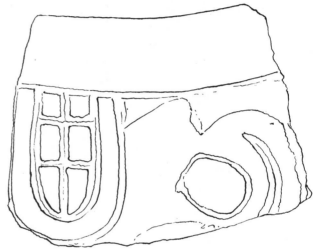

FIG. 46.—Sherd. (Full size.)

MOUND NEAR DON'S BAYOU, CHOCTAWHATCHEE BAY, SANTA ROSA COUNTY, FLA.

Garnier's Bayou is near the western extremity of Choctawhatchee Bay. Don's Bayou enters Garnier's Bayou on its western side.

In scrub, about 200 yards in a westerly direction from the landing, at the head of Don's Bayou, in a field on Government property showing signs of early cultivation, is a mound of irregular outline, greatly spread by the plough, apparently. The major and minor basal diameters are 80 feet and 50 feet respectively. The present height is 3 feet. Thorough trenching showed the mound to be of sand and probably erected as a dwelling site.

MOUND NEAR BLACK POINT, CHOCTAWHATCHEE BAY, WALTON COUNTY, FLA.

About one-quarter mile in a northwesterly direction from Black Point, in scrub, formerly a cultivated field, on Government property, is a rather symmetrical mound of circular outline with basal diameter of 83 feet.

The diameter of the summit plateau is 46 feet. Thorough trenching showed the mound to have been a place of residence only. Isolated sherds lay here and there in the sand of which the mound was composed, some of excellent quality, undecorated, with the check-stamp, with the complicated stamp and with incised decoration.

MOUNDS NEAR ROCKY BAYOU, CHOCTAWHATCHEE BAY, WALTON COUNTY, FLA.

On the west side of Rocky Bayou, about 1.5 miles up, in scrub, not far from the water's edge, was a mound, circular in outline, 28 feet across the base and 2 feet 3 inches in height. A small trench had been dug through the central part.

This mound, which was demolished by us, was of unstratified sand. Three badly decayed skulls, each with some fragments of other bones, were met with and a few small pieces of bone lying alone.

About 8 inches below the surface, apparently unassociated, was a tobacco pipe of soapstone, similar to those we have found in mounds near the mouth of the St. John's river, Florida, where the orifice for the stem almost equals in size the bowl of the pipe. In shape the pipe forms almost a right-angle with one side 4 inches in length, the other side, 3 inches.

With human remains, near together, were five small vessels of yellow ware, all perforate as to the base. Three are undecorated bowls, each of about one-half pint capacity. Another, semi-globular, 3.6 inches in maximum diameter, has the rim turning inward to leave an aperture of about 1.7 inches. The height is about 2.4 inches. The fifth vessel has the form of a gourd. Its length is 4.6 inches; its height, 2.8 inches. The diameter of aperture is 1.4 inches (Fig. 47). The end of the stem has a small irregular hole which seems to have come through decay.

FIG. 47.—Gourd-shaped vessel. Mound at Rocky Bayou.
(Two-thirds size.)

A graceful "celt," probably of igneous rock, with well-ground edge and rounded end, 8.5 inches in length, lay near the surface.

In various parts of the mound were several vessels, parts of vessels and sherds, of no particular interest.

About 100 yards east of the eastern side of the mouth of Rocky Bayou, in a field formerly cultivated but now overgrown with scrub, is a mound of irregular outline, with basal diameters of 72 feet and 112 feet. The height is 4 feet. Careful trenching gave every indication that the mound had been domiciliary in character.

MOUND NEAR BASIN BAYOU, CHOCTAWHATCHEE BAY, WALTON COUNTY, FLA.

This mound was in thick scrub, about one-quarter mile in a westerly direction from the first habitation on the western side of the bayou, on property of Mr. George Berry, of Portland, Fla. The mound proper had a diameter of base of 40 feet, a height of 6 feet 6 inches. A graded way 28 feet long and 20 feet across, where it joined the mound on its S. W. side, was about 3.5 feet lower than the mound where it united with it.

A hole involving half of the central part of the mound had been dug previous to our visit.

The mound, with the exception of certain marginal parts, was dug through by us. Careful search failed to discover that dark line which we usually recognize as marking the base. The outer part of the mound at the N. E. side was composed entirely of black, loamy sand, rich in organic matter, having a maximum depth of 6 feet. This did not seem to be midden material, but muck from swampy ground near by. The remainder of the mound was of yellow sand, with black sand above it in varying depths, but nowhere approaching the depth of the black sand at the side of the mound.

While the former digger doubtless disturbed certain burials, yet, as the excavations made by him converged considerably, it is not likely a large percentage was affected. It is probable that certain burials had disappeared through decay, as, in addition to some scattered bones, but four burials were met with by us. Three of these consisted of decaying fragments of skull with friable pieces of long-bones, all between 6 and 7 feet in depth. A number of long-bones in fragments lay together.

Five and one-half feet from the surface was a bowl 3 inches in diameter, with perforate base. No remains were found near it, though it is likely a burial had lain with it.

No artifacts were with burials, practically all objects met with by us being near the bottom of the deposit of black loam on the northeastern side of the mound, in which were no burials.

Near together were four undecorated bowls all with base-perforation and all slightly broken in addition. Near them lay many pieces of mica.

Several fragments of excellent yellow paste lay somewhat scattered. Pieced together, they showed a fragment 7.5 inches in height, of a cylindrical vessel with flat base. The design, carefully made with a blunt point, is symbolical. The head of a duck stands out in relief for a handle (Fig. 48). Most careful search was made for the remainder of this vessel throughout the entire deposit of dark sand, and we are forced to believe that the fragments obtained by us represent all that was in the mound, and that this portion of the vessel, as Mr. Fewkes says of another class of objects, "should come under the group of sacrifices called substitutional, or symbolical, a part for the whole." [1]

A number of scattered fragments formed part of a pot decorated with crimson paint.

[1] "Property-right in Eagles among the Hopi," American Anthropologist, October–December, 1900, p. 690.

Also in fragments, rather closely associated, immediately on the base of the black loam deposit was a large part of an effigy-vase of yellow ware. The figure is that of a male in a squatting position. Its height is 9.5 inches. It is 6.5 inches across the shoulders and has a maximum thickness of 5.3 inches. The diameter of the aperture, which is at the top of the head, is 3.4 by 3 inches. The arms, which

Fig. 48.—Fragment of vessel. Mound near Basin Bayou. (About two-thirds size.)

had been fashioned separately and fastened to the body by pressure, are missing. Around the head is a band, part of which has fallen from the forehead and part from the back. Much of the base is wanting. This interesting effigy, taken from the front and from the side, is shown in Figs. 49, 50.

Isolated sherds showed fine ware with incised decoration. The complicated stamp was represented by four varieties.

No use of powdered shell with the paste was noted.

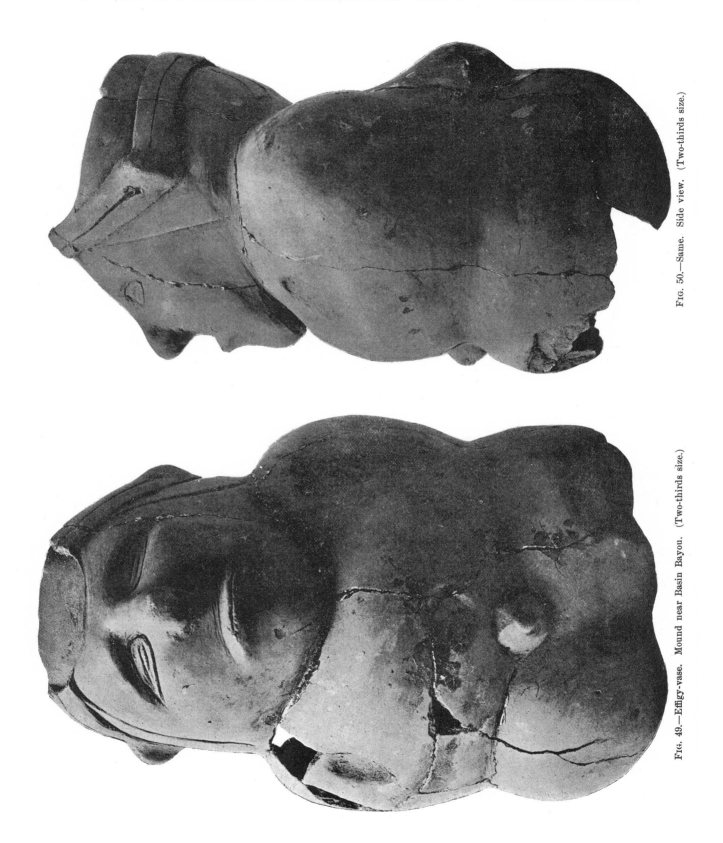

FIG. 50.—Same. Side view. (Two-thirds size.)

FIG. 49.—Effigy-vase. Mound near Basin Bayou. (Two-thirds size.)

Mound near Jolly Bay, Choctawhatchee Bay, Walton County, Fla.

Jolly bay is at the eastern end of Choctawhatchee bay. Landing at the head of Jolly bay, on the north side, and keeping about one mile inland in an N. N. W. direction, a mound is reached in pine woods on the verge of hammock land near a fine stream of water. The mound, on property of Mr. R. L. Burnham, resident on the place, was investigated by kind permission of the owner. The mound had been dug into more extensively than any of its size it has been our fortune to see and, as usual, vain search for treasure was the motive of the wreck. Little beyond the sloping portion of the mound and part of the eastern end remained intact. Fortunately for us, deposits of earthenware in mounds in this section of the country are often marginal, so that we believe little, if any, pottery was destroyed by previous digging. We were informed by Mr. Burnham that he had been present when others were seeking for gold, and had witnessed the finding of but one pot since the digging began, twenty years ago.

The height of the mound as we found it, was 3 feet 9 inches; its diameter east and west was 70 feet and 55 feet north and south. Its summit plateau was 51 feet by 38 feet.

All undisturbed parts of the mound which was composed of unstratified sand, were dug through by us.

Twenty-seven undisturbed burials were met with. These were lone skulls; skulls with a few fragments of long-bones, and, occasionally, long-bones without the skull, all badly decayed.

With one skull was a lancepoint 5 inches in length. Another skull had eight arrowpoints or knives, five of quartzite, three of jasper.

With a burial was a piercing implement made from the column of a *Fulgur*.

A small chisel of undetermined rock, a broken "celt" and several arrowpoints, one of blue quartz, lay loose in the sand.

On the southern side of the mound, beginning at the general level, dark sand extended below the surface, continuing into the slope for a considerable distance. In this sand were several vessels, and burials also were present in it.

In all, fourteen vessels were met with, all but one or two in the sloping portion of the mound, and none much farther in than the margin of the summit plateau.

We give in detail a description of the vessels.

Vessel No. 1.—A little below the surface, almost at the beginning of the upward slope, with no bones in association, lay an interesting dish of yellow ware, five pointed, with basal perforation. The decoration, which is incised and punctate, is evidently symbolical. Maximum diameter, 7.5 inches; depth, 2.3 inches (Fig. 51).

Vessel No. 2.—2 feet 10 inches down, inverted over the skull of an infant, with other bones near by in a condition resembling sawdust, was a bowl with incised decoration much the same as that on Vessel No. 20 (Fig. 23) from the Walton's Camp mound. Maximum diameter, 8.8 inches; depth, 4 inches. The base is imperforate. On the sides of the bowl is much soot indicating use for domestic purposes.

Vessel No. 3.—3 feet 3 inches down, upright, unassociated, was an undecorated, perforate bowl of excellent ware. The rim, thickened, projects horizontally about .5 inch. Maximum diameter, 6.5 inches; depth, 2.7 inches.

FIG. 51.—Vessel No. 1. Mound near Jolly Bay. (About full size.)

Vessel No. 4.—This vase, with perforate base, undecorated, of about one quart capacity, has a globular body and an upright neck, slightly expanding, 1.25 inches high.

Vessel No. 5.—A rude, undecorated bowl of about one quart capacity.

Vessel No. 6.—A bowl, 3 feet down, inverted over a fragment of human bone. The ware is inferior. The decoration is incised. From one side a head, probably representing that of a frog, projects. Opposite, a tail, apparently, has been lost through breakage (Fig.52). Maximum diameter, including head, 3.6 inches; depth, 1.8 inches.

FIG. 52.—Vessel No. 6. Mound near Jolly Bay. (Full size.)

Vessel No. 7.—3 feet down, lying on its side, unassociated, was a perforate vessel with undecorated, globular body and upright neck, slightly flaring, 2 inches in height. The neck has a poorly defined check-stamp decoration.

Vessel No. 8.—This bottle, imperforate, of dark ware, is probably the most

FIG. 53.—Vessel No. 8. Mound near Jolly Bay. (Full size.)

interesting vessel taken by us from the Florida coast.   It fell with caving sand, so that data as to its association with human remains were not obtainable.   The body, which tapers to a flat base 1.8 inches across, has a maximum diameter of 5 inches.

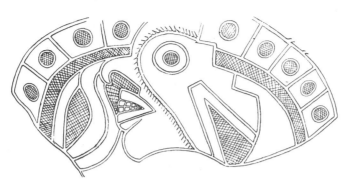

FIG. 54.—Engraved decoration on Vessel No. 8.   (Half size.)

The undecorated upright neck expands slightly.   The height is about 4.5 inches.   The decoration, carefully engraved, represents, on one side of the body of the bottle, a head wearing a grotesque mask having the beak of a bird and the bird's eye so often shown on aboriginal work. Above the head is a conventionalized serpent marking. The engraved decoration is shown on the half-tone representation of the bottle (Fig. 53) and diagrammatically in Fig. 54.

On the opposite side of the bottle is an engraved design representing an eagle

FIG. 55.—Vessel No. 8. Opposite side. (Full size.)

with extended wings and head turned to the reader's left (Figs. 55, 56). Two vertebræ of a child were in the sand within this bottle.

Fig. 56.—Engraved decoration on Vessel No. 8. Opposite side. (Half size.)

Vessel No. 9.—Fragments of part of a bowl.

Vessel No. 10.—Bowl, perforate base, inferior ware with four incised, encircling, parallel lines. Maximum diameter, 8.25 inches; depth, 5.2 inches. From the rim, projecting obliquely upward, are six rude animal heads, much resembling in style those shown on Vessel No. 13, this mound.

Vessel No. 11.—A bowl with rough, incised decoration and in-turned rim a little less than 1 inch in width. From the body are four projections. This vessel, which rudely represents a life-form, lay tilted on its side 2 feet below the surface. No bones were in association. The base is perforate (Fig. 57).

Fig. 57.—Vessel No. 11. Mound near Jolly Bay. (About half size.)

Vessel No. 12.—A rather rude, imperforate bowl with bird-head handle and conventional tail on the opposite side. The decoration on the upper part of the bowl, which is slightly thicker than the lower part, is incised. Diameter of body, 7 inches; depth, 4.75 inches.

Vessel No. 13.—A bowl of inferior ware, perforate, with undecorated body and four projections, rude representations of animal head (Fig. 58). Maximum diameter, 7.6 inches; depth, 4.4 inches. This bowl has been used for culinary purposes.

Vessel No. 14.—Soon after our work on this mound began, parts of a vessel of dark ware, the body surrounded by several incised lines, were thrown out by a digger. Somewhat later other parts were met with. About two hours after this the same digger found several other fragments of this vessel, much farther in. At the end, almost the entire vessel was present and such small parts as were missing no doubt escaped our attention and that of the digger. From all this it would

FIG. 58.—Vessel No. 13. Mound near Jolly Bay. (Half size.)

FIG. 60.—Handle of vessel. Mound near Jolly Bay. (Full size.)

FIG. 59.—Handle of vessel. Mound near Jolly Bay. (Full size.)

seem that an entire vessel had been broken and its parts scattered on the sand during the construction of the mound.

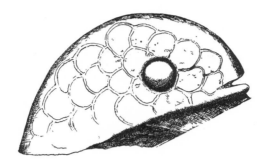

FIG. 61.—Handle of vessel. Mound near Jolly Bay. (Half size.)

Loose in the sand were three handles of vessels; two representing human heads (Figs. 59, 60), and one the head of a fish, neatly executed (Fig. 61.)

MOUNDS NEAR BLACK CREEK, CHOCTAWHATCHEE BAY, WALTON COUNTY, FLA. (3).

These mounds lay in sight of each other in an old field about 2.5 miles up Black Creek and one mile inland in a southwesterly direction from Mr. David Evans' lower landing.

The mounds had all been under cultivation, and evidently all had been greatly spread by the plough. The smallest was less than one foot in height. The others were 70 feet and 96 feet in diameter and 1.5 feet and 4 feet in height, respectively. All these mounds were carefully trenched with no result, save to indicate their former use as places of domicile.

MOUND NEAR POINT WASHINGTON, CHOCTAWHATCHEE BAY, WASHINGTON COUNTY, FLA.

This mound was about two miles in a westerly direction from Point Washington, near a spring of excellent water. The spring feeds a pond from which a narrow creek, navigable for small boats, runs to the bay, somewhat over a mile distant. The mound, on the property of Mr. Simeon Strickland, Sr., of Point Washington, who kindly permitted us to dig, was of circular outline, 36 feet across the base and 6 feet high. Previous diggers, treasure seekers, we were told, had made a large hole in the center, probably 8 feet in diameter, and had driven a trench in from the margin.

The mound, of yellow sand without stratification, was demolished by us.

Burials were central to a certain extent, the first being met with 8 feet in from the margin. In all eleven were met with by us at depths varying from 2 feet to the base of the mound, and doubtless a considerable number was destroyed by the hunters for gold. The form of burial was the solitary skull, sometimes accompanied by a few fragments of other bones or, occasionally, long-bones without the skull were met with. On the center of the base of the mound, 6 feet down, was the only skeleton found, being the bones of an adolescent lying at length to the knees, with the lower legs flexed under.

With the exception of a thick sheet of mica below this skeleton, no artifacts were met with in the mound in direct association with the dead. Two arrowheads were loose in the sand, as was a ball of galena, about 2 inches in diameter. There was present, also, a part of a small disc of copper, or of brass, too minute and too corroded for determination.

While no tributes were placed immediately with burials, yet, as we have seen to be the case elsewhere, there was in this mound a large deposit of earthenware, marginal in the main, placed generally.

In the N. E. part of the mound, not far from the margin, where the mound was a trifle over two feet in height, was sand much darker than the rest, though not so markedly in contrast as was the black loam in the marginal part of the mound near Basin Bayou. In this sand in the Point Washington mound, in close association, in contact even or, at times, one placed partly within another, were ten vessels of from one pint to two quarts capacity, approximately, the under ones lying on the base of the mound. A short distance away were five additional vessels while, a little further in, lay a number of others. In all, thirty-eight vessels of earthenware came from the mound, all, save two, from or from the vicinity of, the place we have noted. Of the two exceptions, one was from the margin, but several yards distant from the rest, while the other fell with caving sand from near the surface. This vessel was imperforate as to the base and was the only one met with by us in the mound clearly without mortuary mutilation, though several were too fragmentary for determination.

One of the groups of vessels lay with their bases resting upon great fragments of much larger vessels, as on a floor.

In two cases vessels whose bodies tapered to the base, had the base entirely knocked away instead of perforated simply. In one case, the base was found later, some distance from the vessel to which it belonged.

Of the thirty-eight vessels found by us none exceeded two quarts in capacity, and in none was admixture of powdered shell apparent. The paste, yellow, as a rule, ranged from inferior to most excellent quality, resembling the ware of peninsular Florida. Many were undecorated; others offered no novelty in shape or ornamentation, while others, again, were crushed to fragments. We shall, therefore, confine ourselves in description to vessels worthy of especial notice.

Vessel No. 1.—This vessel, of excellent ware, was found in a number of pieces and without a base. The design is incised (Fig. 62).

Fig. 62.—Vessel No. 1. Mound near Point Washington. (Half size.)

Vessel No. 2.—This vase has the lower half of the body hemispherical; the upper part somewhat constricted. The neck is slightly flaring. There have been four small projections from the rim, of which two remain. Encircling the rim on the upper surface is an incised line. The ornamentation, incised, is a cross-hatch beneath two arching parallel lines. Maximum diameter, 5.5 inches; height, 4.5 inches (Fig. 63).

FIG. 63.—Vessel No. 2. Mound near Point Washington. (Half size.)

Vessel No. 5.—A vase of thick ware with flat base, and quadrilateral as to the lower part of the body. The upper part turns inward. The neck is upright. The ornamentation, incised and punctate, shown on the two sides in Fig. 64, is repeated on the other two sides. Capacity about one pint.

Vessel No. 6.—An acorn-shaped vessel of less than one pint capacity, with pinched decoration, perhaps intended to imitate the acorn (Fig. 65).

FIG. 64.—Vessel No. 5. Mound near Point Washington. (Full size.)

Vessel No. 14.—This vase, of inferior ware, resembles Vessel No. 5, this mound, as to shape of body which, in this case, is undecorated. The vessel, which

FIG. 65.—Vessel No. 6. Mound near Point Washington. (Two-thirds size.)

FIG. 66.—Vessel No. 14. Mound near Point Washington. (Half size.)

flares slightly at first and then becomes upright, has six parallel circles of punctate markings. Capacity about one quart (Fig. 66).

Vessel No. 18.—This interesting vessel of thick and excellent ware, a light yellow with many traces of crimson paint, somewhat resembles in shape of body Vessel No. 5. The head of an owl projects horizontally from one side. On either

FIG. 67.—Vessel No. 18. Mound near Point Washington. (Full size.)

side, behind the head, are deeply incised representations of wings. An incised tail is opposite the head. Just above the tail is a neatly made perforation as for suspension. Presumably a corresponding one on the opposite side has been omitted. The capacity is less than one pint (Fig. 67).

FIG. 68.—Vessel No. 19. Mound near Point Washington. (Full size.)

Vessel No. 19.—This vessel,· of good yellow ware, bearing traces of crimson paint, has a double compartment with a human head between for a handle. The decoration, incised and punctate, is confined to one compartment. The closing of the scroll is a treatment similar to that found on vessels from Yucatan (Fig. 68).

Vessel No. 21:—The body is semi-globular, with high and slightly expanding neck. The base is flat. The body is undecorated. Around the neck is an interesting complicated decoration conferred by the use of a stamp. Maximum diameter, 5.75 inches; height, 6 inches (Fig. 69).

Vessel No. 22.—A bowl with semi-globular body and thickened rim, of about three pints capacity. The interior has a coat of crimson paint, as has part of the outside.

Vessel No. 25.—A vase of flattened outline, of most excellent yellow ware

FIG. 69.—Vessel No. 21. Mound near Point Washington. (Three-quarters size.)

and with gracefully rounded rim. The complicated decoration, beautifully carved, confined to the upper portion, is practically all shown in Fig. 70. Fig. 71 gives the outline of the side. Maximum diameter, 6 inches; height, 3 inches; diameter of aperture, 3.5 inches.

Vessel No. 27.—A pot with two encircling lines of punctate markings (Fig. 72).

Vessel No. 29.—A pot with ovoid body, of about two quarts' capacity. A thick rim flares slightly. A border .5 inch in diameter, consisting of complicated stamp decoration, is just below the rim. Diameter, 5.6 inches; height, 6.8 inches (Fig. 73).

Vessel No. 35.—In shape an inverted truncated cone. The ware, bright yellow, has been colored crimson about one inch below the rim. Next follows a band about 1.75 inches broad, without paint, with incised decoration. The remainder of the vessel is crimson. Parts are missing. Height, 6 inches; maximum diameter, 4.5 inches (Fig. 74).

FIG. 70.—Vessel No. 25. Mound near Point Washington. (About one-sixth oversize.)

FIG. 71.—Section of Vessel No. 25. (Half size.)

FIG. 72.—Vessel No. 27. Mound near Point Washington. (Half size.)

FIG. 73.—Vessel No. 29. Mound near Point Washington. (One-third size.)

FIG. 74.—Vessel No. 35. Mound near Point Washington. (One-third size.)

FIG. 75.—Vessel No. 38. Mound near Point Washington. (Half size.)

Vessel No. 38.—A fragment of a vessel of eccentric form, of very superior ware, beautifully decorated. Traces of crimson paint remain (Fig. 75).

CEMETERY NEAR POINT WASHINGTON, CHOCTAWHATCHEE BAY, WASHINGTON COUNTY, FLA.

Over a score of years ago, we were told, persons living at Point Washington noticed earthenware vessels, or parts of vessels, projecting above the ground in a hammock about 3.5 miles west of their settlement. Incidentally, it may be said that the word hammock is used in certain parts of the Southern United States to describe a tract of land on which grow the palmetto, the oak and certain other trees, in contradistinction to the pine barrens, the swamp, the marsh, or the prairie. This hammock, which is about three acres in extent, lies in from the bay and is surrounded by pine woods. It is said that former visitors from the town obtained a number of vessels at this place, though we saw but little evidence of former digging, either on or below the surface.

Four and one-half days were passed by us at the cemetery with ten men to dig and three men to supervise.

About one-quarter of an acre was dug through by us and it is our belief that that part of the hammock containing burials was thoroughly dug by us, the limit being determined not only by the spade but by sounding rods of iron which we found so useful in our work at the aboriginal cemetery at Durand's Bend, Alabama river.

The cemetery near Point Washington was not exactly level, there being a number of irregular rises in the ground with flat spaces between. These rises, which probably did not exceed a foot in height, in three cases contained large deposits of human bones, solid masses with outlying bones here and there, these bones not being enough apart to call them separate burials, nor yet so closely associated that they might be considered one interment. One of these deposits had seventeen skulls, all of adults but one, as to which we had not sufficient data to judge. Numbers of long-bones accompanied the skulls. In other parts of the cemetery were single skulls, others with long-bones and, in a few cases, long-bones without the crania, in addition to the burials found under earthenware vessels, which will be taken up later.

Certain skulls from the cemetery showed marked flattening as by compression. Captain Bernard Romans, in his " A Concise Natural History of East and West Florida,"[1] page 82, tells us, speaking of the Choctaws, " their women disfigure the heads of their male children by means of bags of sand, flattening them into different shapes, thinking it adds to their beauty."

Artifacts other than vessels of earthenware were not numerous. A piece of iron lay near a skull and glass beads were with a number of burials. There were also: shell beads in many places; several undecorated gorgets of shell; a hoe-shaped implement of calcareous lime-stone, much disintegrated, with one of the masses of skulls; a large hone with a burial; eleven bits of chert and two arrowpoints together, with human remains; two glass finger-rings loose in the sand; two pendants of shell resembling barbless arrowpoints in shape, with a burial; a piercing implement of shell, wrought from a columella, with two circular grooves.

While the burials without earthenware covering were largely in the low mounds, burials under vessels were chiefly in the slopes of the mounds or in the levels and depressions between them.

At certain places in the cemetery, from a few inches to one foot below the surface, as in other cases reported by us, but still more noticeably so, lay quantities of earthenware over considerable areas. No burials were with or beneath these deposits which, at places, were so near together as almost to resemble a floor. These deposits were made up of fragments of vessels, some very large; occasionally a small, well-made vessel, usually with some imperfection; or bowls rarely over one quart in capacity, of poor material, often undecorated and sometimes broken in addition.

During our entire investigation, though particular care was exercised and

[1] New York, 1775.

the matter was constantly kept in view, no vessel of any size was reconstructed from pieces present in these deposits. Parts of smaller vessels, probably intended for domestic use, lay among the sherds. It has suggested itself to us that possibly vessels broken in domestic use were put aside and carried in numbers to the cemetery, where these fragments were spread upon the surface with small, unbroken vessels, not with, but near, the burials. In lapse of time leaf mould and shifting sand could readily account for the superficial depth at which these deposits were found. Fragments, during conveyance and deposit, would become greatly mixed, which would account for our inability to find full complement of parts of vessels and, moreover, as it seemed to us that decorated portions predominated, it may be that such parts were more carefully preserved. A definite method to settle this question, to which we have already referred in our account of the mounds at Bear Point and at Walton's Camp, would be to preserve each fragment of ware found during an investigation and, at the end, to endeavor to restore vessels from parts found at various points. This herculean task, however, could be attempted reasonably only in the case of a cemetery which had never undergone previous disturbance.

The earthenware at the cemetery contained practically no admixture of pounded shell, though here and there a small amount was present locally in vessels as was the case with those in the mound at Walton's Camp.

When bowls lay inverted over burials, such burials were from 1 to 3.5 feet in depth.

Vessel No. 1.—A life-form of coarse yellow ware, imperforate. The decoration is punctate. There are small holes at either end for suspension. Length, 4.1

FIG. 76.—Vessel No. 1. Cemetery near Point Washington. (Full size.)

inches; maximum diameter, 2 inches; depth, 1.6 inches (Fig. 76). A small part of the tail was broken by a trowel. This interesting little vessel lay apart from burials with many pieces of broken ware.

Vessel No. 2.—A bowl found in fragments but since pieced together. The base is perforate; the decoration, incised. Maximum diameter, 10 inches; depth, 5 inches (Fig. 77). No human remains were found with this bowl though probably they had disappeared through decay.

Vessel No. 3.—Found lying on its side, crushed to fragments.

Vessel No. 4.—Inverted, crushed to fragments, parts missing.

Vessel No. 5.—Inverted, imperforate base. The decoration is a partially interlocked scroll rudely done. There are notches around the rim. Maximum diameter, 12.75 inches; depth, 7 inches.

FIG. 77.—Vessel No. 2. Cemetery near Point Washington. (One-third size.)

FIG. 78.—Vessel No. 7. Cemetery near Point Washington. (One-third size.)

Vessel No. 6.—One half of a large star-shaped dish lying inverted over a fragment of a skull, three large shell beads and two pebbles.

Vessel No. 7.—A pot three pints in capacity, perforate, with rough decoration on the neck (Fig. 78). This pot lay inverted just beneath the surface.

Vessel No. 8.—About the same size as Vessel No. 7 and lying in fragments near it.

Vessel No. 9.—A vessel of eccentric shape with incised and punctate decoration, perforate and with two small holes for suspension. Length, 6 inches; maximum diameter, 2.7 inches; height, 1.7 inches; diameter of aperture, 1.3 inches (Fig. 79).

FIG. 79.—Vessel No. 9. Cemetery near Point Washington. (Half size.)

FIG. 80.—Vessel No. 10. Cemetery near Point Washington. (Half size.)

Vessel No. 10.—A water-bottle of black ware, interestingly incised on body and on base. A white material has been rubbed into the lines. The base is perforate. There are two small holes for suspension, at the rim. Maximum diameter, 4 inches; height, 4 inches; aperture, 1.2 inches (Fig. 80). This bottle lay with the seventeen skulls and the mass of bones to which we have referred.

Fig. 81.—Vessel No. 11. Cemetery near Point Washington. (Full size.)

Fig. 82.—Vessel No. 12. Cemetery near Point Washington. (Full size.)

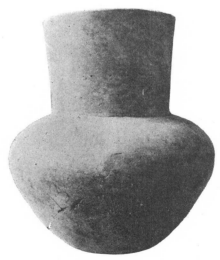

Fig. 83.—Vessel No. 13. Cemetery near Point Washington. (One-third size.)

Vessel No. 11.—A bottle similar to Vessel No. 10, with base perforation, holes for suspension and white material in the incised lines. Maximum diameter, 4.6 inches; height, 4.4 inches; aperture, 1.4 inches (Fig. 81). This bottle lay almost in contact with one of the skulls to which we have referred.

Vessel No. 12.—A bottle of inferior ware, rudely incised. The base is imperforate. Maximum diameter, 2.5 inches; height, 3.1 inches; aperture, 1 inch (Fig. 82). This bottle lay about 2 feet 8 inches down and about 9 inches below the mass of bones to which reference has been made. With it were small fragments of human remains.

Vessel No. 13.—An undecorated, wide-mouthed bottle with body heart-shaped in outline. The base is perforate. This bottle lay almost inverted. No bones remained near it. Diameter of body, 6.6 inches; height, 7.5 inches; diameter of aperture, 3.8 inches (Fig. 83).

Vessel No. 14.—An imperforate bowl partly crushed by a large root, since pieced together. The decoration, incised, represents highly conventionalized bird-wings though, in this case, the head and the tail of the bird do not appear

FIG. 84.—Vessel No. 14. Cemetery near Point Washington. (One-third size.)

on the bowl. In one instance, to the reader's left, on the bowl (Fig. 84) the circle has not been filled in as have the others. Maximum diameter, 13 inches; depth, 6.3 inches. This bowl lay inverted over the skull of an adult. Beneath the skull were a number of long-bones while one foot lower down was another skull. These bones were apparently the advance guard of a mass of remains behind and to one side of them which formed the deposit with the eleven crania to which we have referred.

Vessel No. 15.—Possibly part of a small bottle, though the aperture seems too smooth to mark the presence of a fracture. The decoration, incised and punctate, confined to the top of the body, is given, with section, in Fig. 85.

Vessel No. 16.—A large fragment lying by the side of Vessel No. 17. The decoration, a common one, consists of a series of concentric diamonds with central circles.

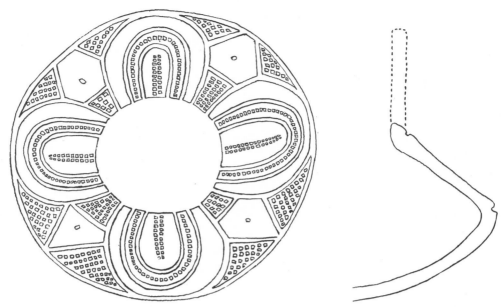

FIG. 85.—Vessel No. 15. Top view and section. Cemetery near Point Washington. (Full size.)

Vessel No. 17.—An imperforate bowl of black ware found, badly crushed, inverted over a human skull with a fragment of clavicle and some vertebræ. With these was a chisel of iron or of steel. This bowl, put together with the exception of a small part of the rim, which is wanting, has an incised decoration shown in Fig. 86. Maximum diameter, 15.5 inches; depth, 6.4 inches.

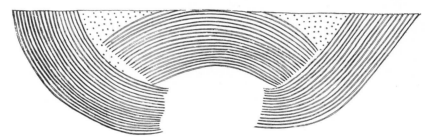

FIG. 86.—Decoration, Vessel No. 17. Cemetery near Point Washington. (One-third size.)

Vessel No. 18.—A bowl, badly crushed, found turned over the skull of an adult, about 2 feet from Vessels Nos. 16 and 17. This bowl, 3 feet 6 inches down, lay at a considerably greater depth than the vessels ordinarily. The decoration, incised, is a form of the partially interlocked scroll. The fragments of this bowl were sent to the Davenport Academy of Natural Science, Davenport, Iowa.

Vessel No. 19.—A bowl found upright in one of the deposits of sherds. The base is perforate. The decoration is incised scroll and punctate, much like that of Vessel No. 24 (Fig. 24) from the mound at Walton's Camp. Maximum diameter, 9.5 inches; depth, 4.5 inches.

Vessel No. 20.—A bowl with perforate base, lying just beneath the surface with no associated remains. The decoration, incised, is in the main similar to that of Vessel No. 40 from this cemetery. Maximum diameter, 6.8 inches; depth, 3 inches.

Vessel No. 21.—A large fragment of a vessel, lying over a skull.

Vessel No. 22.—Found just below the surface, lying on its side in the deposit of sherds, containing, and surmounted by, parts of other vessels, was a vessel of two compartments, which, we believe, represents the open bivalve rather more conventionalized than is sometimes seen in the ware of the Mississippi district, a good example of which may be found on Plate VI in Thruston's excellent

FIG. 87.—Vessel No. 22. Cemetery near Point Washington. (About seven-elevenths size.)

"Antiquities of Tennessee." The decoration on the body consists of a form of incised scroll. On the base of one compartment are concentric circles. On the other base, these circles begun, have not been completed. There are no basal perforations (Fig. 87).

Vessel No. 23.—An imperforate bowl inverted over fragments of the skull of a child or of an infant, 11.5 inches maximum diameter, 6.5 inches in depth. The decoration, incised, is shown in Fig. 88. By a small crack near the rim three holes, intended to allow a sinew or a cord to strengthen the parts, have been begun but not completed.

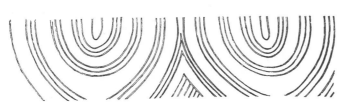

FIG. 88.—Decoration, Vessel No. 23. Cemetery near Point Washington. (About one-third size.)

Vessel No. 24.—A large fragment from the pottery layer, having on one side an animal head for a handle.

Vessel No. 25.—A perforate bowl inverted over the skull of an old person, which showed marked artificial flattening. Maximum diameter, 13.2 inches; depth, 6 inches. The decoration is shown in Fig. 89. This bowl, mounted over the skull which was found beneath it, placed upon sand and roots from the cemetery, has been sent to the Museum at Memorial Hall, Fairmount Park, Philadelphia.

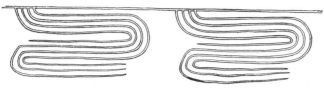

FIG. 89.—Decoration, Vessel No. 25. Cemetery near Point Washington. (One-third size.)

Vessel No. 26.—A little above Vessel No. 25 and to one side of it was an unbroken, imperforate bowl, lying over the skull of an adult with which were one piece of tibia, one ulna, one clavicle, part of a humerus, a piece of a pelvis and one half of a lower jaw. On the upper part of the bowl is incised decoration, evidently symbolical, while designs representing animal legs and paws encircle the body of the bowl. Maximum diameter, 15 inches; depth, 6.8 inches. This bowl, mounted over the burial found beneath it (Fig. 90) is at the Academy of Natural Sciences of Philadelphia, where may be seen the principal part of all our collections.

Vessel No. 27.—Immediately under the burial with Vessel No. 26 lay an imperforate bowl over the skull of a woman. The incised decoration is a combination of the favorite scroll. Maximum diameter, 11 inches; depth, 5 inches. This bowl with its skull and with sand from the cemetery, has been sent to the Free Museum of Science and Art, University of Pennsylvania, Philadelphia.

FIG. 91.—Vessel No. 28. Outline. Cemetery near Point Washington. (Half size.)

FIG. 92.—Same vessel, top decoration. (Half size.)

FIG. 93.—Same vessel, decoration of body. (Half size.)

Vessel No. 28.—This little vase was found, upright, slightly mutilated, in a layer of fragments. Incised decoration is on top and interesting incised symbolical decoration surrounds the body. Maximum diameter, 3.2 inches; height, 3 inches; aperture, 1 inch (Figs. 91, 92, 93).

Vessel No. 29.—This little vase was found inverted but apart from human remains. A part of the base was knocked in by the blow of a spade. There is rude, incised decoration of curved lines on the body and on the neck. Maximum diameter, 2.7 inches; height, 3.5 inches (Fig. 94).

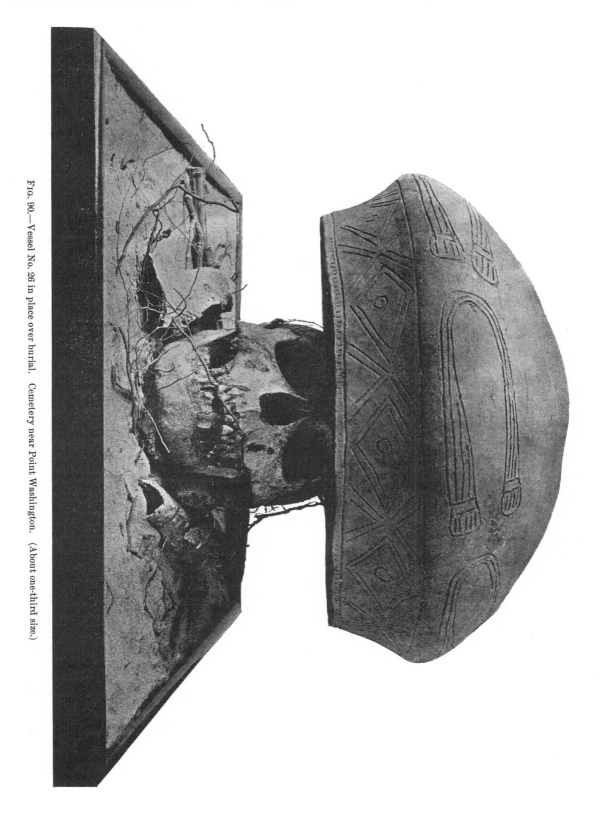

FIG. 90.—Vessel No. 26 in place over burial. Cemetery near Point Washington. (About one-third size.)

FIG. 94.—Vessel No. 29. Cemetery near Point Washington. (Full size.)

Vessel No. 30.—This interesting, imperforate, dipper-shaped vessel lay inverted over fragments of the skull of an adult. Incised decoration of diamonds, circles and straight lines surrounds the upper part of the body. A solid handle, 3 inches in length, projects horizontally from one side. Diameter of bowl, 8 inches; depth, 3.4 inches (Fig. 95).

Vessel No. 31.—This graceful, imperforate vessel, evidently modelled after a section of a gourd, lay inverted over the skull of an adolescent, about one-half foot distant from Vessel No. 30. At the end of the handle is a small hole for suspension. The incised decoration is shown on Fig. 96. Diameter of body, including handle, 10.3 inches; breadth of body, 7.1 inches; depth, 3 inches.

Vessel No. 32.—This vessel, representing an owl with the head and conventional tail and incised decoration of conventionalized wings, lay somewhat crushed by roots over a skull in fragments (Fig. 97). Maximum diameter, 11.5 inches; depth, 4.8 inches.

Vessel No. 33.—This bowl lay over the skull of an adult, in contact with Vessel No. 32. The upper part of the body is surrounded with incised decorations,

FIG. 95.—Vessel No. 30. Cemetery near Point Washington. (About seven-elevenths size.)

FIG. 96.—Vessel No. 31. Cemetery near Point Washington. (About seven-tenths size.)

FIG. 97.—Vessel No. 32. Cemetery near Point Washington. (Half size.)

among which may be recognized the usual aboriginal bird's eye and symbolical designs often found on vessels representing fish. The base of the bowl is imperforate (Fig. 98). Maximum diameter, 18.8 inches; depth, 9 inches.

Vessel No. 34.—This bowl lay inverted on one side of the base of Vessel No. 35. The base was imperforate, but a piece has been knocked out by a blow from a spade.

Vessel No. 35.—A perforate bowl of light-colored ware, found inverted over a few fragments of a skull. The incised design is much like that on Vessel No.

FIG. 98.—Vessel No. 33.   Cemetery near Point Washington.   (One-third size.)

50, from this cemetery, which, however, has projecting heads.   Maximum diameter, 14.3 inches; depth, 5.5 inches.

Vessel No. 36.—This interesting bowl, of excellent ware, perforate as to its base, has on one, side projecting slightly, what seems to be a representation of the

FIG. 99.—Vessel No. 36.   Cemetery near Point Washington.   (About seven-fifteenths size.)

head of a frog much in the manner of heads we see on bowls from Nicaragua. Below are incised designs intended for legs and feet. Symbols encircle the upper part of the bowl. Maximum diameter, 15.7 inches; depth, 7.2 inches (Fig. 99).

Vessel No. 37.—This bowl, badly crushed by roots, lay inverted over the skull of an adult. Restored, the base shows a perforation. The decoration, the well-known scroll, has a pink material inset in the lines (Fig. 100). Maximum diameter, 15.5 inches; depth, 7 inches.

FIG. 100.—Vessel No. 37. Cemetery near Point Washington. (One-third size.)

Vessel No. 38.—Inverted, but with the rim slightly tilted upward, were two halves of a bowl over a skull in fragments with a few long-bones. These two halves did not lie as though placed in the mound as a whole, and subsequently

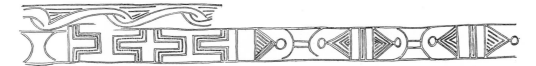

FIG. 101.—Decoration, Vessel No. 39. Cemetery near Point Washington. (One-third size.)

fractured, since a broken margin of one side was turned away from the corresponding margin of the other side.

Vessel No. 39.—This beautiful little bowl of black ware, imperforate, lay on its base, unassociated. The decoration, incised, is shown in Fig. 101. The upper part, the partially interlocked scroll, is uniform throughout. Below, the designs would seem to connect the vessel with that class bearing projecting heads and tails of fish, on which some of these symbols often appear. Maximum diameter, 5.5 inches; depth, 2 inches.

Vessel No. 40.—Resting on its base was a perforate bowl (Fig. 102), 15.8 inches in maximum diameter and 8.2 inches in depth. The incised decoration represents a conventional animal head with other parts of the body. Within this

FIG. 102.—Vessel No. 40. Cemetery near Point Washington. (Half size.)

FIG. 103.—Vessel No. 45. Cemetery near Point Washington. (About five-sixths size.)

bowl were decaying fragments of a skull and other bones. Capping the bowl was a large fragment of a vessel, inverted. Here for the first time on the Florida coast we find the regular enclosed burial so often described by us as present along the Alabama river and in mounds of the Georgia coast.

Vessel No. 41.—This imperforate bowl was found inverted over fragments of a skull of an adult. Part of the ware had been crushed in by a large root and the bowl received a blow from a spade, in addition. The incised decoration is a variety of scroll similar to that on Vessel No. 20 (Fig. 23) from the mound near Walton's Camp. Maximum diameter, 16.3 inches; depth, 8.3 inches.

Vessel No. 42.—A bowl crushed to fragments by a large root, inverted over the fragments of a skull of an adult. To one side lay a single shell bead. This bowl was sent to the Peabody Museum, Cambridge, Mass.

Vessel No. 43.—A perforate, six-pointed, or star-shaped, dish of black ware with the decoration usual on these dishes, somewhat rudely executed, lay turned over some fragments of bone resembling sawdust more than anything else. Maximum diameter, 17.2 inches; depth, 4.2 inches. Holes have been drilled on either side of a crack to permit the lashing together of the parts. This vessel, which, as we have said before, is of an entirely new type, has been sent to the National Museum, Washington, D. C.

Vessel No. 44.—A bowl of yellow ware, badly crushed by roots. The decoration is a form of the favorite scroll.

Vessel No. 45.—A bowl found in contact with Vessel No. 44, having for handles on one side, three rude models of birds' heads, one looking in, two looking out, and on the other, the conventional bird's tail. The incised decoration, as might be expected, represents conventional bird-wings (Fig. 103). Diameter of body, 7.75 inches; height, 2.7 inches. This vessel, part of which was badly crushed by roots, lay over minute fragments of bone.

Vessel No. 46.—An imperforate dish of yellow ware, of the six-pointed type, found over certain bones of a child, with shell beads. This dish, badly crushed when found, has been pieced together, showing the usual decoration on vessels of this type. Maximum diameter, 18 inches; depth, 4.7 inches.

Vessel No. 47.—A bowl with basal perforation, found lying over a skull, occiput down. Pressure against the chin had caused the side of the bowl to give way. One foot distant and a little above the level of the inverted rim of the bowl were certain long-bones. The skull, which was much better preserved than were most from this cemetery, was sent with the bowl and sand for mounting, to the Peabody Museum, Cambridge, Mass. The decoration on the bowl is similar to that on Vessel 41 (Fig. 35) from the mound at Walton's Camp.

Vessel No. 48.—A bowl found crushed to fragments, lying over the skull of an adult. The pieces, carefully collected, were sent to the American Museum of Natural History, New York City.

Vessel No. 49.—A pot, imperforate, with notches around the rim and a six-pointed margin. This pot was found inverted (Fig. 104). Maximum diameter, 5.5 inches; depth, 3.7 inches.

Vessel No. 50.—An imperforate

FIG. 104.—Vessel No. 49. Cemetery near Point Washington. (Half size.)

bowl of light-colored clay, found, badly crushed, turned over the skull of an adult. The incised decoration consists of diamonds, small circles, etc., similar to other vessels already figured. From either side a head, presumably that of a frog, projects (Fig. 105). Again we would call attention to bowls of Nicaragua in connection with these small heads, projecting from the side. Maximum diameter, 14.5 inches; depth, 6.8 inches.

Vessel No. 51.—A bottle of black ware, found lying on its side with a deposit of scattered bones. Incised decoration shown in Fig. 106, covers the body and imperforate base. Diameter of body, 3.9 inches; length of neck, 1.2 inches; height, 4.8 inches.

Vessel No. 52.—This handsome bowl of black ware, imperforate (Fig. 107) has

FIG. 105.—Vessel No. 50. Cemetery near Point Washington. (One-third size.)

incised decoration, with light colored material inset in the lines (Fig. 108). It lay in a mass of human bones loosely scattered. Maximum diameter, 4.9 inches; depth, 3.5 inches.

Vessel No. 53.—An imperforate bowl with lined decoration and conventional legs and paws below, lay inverted in the same mass of bones as Vessel No. 52 and about one yard from it (Fig. 109).

Vessel No. 54.—This vase, of inferior yellow ware, lay on its side in the same mass of bones from which came Vessel No. 51. The decoration is punctate with

FIG. 106.—Vessel No. 51. Cemetery near Point Washington. (Full size.)

FIG. 107.—Vessel No. 52. Cemetery near Point
Washington. (Two-thirds size.)

the favorite scroll (Fig. 110). There is a basal perforation made previous to baking. Maximum diameter, 3.6 inches; height, 3 inches.

FIG. 108.—Decoration, Vessel No. 52. Cemetery near Point Washington. (One-third size.)

FIG. 109.—Vessel No. 53. Cemetery near Point Washington. (About seven-twelfths size.)

FIG. 110.—Vessel No. 54. Cemetery near Point Washington. (Full size.)

Vessel No. 55.—A bowl, imperforate, with symbolical decoration rudely executed (Fig. 111). Maximum diameter, 6.5 inches; depth, 3.5 inches. This bowl, one side of which was crushed by a blow from a spade, lay over the skull of a child.

Vessel No. 56.—This vessel lay on its side, in the pottery deposit just beneath the surface. The ware is poor and rather rudely decorated. The rim has two perforations for suspension, a feature seldom met with in this section. A basal perforation lies to one side of the center. Parts of the vessel are missing. Maximum diameter, 5.3 inches; height, 4 inches; aperture, 4.5 inches (Fig. 112).

Vessel No. 57.—This small, six-pointed dish of bright yellow ware, perforate as to the base, lay in a deposit of pottery and, like nearly all vessels from such deposits, it is imperfect, having one corner missing.

FIG. 111.—Vessel No. 55. Cemetery near Point Washington. (Half size.)

FIG. 112.—Vessel No. 56. Cemetery near Point Washington. (Half size.)

Fig. 113 shows a number of handles of vessels from the cemetery near Point Washington. The heads of various birds are shown in *a, b, c, f, h,* and *i.* An unusual form, two birds' heads, each looking in an opposite direction, is shown in *g.* The head of a turtle is poorly represented by *j.* In reality the head is very life-like, being of black ware decorated with red paint. The animals represented in *d* and *e* are doubtless dogs. Cabeça de Vaca, during his travels, met with many aboriginal dogs.

In Fig. 114 we have additional handles of vessels from the cemetery. Heads of owls, presumably, are shown in *a* and *c.* We have in *b* an entire bird with a head disproportionately large. A bird's head is shown in *d.* Another dog is figured in *e.*

Fig. 115 shows symbolical decoration on a large sherd.

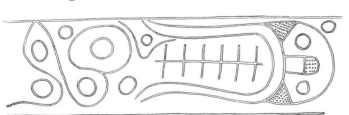

FIG. 115.—Decoration from part of vessel. Cemetery near Point Washington. (One-third size.)

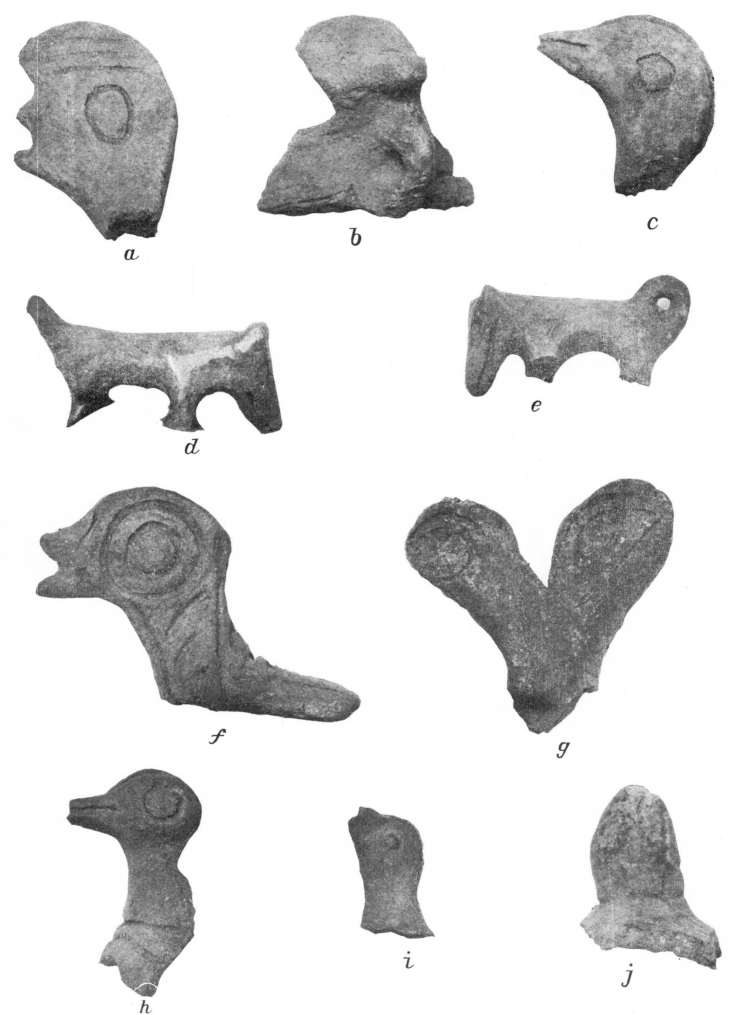

FIG. 113.—Handles of Vessels. Cemetery near Point Washington. (Full size.)

FIG. 114.—Handles of Vessels. Cemetery near Point Washington. (Full size.)

The head of an owl, a handle on a vessel, is shown in Fig. 116. The ware is most excellent and there is decoration with red paint.

Fig. 117 gives a large frog's head.

In Figs. 118, 119, we have two views of a part of a vessel which has had the head of a bird projecting upward and wings extending horizontally as handles.

A human head belonging to a bowl is shown in Fig. 120. This head is hollow and small objects within rattle when shaken. Fig. 121 represents a fragment of a vessel having for a handle the head of a serpent. To the reader's left may be seen a place on the vessel from which another head, presumably that of a serpent also, has disappeared. To one familiar with the markings on a Florida rattlesnake, the diamond-shaped design on the vessel must be highly

FIG. 116.—Sherd. Cemetery near Point Washington. (One-third size.)

FIG. 117.—Sherd. Cemetery near Point Washington. (About two-thirds size.)

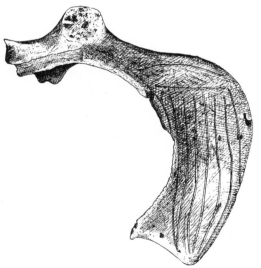

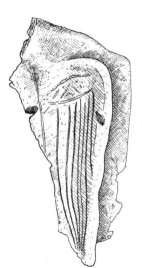

FIG. 118.—Sherd. Cemetery near Point Washington. (Half size.)

FIG. 119.—Same. Another view. (Half size.)

suggestive. The aborigines of Florida, in common with those of many other places, held the serpent in high esteem. " Nor have I seen a savage who would willingly kill a snake," says Captain Bernard Romans in his " Concise Natural History of East and West Florida."[1]

FIG. 120.—Handle of Vessel. Cemetery near Point Washington. (Full size.)

William Bartram, who travelled in Florida before our Revolutionary War, tells most amusingly of how a rattlesnake, having full possession of an Indian village,

FIG. 121.—Sherd. Cemetery near Point Washington. (One-third size.)

was killed by him, and how, afterward, certain braves feigned a fierce attack upon him, with much noise, that the manes of the snake, believing them to be his avengers, might be appeased.[2]

We have found a small effigy of a snake in copper in the mound at Mt. Royal, St. John's river, Florida, which place we believe to be the site of the town of the great King, near the lake

[1] Page 101.
[2] Travels. Dublin, 1793, p. 258 et seq.

(Lake George) visited by part of the colony of Huguenot French on their journey up the river, the rest remaining at Fort Caroline near the river's mouth.

Mound near Hogtown Bayou, Choctawhatchee Bay, Washington County, Fla.

At Hogtown Bayou are the principal shell deposits of Choctawhatchee bay, which are extensive, but in no wise comparable with those of the St. John's river, or with many on the Florida east coast, or on parts of the west coast, farther south.

It is our belief that a cemetery lies undiscovered at this place, as previous search by others has failed to locate a mound there, and careful investigation on our part availed only to find a small mound near the water's edge, about one mile up the bayou on the south side. This mound contained no burials.

The results of our exploration of the northwest Florida coast, so far as we have gone, that is from the Alabama boundary to the easternmost extremity of Choctawhatchee bay, are of considerable interest.

A new form of burial has been met with in our work, namely, that where a lone skull or a skull with a few bones lies beneath a down-turned vessel of earthenware. In but one case was the enclosed form of burial found, i. e., where human remains placed in a vessel are covered by an inverted dish, bowl or large fragment of earthenware. Incidentally, we may say the inverted vessel over human remains lying on sand prevails in Georgia, but these remains have been cremated, while cremation has not been met with on that part of the northwest Florida coast investigated by us.

Little of interest but earthenware has come from the mounds and cemeteries lately explored by us, but of earthenware a most striking collection has been obtained. This ware is purely aboriginal in style, no trace of European influence appearing in its make or decoration, which latter is largely symbolical. A mixture of cultures is plainly apparent in this ware. We have many of the life-forms of the ware of the middle Mississippi district, but the admixture of coarsely powdered shell in use in that section is wanting in the clay of vessels here. We find the complicated stamp decoration of Georgia and of Carolina, but the tempering of the clay with small pebbles forming "gritty ware" is not met with. We encounter in this northwest Florida district, ware from the soft paste of the kind so well known in peninsular Florida to the eastward, while, on the other hand, we find the black, polished ware of Mississippi and districts to the westward of our field of research.

The small check-stamp found everywhere else by us is also abundantly present in the district we have lately explored.

Perforation of the base of earthenware interred with the dead, so widely practised in peninsular Florida and occasionally met with in lower Georgia and Alabama, though unknown, we believe, in the middle Mississippi district which seems so greatly to have influenced the ware of the northwest Florida coast, is very prevalent in this coast district. This mutilation of base consisted in the knocking out of a small portion before interment with the dead in fulfilment of some ceremonial rite. In peninsular Florida, as we have already pointed out in this Report, the aborigines went a step farther and prepared in advance, presumably, flimsy mortuary ware with a base-perforation made during process of manufacture. This ready made mortuary perforation, which we have never encountered in Alabama, Georgia or Carolina, was met with by us, in our researches this season in very few instances and to the eastward of Pensacola bay only. It might seem that the custom to perforate the base of earthenware by fracture, originating in Florida, or brought there from we know not where, spread upward and sideward to a limited extent and that ready made mortuary perforation, probably a refinement and an afterthought, was less widely disseminated. All this, however, before final conclusion, had best await results of work we hope to be able to do the coming season.

Certain Aboriginal Remains of the Northwest Florida Coast, Part II

BY

CLARENCE B. MOORE

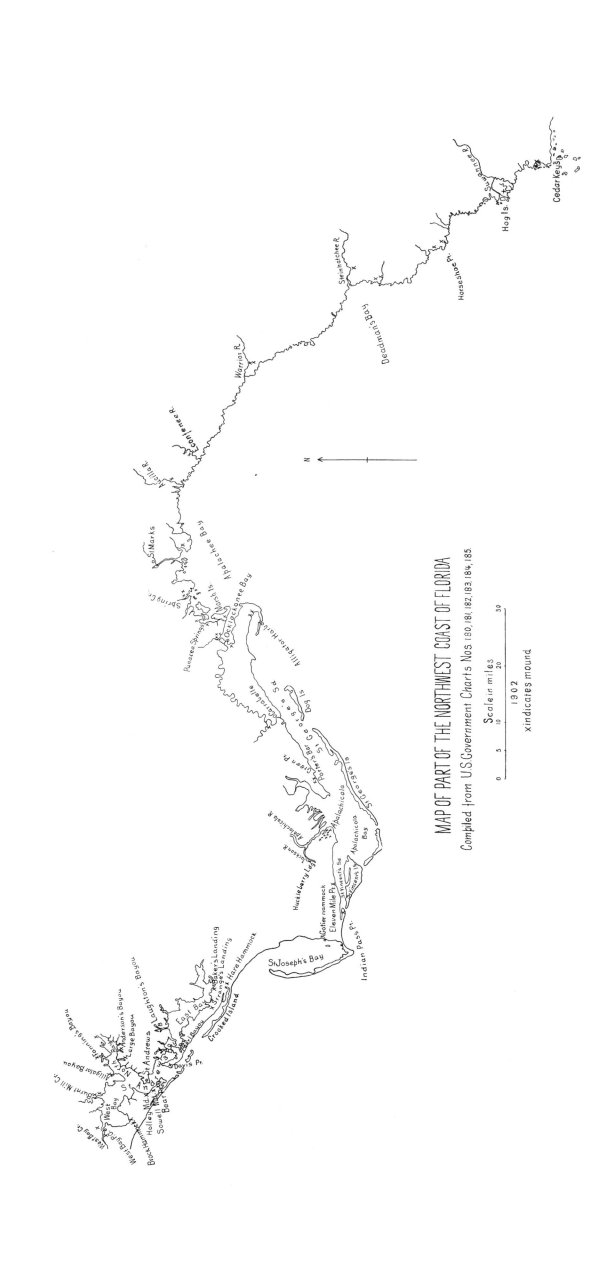

MAP OF PART OF THE NORTHWEST COAST OF FLORIDA

Compiled from U.S.Government Charts Nos.180,181,182,183,184,185.

Scale in miles

0   5   10   20   30

1902

x indicates mound

Cedar Keys

Hog Is.

Suwanee R.

Horseshoe Pt.

Steinhatchee R.

Deadman's Bay

Warrior R.

Econfenee R.

Aucilla R.

St Marks

Apalachee Bay

Marsh Is.

Spring Cr.

Panacea Springs

Ocklockonee Bay

Alligator Harbor

Dog Is.

Ochlockonee R.

Turkey Pt.

St. George's Sd.

Dog Is.

Potter's Bar

Green Pt.

St. George's Is.

Apalachicola R.

Jackson R.

Apalachicola

Apalachicola Bay

St Vincent's Sd.

St Vincent's Is.

Huckleberry Ld.

Gotier Hammock

Eleven Mile Pt.

Indian Pass Pt.

St Joseph's Bay

Baker's Landing

Strange's Landing

Hare Hammock

Crooked Island

East Bay

Anderson's Bayou

Laughton's Bayou

St Andrews

Large Bayou

Horning's Bayou

Alligator Bayou

Davis Pt.

Burnt Mill Cr.

West Bay

Sowel Beach

Holley Md.

Brock Hammock

West Bay Cr.

Old Bay

N

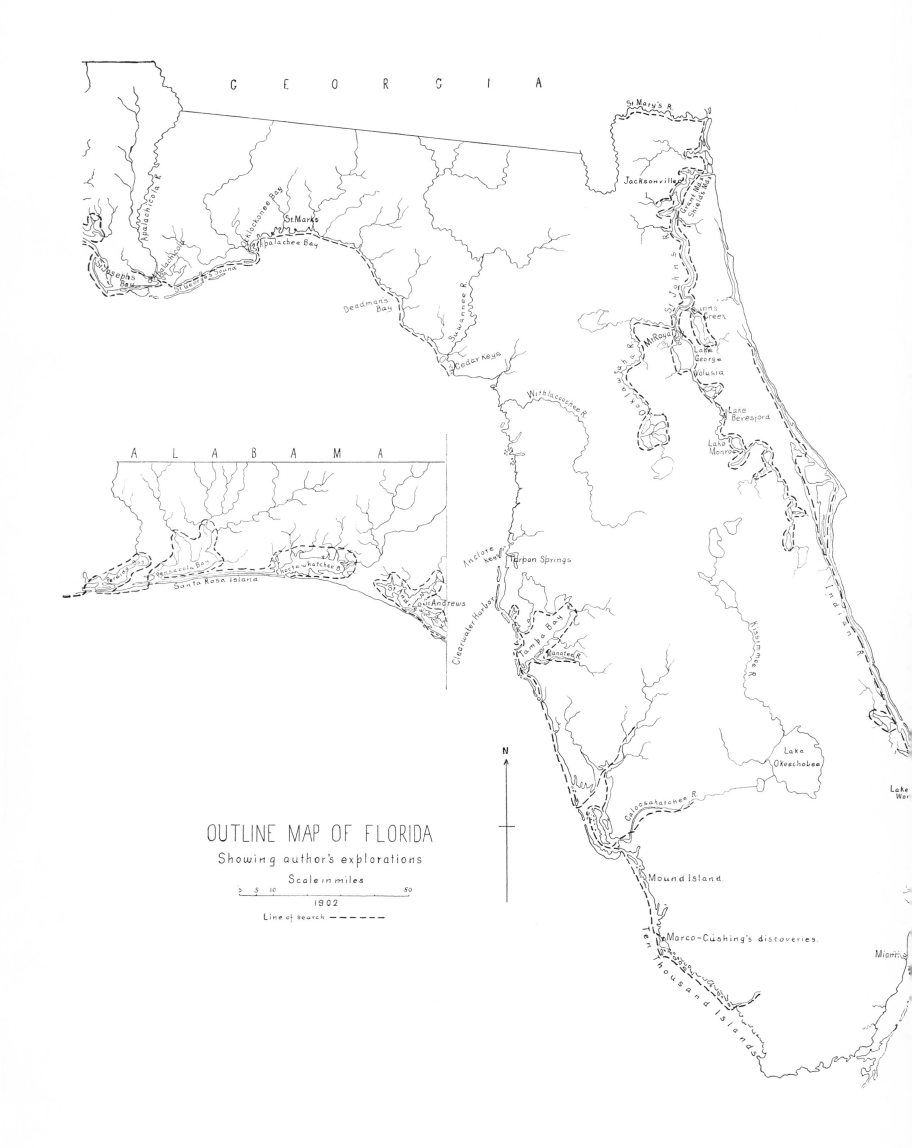

GEORGIA

ALABAMA

St Mary's R.

Jacksonville

Grant Md.
Shields Md.

Apalachicola R.
St Joseph's Bay
Aspalaga
St George's Sound
Ocklockonee Bay
St Marks
Apalachee Bay

Deadman's Bay

Suwannee R.

Cedar Keys

Withlacoochee R.

St Johns R.

Ocklawaha R.
Mt Royal
Dunns Creek
Lake George
Volusia

Lake Beresford

Lake Monroe

Perdido Bay
Pensacola Bay
Santa Rosa Island
Choctawhatchee B.
St Andrews
Clearwater Harbor

Anclote Key
Tarpon Springs

Indian R.

Kissimmee R.

Tampa Bay
Manatee R.

N

Lake Okeechobee

Lake Wor...

Caloosahatchee R.

OUTLINE MAP OF FLORIDA

Showing author's explorations

Scale in miles

0 5 10   50

1902

Line of search — — — — —

Mound Island

Marco-Cushing's discoveries.

Miami

Ten Thousand Islands

CERTAIN ABORIGINAL REMAINS OF THE NORTHWEST FLORIDA COAST.

PART II.

BY CLARENCE B. MOORE.

In the first part of this report, of which this is the second and concluding part, we gave the result of our investigations along a portion of the northwest coast of Florida, beginning at Perdido bay, the coast-boundary between Alabama and Florida, and continuing eastward along Pensacola bay, Santa Rosa sound and Choctaw-hatchee bay.

In this second part we describe the result of our work going eastward and later, southward, along St. Andrew's bay, St. Andrew's sound, St. Joseph's bay, St. Vincent's sound, Apalachicola bay, St. George's sound, Alligator Harbor, Ocklockonee bay, Apalachee bay, Deadman's bay and the rivers and Gulf coast to Cedar Keys.

Mr. J. S. Raybon, captain of the flat-bottomed steamer from which our researches are always conducted, with a companion, spent a number of months previous to our visit in going over all the territory later investigated by us, locating all known aboriginal remains along our intended route. The names and addresses of owners[1] were sent to us in advance that, permission to dig being obtained previous to our visit, there might be no delay when we found ourselves on the ground. In fact, by traveling after working hours no time was wasted and the four months of the season of 1902 were taken up almost entirely in digging.

From St. Andrew's bay to Apalachee bay, inclusive, with one exception, we investigated every mound the most careful search could locate and, we believe, all that existed, save several small, flat, circular heaps in open pine woods, which experience has taught us were not intended for burial purposes, but as sites for tepees.

Along the coast between the eastern end of Apalachee bay and Cedar Keys, we investigated all the mounds that persistent search had located, but as the shore is swampy in many places and the water is shoal and often studded with masses of lime rock, access is difficult and hence inhabitants from whom inquiries as to mounds can be made are few. Therefore, it is likely some mounds escaped us, but such as were dug by us were probably representative.

We know of no previous scientific work in the district we have gone over; but

[1] Our sincere thanks are tendered owners of mounds investigated by us, who, almost without exception, gave full permission to dig.

unfortunately the mounds were not intact.   Not treasure seekers alone have dug into the mounds of St. Andrew's and of Apalachicola, bays, but individuals seeking curiosities to sell, some of whom have come under our personal notice.   Still, the size of the mounds in some instances has been a partial protection against a single digger, while ignorance as to where to search has often saved contents of smaller mounds.

As markedly as was the case in the first part of this report, the result of our work this season resolved itself into little more than a study of the aboriginal earthenware of the coast-district investigated by us.   Lewis Morgan, sometime an honored correspondent of our Academy of Natural Sciences, has said, we believe, in his "League of the Iroquois", that the advent of earthenware marks the line between savagery and barbarism.   Hence it may be considered, in view of the importance of earthenware as an aid to the study of the people, that the returns of our season's work have been sufficient.

All measurements of earthenware reported in this volume are approximate.

It must be borne in mind in respect to process work that reductions in size are made with regard to diameter and not area.   If a diagram four inches by two inches is to be reduced one-half, each diameter is divided by two and the reproduction, which is called half size, is two inches by one inch.   The area of the original diagram, however, is eight square inches, while that of the so-called half size reproduction is two square inches, or one-quarter the area.   To find the actual size of a design shown in diagram, multiply the length and the breadth by two, if the diagram is given "half size"; by three, if "one-third size", and so on.

In a few cases partial restoration of vessels has been attempted, but always in a material differing in color from the original so that the restoration may be readily recognized, and it has been done only when the remainder of the vessel clearly indicated the size and shape of the missing part.   All objects found by us, with the exception of certain duplicates sent to the museum of Phillips Academy, Andover, Mass., may be seen at the Academy of Natural Sciences of Philadelphia.

Dr. M. G. Miller, who has been with us in all our previous mound work, determined as to human remains this year and lent his assistance in a general way to all the field work and in putting this report through the press.

Mounds Investigated.

Mound near West Bay post-office, St. Andrew's bay.
Mound near West Bay creek, St. Andrew's bay.
Mound in Brock Hammock, St. Andrew's bay.
Larger Mound near Burnt Mill creek, St. Andrew's bay.
Smaller Mound near Burnt Mill creek, St. Andrew's bay.
Mound near Alligator bayou, St. Andrew's bay.
Mound near Fanning's bayou, St. Andrew's bay.
Mound near head of North bay, St. Andrew's bay.
Mound near Anderson's bayou, St. Andrew's bay.
Mound near Large bayou, St. Andrew's bay.

Holley Mound, St. Andrew's bay.
Sowell Mound, St. Andrew's bay.
Mounds near Bear Point, St. Andrew's bay (4).
Cemetery at St. Andrew's, St. Andrew's bay.
Mound at St. Andrew's, St. Andrew's bay.
Mound near Davis Point, St. Andrew's bay.
Mound near Pearl bayou, St. Andrew's bay.
Mounds near Laughton's bayou, St. Andrew's bay (2).
Mound near Strange's Landing, St. Andrew's bay.
Mound near Baker's Landing, St. Andrew's bay.
Mounds near Hare Hammock, St. Andrew's sound (2).
Mound in Gotier Hammock, St. Joseph's bay.
Mound near Indian Pass Point, St. Vincent's sound.
Mound at Eleven Mile Point, St. Vincent's sound.
Cool Spring Mound, Apalachicola bay.
Mounds near Apalachicola, Apalachicola bay (2).
Pierce Mounds, near Apalachicola, Apalachicola bay (5).
Singer Mound, near Apalachicola, Apalachicola bay.
Jackson Mound, near Apalachicola, Apalachicola bay.
Mound near Huckleberry Landing, Jackson river.
Mound near Porter's Bar, St. George's sound.
Mound near Green Point, St. George's sound.
Mound on Carrabelle river.
Tucker Mound, Alligator Harbor.
Yent Mound, Alligator Harbor.
Mound at Marsh Island, Ocklockonee bay.
Nichols Mound, Ocklockonee bay (2).
Mound near Ocklockonee bay.
Hall Mounds, Apalachee bay (2).
Mound near Spring creek, Apalachee bay.
Mound near the Mound Field, Apalachee bay.
Mound near St. Mark's, Apalachee bay.
Mound near the Aucilla river.
Mounds near the Econfenee river (2).
Mounds near the Warrior river (2).
Mound near the Steinhatchee river.
Mounds near Goodson's Fish-camp, Gulf coast (2).
Mound near Murphy Landing, Gulf coast.
Mounds near Horseshoe Point, Gulf coast (3).
Mound on Hog Island, Gulf coast.
Mound on Pine Key, Gulf coast.
Mound near the Shell-heap, Gulf coast.

17 JOURN. A. N. S. PHILA., VOL. XII.

Mound near West Bay Post-Office, Washington County.

About one-quarter of a mile WNW. from the village known as West Bay post-office, in a field formerly under cultivation, on property of Mr. George W. Lee of Point Washington, Florida, was a mound about 8 feet in height and 58 feet through the base. This mound, formerly a truncated cone, had been considerably dug into superficially and to a certain extent in a more serious way, but not sufficiently to disturb more than a small portion of the mound.

The mound was totally demolished by us, including its extreme marginal parts.

No interments were found until the central parts of the mound were reached and such as were met with were so badly decayed that almost no trace of them remained. Owing to this it was impossible to determine the form of interment, but a small fragment of femur, lying just beneath the crowns of certain teeth, indicated a bunched burial in that case at least.

Over certain burials, as is often seen in Florida mounds, were deposits of charcoal which cannot have been the remains of continued fires since the bones were not calcined nor the sand reddened by heat.

With one burial was a knife or arrowhead of chert; with another, a thick sheet of mica. In caved sand was a hone of ferruginous sandstone[1] and a large "celt".

Incidentally, we may say that in this report the rocks from which the "celts" discovered by us were made will not be stated. Apparently no new features were presented and in many cases these implements were given to owners of mounds, who wished souvenirs from them.

Beginning almost directly at the margin of the NE. part of the mound, on or near the base, as a rule, vessels of earthenware were met with, sometimes singly and again a number together. This deposit, continuing and broadening to the eastward, extended under the slope of the mound almost to the margin of the summit plateau, where the burials began. At times vessels and quantities of fragments of vessels lay together. These fragments, when collected, often failed to furnish full complement of the vessels to which they belonged, but as parts were found widely separated sometimes, it is likely many vessels had been broken first and then scattered through the mound while it was in process of construction, a custom we have noted in the first part of this report. An example of this practice was noticed in the case of a vessel with five compartments, which had been broken into four parts. One of these parts was met with in digging, several hours before the others which, themselves, were somewhat separated and many feet nearer the center of the mound.

As we had found the case to be before along the northwest coast, the sand in that part of the mound in which the earthenware deposit lay was much darker in color than that of the rest of the mound. During our investigations the present sea-

[1] Our thanks are tendered Messrs. Theodore D. Rand and Lewis Woolman, of our Academy of Natural Sciences, for all determinations of rocks mentioned in this report. As it was not expedient to mutilate specimens for microscopic slides, determinations have not been made with the certainty that otherwise would have been the case.

son so universal was this occurrence of blackened sand in which no particles of charcoal were apparent that a certain amount from the Hall mound, near Panacea Springs, was put aside by us and afterward submitted to Prof. Harry F. Keller, Ph. D., of Philadelphia, who, under date of June 28, 1902, reports as follows:

"The chemical and microscopic examination of the black sand from the mound at Panacea Springs, Fla., shows that the dark color is due to carbonaceous matter which is very probably of animal origin.   Most of it is in the form of very minute black particles adhering to the sand.   These particles show no distinct structure and are certainly not wood charcoal.   When the sand is strongly heated in air, the carbon burns off, leaving a residue nearly white.   The black particles are soluble to a considerable extent in caustic potash and in nitric acid, imparting a deep brown color to these solvents, an indication that organic matter is present.   A few larger particles which I succeeded in picking by the aid of a lens were incinerated, and the residue gave a strong reaction for phosphoric acid.   Could this matter be the product of partial charring or slow decomposition of bone?"

Dr. H. F. Keller submitted the sand to Dr. I. Keller, an expert microscopist, who concurred in the belief that the carbonaceous matter was of animal origin and stated, "I cannot think of anything in the vegetable line that could have produced this result."

Many of the vessels and parts of vessels found by us in this mound, being of ordinary form, of inferior ware and undecorated, will not be particularly described.

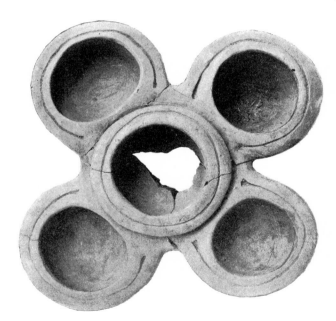

FIG. 1.—Vessel No. 1.   Mound near West Bay P. O.   (One-third size.)

Vessel No. 1.—In Fig. 1 is shown a vessel with five circular compartments, a central one being somewhat raised above the surrounding four.   The only decoration is an incised line encircling the middle compartment and one almost surrounding each of the others.   The ware is thick and of fairly good quality.   The central compartment alone has the basal perforation.   Maximum diameter of vessel, 9.5 inches; height, 2.1 inches.   We have not met with compartment vessels of this character west of this place.

Vessel No. 2.—Fig. 2 shows an entirely new type, we believe, a combination of the compartment vessel and the life-form.   The head, body and tail are represented by the outlines of the three compartments and to make the resemblance still stronger, horns or "feelers," have projected from the head.   Parts of these, missing when found, have been restored.   The ware, which is thick and fairly good, has traces of crimson pigment at various points.   The middle compartment only has the base-perforation. Length, 9.5 inches; height, 2 inches.

FIG. 2.—Vessel No. 2.   Mound near West Bay P. O.   (Three-fourths size.)

Vessel No. 3.—This vessel, shown in Fig. 3, perforate, undecorated, has a globular body and slightly expanding neck.   The rim is trilateral.   Height, 8.5 inches; maximum diameter, 7 inches; opening, 5.2 inches.

FIG. 3.—Vessel No. 3.   Mound near West Bay P. O.   (Half size.)

Vessel No. 4.—Seems to be a lifeform, though the mouth is peculiarly placed in relation to the ridge on the back if this latter is intended to represent a dorsal fin.   The opening has a portion missing at one side, but as the margin is unimpaired a part of the way, it is not likely much has been broken off.   There are traces of crimson paint on the vessel inside and out (Fig. 4).   Length, 11.2 inches; height, 6 inches; width, 6.5 inches.

Vessel No. 5.—In Fig. 5 is shown a vessel which, expanding slightly from the base upward, ends in an oblate spheroid.   On the lower part of the vessel are incised encircling lines and punctate decoration.   Two lines of punctate markings are below

FIG. 4.—Vessel No. 4.   Mound near West Bay P. O.   (Three-fifths size.)

FIG. 5.—Vessel No. 5.   Mound near West Bay P. O.   (Five-sixths size.)

the rim.   On the other side are small holes for suspension.   A mortuary perforation of base is present.   Height, 6 inches; maximum diameter, 5.8 inches.

FIG. 6.—Vessel No. 6.   Mound near West Bay P. O.   (Full size.)

Vessel No. 6.—Part of a compartment vessel of a type new to us is shown in Fig. 6. • We cannot say how many divisions there have been.   In the part remaining a small one is shown within another.

Vessel No. 7.—A perforate bowl is shown in Fig. 7 giving a good example of handsomely executed pinched decoration, eight rows of which surround the body. Height, 4 inches; maximum diameter, 5.8 inches.

Vessel No. 8.—An interestingly decorated vessel shown in Fig. 8 of somewhat less than 1 pint capacity.   The upper part of the body is quadrilateral.   The lower part tapers to what was a flat base previous to the mortuary mutilation.   The rim projects horizontally with a small handle on two opposite sides.

Vessel No. 9.—A perforate bowl of rather poor ware, of about 1 gallon capacity, has below the rim four encircling rows of impressions made by a triangular point, between two incised lines.

Vessel No. 10.—The upper portion of a vessel of good ware, having below the rim incised and punctate decoration.   The design, which shows an animal head with eyes, is once repeated on the vessel (Fig. 9).

Vessel No. 11.—A bowl of about 3 pints capacity, of uniform decoration, incised and punctate. A small animal head projects vertically from the rim (Fig. 10).

FIG. 7.—Vessel No. 7. Mound near West Bay P. O. (Four-fifths size.)

Vessel No. 12.—A vessel of about 1 quart capacity, in form an ovoid truncated at either end, with a flaring five-pointed rim, is shown in Fig. 11.

FIG. 8.—Vessel No. 8. Mound near West Bay P. O. (Half size.)

Vessel No. 13.—A jar of about 3 pints capacity, badly crushed when found. The fragments have been cemented together with partial restoration. The ware is inferior and the incised decoration is rude. A handle or lip projects obliquely from the rim (Fig. 12).

Vessel No. 14.—A vessel of about 3 quarts capacity, found in fragments a number of which were not recovered. The parts have been cemented together and certain restoration has been attempted. The body of the vessel has an oval transverse section; the opening is oval. From one end of the vessel projects a large head, perhaps intended to represent that of a panther. It certainly bears no resemblance to the head of a bear, of a wolf, or of an aboriginal dog. There is interesting incised and punctate decoration, in part representing conventionalized fore-legs and hind-legs (Fig. 13).

Vessel No. 15.—This vessel, of about the same shape as the one just described, was found broken to fragments from which certain parts of the vessel are missing.

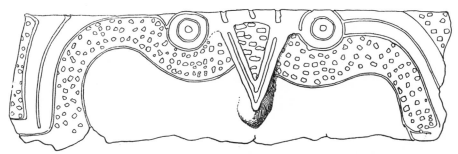

FIG. 9.—Vessel No. 10. Decoration. Mound near West Bay P. O. (Half size.)

Cementing and partial restoration show the body to have been of about 2 quarts capacity, with decoration, incised and punctate, in part representing wings. As the design varies somewhat on either side, complete restoration has been impossible. At either end is a bird's head from which the bill has been broken in part (Fig. 14). On

FIG. 10.—Vessel No. 11. Mound near West Bay P. O. (Half size.)

FIG. 11.—Vessel No. 12. Mound near West Bay P. O. (Half size.) FIG. 12.—Vessel No. 13. Mound near West Bay P. O. (Half size.)

Fig. 13.—Vessel No. 14. Mound near West Bay P. O. (Seven-eighths size.)

Fig. 14.—Vessel No. 15.   Mound near West Bay P. O.   (Two-thirds size.)

this vessel are a number of symbols, perhaps representing feathers.   Symbols of this class are found on practically all bird-vessels and consist of straight or curved lines with circular or triangular enlargement at one end or at both ends.

Fig. 15.—Vessel No. 16.   Mound near West Bay P. O.   (Two-thirds size.)

These bird-symbols are sometimes found on vessels apparently having no connection with bird forms, though they may indicate some connection with the bird.   On the other hand, as Professor Holmes has shown, the aborigines were not always consistent and the bird symbol at times may have degenerated into an ornament.   At all events, the symbols we have described belong normally to the bird.

Fig. 16.—Handle of vessel.   Mound near West Bay P. O.   (Eight-ninths size.)

Vessel No. 16 is a graceful vessel of about 2 quarts capacity found in small fragments and partly restored.   Seemingly, the decoration, incised and punctate, is not uniform.   This vessel, made up of four lobes, is shown in Fig. 15.

Figs. 16, 17, 18, 19 represent four bird-head handles from this mound.

On the base, in the central part of the mound, sometimes together in twos and threes, apart from burials, were sixteen vessels of ordinary type and inferior ware.   Some were undecorated; some had an indistinct,

Fig. 17.—Handle of vessel.   Mound near West Bay P. O.   (Eight-ninths size.)

complicated stamp; a few had scalloped margins.   All had the basal perforation which we believe, without exception, was the case with the vessels of this mound.

These vessels, which in capacity ranged between 2 quarts and four times that amount, were so water soaked and so hopelessly crushed that all hope of saving them was abandoned.

FIG. 18.—Handle of vessel. Mound near West Bay P. O. (Eight-ninths size.)

FIG. 19.—Handle of vessel. Mound near West Bay P. O. (Eight-ninths size.)

MOUND NEAR WEST BAY CREEK, WASHINGTON COUNTY.

This mound, in pine woods on property of Mr. W. M. Sowell of Point Washington, Florida, is about one-half mile in a northeasterly direction from the northern side of the western extremity of West bay, which is one of the subdivisions of St. Andrew's bay (see map). Its diameter of base was 45 feet; its height, 2 feet 9 inches. Careful investigation led to the conclusion that this mound belonged to the domiciliary class.

MOUND IN BROCK HAMMOCK,[1] WASHINGTON COUNTY.

This mound, about 2.5 feet high and 38 feet across the base, was about 3 miles in a S. direction from West Bay post-office and 300 yards, approximately, from the water, on land said to belong to the United States Government. A large excavation had been made in the center previous to our visit. Extensive trenching by us yielded a small, imperforate, undecorated bowl of poor quality and several sherds, bearing the small check stamp or the complicated variety.

Human remains, which were no doubt central, had probably fallen to the lot of the previous digger.

LARGER MOUND NEAR BURNT MILL CREEK, WASHINGTON COUNTY.

This mound, which the owner, Mr. Marion Shypes, who lives nearby, informed us had been ploughed over ten years, stood in a cultivated field on the north side of the creek about 1 mile from the mouth and 200 yards from the water, approxi-

[1] The word hammock, used by Captain Bernard Romans in the latter half of the XVIII century, in his "Concise Natural History of East and West Florida," stands for territory on which grow palmetto, oak and other woods in contradistinction to pine lands, the prairie, the swamp and the marsh. The word is widely employed in Florida.

mately. Its height was a trifle over 4 feet; its basal diameter, 50 feet. Its shape had been the usual truncated cone.

The mound, which showed no trace of previous digging, was totally demolished by us.

Human remains, which were almost reduced to the consistency of paste, were found at eleven points, beginning about 15 feet from the center and consisted of single skulls and skulls with a few long bones.

Once human remains lay near a deposit of earthenware and once a few thin sheets of mica were in association.

In this mound earthenware was met with near the margin of the northeastern side and continued in, on or near the base, singly or in larger deposits of five, seven and ten vessels together until within ten or twelve feet of the center of the mound. But two or three fragments of vessels came from other portions of the mound.

In all, 39 vessels were noted by us, though it is likely some, broken into small pieces and mixed together, were neglected in our count. Many vessels were hopelessly wrecked through the action of water on the inferior ware, while others, taken out entire, are not of a character to merit particular description.

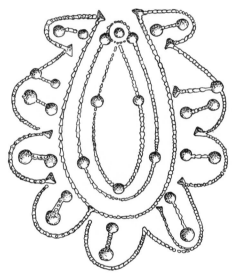

FIG. 20.—Vessel No. 4. Decoration. Larger mound near Burnt Mill Creek. (Half size.)

Vessel No. 4.—A small cup with rounded base having incised decoration on part of the body and on the base, shown diagrammatically in Fig. 20, where it has been necessary to allow a certain expansion to the design on account of its position. Hence the scale given is approximate only.

Vessel No. 5.—An undecorated jar almost cylindrical but expanding slightly at the opening. Height, 9 inches; maximum diameter, 5.7 inches.

Vessel No. 8.—About 1 quart capacity, heart-shaped in section as to the body, with constricted neck and flaring four pointed rim. The decoration, made up of encircling, undulating lines, is similar to that on Vessel No. 5 from the Hall Mound, to be described later.

Vessel No. 15.—Globular with thickened rim, undecorated, of about 2 quarts capacity.

Vessel No. 16.—A hemispherical body with slightly elongated base, part of which has been lost through mortuary breakage. The ware is yellow. The decoration consists of crosshatch design finely incised. At the corners of the spaces between the designs are imprints of a tubular implement, probably a reed (Fig. 21). Maximum diameter, 10.5 inches; present height, 5 inches; diameter of opening, 6.5 inches.

Vessel No. 18 is rather an image of earthenware, almost solid and of considerable weight. This image, representing a male wearing a breech clout, ends at the knees, apparently. The arms are folded across the chest. There are traces of crimson paint on various parts of the body. The upper part of the head, which had begun to crumble owing to the dampness of the mound, received, in addition, a blow from a spade (Fig. 22).

FIG. 21.—Vessel No. 16. Larger mound near Burnt Mill Creek. (About two-thirds size.)

Vessel No. 27.—Of about 1 quart capacity with a body heart-shaped in outline and a neck flaring slightly. The decoration consists of four encircling rows of punctate impressions above an incised line.

Vessel No. 31.—Seemingly, when found, a solid full-length image of the human form which, on removal, fell into an infinite number of small bits of the consistency of paste. These, on drying, became extremely friable and past all hope of restoration.

Vessel No. 32.—This most interesting vessel of the readymade mortuary type, was found in fragments which have since been cemented together with great care and a few missing portions restored, including the upright rim, as to the original shape of which we are uncertain.   The ware is thin and covered with crimson pigment. In addition to the hole in the base, made before baking, there are many other orifices, varying in size and shape, made at the same time as the basal perforation, inaugurating

FIG. 22.—No. 18.   Image of earthenware.   Larger mound near Burnt Mill Creek.   (Three-fourths size.)

a type not found by us to the westward, and but infrequently met with until much farther east along the coast.   At either end of the body, which has an elliptical transverse section, probably modelled after the body of a bird, is a bird's head projecting horizontally outward.   Below, on one side, a hole has been made with the outline of a wing, which design is not repeated on the opposite side (Fig. 23).   Length, 9.5 inches; width, 5.5 inches; height, 9 inches.

Vessel No. 33.—A bowl, oblate spheroid in shape, much flattened, of about 3 quarts capacity, with incised decoration, half of which is shown diagrammatically in Fig. 24, the other half being similar.   This vessel, found crushed to bits, has been cemented together and somewhat restored.

Vessel No. 34.—This vessel, found crushed to fragments, parts of which were not recovered, has had a flat base, most of which is now missing through the mortuary mutilation common to the vessels of this mound.   The lower part, a truncated cone reversed, supports the body which is made up of three projecting bosses surmounted by incised lines. The neck slopes inward slightly (Fig. 25).   Height, 8 inches; maximum diameter, 6.5 inches.

Vessel No. 35.—A quadrilateral vessel of about 1 pint capacity, tapering to the base, part of which has been knocked out.   Two sides are undecorated.   Of the other two sides, which have incised decoration, one is shown in the representation of the vessel (Fig. 26); the other, diagrammatically in Fig. 27.

Vessel No. 39.—A jar of about 1 quart capacity with semiglobular body and neck first slightly constricted, then flaring.   The decoration, which is between two

FIG. 23.—Vessel No. 32.   Larger mound near Burnt Mill Creek.   (Nine-elevenths size.)

FIG. 24.—Vessel No. 33.   Decoration.   Larger mound near Burnt Mill Creek.   (One-third size.)

Fig. 25.—Vessel No. 34.   Larger mound near Burnt Mill Creek.   (Nine-tenths size.)

incised encircling lines, is made up of linear impressions around the neck, six deep in places, in others, seven.

FIG. 26.—Vessel No. 35. Larger mound near Burnt Mill Creek. (Half size.)

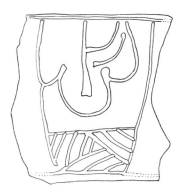

FIG. 27.—Vessel No. 35. Decoration. Larger mound near Burnt Mill Creek. (Half size.)

SMALLER MOUND NEAR BURNT MILL CREEK, WASHINGTON COUNTY.

The mound, said to be on property belonging to the State of Florida, is on ground formerly cultivated, about 1 mile in a northerly direction from the mouth of Burnt Mill creek. This mound, which was leveled by us, had a basal diameter of 28 feet; a height of about 2.5 feet. A hole in the center dug prior to our coming, involved about one-quarter of the mound. If human remains had been spared by decay, they must have occupied this central space as no trace of bones was met with by us. Nor was charcoal present or blackened sand.

FIG. 28.—Sherd. Smaller mound near Burnt Mill Creek. (About two-thirds size.)

Near the margin of the NE. part of the mound, continuing in under the sloping portion, was a deposit of earthenware vessels all within an area not over 7 feet in diameter and, as a rule, in, or almost in, actual contact, many being crushed one into the other. Of these, 29 vessels were recognized as whole or having been entire or nearly so before they were crushed by weight of sand. In addition to our count, however, must be included many other vessels hopelessly broken to small fragments and intermingled. These vessels, with four exceptions, were bowls, pots and jars, of ordinary type from 1 pint to 2 gallons capacity, approximately, mostly of thin and inferior ware which a long period of soaking had reduced to a sodden condition, unable to withstand the pressure of surrounding sand. A few vessels, however, were of somewhat better quality.

Certain of these vessels had a complicated stamp decoration more or less faint and one, encircling rows made up of oblong imprints about .75 of an inch in length. One had decoration of crimson paint interiorly while others were undecorated.   All whose condition allowed determination were noted as having the usual basal perforation, with the exception of a small jar of coarse ware.   Certain sherds had circular punctate decoration and one had scroll work deeply incised (Fig. 28).

FIG. 29.—Vessel of earthenware. Smaller mound near
Burnt Mill Creek. (Half size.)

FIG. 30.—Vessel of earthenware. Smaller mound
near Burnt Mill Creek. (Half size.)

Of vessels found outside the usual run, one undecorated, and of fairly thick ware, is boat-shaped with projections at the extremities.

A vessel of about 1 quart capacity has a spherical body with elongated base. Below the rim is an incised line.   There have been four small projections, like rudimentary handles, one on each side a little below the rim, two of which are missing. The decoration is incised and punctate (Fig. 29).

Fig. 30 shows a vessel of about 1 pint capacity, with decoration made with an implement though such decoration is often considered cordmarked.

A sherd with complicated stamp is shown in Fig. 31.

Among the farthest in was a bowl of fairly good ware which pressure of sand had split. This bowl, which lay on its base, still kept an upright position.   Standing in the bowl and to a certain extent protected by it, was a rude effigy-vessel of yellow ware, representing a male figure, shown in

FIG. 31.—Sherd. Smaller mound near Burnt
Mill Creek. (Half size.)

two positions in Figs. 32, 33.   The lower part is wanting through the usual basal mutilation.   Present height, 7.5 inches; maximum width, 4.4 inches.

A broken arrowhead or knife, of chert, lay unassociated in the sand.

FIG. 32.—Effigy-vessel, front view. Smaller mound near Burnt Mill Creek. (About full size.)

FIG. 33.—Effigy-vessel, rear view. Smaller mound near Burnt Mill Creek. (About full size.)

MOUND NEAR ALLIGATOR BAYOU, WASHINGTON COUNTY.

Alligator bayou joins North bay, a part of St. Andrew's bay on the W. side, about 2 miles up the bay.

The mound, near the head of the bayou which is about one-half mile in length, was on the property of Mrs. Elizabeth J. Daniels, who lives on the place. The mound on low-lying ground and partly surrounded by not far distant water, was very moist as to the sand composing it and in a condition to facilitate decay. It was oblong in shape, 76 feet E. and W. through the base and 50 feet N. and S. Its height was 6 feet 5 inches. It had received but little previous attention from the treasure seekers of the bay. The mound was completely levelled by us.

FIG. 34.—Vessel No. 15. Mound near Alligator Bayou. (Half size.)

Owing to the dampness, no doubt, no trace of human remains was met with by us.

At one place, in a mass of sand of almost inky blackness from admixture of organic matter, was a wooden object resembling a tine of a stag's antler, overlaid with copper. This interesting object, which doubtless accompanied a burial, unfortunately received a blow from a spade.

In another portion of the mound was a pocket of sand made crimson from admixture of hematite. This deep-colored sand called to mind the great deposits at various points in the mound at Mt. Royal described in our reports on the St. John's River Mounds, the rich crimson color differing considerably from the pink tint found in sand having the usual slight admixture of the red oxide of iron.

A barbed arrowpoint of chert, a sheet of mica to which had been given, rather rudely, the outline of an arrowhead and a shell drinking cup were the only other artifacts in the mound, exclusive of earthenware.

About 13 feet in from the margin, on the eastern side of the mound, in sand, which by its dark admixture of organic matter, contrasted with the yellow sand of other parts of the mound, began a deposit of earthenware, 4 feet across, which, continuing in, on or near the base, broadening to the N. and S., and contracting again, ended about 11 feet from the center, thus having a length of about 14 feet.

The vessels, of which we counted sixty-six, and doubtless some badly crushed and intermingled were left from the score, were upright or tilted at almost any angle, and nearly always in groups crushed into each other or separated by very

FIG. 35.—Vessel No. 24.   Mound near Alligator Bayou.   (About seven-eighths size.)

small space.   All but two, which will have reference later, had the usual basal perforation, at least all whose condition allowed us to determine.

Greatly to our disappointment, the vessels, which in size ranged from a toy bowl holding hardly more than a thimble-full to pots of at least four gallons capacity, were almost exclusively kitchen ware of ordinary shapes and of flimsy material. The majority were undecorated.   On but two were incised designs.   One vessel was covered with crimson pigment.   Many vessels had the complicated stamp but, as a rule, the impress was faint though several patterns new to us were present in the mound. The small check stamp was absent. Scalloped margins abounded. The condition of most of this pottery, thin and of inferior ware, ground together by pressure of sand after continued soaking for a long term of years, can well be imagined. In most cases our efforts to preserve the fragmentary vessels was baffled, while but few of those saved merit special mention.

Vessel No. 5.—A globular undecorated body of about 1 pint capacity with part of what had been a solid handle projecting upward at an angle. This vessel is of the class modelled after gourds.

Vessel No. 15.—A globular body of yellow ware, which probably had a flat base. Almost the entire neck, which was flaring, is missing through an old fracture. The decoration, incised, is made up of a series of two concentric circles surrounded by other designs as shown in Fig. 34. Maximum diameter, 8.2 inches.

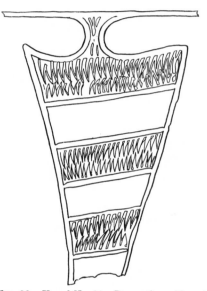

FIG. 36.—Vessel No. 24. Decoration. Mound near Alligator Bayou. (Half size.)

Vessel No. 24.—Of yellow ware, almost semi-globular body, tapering somewhat at the base. The rim flares slightly. The interesting incised decoration consists of two large similar designs on opposite sides, one of which is shown in Fig. 35. There are two smaller designs, also alike, one of which is given in diagram, Fig. 36. Maximum diameter, 7 inches; height, 5.5 inches.

Vessel No. 34.—A small vessel almost a perfect globe, with small aperture and slightly projecting rim. This vessel, of about a pint capacity, when removed from the wet sand was of a bright crimson which faded when dry.

Vessel No. 35.—A pot of yellow ware with scalloped margin. The decoration, a complicated stamp, is distinctly impressed (Fig. 37). Height, 10 inches; maximum diameter, 9 inches.

Vessel No. 44.—Badly crushed, had four small feet.

Vessel No. 64.—A pot of yellow ware expanding slightly toward the rim, which is scalloped. The decoration is a zigzag stamp identical with that shown on a sherd from this mound. Maximum diameter, 10 inches; height, somewhat impaired by loss of the base, 9.8 inches.

Vessels Nos. 65 and 66.—Toy bowls, 2.3 inches and 1.8 inches in diameter, respectively, found together a little apart from the main deposit.

Three sherds with complicated stamp decoration are shown in Figs. 38, 39, 40.

MOUND NEAR FANNING'S BAYOU, WASHINGTON COUNTY.

Fanning's bayou joins North bay from the north about five miles up the bay.

The mound, which had been dug into to a small extent only, was on the edge of a hammock, about one mile in a NW. direction from Anderson P. O., which is

Fig. 37.—Vessel No. 35. Mound near Alligator Bayou. (Half size.)

Fig. 38.—Sherd. Mound near Alligator Bayou. (Half size.)

Fig. 39.—Sherd. Mound near Alligator Bayou. (Half size.)

about two miles up the bayou. The mound was about 3 feet high and about 40 feet in basal diameter. The ownership of the property is in dispute.

The mound, which was totally demolished by us, contained nineteen burials, single skulls with a few long-bones, or long-bones without skulls, or in two cases, two skulls with long-bones. Above certain of these burials was charcoal.

With one burial was a shell drinking cup. Another burial lay near certain vessels of earthenware, but as these vessels were a continuation of a deposit beginning at a considerable distance from the remains, we do not believe the earthenware had any direct connection with them.

An arrowhead of chert and two rude imitations of spearheads in mica were found, not in immediate association with the dead.

FIG. 40.—Sherd. Mound near Alligator Bayou. (Half size.)

The result of our investigation in this mound was the old story with which we have become so familiar. In the extreme margin of the eastern part of the mound, preceded by a deposit of miscellaneous sherds and continuing at intervals to the center, were numerous vessels, broken and whole, undecorated in the main, some having the small check stamp, others incised and punctate decoration. Three vessels only had the complicated stamp and that around the neck alone. A complicated stamp decoration on a sherd is shown in Fig. 41.

FIG. 41.—Sherd. Mound near Fanning's Bayou. (Three-fourths size.)

All vessels, broken or whole, as far as we could determine, had the usual base-perforation and all lay in masses of sand far darker than the yellow sand of the rest of the mound.

We shall now describe in detail the more interesting vessels from the mound, some of which, taken out in pieces, have been carefully cemented together.

Vessel No. 1.—A vessel of about 3 pints capacity has a circular neck, flaring into a square outline at the rim. The incised decoration, which is repeated on the opposite side with but slight variation, is shown in Fig. 42.

Vessel No. 2.—A bowl of curious outline recalling that of a horseshoe were the extremities joined.   The body is undecorated.

FIG. 42.—Vessel No. 1.   Mound near Fanning's Bayou.   (Half size.)

Notches extend around the margin of the curved portion, while an incised line resembling the symbol of the bird, which, seemingly, is not always confined to bird-vessels, stretches across the straight portion (Fig. 43).

Vessel No. 3.—A gracefully made semiglobular vessel with short, upright, rounded rim, of excellent ware, has four encircling lines of punctate markings around the upper part of the body, about 1 inch apart. Maximum diameter, 10.5 inches; height, 6.5 inches.

Vessel No. 4.—A jar of inferior ware (Fig. 44), 6 inches in maximum diameter with a present height of 9 inches, bears a curious punctate and incised decoration, probably some highly conventionalized figures among which may be recognized the symbol of the bird.   The decoration is shown diagrammatically in Fig. 45.

Vessel No. 5.—A bowl of yellow ware of about 1 quart capacity with rude line and punctate decoration as shown in Fig. 46.

Vessel No. 6.—A vase roughly globular as to the body with neck flaring outward and upward. Where the neck joins the body on the outside are two encircling rows of pinched decoration (Fig. 47). Maximum diameter, 7.5 inches; height, 5.5 inches.

Vessel No. 7.—In the central deposit was a curious vessel of thick ware rather carelessly made, the upper portion leaning to one side. On the upper part of the vessel is punctate decoration. There are two holes for suspension (Fig. 48). Height, 7 inches; maximum diameter, 5.8 inches.

FIG. 43.—Vessel No. 2. Mound near Fanning's Bayou. (Half size.)

Vessel No. 8.—A vase of yellow ware of about 1 quart capacity, found broken into many pieces, a few of which, not recovered, have since been restored (Fig. 49). The decoration, incised, is carefully executed. One-half of it is shown diagrammatically in Fig. 50, the other half being a repetition.

FIG. 44.—Vessel No. 4. Mound near Fanning's Bayou. (Half size.)

Vessel No. 9.—A bowl of inferior ware, about 1 quart capacity, has a cross-hatch design rudely executed. An upright protuberance about .25 of an inch in height, projects from the rim on one side.

Vessel No. 10.—This vessel, of rather soft yellow ware, found badly crushed with certain parts missing, presumably, since the sand was carefully sifted, would hold about 3 quarts. The lower part is semiglobular, slightly flattened at the base. The upper part of the body is hexagonal. The neck expands slightly. The decoration consists of six semicircles over curious incised designs varying but slightly one from another, in fields of punctate markings. Impressions of points fill the spaces between the junction of the ends of the semicircles and the neck (Fig. 51).

Vessel No. 11.—A jar of graceful outline, unfortunately much broken at the base, bearing the check stamp decoration (Fig. 52). Present height, 14.5 inches; maximum diameter, 7.5 inches.

Vessel No. 12.—A bowl with quadrilateral rim bearing incised and punctate decoration as shown in Fig. 53.

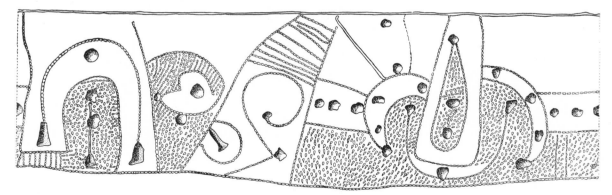

FIG. 45.—Vessel No. 4. Decoration. Mound near Fanning's Bayou. (One-third size.)

Fig. 46.—Vessel No. 5. Mound near Fanning's Bayou.
(Half size)

Fig. 47.—Vessel No. 6. Mound near Fanning's Bayou.
(Half size.)

Fig. 48.—Vessel No. 7. Mound near Fanning's Bayou. (About three-fourths size.)

FIG. 49.—Vessel No. 8. Mound near Fanning's Bayou. (Full size.)

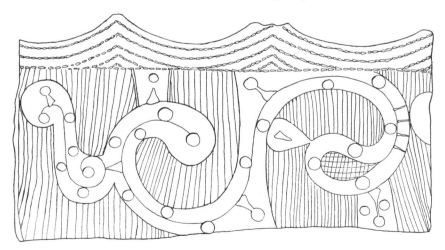

FIG. 50.—Vessel No. 8. Decoration. Mound near Fanning's Bayou. (Half size.)

FIG. 51.—Vessel No. 10.   Mound near Fanning's Bayou.   (Half size.)

FIG. 52.—Vessel No. 11.   Mound near Fanning's Bayou.
(One-third size.)

FIG. 53.—Vessel No. 12.   Mound near Fanning's Bayou.   (Half size.)

MOUND NEAR THE HEAD OF NORTH BAY, WASHINGTON COUNTY.

This mound, seemingly intact, was in pine woods about one-half mile in a WSW. direction from the home of Mr. W. M. Brooks, the owner, on the shore near the head of North bay.

The mound, about 2 feet in height and 38 feet across the base, was entirely dug through by us.

Human remains were met with in sixteen places and consisted of single skulls, skulls with long-bones, etc.   No artifacts lay with the burials.

Unassociated, was an arrowpoint or knife, of red chert and, near the surface, lay a cube of lead sulphide about 2.5 inches in each of its dimensions.

Vessel No. 1 was met with at the extreme verge of the NW. side of the mound. The body is rounded, the rim flares slightly. The ware is most inferior. This vessel, which has four feet and faint traces of decoration, is without the basal perforation.

In the margin of the eastern part of the mound were numbers of sherds, several of good ware, many bearing the small check stamp. Among these, several feet apart, were portions of a dish of excellent ware, undecorated. In common with all the vessels in this mound, except the one first described, it had the basal perforation.

Vessel No. 3.—Triangular, with rounded corners, with slight traces of punctate and incised decoration. A handle fastened by pressure on the clay before baking is missing and was not present with the vessel. Length, 4.5 inches; height, 2 inches.

Ten other vessels were in the same deposit, all within a few feet of each other. Some were broken; all were of ordinary form, without decoration or with a rude check stamp, or, in one case, with rough incised lines.

There was no central deposit in this mound, but considerably farther in than the vessels just noted were two others, or parts of them, in fragments. Their decoration, seemingly, was conferred by basket work.

MOUND NEAR ANDERSON'S BAYOU, WASHINGTON COUNTY.

Anderson's bayou joins the E. side of North bay about 5 miles up. The mound, on property belonging to Mr. A. J. Gay, whose home is not far distant, is in thick hammock about 50 yards from the eastern side of the bayou and about one-quarter of a mile up. The height of the mound was 2 feet 4 inches; its basal diameter, 55 feet. The mound, into which three comparatively small holes had been dug prior to our visit, was completely leveled by us. It proved to be of yellow sand, except in the neighborhood of earthenware, where the sand had the customary darkened appearance.

Presumably, human remains to a certain extent had disappeared through decay as burials were found in four places only. These consisted of three skulls, together; certain small pieces of a skull; a skull with a few pieces of long-bone; and several fragments of long-bones without a skull. There were also in the mound a few bits of calcined bone, but none of a size large enough to determine whether they were human or otherwise.

There were present in the mound, unassociated with human remains, though bones may have decayed in their immediate vicinity : a bead of red argillite, nearly cylindrical, .85 of an inch in length and .55 of an inch in maximum diameter; two small fragments of sheet copper, near the surface; a sheet of mica; four bits of rock together. In association were bits of rock, pebble-hammers, smoothing stones, broken hones, four bits of *Fulgur;* a pebble with a semicircular space worn in the side, and numerous pebbles.

We have frequently found in the mounds round or cylindrical pebbles seemingly too small for use as pebble-hammers. These pebbles, often lying together as though at one time deposited within a receptacle, we believe to have been sling-stones. Cabeça de Vaca [1] says the Indians began " to throw clubs at us and to sling

---

[1] Chapter X, p. 37. Buckingham Smith's translation.

stones."   In the original Spanish the words " *tirar piedras cō hondas* " are used, so there can be no doubt as to the meaning of the author.

Two bits of pottery with small check stamp were in the body of the mound.

In the margin of that part of the mound embraced between NE. and S. of E.,

FIG. 54.—Vessel of earthenware.   Mound near Anderson's Bayou.   (About four-fifths size.)

the usual deposit of pottery, made for the dead in common, began and continued in, at intervals, to the center of the mound.   The vessels, which lay along the base and were unassociated with burials, all had, as far as noted, the usual basal perforation. Many were badly crushed and the ware of nearly all was most inferior.   With two exceptions, no incised decoration was present in the mound, all other vessels being undecorated, or bearing the complicated stamp.

A feature in the mound was the presence of a number of bases of vessels lying unassociated, which showed that the knocking out of basal portions in fulfilment of the mortuary rite was sometimes attended to at the mound and the bases scattered throughout the sand.

A quadrilateral vessel, with sides tapering somewhat to the base, which is flat, has a decoration similar on each side, shown in Fig. 54. Height, 9 inches; maximum diameter, 7 inches.

With the vessel just described, which came almost exactly from the center of the mound, was another with decoration of broad, incised lines, shown in Fig. 55.

Three sherds with complicated stamps are shown in Figs. 56, 57, 58; also a vessel with the same type of decoration, which we believe came from this mound, though the label formerly upon it has disappeared (Fig. 59).

FIG. 55.—Vessel of earthenware. Mound near Anderson's Bayou. (Half size.)

FIG. 56.—Sherd. Mound near Anderson's Bayou. (Four-fifths size.)

FIG. 57.—Sherd. Mound near Anderson's Bayou. (Four-fifths size.)

FIG. 58.—Sherd. Mound near Anderson's Bayou. (Four-fifths size.)

FIG. 59.—Vessel of earthenware. Mound near Anderson's Bayou. (Six-sevenths size.)

MOUND NEAR LARGE BAYOU, WASHINGTON COUNTY.

Large bayou unites with North bay about 3 miles up, on the E. side of the bay. The mound, on property of Mr. A. J. Gay, owner of the Anderson's bayou mound, is in an old field about one-half mile in a southerly direction from the head of the bayou.

This mound, about four feet high and fifty feet across the base at the present time, has been dug into for years and objects of interest are reported to have been taken from it. Much of the remainder was dug down by us.

Ten bunched burials were met with, one having two skulls.

On the base, below human remains, well in on the western slope of the mound, was a quadrilateral vessel with incised decoration similar on each side. Maximum diameter, 5.4 inches; height, 3.3 inches.

Near a burial was a considerable number of sherds, probably a vessel crushed to fragments.

Also with a burial was an undecorated toy pot, having a perforation of the base, as had all vessels found by us in this mound.

Well in on the western side, on the base, together, both badly crushed, were a pot with a complicated stamp decoration and an undecorated bowl, also mica. No bones were present with these, but presumably a burial had disappeared through decay.

At the very verge of the eastern part of the mound, with no bones associated, were a number of vessels extending in and over toward the NE. These vessels, pots and bowls, were undecorated or bore the small check stamp. Many were badly crushed. It is impossible to say how far into the mound this deposit may have extended, owing to the great amount of previous digging.

There were also in the mound portions of two compartment vessels; a pebble-hammer and a smoothing stone.

HOLLEY MOUND, WASHINGTON COUNTY.

This mound, about two miles in a westerly direction from Bear Point, in an old field, the property of Mr. John C. Holley, who lives on the place, is about 100 yards from the water. According to Mr. Holley the mound had sustained no previous digging, with the exception of two small holes dug by members of his family, which yielded nothing except a few bones in fragments.

This mound, 2.5 feet high and 50 feet across the base, was totally dug down by us.

Seven burials were met with, the first 11 feet in from the NE. margin of the mound, on the base as were all with one exception. The remaining burials continued in at intervals until the center of the mound was reached.

Burial No. 1.—Part of a pelvis covered by a *Fulgur perversum* having the mortuary perforation. Presumably other bones of the deposit, not thus protected, had disappeared.

Burial No. 2.—Small decaying fragments of a femur and of a tibia, side by side.

Burial No. 3.—In a shallow grave below the base of the mound were fragments of a skull and bits of two femurs.

Burial No. 4.—A small fragment of decaying bone.

Burial No. 5.—Bits of two femurs and of one tibia.

Burial No. 6.—The remains of a skull.

Burial No. 7.—Decaying fragments of a cranium.

We believe that other burials had disappeared from the mound through decay, but think such were from the neighborhood of those we have described, as no discolored earth or sign of interment of any sort was found in other portions of the mound.

Exactly in the same line with the burials, but beginning at the margin, in blackened sand, were many sherds, and fourteen vessels, three or four together at times, some whole, some crushed to pieces.

Vessel No. 1.—An imperforate bowl of about 1 quart capacity, of inferior yellow ware, having an almost uniform incised and punctate decoration around the upper part (Fig. 60). This vessel, unlike all others in the mound, had no basal perforation.

FIG. 60.—Vessel No. 1. Holley mound. (Half size.)

Vessel No. 2.—A compartment vessel with four divisions on one plane and a fifth in the center, somewhat above the rest (Fig. 61). The central compartment has a basal perforation which does not show in the half-tone. Length, 8.7 inches; width, 7.1 inches; height, 2.3 inches.

Vessel No. 3.—A pot of about 1 quart capacity, undecorated, almost cylindrical, expanding slightly toward the base which is flat.

FIG. 61.—Vessel No. 2. Holley mound. (About three-fourths size.)

FIG. 62.—Vessel No. 8.   Holley mound.   (Half size.)

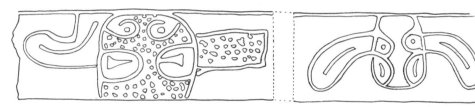

FIG. 63.—Vessel No. 8.   Decoration.   Holley mound.   (Half size.)

FIG. 65.—Sherd.   Holley mound.   (Three-fourths size.)

FIG. 64.—Vessel No. 12.   Holley mound.   (Half size.)

Vessel No. 4.—Globular, about 3 quarts capacity, thickening at the rim. The decoration is a faint complicated stamp.

FIG. 66.—Sherd. Holley mound. (Half size.)

Vessel No. 8.—Quadrilateral, of yellow ware, broken into many fragments when found. The rim, which turns inward nearly at right angles, has incised decoration. There are incised and punctate designs on three sides, that on the fourth having been worn away. The bowl with the decoration on one side is shown in Fig. 62, while the designs on two other sides are given diagrammatically in Fig. 63.

Vessel No. 12.—A vase made to hold about 3 quarts, with hemispherical body and neck at first constricted, then flaring, around which is a complicated stamp decoration (Fig. 64). With this vessel were sheets of mica.

The complicated stamp designs on two sherds are shown in Figs. 65, 66.

SOWELL MOUND, WASHINGTON COUNTY.

This mound, on property of Mr. Jesse Sowell of West Bay P. O., Florida, is in scrub about 1 mile in a westerly direction from Bear Point. Previous to our visit a trench 12 feet across had been dug from the northern margin of the mound almost to the center. The height of the mound was 4.5 feet; the basal diameter, 50 feet. A great depression whence the sand for the mound had been taken was at its southern margin. All parts of the mound, not before dug, were carefully gone through by us, beginning at the extreme outer limit.

On the extreme eastern margin burials were encountered consisting of flexed skeletons, bunched burials, scattered bones and masses of bones, one of these masses having no less than six skulls. These burials extended without intermission until the center of the mound was reached.

At first the attempt was made to keep count of the burials, but the difficulty to determine where one ended and another began forced us to limit ourselves to a tally of skulls only, and of these there were one hundred and twenty-one.

All burials but three were confined to the eastern part of the mound between the margin and the center, and were, to a certain extent, superficial, lying between a few inches and 2 feet from the surface. Three burials came from the western part of the mound, one 19 feet from the margin, the other two a few feet farther in. Two of these burials were on the base. One was about 2.5 feet from the surface.

The bones in this mound were in a far better state of preservation than are those usually found by us, and, in consequence, a number of crania, now belonging to the Academy of Natural Sciences, were saved.

Many of these skulls showed great antero-posterior flattening as by compression from boards, while some gave evidence of early constriction by a band, a concave depression being evident. A selected skull from this mound is shown in Fig. 67. Captain Bernard Romans, who was familiar with this part of Florida, writing in the

FIG. 67.—Skull showing artificial flattening. Sowell mound. (Two-thirds size.)

latter part of the XVIII century, tells[1] us that in his time the Choctaws bound bags of sand to the heads of male children. In this mound, however, all skulls which were in a condition to allow determination, showed flattening.

All skeletons but one which lay on the back with the legs drawn up under the thighs, were closely flexed, some lying on the right side, some on the left. With certain burials were a small number of oyster shells.

[1] "Concise Natural History of East and West Florida."

With the skeleton of a child were many small shells (*Marginella apicina*),[1] perforated for use as beads.

A pendant of igneous rock was found unassociated with human remains and a smoking pipe of steatite lay in sand thrown out by previous diggers.

Beginning with the burials and continuing with them until the end, were great numbers of sherds, parts of vessels and vessels unbroken or crushed but with full complement of parts.   This deposit of earthenware, which included 53 vessels entire or, when broken, with all but small parts present, began at the margin with great numbers of sherds, undecorated or having the check stamp as a rule.   Next came a few scattered vessels and, shortly after, the first burials were found.   Thence on, earthenware and burials continued more or less closely associated, a burial at times being almost in direct contact with two or three vessels.

All earthenware in this mound, as far as noted, had the usual base-perforation, as did a shell drinking cup associated with the pottery, and lay in sand blackened with organic matter.

Though much of the ware in this mound was broken, perhaps through close contact, vessels sometimes being one within another, and once even a vessel, contained in another, itself held a third, yet a considerable amount was recovered intact, or nearly so.   Unfortunately, the decoration, mainly incised and punctate, only four vessels having the complicated stamp, does not average as high from an artistic point of view as does that from certain other mounds in this district.

FIG. 68.—Vessel No. 1. Sowell mound. (Full size.)

We shall now describe the more notable vessels from this mound.

Vessel No. 1.—Almost an inverted truncated cone in shape with punctate decoration shown in Fig. 68.   There are holes on opposite sides for suspension.   Height, 3.1 inches; maximum diameter, 2 inches.

Vessel No. 3.—Of ordinary form with two encircling bands, the upper formed of three rows of upright linear impressions; the other, a little less than 1 inch below, of two rows of larger impressions of the same style.

Vessel No. 5.—A pot of about 1 pint capacity, covered with rows of small circular impressions, probably made with the end of a reed.

Vessel No. 14.—Oblate spheroid with incised and punctate decoration as shown in Fig. 69.   Height, 4.3 inches; maximum diameter, 10.5 inches.

Vessel No. 18.—Ovoid, has for decoration three encircling rows of punctate linear impressions.   In addition to the basal perforation, two others have been made on the side.

[1] All shells referred to in this report have been determined by Dr. H. A. Pilsbry, of the Academy of Natural Sciences.

22 JOURN. A. N. S. PHILA., VOL. XII.

FIG. 69.—Vessel No. 14. Sowell mound. (Two-thirds size.)

Vessel No. 19.—A jar of about 1 quart capacity, undecorated but of somewhat unusual form.   Part of the neck is missing.   There are two perforations, which may have been for suspension.

Vessel No. 23.—An undecorated vessel holding about 1 pint, in shape resembling two much-flattened spheres, one upon the other.   There have been two perforations for suspension, one of which is now included in a broken portion.

Vessel No. 25.—A pot of inferior ware of about 6

FIG. 70.—Vessel No. 25. Sowell mound.
(One-quarter size.)

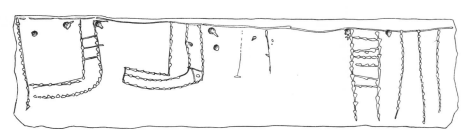

FIG. 71.—Vessel No. 28. Decoration. Sowell mound. (One-third size.)

quarts capacity, having around the upper part of the body a series of roughly incised designs, all similar, consisting of diagonal parallel lines between parallel upright ones (Fig. 70).

Vessel No. 28.—A pot of about 1 quart capacity, with rude decoration shown diagrammatically in Fig. 71.

Vessel No. 29.—A pot rather rudely decorated with incised horizontal and diagonal lines, which enclose similar designs on two opposite sides of the vessel (Fig. 72).

Vessel No. 31.—A three-lobed vessel holding about 1 quart, with three rudimentary bird-heads on the rim at the junction of the lobes (Fig. 63). The decoration, incised, extending over the sides and bottom of the vessel, is shown diagrammatically in Fig. 74.

Vessel No. 32.—Has for decoration a series of parallel diagonal lines at angles to each other, rudely executed.

Vessel No. 33.—Of about 2 quarts capacity, had a piece missing, the result of aboriginal breakage, as a perforation for repair is near the margin of the fracture. The missing portion has since been restored by us (Fig. 75). The incised design is repeated around the vessel.

FIG. 72.--Vessel No. 29. Sowell mound. (Half size.)

FIG. 73.--Vessel No. 31. Sowell mound. (Full size.)

Vessel No. 36.—Of about one-half pint capacity, tapering sharply to the base and somewhat toward the aperture. There is a faint decoration of incised curved lines (Fig. 76).

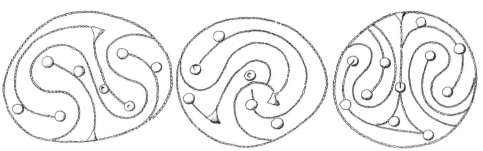

FIG. 74.—Vessel No. 31.   Decoration.   Sowell mound.   (One-third size.)

Vessel No. 41.—A small triangular bowl, undecorated and of inferior ware.

Vessel No. 43.—A vessel of oval section longitudinally, of about 3 pints capacity, covered with crimson pigment inside and out, having at one end a fantastic representation of the head of a bird and, at the other, the conventional tail (Fig. 77).

FIG. 75.—Vessel No. 33.   Sowell mound.   (Seven-eighths size.)

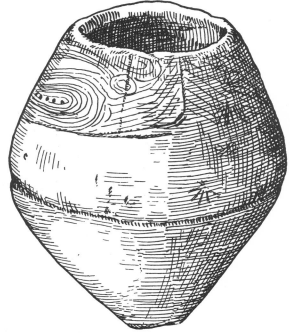

FIG. 76.--Vessel No. 36.   Sowell mound.   (Full size.)

FIG. 77.--Vessel No. 43.   Sowell mound.   (Half size.)

FIG. 78.--Vessel No. 46.   Sowell mound.   (Half size.)

FIG. 79.--Sherd.   Sowell mound.   (Four-fifths size.)

Vessel No. 44.—An undecorated vessel of inferior ware, holding about 1 pint, with globular body and upright quadrilateral neck.

Vessel No. 46.—Rather heart-shaped in outline of body, with neck slightly expanding and surrounded by incised parallel lines. From the rim extend four equidistant horizontal projections. The ware is inferior (Fig. 78). Height, 7 inches; diameter of body, 6.6 inches.

Vessel No. 49.—A flattened sphere with upright rim, with decoration much similar to that on Vessel No. 14 from this mound.

A sherd with complicated stamp decoration is shown in Fig. 79.

In the pottery deposit were several parts of a vessel of better quality of ware and more artistic decoration than characterized any other earthenware from this mound. On one fragment is the head of a duck, not projecting from the rim but in relief on the side.

Mounds near Bear Point, Washington County.

In thick hammock, about 100 yards from the water and one-quarter of a mile from Bear Point, approximately, on property of Lieutenant-Commander Francis H. Sheppard, U. S. N., retired, of St. Andrews, Fla., was a mound which had undergone but little digging previous to our visit. Its basal diameter N. and S. was 60 feet and 50 feet E. and W. Its position on a slope made its height somewhat deceptive. On one side the altitude was but 20 inches. On the opposite side, the east, its height was about 4 feet. It was completely dug down by us.

The first burial was found in the NE. part of the mound, 7 feet in from the margin. Other burials were met with in the same direction, continuing in or a little to the eastward or to the NNE. Near the center one burial to the N. was noted. One lay in the center. These burials, twelve in all, had occasionally a few oyster shells in the sand above them. Three skeletons were closely flexed on the right side and one on the left. One skeleton occupied a squatting position. There were three bunched burials and scattered bones were found in three places. A few decaying fragments were all that remained of one burial.

All bones were badly decayed. No skulls were saved, though fragments were met with sufficiently large to show that cranial compression had been practised.

A "celt" of volcanic rock lay with a burial. Another, about 4 feet distant from human remains, also of volcanic rock, 9 inches long and two inches across the cutting edge, tapered gracefully to a blunt point .5 inch in diameter at the other end.

A ball of lead sulphide was found unassociated.

A number of sherds, undecorated, with the check stamp or with the complicated stamp, were in the NE. margin of the mound and continued into the mound, lying here and there. Near the center of the mound was an undecorated vessel in fragments and at the center was a small undecorated vessel, resembling the longitudinal section of a gourd. Part of the handle, which was solid, is missing. There is a basal perforation.

Near this mound, to the westward, is a considerable shell deposit composed of irregular ridges having a maximum height of 7 feet.   There is also a circular enclosure of shell.   These deposits are said to be the largest of the kind until the great shell-heaps begin a few miles to the north of Cedar Keys, and this was confirmed by our observations later.

Still farther westward are three flat mounds, which careful digging indicated to belong to the domiciliary class.

CEMETERY AT ST. ANDREWS, WASHINGTON COUNTY.

For a considerable time citizens of St. Andrews and visitors to that town have admired a collection of aboriginal earthenware in the possession of Mr. Isaac Godard, living at that place.   Mr. Godard informed us that while digging in an enclosure adjoining his home, he had come upon vessels of earthenware and, with the aid of a rod, he had located and secured about twenty of them.

FIG. 80.--Vessel of earthenware.   Cemetery at St. Andrews.   (About two-thirds size.)

According to Mr. Godard, certain smaller ones among these vessels lay with burials, while others, bowls, were over skulls.   In two cases human remains lay in bowls each covered by an inverted vessel.

With Mr. Godard's permission, the field, a small one, surrounded by an irregular, circular shell ridge, 2 feet to 4 feet high and about 170 feet in diameter, was carefully sounded by us.   Mr. Godard's search, however, had been a thorough one and only a single vessel rewarded our investigation.   This one, a bowl, lay base uppermost about 3 feet from the surface.   No bones were found beneath it, but it is our confident belief that infant remains, placed there originally, had disappeared through decay.

The bowl, of a type very familiar to us during our investigations of the preceding year, is dark in color with incised decoration representing, probably, a highly conventionalized animal head with a circle presumably intended for an eye.   This design occurs six times.   In addition, there are two pairs of curved figures, possibly representing legs, while two sets of animal jaws and teeth, in combination, appear but once (Fig. 80).   This last is a new feature to us, though single sets of jaws on bowls in the district to the westward are common enough.   Maximum diameter, 11 inches; height, 5.5 inches.

This discovery of a cemetery is of some interest, establishing, as it does, the existence of urn-burials at a point farther to the eastward than had been noted before.

Mound at St. Andrews, Washington County.

This mound, in the western limits of the town, on property of Mr. J. A. Moates, living nearby, literally has been dug to pieces.   After a short trial, investigation was abandoned by us.   The mound seems to have been elliptical in outline originally, about 110 feet along the base NE. and SW. and 58 feet NW. and SE.   The height, probably, was about 7 feet.

Mound near Davis Point, Calhoun County.

This mound, much dug into before our visit, lay in hammock land on property of Mr. Hawk Massaliner, colored, who lives on the place.   Its height was about 2 feet 9 inches; the basal diameter, 45 feet.   It was completely dug down by us.

On the extreme eastern margin were burials and numbers of parts of different vessels, mostly undecorated, some bearing the check-stamp.   The burials and earthenware continued in to the center of the mound, the area of deposit broadening somewhat to the SE.

As the digging continued burials became more numerous for a while, and several were found included between the limits NE. and W. by S., though the deposit of earthenware which farther in included whole vessels and broken vessels of which all parts were present, and many sherds, was not present with burials in that part of the mound.

One small vessel, however, lay SW. of the center.

The mound was largely composed of sand blackened by admixture of organic matter, thus excavations made and filled previous to our visit were hard to locate, the sand being of the same color, therefore data, burial by burial, were not collected. The closely flexed form, the bunch, scattered bones and masses of bones were found in abundance.   No skulls were recovered entire, but large fragments showed flattening of the frontal and occipital portions.

One burial, a bunch, lying under oyster-shells, as was often the case with interments in this mound, had a left femur which had sustained fracture at an early period and had united with little inconvenience to the subject, an occurrence somewhat out of the usual run in aboriginal times, judging from other fractures found by us in mounds.   This femur was sent to the United States Army Medical Museum, Washington, D. C.

With one or two burials in the mound were parts of human bones, some discolored by fire, some charred and one or two calcined, but this evidence of the use of fire in no case extended to the entire burial, nor even to a considerable part of it, making it evident that cremation had not been practised, but rather the use of fire, ceremonially, which had occasionally burned a small portion of the bones.

Of artifacts in the mound there were, exclusive of earthenware, a mass of rock about twice the size of a closed hand, having on one side a pit 2.5 inches in depth and about 1.5 inches in diameter, and on the other side three small pits and a concave area produced by wear; a mass of lead sulphide, pitted on one side, evidently by use as a hammer; two graceful celts, one found with a burial, the other in caved sand; thirty-seven pointed columellæ of large marine univalves, found with a burial.

There were also in caved sand a small fragment of sheet copper badly carbonated, and a piece of sheet copper about 7 inches square, broken on three sides, which had formed part of a square or oblong ornament with a central perforation surrounded by punctate markings.   The margin of the sheet had been carefully turned over and hammered down.   On the metal were traces of a vegetable fabric in which the bones, which the copper accompanied, had been wrapped.

The copper, analyzed by Prof. Harry F. Keller, Ph.D., contained small quantities of iron and a faint trace of silver.   Lead, arsenic, antimony, bismuth, nickel, etc., were entirely absent.   This copper, then, is native copper, of a purity above that of any copper made from the sulphide ores found in Europe, especially in former times.

Incidentally we may say it is now eight years since we made public in the second part of our " Certain Sand Mounds of the St. Johns River, Florida," results of many careful analyses of native copper and of copper from the mounds, and showed chemically that most of the copper of the mounds could not have been produced in Europe, but was native copper, hammered out from nuggets or masses by the aborigines.   These conclusions were accepted, we believe, by all who do not prefer an unsupported opinion to weight of evidence.   At all events, no effort has been made, based on analyses, to controvert our deductions.

The Davis Point mound was filled with roots of the palmetto, doubly destructive to earthenware in that, while tearing it apart themselves, they compel from the investigator heavy blows of axe and spade, fatal to neighboring earthenware.   This fact and the aboriginal custom to break vessels and scatter their parts throughout the mound, which markedly had prevailed in this mound, made it so that but three vessels were taken out unbroken, even as to parts unaffected by basal perforation. This is especially to be regretted as the ware of this mound, if we exclude the check-

23 JOURN. A. N. S. PHILA., VOL. XII.

stamp on certain coarse sherds, was of the incised and punctate variety which demands more originality and artistic ability than does the complicated stamp so prevalent in the mounds of this district.

Vessel No. 1.—This vessel, of excellent yellow ware, shown in Fig. 81, lay with a mass of bones. On the upper portion punctate markings constitute a field on which two rattlesnakes with highly conventionalized heads appear in relief. In this connection it is interesting to compare the rattlesnake decoration on the two vessels from the Hall mound, described and figured later, where heads much

FIG. 81.—Vessel No. 1.   Mound near Davis Point.   (About six-sevenths size.)

less conventionalized are given. Between the rattlesnakes, on either side, is an incised figure somewhat resembling a flying bird, shown in diagram (Fig. 82). The wings, if such they are, of one point downward; one wing of the other is raised. On examining the vessel, however, one can see the outline, faintly incised, of a lowered wing, which could not be completed owing to lack of space and, therefore, a raised wing was substituted. Beneath one rattlesnake is a rude cross shown in the half-tone. There are handles projecting obliquely from the rim, connecting with the heads of the snakes. Maximum diameter, 7 inches; height, 5.5 inches.

Vessel No. 4.—A small cup shown in Fig. 83.

Vessel No. 7.—A rude life-form of about 1 quart capacity (Fig. 84).

Vessel No. 8.—A vessel of about 1 quart capacity with rounded body and neck first constricted, then flaring.   The decoration consists of incised perpendicular lines, probably intended to be parallel (Fig. 85).

FIG. 82.—Vessel No. 1. Decoration. Mound near Davis Point. (Half size.)

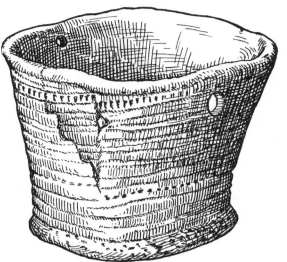

FIG. 83.—Vessel No. 4. Mound near Davis Point. (Full size.)

Vessel No. 11.—Part of a vessel with interesting incised decoration shown in Fig. 86.

Vessel No. 12.—A jar of excellent red ware with a body of heart-shaped section and a neck first constricted, then expanding.   There are two similar groups of incised decoration on the neck. A part of the rim has been restored (Fig. 87). Height, 8.5 inches; maximum diameter, 6.2 inches.

Vessel No. 14.—The lower half of a small effigy-vessel (Fig. 88), which has represented a human figure wearing a breach-clout adorned with ornaments on the

FIG. 84.—Vessel No. 7. Mound near Davis Point. (Half size.)

FIG. 85.—Vessel No. 8. Mound near Davis Point.   (Half size.)

side and back.   Careful, but unsuccessful, search was made for the missing portion of the figure.

Vessel No. 17.—This vessel, globular in shape, with oval aperture (Fig. 89) has a capacity of about one quart.   The decoration, incised, representing wings and tail,

FIG. 86.—Vessel No. 11.   Mound near Davis Point.   (Twelve-thirteenths size.)

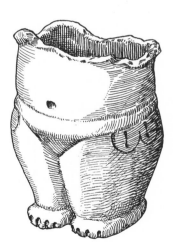

FIG. 88.—Vessel No. 14.   Mound near Davis Point.
(Two-thirds size.)

FIG. 87.—Vessel No. 12.   Mound near Davis Point.   (Half size.)

includes a design on the breast (Diagram, Fig. 90).   The head of a bird projects from one side.

Vessel No. 18.—A jar with faint check-stamp ornamentation (Fig. 91).   Height, 11 inches; maximum diameter, 4.8 inches.

Vessel No. 19.—This vessel, of unusual shape, found crushed to bits and with portions missing, has been cemented together with restoration.   The decoration is coarsely done (Fig. 92).

FIG. 89.—Vessel No. 17.   Mound near Davis Point.   (About full size.)

Vessel No. 20.—A bowl of about 2 quarts capacity, found broken into many pieces, some of which were not present with the rest.   The decoration, which is on the upper part, consists of a zigzag and a meander, in places, running through a field alternately cross-hatch and punctate.

In Fig. 93 is shown a bird-head handle which, when found, contained nine flat bits of earthenware constituting a rattle within the head.   Rattling vessels of this sort are rare along the northwest Florida coast, one having been found by us last year and three during the present season.

In Fig. 94 is shown a sherd of most excellent ware with bird-head handle and incised representation of a wing.

FIG. 90.—Vessel No. 17.   Decoration.   Mound near Davis Point.   (Half size.)

FIG. 91.—Vessel No. 18.   Mound near
Davis Point.   (One-fifth size.)

FIG. 92.—Vessel No. 19.   Mound near Davis Point.   (Full size.)

FIG. 93.—Handle of vessel.   Mound near
Davis Point.   (Three-fourths size.)

FIG. 94.—Sherd.   Mound near Davis Point.   (Half size.)

MOUND NEAR PEARL BAYOU, CALHOUN COUNTY.

Pearl bayou joins East bay, a part of St. Andrew's bay, on the south side about 5 miles from the entrance to East bay. The mound, as to whose ownership we are in ignorance, is within sight of the water in a field formerly cultivated, but now overgrown, about 1 mile in an easterly direction from Pearl bayou.

The mound formed no exception to those of this district, having been dug into in many places. It was 40 feet across the base and about 3.5 feet in height. It

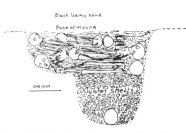

FIG. 95.—Section of grave. Mound near Pearl Bayou.

was completely dug through by us with the exception of a part of the western portion, where digging was discontinued after a large percentage had been gone through without finding burial or artifact.

Burials and numerous sherds were encountered in the eastern margin. The burials which, later, extended in a scattering way to the SE. and one even so far as N., continued to be met with in great numbers in the eastern part of the mound until the center was reached, after which none was found. The marginal burials were closely flexed on the right side or on the left, but later such a mass of bones was present that the form of burial was hard to determine. Presumably, the burials were of the flexed variety, overlapping and underlying each other in greatest confusion. No skull was saved, though some were sufficiently entire to allow determination as to cranial compression. This compression, plainly distinguishable in some, was much less so in others, while certain ones showed no trace of it.

In the outer portion of the mound, especially, though their presence was noted among the burials farther in, were many small shallow graves into which the burials had been forced. A number of interments were covered with oyster-shells. Under

FIG. 96.—Lancehead of chert. Mound near Pearl Bayou. (Full size.)

a mass of burials with which were numbers of shell drinking cups, some perforated as to the base and some not, was a grave containing a single skeleton, running below the base, filled with oyster-shells (Fig. 95).

A feature in this mound was the number of shell drinking cups present, numbers being found together at times.

Usually closely associated with burials were eight celts, gracefully shaped as a rule and tapering to a blunt point opposite the cutting edge, the longest having a length of 10.2 inches. One had an edge so blunt, though smooth and rounded, that it would seem to have been made for a purpose other than to cut.

There were also in the mound: a barbed arrowhead of chert, found with a burial; mica in several places; a large hammer-stone.

In caved sand was a beautifully wrought barbed lance-head of chert, 5.6 inches in length and .25 of an inch in maximum thickness (Fig. 96).

After the marginal sherds, a few feet farther in, associated with a great mass of bones, continuing to the center of the mound from the eastern part, at times extending to the NE. on one side, to ESE. on the other, were numbers of vessels and parts of vessels and deposits of sherds mixed together. Many of the fragments,

FIG. 97.—Sherd. Mound near Pearl Bayou.
(Four-fifths size.)

FIG. 98.—Sherd. Mound near Pearl Bayou.
(One-third size.)

no doubt, belonged to vessels intentionally broken and scattered through the mound by the aborigines at its building.

Thirty-three vessels were noted by us as found entire or having nearly a full complement of fragments. As a rule the ware was inferior and little care seemed to have been taken with the decoration. The check-stamp was present on a few vessels and on many sherds. The complicated stamp was sparingly represented. Two specimens are shown in Figs. 97, 98.

We shall now take in detail the most noteworthy vessels, all of which but three had the basal perforation.

Vessel No. 2.—A pot with a small check-stamp as decoration. The ware is extraordinarily thick and heavy.

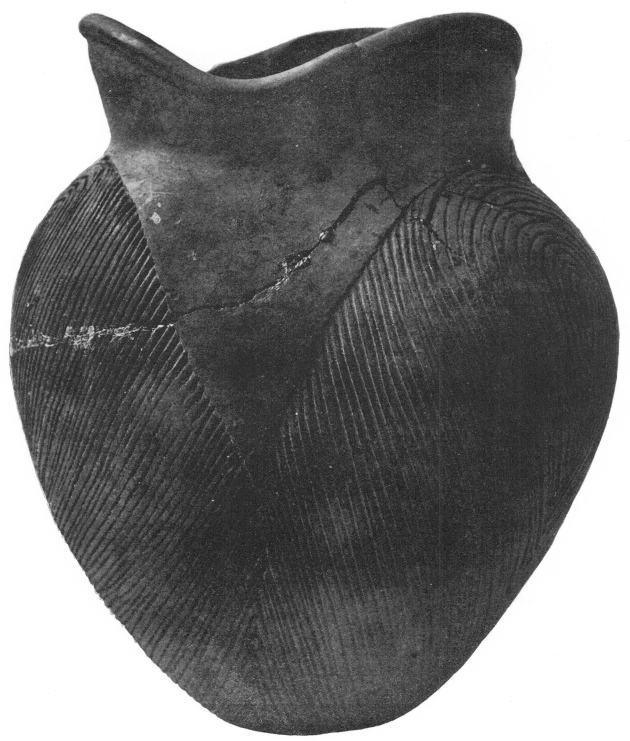

Fig. 99.—Vessel No. 10.   Mound near Pearl Bayou.   (Full size.)

Vessel No. 6.—A small cup or bowl with four rudimentary feet.   A line of punctate markings surrounds the rim.   On opposite sides are perforations for suspension.

Vessel No. 10.—A most artistically shaped vessel of superior ware, of about 2

FIG. 100.—Vessel No. 11. Mound near
Pearl Bayou. (Half size.)

FIG. 101.—Vessel No. 13. Mound near Pearl Bayou. (Half size.)

quarts capacity.   The body is almost trilobate, the upright neck is nearly circular with undulating margin.   The base is flat.   The decoration, carefully done, consists of a series of incised lines (Fig. 99).

Vessel No. 11.—A cup almost cylindrical, flaring slightly.   At four equidistant points on the rim have been small protuberances, probably rudimentary bird-heads, of which three yet remain.   The decoration, which is uniform all around, consists of various designs made of combinations of the symbol of the bird (Fig. 100).

Vessel No. 13.—A bowl without basal perforation, an elongated oval in longitudinal section.   A line of punctate impressions is below the margin,

FIG. 102.—Vessel No. 15. Decoration. Mound near
Pearl Bayou. (One-third size.)

FIG. 103.—Vessel No. 23. Mound near Pearl Bayou.
(Half size.)

also a rather rude incised decoration on either side and the length of the base. There is but one hole for suspension (Fig. 101).

Vessel No. 15.—Is of about 2 quarts capacity and semi-globular as to the lower part.   The upper portion, on which is incised decoration, shown in diagram in Fig. 102, turns inward.

Vessel No. 23.—Roughly heart-shaped with flattened base (Fig. 103).   The aperture is elliptical.   Two and one-half inches apart, on the same side, are perforations for suspension, a method of placing these holes new to us when this vessel was found, but met with by us a number of times afterward, along the coast.   The decoration consists of crimson paint at either end of the vessel, on the outside.

FIG. 104.—Vessel No. 28.   Mound near Pearl Bayou.   (Eight-ninths size.)

Between, at first glance, seems to be an undecorated space, though, on closer inspection, traces of pigment are apparent, and might indicate that a band had surrounded the vessel, friction against which had worn away the paint.

Vessel No. 27.—A bowl of red ware found in many pieces.   The decoration consists of two incised curved lines on one side and on the other, two designs roughly made composed of four concentric circular lines around a number of punctate markings.

Vessel No. 28.—A vessel found in fragments and since put together with slight restoration is a life-form representing a duck with head in relief, *repoussé* wings and tail on which is incised and punctate decoration including the symbol of the bird (Fig. 104).

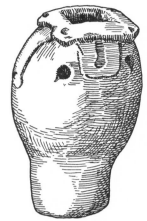

FIG. 105.—Vessel No. 29. Mound near Pearl Bayou. (Two-thirds size.)

FIG. 106.—Vessel No. 33. Mound near Pearl Bayou. (Half size.)

Vessel No. 29.—A rudely made quadrilateral vessel with imperforate base and two holes for suspension beneath the rim on the same side. The decoration consists of circular punctate markings at each corner of the almost square aperture and designs in relief on the four sides below the rim (Fig. 105).

Vessel No. 33.—An undecorated quadrilateral vessel with flat base and a projection at each corner. There are perforations for suspension on opposite sides (Fig. 106).

One bowl, broken when found, held a pot in which was a still smaller one lying on its side.

MOUNDS NEAR LAUGHTON'S BAYOU, WASHINGTON COUNTY. MOUND A.

Laughton's bayou unites with East bay on the north side about seven miles up. The mound was about one-half mile in a southerly direction from the head of the bayou, in a field, the property of Messrs. P. F. and C. T. Parker, of Parker P. O., Florida.

The mound, which had sustained a considerable amount of previous digging, was, before its complete demolition by us, 3.5 feet in height and 45 feet across the base.

In the same field were considerable shell deposits much spread by the plough, including a circular shell enclosure.

As we had anticipated, sherds and large parts of vessels were encountered at the very margin of the eastern slope of the mound. The deposit continued in 4 or 5 feet, accompanied here and there by complete vessels or some from which small parts only had been broken, and by a number of pots and bowls or considerable parts of them, very badly crushed. No other earthenware was met with in the mound.

Of the nine vessels recovered in fair condition, three only call for description.

Vessel No. 2.—A quadrilateral bottle with flat base and upright neck, around which is decoration in relief (Fig. 107).

Vessel No. 3.—Has a globular body somewhat elongated toward the base, which is flat. The upper part is surrounded by a complicated stamp rudely impressed.

Vessel No. 6.—A small bowl of inferior ware decorated with a sort of meander made up of a number of almost parallel lines rudely incised.   In this mound was no check-stamp decoration, though the complicated stamp, one example of which is shown in Fig. 108, was abundantly found.   All vessels were of inferior ware and decoration, and all had the basal perforation.   Near certain vessels lay sheets of mica.

FIG. 107.—Vessel No. 2. Mound A, Laughton's Bayou.
(Full size.)

FIG. 108.—Sherd.   Mound A, Laughton's Bayou.
(Three-fourths size.)

No human remains were met with until within a few feet from the center when burials were encountered once to the N. and six times to the NE. and E., all badly decayed, at times traces alone remaining in the sand.   Two skulls lay together; one lay alone.   One skull had traces of bones in association.

MOUNDS NEAR LAUGHTON'S BAYOU, WASHINGTON COUNTY.   MOUND B.

This mound, in hammock land, on the eastern side of the creek which enters the bayou at its head (mound A was on the W. side) was about one-half mile in a SW. direction from the head of the bayou, also on property of the Messrs. Parker. A trench about 5 feet broad had been carried in from the western margin to the center of the mound, previous to our visit.   The mound, which was 7 feet high and 43 feet in basal diameter, was entirely dug through by us with the exception of the former trench and a small part of the mound bordering it.

The inevitable deposit of sherds and broken vessels was encountered at the extreme verge of the eastern slope, but in less numbers than was usually the case. The full complement of fragments of not over ten or twelve vessels were found, but none was recovered entire.   These vessels, which were of inferior ware and decoration, continued on toward the center of the mound, never immediately with burials, but sometimes in their vicinity, perhaps two or three feet away.

FIG. 109.—Vessel No. 1.   Mound B, Laughton's Bayou.   (Six-sevenths size.)

A number of fragments of vessels had the basal perforation made before baking.

But two vessels worth detailed description were taken by us from this mound.

Vessel No. 1.—This vessel, of eccentric form, elliptical in cross section, bears traces of crimson pigment inside and out ; on one side is raised decoration, on the other, the same pattern is shown but with deeply incised lines.   Two holes are on the same side of the vessel for use for suspension or attachment (Fig. 109).   Perforations thus placed, the reader will recall, were found by us in a vessel in the mound at Pearl bayou. From this time on we were destined to meet a number of them.

Vessel No. 2.—A fine example of the "freak," or ceremonial, ready-made, mortuary ware, having not only a perforation made in the base before baking, but holes throughout the body of the vessel.   The vessel represents a horned owl with feather markings around the head, *repoussé* wings and the conventional tail (Fig. 110).   One horn, missing from the vessel, has been restored.   Height, 10.3 inches ; maximum diameter, 7.3 inches.

Part of a vessel with a rude bird-head projecting from the end has a number of circular holes at either side of the neck (Fig. 111).

Burials, nine in number, were confined to the E., SE. and ENE. parts of the mound, beginning near the margin and continuing in to the center.   Some were badly decayed, rendering impossible a determination as to the form of burial. The closely flexed burial and the bunched were present in the mound in several instances.   In some cases oyster-shells lay over burials in the mound and once over a shallow grave beneath the base.

With two burials were gracefully shaped "celts", near one of which lay also a number of shells (*Marginella apicina*), pierced for use as beads.

The ceremonial use of fire was clearly emphasized in this mound.   Near one burial lay a mass of charcoal and the sand was discolored by heat, though the bones showed no trace of it.   The central portion of the mound, extending several feet in

FIG. 110.—Vessel No. 2.   Mound B, Laughton's Bayou.   (About six-sevenths size.)

all directions, seemed to be discolored by fire, though charcoal in masses was not present, and made into a sort of cement through admixture of ashes. The material was so tough that a pick rather than a shovel was needed.

FIG. 111.—Sherd.   Mound B, Laughton's Bayou.   (About half size.)

No trace of human remains was present in other parts of the mound. We are constrained to believe that cemeteries exist around St. Andrew's bay, whose position we have been unable to locate.

MOUND NEAR STRANGE'S LANDING, CALHOUN COUNTY.

This mound, in hammock land, about one-half mile in a westerly direction from the landing, on East bay, is on property belonging to Mr. William Strange, living nearby.

The mound, which was about 4 feet high and 38 feet across the base, was the

FIG. 112.—Vessel No. 1.   Mound near Strange's Landing.   (About full size.)

usual truncated cone in shape and had been very symmetrical until persons previous to our visit dug a trench 22 feet long and 6 feet broad from the western margin toward the center. The remaining parts of the mound were largely dug through by us.

At the very edge of the slope of the eastern side of the mound was the usual deposit of sherds and large fragments of vessels with whole vessels and others somewhat broken. This deposit continued in along the base until the former trench was reached, not far from the center of the mound, and was made up of vessels placed in the sand singly or in twos or threes. The deposit lay apart from the burials and was evidently a general one put in for the dead in common. Among the sherds some bore the check-stamp and a few examples of the complicated stamp also were present. All vessels had the basal perforation.

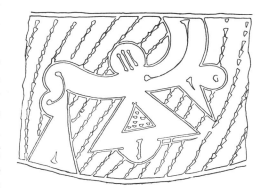

FIG. 113.—Vessel No. 1. Decoration. Mound near Strange's Landing. (Half size.)

Vessel No. 1.—A life-form representing a bird, ovoid in shape with circular

FIG. 114.—Vessel No. 2. Mound near Strange's Landing. (Eight-ninths size.)

FIG. 115.--Vessel No. 5.   Mound near Strange's Landing.   (About full size.)

FIG. 116.--Vessel No. 6.   Mound near Strange's Landing.   (Six-sevenths size.)

aperture. The head projects from one end, the wings are circular and in relief; the decoration is punctate and incised (Fig. 112). The incised decoration representing the tail is shown in diagram in Fig. 113. Length, 7 inches; width, 5 inches; height, 4 inches.

FIG. 117.—Vessel No. 7. Mound near Strange's Landing. (Full size.)

Vessel No. 2.—Shown in Fig. 114 is another life-form, also a bird with projecting head and tail and incised and punctate decoration. The wings and legs are plainly shown. A part of the bill has been restored by us.

Vessel No. 4.—A gourd-shaped vessel, of excellent ware, with oval aperture, undecorated.

Vessel No. 5.—A bowl of light-colored ware, decorated on the upper part with five crescentic figures enclosing a crosshatch design (Fig. 115).   Maximum diameter, 7.5 inches; height, 3.8 inches.

Vessel No. 6.—A handsome globular vessel of about 2 quarts capacity, of excellent ware, decorated with a meander running through a field of punctate markings (Fig. 116).

Vessel No. 7.—In shape an inverted, truncated, four-sided pyramid with slightly rounded corners and edges.   The rim, about 1 inch in breadth, projects inward horizontally (Fig. 117).   The decoration, incised, is similar on two sides.   Of the three different designs, one is simple cross-hatch, one is shown in the half-tone, and the third is given diagrammatically in Fig. 118.

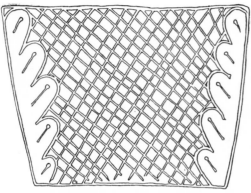

FIG. 118.—Vessel No. 7.   Decoration.   Mound near Strange's Landing.   (Half size.)

But five burials were met with, and these were in the NE. and N. parts of the mound.

Burial No. 1.—In a shallow grave below the base was a skeleton closely flexed under oyster-shells, with the skull badly crushed, as were all found by us in this mound.

Burial No. 2.—A bunch of bones with four skulls, under oyster-shells.

Burial No. 3.—A closely flexed skeleton lying on the base of the mound, with no shells in association.

Burial No. 4.—In a shallow grave, closely flexed, was a skeleton with skull badly broken, but not sufficiently so to prevent evidence of flattening being apparent. This burial did not lie under oyster-shells, but was covered with a mass of small conchs (*Fulgur pugilis*).

Burial No. 5.—A closely flexed skeleton covered by sand alone.

A large and well-made " celt " lay within a few feet of one of the burials.

MOUND NEAR BAKER'S LANDING, CALHOUN COUNTY.

The mound, about 400 yards WSW. from the landing, East bay, is in hammock land, on property of Mr. Jonah Baker, living nearby.

The mound, which was 5 feet 4 inches high and 72 feet in basal diameter, had been woefully dug into.   Besides several trenches, a hole in the center, 22 feet by 25 feet, involving the entire summit plateau, had been put down by former diggers. The eastern slope, however, was practically intact.   Deep depressions at points adjoining the base of the mound showed whence material for its making had come. In an adjoining field was a shell deposit including a circular enclosure of shell, now almost ploughed away.

Nearly the remainder of the mound was dug through by us resulting in the finding of nine burials, all but one under considerable quantities of oyster-shells.

These burials were : one at full length on the back ; one on the back, extended to the knees, the legs being flexed back ; one flexed on the left side with the legs at right angles ; one cut off at the knees by the aborigines in making another grave ;

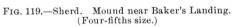

FIG. 119.—Sherd. Mound near Baker's Landing. (Four-fifths size.)

FIG. 120.—Sherd. Mound near Baker's Landing. (Half size.)

three too decayed for determination ; scattered bones in shell above a burial ; a single skull lying on the base of the mound, without the usual covering of shell.

While no skulls were in a condition to preserve, those in a partial state of preservation showed no flattening.

But one burial, the lone skull, lay in the eastern part of the mound, the others being mainly in the western.

A few sherds lay at the beginning of the eastern slope and farther in, here and there, the last near the center, were seven or eight vessels of inferior ware, all in fragments but two. The majority were undecorated, the check stamp and incised decoration not being found by us in this mound. Several bore complicated stamps, one of which resembles that on a sherd shown by us in Part I of this report as coming from the great mound at Walton's Camp. Two sherds with complicated stamp decoration are shown in Figs. 119, 120.

LARGER MOUND IN HARE HAMMOCK, CALHOUN COUNTY.

St. Andrew's sound, so-called, is a long arm of water between the mainland and a narrow strip of land bordering the sea, known as Crooked Island. As these are the names made use of on the chart, we have adopted them, though the filling of a pass at the eastern end of the strip of water made it a sound no longer and joined Crooked island to the mainland.

The mound lay about one-half mile inland from a point near the eastern extremity of the sound, on property of Mr. Joseph Dyer, of Wetappo, Florida. The mound, which was pleasingly symmetrical, the usual truncated cone in shape, with a height of 7.5 feet and a basal diameter of 56 feet, had escaped the ravages common to the mounds of this district, partly through being more difficult of access than others, and partly through the presence of modern burials in the summit plateau. The only signs of previous digging were two or three small holes and a narrow trench on the western side, which continued superficially across the top.

The mound was levelled by us with the exception of a small part of the western margin and of a portion 10 feet square in the western part of the body of the mound, where modern burials were thickest. During a long period before our digging was discontinued no trace of earthenware or aboriginal interments had been found.

Aboriginal burials, as noted by us, numbered thirty-one and included, as to form, the lone skull; the bunch; close flexion on the side; one skeleton in a squatting position; scattered bones; and masses of bones continuing in on the same level. These masses, though each counted as one burial, in all cases represented a number of individuals.

Certain skulls showed flattening while in others it was not marked.

The first interment was found at the margin of the mound, almost due east and as the digging continued, burials were met with exceptionally as far to either side as north and south, though the great majority lay with a deposit of earthenware in the eastern and southeastern parts of the mound. No burial was met with farther than 16 feet from the margin.

The burials in nearly every case lay beneath masses of shells, not oyster-shells, however, such as we have found to be the case in other mounds, but small conchs (*Fulgur pugilis*).

With a number of burials were shell drinking cups (*Fulgur perversum*), sometimes immediately on the skull, and with certain interments were "celts," two in one instance. In all, seven of these hatchets and part of another were met with, some not immediately with burials.

There were present also in the mound, exclusive of earthenware: a fossil shark's tooth; mica; a fragment of a graceful, barbed lancehead, 4 inches long; a gorget of ferruginous sandstone with two perforations for suspension (Fig. 121).

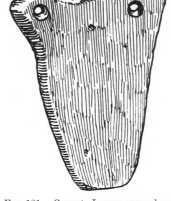

FIG. 121.—Gorget. Larger mound near Hare Hammock. (Full size.)

The earthenware of this mound was in better condition than usual in this district, while the decoration was much above the average. The deposit began in contact with the first burial in the eastern margin of the mound, as stated, and continued in about 15 feet, sometimes associated with burials and sometimes at a distance from them, but always in an area where they were most frequent. Incised and punc-

Fig. 122.—Vessel No. 1. Larger mound near Hare Hammock. (About five-sixths size.)

Fig. 123.—Vessel No. 1. Decoration. Larger mound near Hare Hammock. (Half size.)

tate decoration was largely represented; the complicated stamp less frequently; while the check stamp was found with a deposit of sherds in the beginning.

Of the twenty-four vessels met with by us, some of which were badly broken but have since been cemented and restored, we shall describe only the more noteworthy, omitting fragments with ordinary decoration and vessels of common type.

Vessel No. 1.—This vessel, shown in Fig. 122, is almost cubical, with the upper part inverted and ascending to an elliptical opening. On two opposite sides have been bird-head handles, one of which, missing when found, has been restored. The

Fig. 124.—Vessel No. 2. Larger mound near Hare Hammock. (About full size.)

decoration, incised, is nearly identical on two sides, one of which is shown in the half-tone. On the other sides are striking designs to a certain extent recalling the swastika. It will be noted by referring to the diagram (Fig. 123) that one-half of the swastika is represented on each design, but the remaining half not alone has its extremities in the form of loops, but these loops turn in the wrong direction. Length, 7.8 inches; width, 7 inches; height, 5.7 inches.

Vessel No. 2.—A handsome vessel of yellow ware with hemispherical body and inverted rim, on which is punctate decoration and two small horizontal projections. Somewhat below the rim there is an encircling projection, octagonal, tending slightly

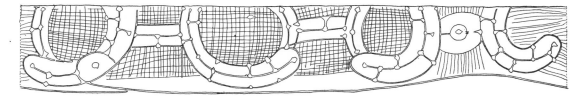

FIG. 125.—Vessel No. 2. Decoration. Larger mound near Hare Hammock. (One-third size.)

FIG. 126.—Vessel No. 6. Larger mound near Hare Hammock. (Full size.)

upward (Fig. 124). The decoration of the body, incised, not uniform, is shown in diagram in Fig. 125.

Vessel No. 4.—A pot with decoration about 2 inches broad below the rim, consisting of encircling rows of roughly triangular punctate markings, finely lined at the base.

FIG. 127.—Vessel No. 11. Larger mound near Hare Hammock. (Full size.)

Vessel No. 6.—An effigy-vase representing a male figure, which, in addition to several parts missing through early breakage, unfortunately lost one part of the head through a blow from a spade, necessitating restoration. The figure is in a squatting position with folded arms. A breech-clout encircles the loins and runs

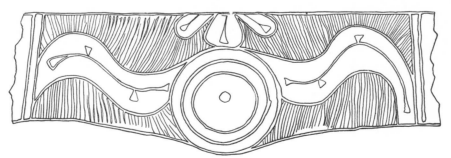

FIG. 128.—Vessel No. 11. Decoration. Larger mound near Hare Hammock. (Half size.)

between the legs. An unusual feature is that the head extends upward several inches above the rear portion of the vessel. The capacity is about 1 quart. There are four perforations for suspension (Fig. 126).

Vessel No. 8.—A bowl of somewhat over 1 quart capacity, triangular in horizontal section with rounded corners. The sole decoration consists of two encircling incised lines about one-half inch apart, below the rim.

Vessel No. 9.—A vessel of about 1 pint capacity, undecorated, with globular body, slightly expanding neck and oval aperture. The rim has been elongated into two projecting points, one of which is missing.

Vessel No. 10.—A small, undecorated cup, the only vessel without basal perforation coming from this mound. It lay directly with human remains, somewhat beyond the area of the earthenware deposit.

FIG. 129.—Vessel No. 13. Larger mound near Hare Hammock. (About full size.)

Vessel No. 11.—A vessel of about 1 pint capacity, diamond-shaped with rounded corners, with aperture of similar outline and base almost flat (Fig. 127). The decoration, incised, shown diagrammatically in Fig. 128, covers one-half of the vessel and probably represents a bird with head and body much conventionalized.

Vessel No. 13.—A vase with globular body and flaring neck surmounted by a thickened hexagonal rim (Fig. 129). The decoration, incised and not uniform, is shown diagrammatically in Fig. 130. Height, 4.8 inches; maximum diameter, 5 inches.

Vessel No. 14.—This unique vessel of excellent red ware, almost a truncated pyramid in form, has on one side a *repoussé* human figure standing with back turned to the observer, grasping with either hand the rim of the vessel (Fig. 131). The opposite side, showing the head and the face looking across the rectangular aperture, is shown in Fig. 132. The decoration on the two remaining sides of the vessel is given in Fig. 133. There are two holes, on the same side, for suspension.

Vessel No. 16.—A vessel of superior ware, in shape a truncated sphere, undeco-

FIG. 130.—Vessel No. 13. Decoration. Larger mound near Hare Hammock. (Half size.)

rated as to the body. The rim, which bears four incised designs, is inverted and slightly depressed. Capacity about 3 quarts (Fig. 134).

Vessel No. 17.—A bowl of superior ware, of elliptical longitudinal section, with thick rim slightly projecting laterally and rounded points at either end. The decoration consists of crimson paint on the inside. Maximum diameter, 9.3 inches; width, 7.8 inches; height, 3 inches.

Vessel No. 18.—A thick bowl of excellent ware, undecorated save for traces of crimson pigment on the inside.

Vessel No. 23.—An interesting little vase with globular body and oblong aperture, having a duck's head in relief on each of two sides below the rim. The decoration on the other two sides, which probably represents wings, is almost identical. There are two holes for suspension (Fig. 135). Maximum diameter, 3.7 inches; height, 2.8 inches.

Vessel No. 24.—Globular body with flaring neck around which is a complicated stamp decoration.

Vessel No. 25.—Part of a vessel found in fragments. A portion of the body has been restored. The body, in addition to line and punctate decoration in which the bird symbol often appears, has been covered with crimson paint. From one side an object which seemingly projected somewhat, has disappeared. The opposite side, where, perhaps, was an identical object, was missing. From the rim on the back of the vessel projects an upright bird-head. In front, another head has a hollow bill to allow the passage of a liquid (Fig. 136). This feature is new in all our mound work.

FIG. 131.—Vessel No. 14.   Larger mound near Hare Hammock.   (Full size.)

FIG. 132.—Vessel No. 14. Another position. Larger mound near Hare Hammock. (Full size.)

FIG. 133.—Vessel No. 14. Decoration. Larger mound near Hare Hammock. (Half size.)

FIG. 134.—Vessel No. 16. Larger mound near Hare Hammock. (Half size.)

FIG. 135.—Vessel No. 23. Larger mound near Hare Hammock. (Full size.)

SMALLER MOUND IN HARE HAMMOCK, CALHOUN COUNTY.

This mound, in dense growth of trees and vines, lay about 400 yards from the larger mound.   Its basal diameter in an easterly and westerly direction was 50 feet and 36 feet in a northerly and southerly.   It had escaped all previous digging.

Owing to unavoidable circumstances a portion of the eastern end only of the mound was dug by us.   However, the earthenware deposit seemed to have come to an end sometime previous to our departure.

With a burial was a handsome weapon of light gray chert, 6 inches long and 1.7 inches in maximum width (Fig. 137).

Not immediately connected with human remains was a thick sheet of mica, roughly given the shape of a spearhead.

FIG. 136.—Vessel No. 25. Larger mound near Hare Hammock. (About full size.)

In the eastern margin were the usual sherds and vessels, broken and whole, of which the following will be particularly described.

Vessel No. 2.—A jar with flat base and body almost cylindrical, expanding slightly. There is slight constriction at the neck and upright rim. Below the rim is a band of rough complicated stamp decoration about 1 inch in breadth.

Vessels Nos. 3 and 4.—Small oblate spheroids found together. One has a decoration of rudely executed incised lines extending from margin to base. The other has carelessly executed incised and punctate decoration extending a distance of about 1 inch below the rim. Both vessels have perforations for suspension, on opposite sides, and both are imperforate as to the base, the only ones from this mound exempt from mutilation so far as noted by us.

Vessel No. 5.—A vessel of rather coarse ware, with an unusual decoration consisting of deep impressions at regular intervals over the entire surface. The base is flat (Fig. 138).   Height, 6.5 inches; maximum diameter, 4.8 inches; orifice, 1.4 inches.

A sherd from this mound, with complicated stamp, is given in Fig. 139.

FIG. 138.—Vessel No. 5. Smaller mound near Hare Hammock.   (Half size.)

FIG. 137.—Weapon of chert. Smaller mound near Hare Hammock. (Full size.)

FIG. 139.—Sherd. Smaller mound near Hare Hammock. (Three-fourths size.)

MOUND IN GOTIER HAMMOCK, CALHOUN COUNTY.

This mound, famous for successful relic searches in it, lay about one-half mile in NE. direction from Conch island, which is near the SE. extremity of St. Joseph's bay. The island is about one-quarter mile from shore and the mound about an equal distance farther in.

The mound, which has been practically dug to pieces, one relic hunter or treasure seeker filling the hole made by another, had been a truncated cone of dark sand. At the time of our visit, when it was completely demolished by us, its height was 5 feet; its diameter of base, 60 feet.

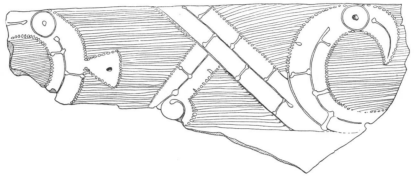

FIG. 140.—Decoration on a sherd. Mound in Gotier Hammock. (One-third size.)

Remnants of the mound found intact by us yielded a few bunched-burials. Several shallow graves below the line of the base, held human remains too badly decayed to determine positively the form of burial, though judging from the restric-

FIG. 141.—Sherd. Mound in Gotier Hammock. (Three-fourths size.)

ted lengths of the graves, they, too, contained the bunched burial. No artifacts were with the burials except a rude, undecorated, imperforate toy bowl.

A coarse, undecorated pot of about three pints capacity, with basal perforation, lay alone.

A four-sided cup with flat base, of about 1 pint capacity, lay in the sand alone.

Unassociated, near the base, was a perforate vessel of about 3 quarts capacity, semiglobular body, upright and slightly flaring rim. Around the neck is complicated stamp decoration.

While all vessels from this mound were of most inferior quality, numbers of sherds were of excellent yellow paste and decorated with crimson paint or with incised designs, showing that the aborigines who built the mound could hold their own in pottery making with any in this region.

One sherd, shown in Fig. 140, lay with others in undisturbed sand.

In Fig. 141 is shown a complicated stamp design from this mound.

MOUND NEAR INDIAN PASS POINT, FRANKLIN COUNTY.

This mound, on property of Mr. James L. Smith, living nearby, lay among sand-blows and dunes near the Gulf shore, about three quarters of a mile in a WSW. direction from the Point. Its outline was irregular. Its height was difficult to determine owing to its irregular surface; perhaps 3 feet would be a fair average. The diameter of base E. and W. was 49 feet and 53 feet N. and S. A small amount of digging had been done by others shortly before our visit. The mound was totally demolished by us. It consisted of white sand, grayish sand, and yellow sand at the bottom with no regularity of stratification.

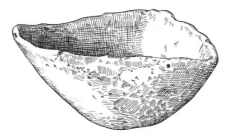

FIG. 143.—Vessel No. 1. Mound near Indian Pass Point. (Half size.)

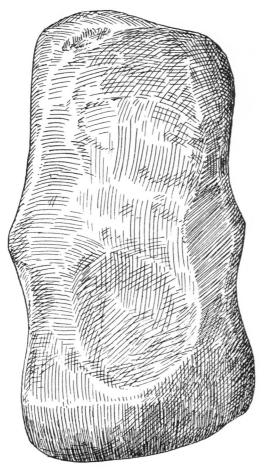

FIG. 142.—Hatchet. Mound near Indian Pass Point. (Full size.)

Burials began at the extreme margin on the south side and in the southeastern part of the mound a little farther in. No burials were found in the western and northern parts until the central portion of the mound was reached.

The burials, which were all of the bunched variety, were very numerous but were not counted by us, as masses of loose bones often lay in contact with each other, making it impossible to say where one burial ended and another began. Many skulls had marked anterior and posterior flattening.

In this mound was no marginal deposit of artifacts, such as were found being almost in immediate contact with burials. There were found : three pebbles lying with one pebble-hammer; conch-shells; several shell drinking cups; one *Fulgur perversum* of the heavy variety, with blunted beak showing use as a tool; a bit of hematite; a hone of ferruginous sandstone, roughly diamond-shape, 17 inches long and 8 inches in its broadest part; two arrowheads or knives, of chert; twenty-seven " celts," some gracefully wrought, others less carefully made. One of these differed markedly from the usual type in that places for fastening were evident on either side (Fig. 142).

The earthenware of the mound was of inferior quality in the main, and, with the exception of a few sherds, began at a considerable distance in. The check stamp was represented on fragments, but no ware bearing the complicated stamp came from the mound. One sherd of good quality showed part of a design in relief. Here and there, as the digging progressed, vessels, mainly undecorated, were found near the burials. At the center of the mound was a deposit of between fifteen and twenty vessels, the majority undecorated, many broken and so mixed as to prevent an exact count.

FIG. 144.—Vessel No. 2. Mound near Indian Pass Point. (Half size.)

The basal perforation is present in all the vessels from this mound, with two or three exceptions.

The most interesting ware will be described separately.

Vessel No. 1.—A three sided, rude, undecorated, imperforate bowl (Fig. 143). Height, 2.2 inches; maximum diameter, 4.5 inches.

Vessel No. 2.—Globular, with a small part missing through an early fracture which has been restored. The decoration is incised (Fig. 144). Maximum diameter, 7 inches; height, 5.7 inches; diameter of aperture, 4.5 inches.

Vessel No. 3.—Undecorated, an inverted acorn in shape. There are holes for suspension below the rim on opposite sides.

Vessel No. 4.—A vase rather heart-shaped in section as to the body, with flaring neck. The surface, with the exception of the neck, is covered with incised decoration including the bird symbol, often repeated. A rudimentary head extends above the rim on one side (Fig. 145). The decoration, shown diagrammatically in Fig. 146, is repeated on the opposite side. Height, 6 inches; maximum diameter, 5.6 inches.

FIG. 145.—Vessel No. 4.   Mound near Indian Pass Point.   (About full size.)

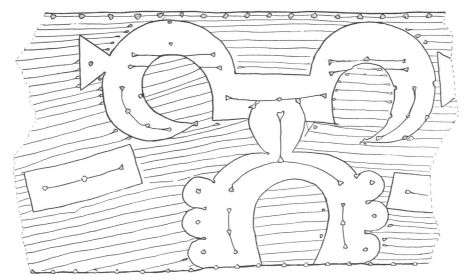

FIG. 146.—Vessel No. 4.   Decoration.   Mound near Indian Pass Point.   (Half size.)

Vessel No. 5.—A truncated globe with rude incised decoration consisting of groups of parallel perpendicular lines about 2 inches long, each group somewhat less than 1 inch apart. This vessel has a capacity of somewhat over 1 quart.

FIG. 147.—Vessel No. 6. Mound near Indian Pass Point. (Half size.)

Vessel No. 6.—A quadrilateral vessel of one quart capacity, with rounded aperture and flat base has for decoration, series of zigzag lines (Fig. 147).

Vessel No. 7.—A quadrilateral vessel of heavy ware, with flattened base and rounded corners, of about 2 quarts capacity. The neck, about 1 inch in height, is upright.

A little below the surface, not associated with human remains, was part of an old-fashioned chisel-pointed spike of brass, of a kind formerly used in ship-building.

MOUND AT ELEVEN MILE POINT, FRANKLIN COUNTY.

This Point, on St. Vincent's sound, taking its name from its distance from the town of Apalachicola, has on it a mound on property of Mr. G. A. Patton, resident on the place. There are various shell deposits in the neighborhood and heaps of shell extend for a distance along the shore.

FIG. 148.—Sherd. Mound at Eleven Mile Point. (Three-fourths size.)

FIG. 149.—Sherd. Mound at Eleven Mile Point. (Two-fifths size.)

The mound, in woods on the verge of a cultivated field, was seamed with trenches and riddled with holes, most of which, however, were superficial.

What was left of the mound had a basal diameter of 50 feet; a height of about

3 feet.   The mound was completely demolished by us.   Beginning at the very margin of the southeastern portion, unassociated with burials, which were more centrally located, were various vessels, singly or in pairs, and parts of vessels and numerous sherds.   These offerings extended a number of feet in toward the center.

FIG. 150.—Vessel of earthenware. Mound at
Eleven Mile Point.   (Half size.)

Still farther in, usually apart from interments, were several other vessels in different parts of the mound.   Sherds were un-decorated; incised, sometimes with cross-hatch; or, in several cases, had a complicated stamp.

FIG. 151.—Vessel of earthenware.
Mound at Eleven Mile Point.
(Half size.)

Two of these are shown in Figs. 148, 149.   Several vessels also bore the complicated stamp and all had the basal perforation.

FIG. 152.—Vessel of earthenware.
Mound at Eleven Mile Point.
(Half size.)

We shall describe in detail the most noteworthy vessels.

A compartment vessel with circular division in the center, in a plane above four similar compartments, one of which, missing when found, has been added with the aid of a mixture composed of beeswax, whitelead, powdered soapstone, resin, linseed oil, and turpentine, which we have found very useful in work of this kind. This vessel has been sent to the Peabody Museum, Cambridge, Mass.

FIG. 153.—Decoration on vessel of earthenware.   Mound at Eleven Mile Point.   (One-third size.)

A four-sided vessel of about one-half pint capacity, otherwise undecorated, has small protuberances at each upper corner of the body and companion ones on the rim immediately above.   The ware is inferior.

A vessel with semiglobular body and short incurving neck has incised decoration as shown in Fig. 150.   The capacity is about 1 pint.

A vessel of eccentric shape, somewhat resembling that of a dumb-bell, undecorated save for an encircling incised line below the rim, has two holes for suspension on opposite sides (Fig. 151).

A bottle with neck curiously disproportionate in length, of inferior ware and rudely made, has a height of 6.7 inches, a maximum diameter of 3.6 inches (Fig. 152).

A vessel made to hold about one quart, has a semiglobular body and a slightly flaring neck about 1.25 inches in height.   There is a curious punctate decoration shown in diagram in Fig. 153.

COOL SPRING MOUND, APALACHICOLA, FRANKLIN COUNTY.

In the western outskirts of Apalachicola is a mound which, as might be expected, has long been the center of attack for avaricious or curious persons.   Material from one trench or excavation has been thrown into others, thus preserving the mound from demolition.   Its present height is about 7.5 feet; its diameter of base, about 90 feet.   On the surface of the mound, where former diggers had thrown them, were many sherds much resembling in material and ornamentation the ware we found during our preceding season's work between Perdido and Choctawhatchee, bays, including a part of a vessel in the form of a frog.

About two-thirds of the mound were dug down by us including much disturbed material.   On the base of the mound and two or three feet above it were a number of burials consisting of trunks of skeletons extended on the back with thighs and legs sometimes drawn up against the body or drawn up at right angles to the trunk, or extended laterally.   These forms, with slight variations, were met with nine times, and burials disturbed by our own or by former diggers indicated a like method of burial.   A single skull and a skull with a humerus were found.   No bones were in a condition to preserve.   The only artifacts encountered with burials were a bit of mica with one skeleton and a well-made lance-head of chert, 4.75 inches in length, beneath the chin of another.

In the marginal part of the mound, which had been dug through by others, were many sherds : undecorated ; with incised and punctate decoration, sometimes in combination ; the complicated stamp, in a few cases ; the check-stamp, once or twice; looped handles ; handles representing heads of quadrupeds or of birds ; animal legs in relief on the sides.   Deeply scalloped margins were abundant.

A " celt " lay unassociated in the sand.

MOUND NEAR APALACHICOLA, FRANKLIN COUNTY.

In a cultivated field, about one-half mile in a westerly direction from the town, on property of the Cypress Lumber Company, of Apalachicola, is a mound much spread by the plow.   Its diameter of base is about 100 feet N. and S. and 80 feet E.

and W., approximately.   The height is about 2 feet.   Nearby is a shell-field while a shell-heap of considerable size is distant about 75 yards in an ENE. direction.

Ten excavations in various parts of the mound yielded no result other than to show the mound to have been built of sand on a base of shell, presumably as a place of abode.

CEMETERY MOUND, APALACHICOLA, FRANKLIN COUNTY.

This mound, in Magnolia Cemetery at Apalachicola, about 5 feet high, was demolished by us, with the courteous permission of the City Council.

The mound, the usual truncated cone, was composed of white sand in places and of grayish sand in others, with oyster-shells centrally, near the base.

The mound, which had sustained much previous digging, seemingly, contained but two whole skeletons and three others from which parts had been cut away.

Unassociated, was a circular ear-plug of lime rock, covered with sheet copper on one side, with a diameter of 1.6 inches, of the type figured by us in a former report as coming from Mt. Royal, Fla.

In midden refuse, near the base, was a bone pin about 8 inches long and from the same deposit, as a rule, came a number of sherds, undecorated or bearing the check stamp.

PIERCE MOUNDS, NEAR APALACHICOLA, MOUND A.

The Pierce Mounds, five in number, lie from 1 mile to 1.5 miles to the westward of Apalachicola, on property belonging to Mr. Alton Pierce of that place.

MOUND A, the southwesternmost of the group, which had undergone but insignificant previous digging, had at base a diameter of 96 feet E. and W. and 76 feet N. and S.   The diameters of the summit plateau in the same directions respectively were 40 feet and 34 feet.   The plateau, however, had been much broadened and the height of the mound somewhat reduced to prepare for interments made in recent times.   The height of the mound which was completely demolished by us, was 8 feet.

The body of the mound was of yellow sand, the basal portion being of sand discolored by fire and by organic matter, often mixed with oyster-shells.   There was no regular stratification, but irregular layers of oyster-shells were present throughout, in places.

Throughout the mound it was noted that the great majority of burials lay in shell, but it seemed to us that this was owing to the fact that the majority of burials were well down toward the base where the shell was, rather than that the association was intentional.   Such burials as were higher in the mound usually lay in the sand.

As the mound was practically undisturbed at our coming, data as to burials were taken with great care.   The relative position of the ninety-nine found by us, which, however, stand for a much greater number of skeletons, is shown in the plan (Fig. 154).   We may say here, and it applies to all other mounds opened by us, that when enough of a bone remains to make its identification certain, we often speak of it as present, for the reason that it was there when the burial took place.   Also, when we write of skeletons in mounds, we do not wish to imply that these skeletons were

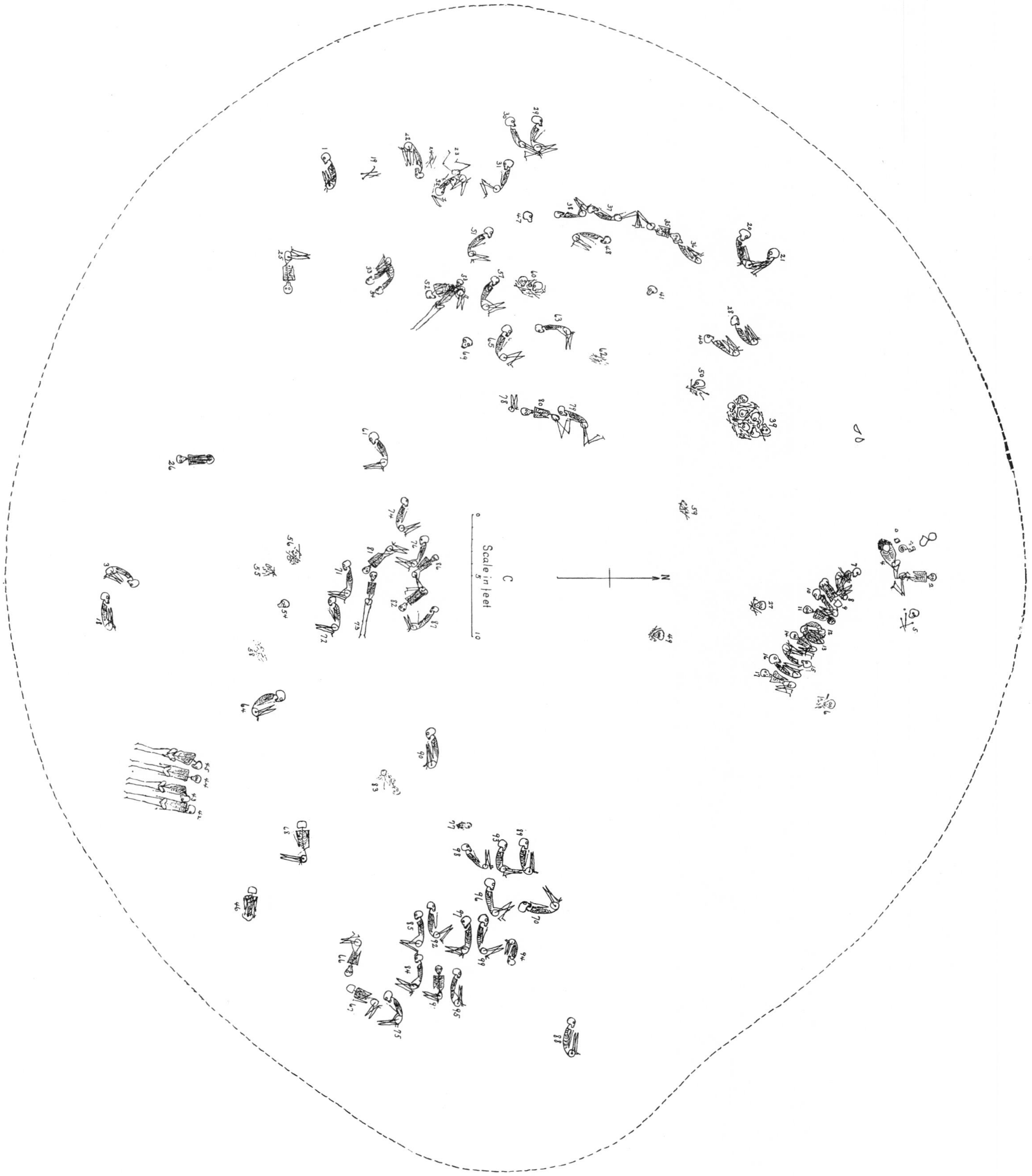

FIG. 154.—Plan of Mound A.   Pierce mounds, near Apalachicola.

interred covered with flesh, but rather, after being exposed for a period, as was the custom with southern aborigines, that they were buried without the flesh but in the main held together by ligaments. Missing bones or bones misplaced, occasionally, show this to be true.

Heads of skeletons pointed in all directions. A few skeletons were closely flexed. The majority, however, had the thighs at right angles to the trunk, with legs drawn up toward the thighs. Unless especially noted, burials were as follows: flexed on the left side, 33; flexed on the right side, 25; flexed on the back, 3; full length on back, 2; infants' skeletons, badly decayed, 2; skulls with fragments of

FIG. 155.—Vessel with Burial No. 2. Mound A. Pierce mounds, near Apalachicola. (About full size.)

bone, 3; lone skulls, 3; scattered remains, 9; aboriginal disturbance, 1; recent disturbance, 1; skull in caved sand, 1.

The following are not included in the above.

Burials No. 7 to No. 17, inclusive, a group comprising eleven skeletons variously flexed with skulls pointing in different directions, but mainly toward the central part of the mound. These skeletons were in a layer of shell, from 1 foot to 1.5 feet in thickness, about 1 foot above the base. With this shell, above the bodies, were blackened masses composed of charcoal, calcined shell, ashes, etc. These masses did not seem to be remains of fires which had been made and allowed to burn at the places where the ashes and charcoal were found, but to have been brought while still burning and placed on or near the skeletons, as such bones only were charred as were in contact with the material. None of the bones was calcined, nor did the sand and shell about these masses of material show evidence of fire. Thoughout the mound were many such places, showing the use of fire away from the mound during the ceremony of interment.

Burial No. 39, a mass of human bones, including seven skulls, lay in the body of the mound, with remains of fire above and sand mixed with shell below.

FIG. 156.--Vessel with Burial No. 2. Mound A. Pierce mounds, near Apalachicola. (Two-thirds size.)

Burials No. 42 to No. 45, inclusive, four skeletons at full length, side by side in a shallow grave beneath the base, with heads in the same direction.

All bones in this mound were in bad condition through decay, but one skull being saved.

Belonging to Burial No. 52 was a femur showing a repaired fracture of the upper third, with some shortening of the bone. This was sent to the United States Army Medical Museum at Washington, D. C.

Seldom before have we found a mound so full of promise as to yield of artifacts at the start, and so disappointing during the remainder of the investigation.

Burial No. 2, (see plan) a skeleton partially flexed on the left side, lay in the northern slope of the mound, 2.5 feet from the surface.   Under the thorax were many fragments of part of a vessel with a decoration of incised lines, and crimson paint in places.   Three feet to the west was a vessel, upright, of about six quarts capacity, of undecorated ware, in fragments through pressure of sand.

Fɪɢ. 157.—Vessel with Burial No. 2.   Another view.   Mound A.   Pierce mounds, near Apalachicola.   (Two-thirds size.)

Immediately back of this one was another of about the same size, undecorated, with part of the bottom knocked out.   About 1 foot farther in the mound, on its side, lay a vessel of yellow paste with two compartments, one of which, crushed by sand and roots, has been cemented together.   The decoration consists of incised lines and bands of crimson paint as shown in Fig. 155.   But one compartment has the basal perforation.   Height, 4.6 inches; maximum diameter, 7.1 inches; diameter of a single aperture, about 3 inches.

In contact with this double cup was a curious spiral vessel shown in two positions in Figs. 156, 157.

Though this vessel, at first glance, resembles a ram's horn, we do not believe it to have been modelled after one.

In the first place, it is our opinion that the origin of the vessel antedates the appearance of sheep in Florida.

Secondly, there are marked points of difference in appearance between the vessel and the horn of a ram. The corrugations are not encircling but leave a smooth space the length of the lower part of the vessel. The distal end is rounded and does not taper to a point as is the case in a horn. As to the aperture, we must bear in mind it is open, of necessity, and may not be called upon to bear testimony as to resemblance.

There are grub-worms in Florida as long as, or longer than, the little finger of a male hand and fully equal in diameter. Their extremities are rounded. The deep corrugations covering their backs and sides end at the belly. As these worms lie dead on the surface, we have seen them in the exact position shown in the vessel. Besides, worms were of some importance along the Gulf coast in early days, being an article of diet at times, according to Cabeça de Vaca.

We are convinced, then, that this vessel represents a life-form and is modelled after the grub-worm. Height, 6.9 inches; maximum diameter of body, 2.9 inches; diameter of opening, about 3 inches; width of entire vessel, 7.8 inches.

About 6 inches distant from the worm-effigy were four arrowpoints or knives, in association, three of chert, one of quartzite, while 10 inches to the south were fragments of an almost cylindrical vessel of yellow ware. The base, which had been flat, is missing. The decoration, punctate and lined, has crimson paint in places, distinguishable in the half-tone (Fig. 158). The diagram (Fig. 159) shows, with other symbols, a pair of open hands, the backs turned outward, the thumbs thrust back. Maximum diameter, 5.1 inches; diameter of opening, 4.3 inches; height of vessel, 5.3 inches.

The widespread emblem of the open hand was found by Mr. Cushing on a mussel shell, among his wonderful discoveries at Marco, and the open hand appears on a vessel from Alabama.[1]

Considering the comparatively large number of burials but few articles lay immediately with the dead.

With Burial No. 60, two skulls with certain bones mingled, lay a "celt" about 11 inches in length, immediately beneath one of the skulls.

Burial No. 63, a skeleton flexed at about right angles on the right side, had near it a beautifully smoothed pendant of a fine grained slate rock, 6.5 inches in length, .6 of an inch in maximum diameter, grooved at one end for suspension, of a type to be figured later in the account of the Yent mound.

In a grave, beneath the eastern slope of the mound, 6 feet below the surface, lay Burial No. 66, flexed at right angles on the left side. Along the right humerus

[1] Report Bureau of Ethnology. 1882–83, p. 433.

FIG. 158.—Vessel with Burial No. 2.   Mound A.   Pierce mounds, near Apalachicola.   (About full size.)

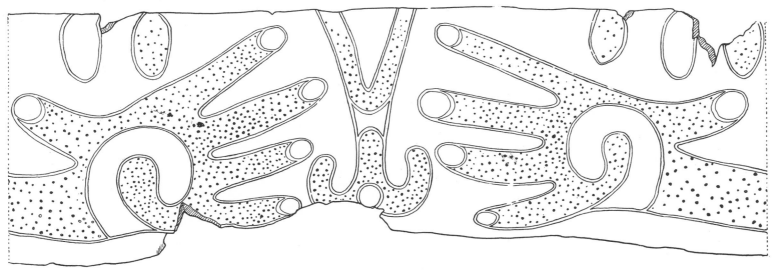

FIG. 159.—Vessel with Burial No. 2.   Decoration.   Mound A.   Pierce mounds, near Apalachicola.   (Half size.)

lay an ornament of sheet copper, 10 inches long and 1.7 inches broad, bent around and overlapping on itself, making a flat tube about .8 of an inch in diameter. The metal, almost entirely transformed into carbonate, fell into bits upon removal. At the neck of the skeleton were found perforated pearls and fragments of others.

Burial No. 81, a skeleton flexed to the right, on the base, 8 feet below the surface, had, at either shoulder a disc of sheet copper so badly carbonated and corroded that the original size could not be determined.

At the center of each of the sheet copper discs, on one surface, is a layer of silver. This layer is not fairly thick, and regular as to its margin as would be the case if a coin or sheet silver had been shaped and fastened on, but is very thin and radiates marginally as though a small nugget, placed on the copper and hammered out, had remained through force of the blows.

We are indebted to Mr. Warren K. Moorehead, whose great discovery of copper objects of aboriginal make in the Hopewell mounds, Ohio, is so well known, for the information that several ornaments of sheet copper were found in the Hopewell altars, which were covered with a thin layer of silver. These may be seen in the Field Columbian Museum, Chicago.

While the existence of sheet copper ornaments of purely aboriginal provenance is now admitted by all who possess a schoolboy's knowledge of chemistry,[1] the presence of silver in a mound, as a rule, shows " white contact " on the part of the aborigines who built the mound, but such is not always the case. Silver is sometimes visibly present in " Lake " copper which is native and Lake Superior is known to have been the main source of aboriginal supply of copper. To cut this free silver from the native copper would be easy, though the supply would be small. Mr. Moorehead informs us that he found in the effigy mound of the Hopewell group a bit of native silver, hammered flat, which is now in the Field Columbian Museum. No indication of contact with Europeans was present in the Hopewell mounds.

While Mr. Moorehead was conducting investigations in 1897 for the Ohio State Archæological and Historical Society, in Pickaway County, Ohio, in a small stone box were found five nuggets of silver, weighing six and one-quarter ounces, in the aggregate. This unique discovery shows the aborigines to have been possessed of silver nuggets in all probability before the coming of the whites, since no artifact of European make was met with during the work.

The method of fastening the silver on the sheet copper ornaments found by us, and the irregular outline and thinness of the hammered silver would, in our opinion, argue aboriginal workmanship and a supply more scanty than would have been the case had silver bullion and coins been forthcoming from the whites through barter or through shipwreck. When to these facts we add that no object surely of white provenance came from the mound in which these ornaments were, there are good grounds to consider these copper and silver ear-plugs to be of purely aboriginal make. They are the first of the kind to be found in Florida, we believe.

[1] "As to Copper from the Mounds of the St. Johns." "Certain Sand Mounds of the St. Johns River, Florida," Part II. By Clarence B. Moore.

A few shell beads lay near a skeleton of an infant.

With Burial No. 93, a skeleton flexed on the left side, were a few shell beads

FIG. 160.—Vessel with Burial No. 93. Mound A. Pierce mounds, near Apalachicola. (Half size.)

near the neck, and at the shoulder, an undecorated, imperforate vessel of about one-half pint capacity (Fig. 160).

A burial had a sheet of mica near the head.

Certain scattered bones lay in sand colored with hematite.

Loose in the sand were : a number of drinkingcups wrought from *Fulgur perversum*, several with perforated bases ; two arrowheads or knives, of chert ; a rude chipped chisel of chert ; a small pendant rather roughly made ; the usual quota of hammer-stones, pebble hammers, pebbles, broken hones, etc. ; two pointed implements made from the axis of *Fulgur ;* a few shell beads in caved sand ; also in caved sand, a fragment of sheet copper with fluted decoration, badly carbonated ; on the base, among the shells, a gorget of bone, elongated oval, made from the femur of a bison,[1] perforated for suspension at one end, 7.1 inches long, 2 inches in maximum width (Fig. 161).

Also unassociated was a small vessel with globular body, constricted neck and flaring rim around which is a series of notches. A rude meander decoration surrounds the body. One of four feet is lost through a basal perforation.

In debris was part of a smoking pipe of earthenware of the platform, or "Monitor," type.

A curious fragment of earthenware lay alone in the sand. The decoration is partly incised and partly made with a crescentic point. Two and five-tenths inches are of solid ware ; above seems to be the beginning of the base of a cup (Fig. 162).

In fallen sand in the SSE. slope of the mound was a globular vessel of about 1 quart

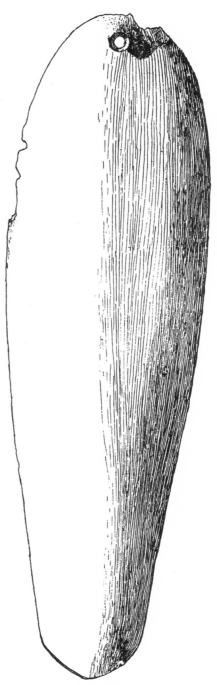

FIG. 161.—Gorget made from the femur of a bison. Mound A. Pierce mounds, near Apalachicola. (Full size.)

[1] Kindly identified by Prof. F. A. Lucas of the U. S. National Museum.

29 JOURN. A. N. S. PHILA., VOL. XII.

capacity, in pieces which have since been cemented together.   The base is perforate.

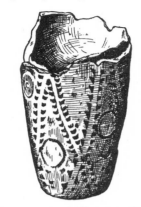

FIG. 162.—Sherd. Mound A. Pierce mounds, near Apalachicola. (Half size.)

The decoration consists of upright parallel bars of crimson paint rudely applied.   With this vessel were many fragments representing parts of three or four vessels, all decorated with crimson pigment.   In association with these was a vessel with the rim slightly broken, which, at first glance, seemed to be an upright cylindrical cup placed within a bowl.   Around the body and even on the base is a repetition of an incised and punctate design with crimson pigment, in addition.   The neck is crimson inside and out.   There is a basal perforation (Fig. 163).   Height, 5.2 inches; maximum diameter of body, 4 inches; diameter of opening, 3 inches.

With fragments of ware were a small undecorated

FIG. 163.—Vessel of earthenware.   Mound A.   Pierce mounds, near Apalachicola.   (Full size.)

FIG. 164.—Vessel of earthenware. Mound A. Pierce mounds, near Apalachicola. (Five-sevenths size.)

imperforate pot with four feet and a rude vessel of about 1 quart capacity, with flaring rim and seemingly cord-marked decoration.   Three of four feet have been removed by a basal perforation.

FIG. 165.—Sherd. Mound A. Pierce mounds, near Apalachicola. (Half size.)

Unassociated, in the eastern slope of the mound, lay the wreck of a curious, undecorated vessel of very inferior ware, which has since been restored.   The body is annular and flattened and has at equidistant points three necks resembling inverted truncated cones (Fig. 164).   Diameter of body, 6.2 inches; central opening, 2 inches.

A sherd with a complicated stamp of a pattern new to us is shown in Fig. 165.

Together, near a great fireplace, on the base of the mound, were: a shell drinking cup; two canine teeth, one of which Prof. F. A. Lucas has identified as the left lower canine of a wolf, *Canis occidentalis*, and the other as the left lower canine of a puma, *Felis concolor ;* and a shell (*Glycymeris americana*, Defr.). Near these or with them were : many fragments of deer bones; one canine of a carnivore; part of a lower jaw of a small rodent; a mass of shell, resembling a large imperforate bead; a rude shell gouge.

A neatly made gouge of shell, with the upper end missing, lay unassociated in the sand.

PIERCE MOUNDS, NEAR APALACHICOLA, MOUND B.

This mound, with a height of 16 feet and a basal diameter of about 100 feet at the present time, showed traces of previous digging on every side. In addition, much of the marginal parts had been hauled away for use in an adjoining cultivated field. On this mound were many palmettoes, much prized by the owner, which precluded a full examination. Such work as was done at various points showed the mound to be of sand with slight admixture of shell. A superficial skeleton lay near the margin.

About fifty yards eastward of Mound B, in a field covered with scattered shells, some trenching was done by us resulting in the discovery of three skeletons at full length. Our work here was discontinued at the request of the owner, who did not wish to have unproductive soil brought to the surface.

In this field is a mound commonly believed to be of shell throughout. It is said by some that the shell extends to a depth of about 2 feet only, after which sand is encountered. As the shell is used for the streets of the town, digging into the mound is not encouraged.

PIERCE MOUNDS, NEAR APALACHICOLA, MOUND C.

This mound, elliptical in outline, with flat top, about 6.5 feet high, has a diameter of 90 feet east and west and of 74 feet north and south.

Starting from the margin, a trench 35 feet long and from 13 feet to 15 feet wide, was continued to within 3 feet of the center. Part of the way, the trench was run along the base of the mound, but it having become evident that the mound was built upon a shell-heap, the useless throwing back of shell was discontinued and the sand alone was removed.

Three skeletons were met with, two flexed, and one, that of an infant, disturbed by the digger. With this skeleton were a few small shells used as beads.

Loose in the sand were various sherds with small check stamp. Pinched decoration and complicated stamp also were represented. One small sherd bore semicircular impressions made, perhaps, by a portion of a reed.

PIERCE MOUNDS, NEAR APALACHICOLA, MOUND D.

This mound, in thick scrub, has a height of 20 inches. The diameter of base is 40 feet. It is composed of sand blackened with organic matter and has local layers of shells of the oyster and of the clam.

The mound, which was about one-half dug away, proved to be a dwelling site.

Sherds of good quality, some with pinched, some with incised, decoration, but mainly of the small check stamp, were present.

PIERCE MOUNDS, NEAR APALACHICOLA, MOUND E.

This mound, which is much spread, has basal diameters of 76 feet N. and S. and 82 feet E. and W.   The height is 3.5 feet.

Fourteen holes, each about 3 feet square, were dug to the base.   The mound is composed of sand of various shades without admixture of shell.   Nothing was found save a single fragment of pottery.   The mound was evidently domiciliary.

SINGER MOUND, NEAR APALACHICOLA, FRANKLIN COUNTY.

This mound, totally demolished by us, was about 1.5 miles in WNW. direction from Apalachicola in a cultivated field, the property of the late Mr. Joseph Singer of that place.

The mound, almost intact, the usual truncated cone in shape, had a height of 5.5 feet; a diameter of base of 65 feet.

The upper portions were of white sand, which probably was the yellow sand of the middle parts of the mound, bleached by sun and rain.   Above the base was a stratum of sand blackened by fire, increasing in thickness until the maximum, about 2.5 feet, was reached in the central part of the mound.

Burials, nineteen in all, were met with from the marginal parts of the mound to the center.   The bones, as a rule, were so decayed that parts only remained.   A few burials were in better condition.

Burial No. 15, the skeleton of a young person, lay in the black layer near the base and was the only burial found at a depth greater than 2.5 feet from the surface. This skeleton was partly flexed on the left side.

Burial No. 10 had been held together in part by ligaments, much of the skeleton being in order, though part of a scapula lay with the legs.   Over this skeleton were a few oyster-shells, as was the case with a number of burials in this mound.

Burial No. 14 was a skeleton at full length on the back with certain other human bones lying across the legs.

All other burials were fragmentary.   Several lone skulls were met with, and once an isolated portion of a femur.

No pottery came from this mound with the exception of a few sherds, undecorated or with the check stamp, evidently introduced with the sand.

Two gracefully wrought celts, each about 8 inches in length, lay separate and unassociated.

JACKSON MOUND, NEAR APALACHICOLA, FRANKLIN COUNTY.

About 2.5 miles in a WNW. direction from Apalachicola, in the verge of woods, on property of Mr. Scipio Jackson, colored, resident on the place, was a mound which was completely demolished by us.   This mound, made of sand of various colors, irregularly placed, had a height of 9 feet. Its basal diameter N. and S. was 72 feet and 66 feet E. and W. Six excavations, all insignificant, had been made previous to our visit.

A feature of the mound was the comparatively central position of the burials. With the exception of a small pocket of calcined fragments of human bones, no trace of human remains was met with until a point 15 feet from the center of the mound was reached, and the majority of the twenty-six burials noted by us were still more central.

FIG. 166.—Smoking pipe of earthenware. With Burial No. 3. Jackson mound. (About full size.)

All burials were badly decayed, sometimes only crowns of teeth, small bits of unidentified bone and even mere traces of bone, remaining in the sand. Single skulls, skulls with a few long-bones and certain long-bones without a skull, were present.

Burial No. 2, a skull and parts of two long-bones, had in association sand colored with hematite and four arrowheads or knives, of chert.

Burial No. 3, a crushed skull on certain long-bones, better preserved than other burials in the mound, lay at a depth of 18 inches from the surface. With this burial were a bit of pottery, one pebble and two smoking pipes of earthenware. One of these pipes (Fig. 166), ornamented around the margin of the bowl and at the base, has a diameter of bowl of 3.5 inches.   The other, with a small, rude decoration of incised lines, is 2.5 inches across the bowl, within which is carbonized material, tobacco or a substitute for it (Fig. 167).   As the other burials in the mound were at considerable depth, some lying on the base, it is possible that this burial was intrusive, especially as the bones were in so much better condition than the others in the mound.   We may say that the presence of smoking pipes with a burial would not of necessity prompt us to consider it a recent interment, since we are convinced that

FIG. 167.--Smoking pipe of earthenware. With Burial No. 3. Jackson mound. (Full size.)

pipes were in the possession of the aborigines long previous to the coming of the whites.   We have personally found pipes in too many mounds in which no article of European make was present, to come to any other conclusion, and it is our belief that a contrary opinion is held by those only who have never engaged in field work.[1]

With the exception of a hammer-stone with one burial and a large, flat pebble with another, no additional artifacts were found with the dead, though it is our belief that certain pockets of very dark sand near the center of the mound, near which objects were met with, were places where burials had been.

In sand blackened by organic matter, 5 feet from the surface, lay a hammer-stone with a small corroded disc of sheet copper or of brass, too badly carbonated for analysis.

Extending a certain distance in from the margin, along the base or just above it, in the E. and NE. parts of the mound, scattered here and there, and not closely associated, were many sherds and numerous vessels of earthenware.   These vessels had the mortuary perforation of base almost without exception.   In the great majority of cases the vessels were imperfect through breakage before interment and

[1] For the opinion of a veteran field worker see "Archæological History of Ohio," page 588, *et seq.*, by Gerard Fowke, Columbus, Ohio, 1902.

the few vessels found whole, with the exception of the mortuary perforation, of course, were, save one, undecorated and of inferior ware. This exception was a vessel bearing a complicated stamp decoration about 2 inches wide, below the margin (Fig. 168). A number of imperfect vessels and sherds also bore the complicated stamp. One of these is shown in Fig. 169.

FIG. 168.—Vessel of earthenware. Jackson mound. (Half size.)

FIG. 169.—Sherd. Jackson mound. (Half size.)

Three vessels, separate, were found more centrally located in the mound, though not immediately associated with burials, than was the general deposit of earthenware which came to an end before interments were met with. One is an undecorated vessel of about 1 pint capacity, of excellent ware, having the form of a gourd. Part of the handle is broken and missing. Another (Fig. 170), with semi-globular body with incised and punctate decoration, had two necks and two orifices, where similar necks, which have since been restored, had been. The base is imperforate. Maximum diameter of body, 6.3 inches; height, with neck, 6.6 inches.

The third vessel, an undecorated pot of about 1 pint capacity, has a certain amount of bitumen which, melted at one time, has hardened on the base. This glue-pot, of necessity, has no basal perforation. We know bitumen to have been in common use among the aborigines, and Cabeça de Vaca tells how he went to what is now the Alabama frontier and acquired in trade various articles, including cement, which was, doubtless, bitumen.

Also in the E. and NE. parts of the mound and comparatively near the margin, presumably deposited for the dead in general were: a soapstone pipe of the common rectangular block pattern and fourteen hatchets, or "celts", ranging in length between 2.5 inches and 11.25 inches.   Many of these are rudely made though some are carefully smoothed and taper gracefully to a blunt point opposite the cutting edge.   Certain of these hatchets lay in pairs.

With the "celts" were two double bladed hatchets, probably of granitoid rock, much weathered, 6 inches and 4.8 inches in length, respectively, showing where a central fastening had held them to a handle.

FIG. 170.—Vessel of earthenware.   Jackson mound.   (Seven-ninths size.)

Also unassociated there came from the mound hammer-stones, whetstones and hones.

Together were: one pebble rudely chipped to resemble a small hatchet; two rounded pebbles; two smooth pebbles; a spear-head with broken point; a pebble grooved at one end for a pendant; and a neat little pendant also grooved at one end.

One pebble-hammer, three pebbles, one chert arrowhead or knife lay closely associated, while eight pebbles and pebble-hammers were found together in another place.

A lance-head of chert, 5.2 inches in length, lay in the outer part of the mound among the hatchets.

Two graceful and keen-pointed arrow-or lance-points of chalcedony, lay together.

Also in the mound were: two arrowheads; one small lance-point; a bit of quartz crystal; a pendant of quartz crystal, with the part above the groove broken off; a mass of galena, 2.5 inches by 2 inches, rounded and flattened at the ends as though by use as a hammer.

A fact worthy of note in this mound is that, with the exception of one small pocket of calcined human bones found by us on the Alabama river, that in the Jackson mound is the westernmost example of cremation met with by us.

Mound near Huckleberry Landing, Franklin County.

Jackson river empties into the Apalachicola about 5 miles above the mouth of the river which enters the bay of that name near the town of Apalachicola.

Huckleberry landing is about 2 miles above the junction.

About 100 yards from the landing, on the south side of the river, in hammock land, on property of Mr. David Silva, resident nearby, was a mound which had undergone a certain amount of previous digging, though not sufficient greatly to impair the scientific value of our investigation.

About 100 yards northwest from the mound were a shell-field and numerous aboriginal shell deposits composed mainly of shells of a small clam (*Rangia cuneata*). One of these deposits, from 1 to 3 feet in height, nearly oval in shape, is 120 feet E. and W. and 180 feet N. and S., inside diameter. Other shell deposits lie to the eastward of the mound.

The mound, which was entirely dug through by us, was 5 feet 4 inches in height and had a basal diameter of 38 feet E. and W. and 52 feet N. and S. It was composed of sand with no regular stratification. In places, especially toward the base, were various deposits of a clayey sand exceedingly tough and forming almost a matrix. In this material often were shells of the kind present in the adjacent shell deposits, while other pockets and small layers of these shells were present in the looser sand also.

Burials, of which we found thirty-four, began near the margin on the eastern side and continued at intervals until the body of the mound was reached, where they became more numerous. In other parts of the mound burials were not met with beneath the slope. A few of the burials were near the surface. Some were 4.5 feet down while one was lower still. So often did the bones lie in the tough clayey material, of which we have spoken, that it seemed as though this clayey sand had been put in expressly with the burials. Those that did not were the superficial burials, with one exception, to be referred to later. Upon several occasions burials of single skulls came from the mound like great balls of clay, the skulls being within the masses.

Eleven burials were of flexed skeletons, some turned to the right, others to the left. The flexion in this mound was much closer in character, as a rule, than was that noted by us in the Jackson mound, though several examples of loose flexion were met with. The heads of the skeletons pointed in all directions. Twelve burials consisted of lone skulls, while the remaining eleven interments were made up of skulls with a few bones; various bones without skulls; several aboriginal disturbances where parts of skeletons had been removed in making place for others; a mass of bones containing three skulls; one burial which fell in caved sand.

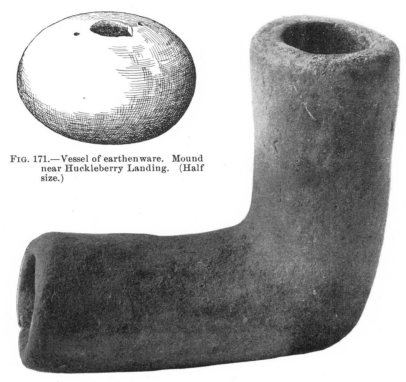

FIG. 171.—Vessel of earthenware. Mound near Huckleberry Landing. (Half size.)

FIG. 172.—Smoking pipe of earthenware. With Burial No. 22. Mound near Huckleberry Landing. (Full size.)

Beneath the center of the base of the mound was a burial included in our list, consisting of a skull, a tibia and a piece of bone belonging to the fore-arm. This burial lay in sand below the level of the clayey deposit and was, perhaps, the initial interment.

Burial No. 1, a flexed skeleton, had marks of serious inflammation, and Burial No. 2, also flexed, showed a similar condition of several bones. This person, the fragmentary condition of whose bones precluded identification as to sex, seemed to have been peculiarly unfortunate as a radius had an ununited fracture whose rough surface with a certain amount of surrounding callous, showed death to have intervened before the parts could unite. This radius was sent to the Army Medical Museum, Washington, D. C.

But few artifacts lay with the bones.   With one was a pebble-hammer; with another a pebble.

Burial No. 8, consisting of a skull and two thigh bones, had somewhat above it a rude, undecorated vessel with perforate base.   Extending from this vessel in a northerly direction for 2.5 feet was a deposit made of several considerable parts of coarse undecorated vessels of ordinary types and many sherds from various vessels, some undecorated, one with a small check stamp and a number with complicated stamps.   On the northernmost sherd, a large one, lay a single skull.

With burial No. 21, one femur and two tibiæ, was an undecorated spheroidal vessel of compact ware, 3.6 inches in diameter and 2.6 inches in height.   The circular aperture is but .8 of an inch in diameter.   On either side are small perforations for suspension.   There is a basal perforation (Fig. 171).

With Burial No. 22, a partial flexion on the right side, was a smoking pipe of earthenware with bowl and portion for the stem, circular in shape and at right angles to each other.   Each orifice is about 1 inch in diameter (Fig. 172).   This burial was fairly well preserved and, being near the surface, may have been an intrusive one.

With Burial No. 23, bones disturbed by caving sand, was a pear-shaped "sinker" or pendant, wrought from a quartzose pebble, with the smaller end grooved for suspension.

Burial No. 26, a skeleton flexed on the left side, lay 4 feet 7 inches down, a few feet from the center of the mound.   At either side of the head, was a disc of sheet copper about 2.7 inches in diameter having a central incused space with a small perforation in the middle, surrounded by a *repoussé* margin.   Behind each disc, that is between the disc and the skull, was a disc of earthenware about 1.7 inches in diameter, having a small central perforation.   On the outside of one of the copper discs there remains a knot formed from a cord or a sinew.   It is evident, then, that these objects were ear-plugs, the copper being worn on the outside of the ear while the earthenware disc, fastened to the copper one, remained at the back of the lobe of the ear.[1]   We are unable to say whether or not the two discs comprising each ear-plug were permanently fastened and the smaller disc buttoned through a hole in the lobe of the ear.   Very likely this was the case since we know the custom among the aborigines to have a great opening in the lobe of the ear, obtained from Peru northward.

Burials Nos. 29 and 30 had each a turtle-shell in association.   These shells, each about 7 inches across, if used for rattles, must have contained perishable material as no pebbles were met with inside.

Burial No. 31 had near it an undecorated vessel of poor material and ordinary type, having the usual basal perforation.

In this mound were no deposits distinctly marginal, as objects put in for the dead in general were found in all parts of the mound and at all depths.

---

[1] We found two earthenware discs of this kind and fragments of sheet copper, in a low mound near Helena, Lake Co., Fla., and described them in our "Certain Sand Mounds of the Ocklawaha River, Florida," Journ. Acad. Nat. Sci., Phila., Vol. X, but did not know their use at that time.

Many sherds found singly and probably of accidental introduction were present, as were numbers of others in close association, probably substitutional offerings. Some were undecorated, two or three bore the small check stamp, while many had the complicated stamp decoration. Three of these are shown in Figs. 173, 174, 175. Incised decoration was practically unrepresented.

FIG. 173.—Sherd. Mound near Huckleberry Landing. (Half size.)

FIG. 174.—Sherd. Mound near Huckleberry Landing. (Half size.)

Seven vessels lay unassociated with burials. Five are undecorated; one, somewhat imperfect, has a complicated stamp and is of material superior to the rest. Five have basal perforations. Five are of ordinary type as to form.

Vessel No. 6, shown in Fig. 176, is undecorated, imperforate, circular in transverse outline.

FIG. 175.—Sherd. Mound near Huckleberry Landing. (Half size.)

FIG. 176.—Vessel No. 6. Mound near Huckleberry Landing. (Half size.)

FIG. 177.—Knife of chert. Mound near Huckleberry Landing. (Full size.)

Vessel No. 7, an urn with slightly scalloped margin of which parts are missing, has a complicated stamp decoration. The base is perforated.

Vessel No. 10, a small pot, undecorated, has four feet.

Rudimentary feet are on the bottom of part of a small vessel found unassociated in the sand and two feet are on half a vessel broken longitudinally.

A smoking pipe of earthenware of the "Monitor" type lay unassociated. Part of the mouth-piece which presumably was as long as the projection on the opposite side of the bowl, is missing through an early fracture. Present length, 4.25 inches; height, 2 inches; diameter of bowl, .7 of an inch.

Throughout the mound were numbers of pebble-hammers, hammer-stones, pebbles and several broken hones. In one instance twenty pebbles and pebble-hammers lay together. There were present also many small masses of chert, possibly "wasters."

Four hatchets, or "celts" lay unassociated.

A sheet of mica lay just below the surface.

With seven pebbles and pebble-hammers was a large flake of chert, probably used as a knife.

Loose in the sand, was a knife of chert, perhaps formerly an arrowhead from which a considerable part had broken longitudinally, involving the margin of the shank. The broken side has been carefully chipped to remove the thick surface left by the fracture (Fig. 177).

Mound near Porter's Bar, Franklin County.

This mound, in thick scrub, is on property of Mr. T. J. Branch, living on the place, situated one mile west of Green Point and a short distance from Porter's Bar.

The mound, which had sustained but little previous digging, had deep depressions in places around it whence the sand used in its building came. Its outline was somewhat irregular, it being much steeper toward the east where it bordered a brook than on the west where it sloped to the level of the surrounding country. Its basal diameters were 60 feet and 78 feet; its height was between 10 feet and 11 feet. It was totally dug down by us.

The mound was composed of irregular strata and masses of sand, sometimes white, sometimes yellow, and in places blackened with organic matter. This black sand was particularly noticeable in the eastern part of the mound from the margin in as long as the principal deposit of pottery was met with.

Beginning at that part of the margin of the mound included between W. and NW. and extending shortly after to SW. was a layer of oyster shells, of irregular thickness, on the base of the mound. This layer, from 1 foot to 2.5 feet in thickness, covering about one-quarter of the area of the mound, was purposely made and not a shell-heap antedating the building of the mound. There were also two or three local pockets of shell, each about 3 feet square and having the same thickness as the principal layer.

Human remains lay in all parts of the mound, which was contrary to our usual experience and, as a rule, were on or near the base, though some were higher in the mound. A certain number lay below the shell layer, while others were just above it. Scattered bones lay here and there among the shells. Superficial burials, after the mound had reached a considerable height, were not present.

There were noted by us in the mound sixty-eight burials, including the closely flexed, the loosely flexed, the bunch, the lone skull, scattered bones, one burial in a

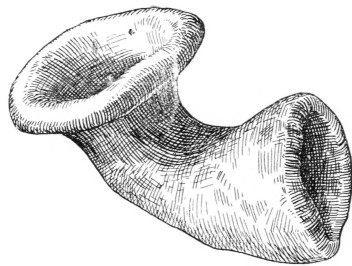

FIG. 178.—Smoking pipe with Burial No. 60. Mound near Porter's Bar. (Full size.)

squatting position and one pocket of calcined fragments of human bones, which resembled the deposits of cremated bones in Georgia where many fragments, all calcined, lie together. Cabeça de Vaca tells [1] us " it is their custom to bury the dead unless it be those among them who have been physicians, and those they burn."

Though the state of the burials was such through decay and pressure of sand that no skulls were preserved, yet a number, though fragmentary, permitted examination as to cranial compression. In but one case was compression noted and then to a moderate degree only.

Burial No. 23 consisted of badly decayed bones in a shallow grave below the base. With them was a rude lancehead.

Burial No. 27, a skull and some badly decayed bones had sand colored with hematite in association, as did a number of other burials in the mound.

Burial No. 49 had teeth alone remaining. With these were a small earthenware vessel and a smoothing stone.

Burial No. 50, a lone skull, had with it a hammer-stone, a small stone pendant, a bit of sandstone, a pebble-hammer and three cutting implements made from columellæ of large marine univalves.

Burial No. 54, a lone skull, had in association a small earthenware vessel (No.

[1] The Narrative of Alvar Nuñez Cabeça de Vaca, translated by Buckingham Smith. Washington, 1851, pg. 49.

87) intact as to the base, which was the case with several pots and bowls, all diminutive, found directly with burials in this mound.

Burial No. 59 was a skeleton in a squatting position on the base. With it were: a pendant of shell; an arrowhead or knife, of jasper; a small undecorated clay smoking pipe; clam shells; six pendants,[1] one bottle-shaped and grooved, made from a quartz pebble, five of ordinary types, one of these of red indurated shale and four of igneous rock.

Burial No. 60, a flexed skeleton, had with it an undecorated smoking pipe of clay with comparatively small bowl and flaring rim (Fig. 178).

Burial No. 63, bones disturbed by caving sand, had nearby five implements, some for cutting, some for piercing, made from columellæ of large marine univalves; three shell gouges, one without a cutting edge; a bit of sandstone and a pebble-hammer.

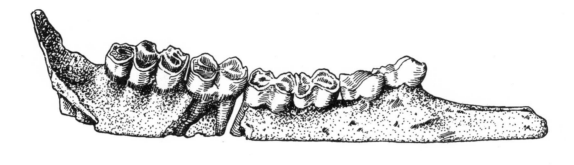

FIG. 179.—Part of deer jaw cut off at base. Two positions. Mound near Porter's Bar. (Full size.)

Burial No. 64, a partly flexed skeleton, lay on the base of the mound. With it were: a small chisel, probably of volcanic rock, somewhat broken; a triangular hammer-stone, rudely grooved for a handle; and four shell gouges.

With other burials were: two "celts;" the small vessels of which we have spoken; and a number of hammer-stones, smoothing-stones and shell drinking cups.

Apart from burials were: three "celts;" a flake of chert, probably a knife; several arrow and lanceheads, some of chert, some of quartzite; mica; shell drinking cups; a lump of galena, of considerable size, apparently having seen service as a hammer; a pendant, probably of ingenous rock; a number of shell implements badly

[1] As to the uses made of plummets, see "Archæological History of Ohio." Fowke, pg. 556, *et seq.*

decayed as a rule; bitumen, in one instance; plumbago; and the quota of hones, hammer-stones, smoothing-stones, pebble-hammers, usually present in mounds.

With a number of artifacts fallen in caved sand and probably at one time associated with a burial, were three jaws of small rodents, also two parts of a lower jaw of a deer, with the base cut away to leave a flat surface (Fig. 179).

We three times found jaws of large carnivores treated this way, in mounds of the Georgia coast and suggested in our report[1] that they had been thus treated to facilitate insertion into wooden masks.

Mr. Cushing at Marco found "certain split bear and wolf jaws neatly cut off"[2] so as to leave the canines and two bicuspids standing. On the jaws were traces of cement. Mr. Cushing believed these jaws to have been let into war-clubs, which may well have been the case with teeth of large carnivores, but hardly so where jaws of deer were used.

Mr. Moorehead found in Ohio mounds human jaws treated in the way we have described, some with perforations in addition, and regards them as ornaments.[3]

From all this, the reader has doubtless come to the conclusion, and rightly, that the use made of these curiously treated jaws is still an open question.

A feature often noticed in the mounds, namely the tendency to place with the dead objects no longer of use to the living, was illustrated in this mound by the finding with a burial, of eight arrow- and lance-points, five of chert, three of quartzite. Of these, five wanted either a shank or a barb; of the remaining three, two were in the rough.

In caved sand was part of an ornament of sheet copper.

Broken into several parts by palmetto roots which had penetrated it, was a curious object of impure kaolin,[4] almost cylindrical, with a certain rounded enlargement at either end. This object, which is 11 inches long and has a middle diameter of 2.5 inches and of 3 inches at either end, had been carefully smoothed at one time and still, in places, shows traces of decoration in low relief. A similar object, found in a much better state of preservation, will be figured and described in our account of Mound B, Warrior river.

Including with whole vessels those which were broken but had full complement of parts, and others from which but small parts were missing, ninety vessels came from this mound. The ware was most inferior, as a rule; the decoration poor in design and rudely executed. Undecorated vessels predominated and, as a rule, when decoration had been attempted, it consisted of the complicated stamp, usually rudely and irregularly applied. The use of this form of decoration, even when carefully executed, is always unfortunate in a mound, since it is likely to take the place of incised design which calls for greater originality. Farthermore, many of the vessels with complicated stamp were not covered as to the entire body, but had only a

[1] "Certain Aboriginal Mounds of the Georgia Coast," pp. 65, 88, 112. Journ. Acad. Nat. Sci. Phila. Vol. XI.

[2] Proc. Am. Philosoph. Soc. Vol. XXXV, No. 153, pg. 45. Phila., 1897.

[3] "Primitive Man in Ohio," pg. 226, et seq.

[4] Kaolin is found in Florida.

comparatively narrow band of the decoration on or below the neck. This form sufficiently ornamental when carefully done, is much less so when the stamp is irregularly and faintly applied.

FIG 180.—Vessel No. 9. Mound near Porter's Bar. (Full size.)

Although a number of sherds and several vessels were found in the southwestern margin of the mound at the very start, yet the great majority of the vessels lay
in the eastern portion and were included within the first fifteen feet of the slope.
With these were the usual sherds. Farther in, in the same direction, were certain
other vessels extending along the base like the rest, but with these were no piles of

FIG. 182.—Vessel No. 9. Decoration. Mound near Porter's Bar. (Half size.)

sherds such as marked the deposit of ware in the outer portion of the mound.
There was no central deposit.

We shall now describe the most noteworthy of the vessels. Unless otherwise
stated, the usual basal perforation is present, all without it being included in our list.

Vessel No. 4.—Has a decoration of vertical parallel lines, rudely executed.

Vessel No. 9.—A bowl of excellent ware, of about 1 quart capacity, colored
crimson inside and out (Fig. 180), with incised and punctate decoration in which
appears the symbol of the bird, shown in diagram (Fig. 181).

Vessel No. 10.—A toy vessel with globular body and flaring quadrilateral neck.

Vessel No. 11.—Is of eccentric shape as shown in Fig. 182. Unfortunately, a part of the neck is missing from an early fracture.

FIG. 182.—Vessel No. 11. Mound near Porter's Bar. (Half size.)

Vessel No. 15.—An undecorated imperforate cup.

Vessel No. 18.—Has a hemispherical body and slightly flaring neck (Fig. 183), around which is an incised and punctate decoration shown in (Fig. 184) in which the punctate markings have been accidentally omitted from the rectangular space in the right upper portion.

Vessel No. 21.—A curious wedge-shaped vessel, a form new to our mound work. The decoration, incised, is practically the same on either side (Figs. 185, 186). Height, 8.5 inches; maximum diameter, 4.8 inches.

FIG. 183.—Vessel No. 18. Mound near Porter's Bar. (Two-thirds size.)

Vessel No. 29.—A little bowl of inferior ware, having below the rim a band about 1.5 inches in breadth, made up of series of rudely incised perpendicular lines, of diagonal lines and of horizontal lines.

Vessel No. 30.—This vessel, undecorated save for a single encircling incised line a short distance below the rim, consists of an upper part somewhat elliptical in horizontal section, placed upon a flattened sphere (Fig. 187).

Vessel No. 33.—This handsome trilateral vessel (Fig. 188), unfortunately found broken into many pieces, probably represents some quadruped in incised and punctate decoration as conventionalized fore-legs and hind-legs are clearly shown (Fig. 189).   An animal head is probably missing from the rim in front.

Vessel No. 35.—A bowl of about one-half pint capacity, with incised decoration on one part only, shown diagrammatically in Fig. 190.

Vessel No. 36.—Portions of a compartment vessel, scattered throughout the mound.   Parts are missing.

FIG. 184.—Vessel No. 18.   Decoration.   Mound near Porter's Bar.   (Half size.)

Vessel No. 60.—An imperforate pot.

Vessel No. 61.—A water-bottle with a most interesting incised design representing some highly conventionalized form.   In addition to the "killing" in the base, a small hole has been knocked in the side of the vessel, involving the decoration to a very limited extent.   Diagram (Fig. 191) shows the design with slight restoration.

FIG. 185.—Vessel No. 21.   Mound near Porter's Bar.
(Half size.)

FIG. 186.—Vessel No. 21.   Another view.   Mound near Porter's Bar.   (Half size.)

FIG. 187.—Vessel No. 30. Mound near Porter's Bar. (Half size.)

FIG. 188.—Vessel No. 33. Mound near Porter's Bar. (Eight-ninths size.)

Vessel No. 63.—The piece knocked from the bottom of this pot was found lying within it, as was the case with another vessel in this mound.

Vessel No. 66.—A bowl of about 1 pint capacity, of red ware, with a handle in the form of a rather rude owl-head looking inward, which, with the exception of crimson paint, inside and out, is the only decoration.

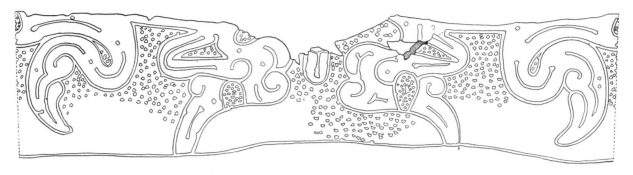

FIG. 189.—Vessel No. 33. Decoration. Mound near Porter's Bar. (One-third size.)

Vessel No. 69.—An imperforate pot with a rough complicated stamp around the neck.

Vessel No. 71.—A graceful undecorated vessel, ovoid in shape, with holes below the rim, for suspension (Fig. 192).

Vessel No. 74.—A shallow bowl 5 inches in diameter, to which a part, missing when found, has been added. There has been incised and punctate decoration over the base, part of which is wanting. A conventionalized animal paw, however, still

FIG. 190.—Vessel No. 35. Decoration. Mound near Porter's Bar. (Half size.)

FIG. 191.—Vessel No. 61. Decoration. Mound near Porter's Bar.
(Half size.)

FIG. 192.—Vessel No. 71. Mound near Porter's Bar.
(Half size.)

remains. The head of an aboriginal dog is represented as looking inward from the rim (Fig. 193). Cabeça de Vaca and the chroniclers of De Soto refer to aboriginal dogs in Florida. Skeletons from the mounds show these dogs to have resembled collies, with somewhat broader jaws.

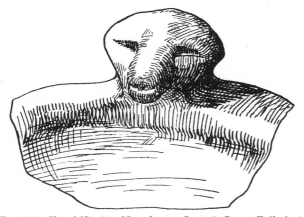

FIG. 193.—Vessel No. 74. Mound near Porter's Bar. (Full size.)

Vessel No. 75.—A life-form from which the head and part of the tail unfortunately are missing, is shown in Fig. 194. The decoration, similar on either side, represents fur and conventionalized fore-legs and hind-legs. Judging from the flat tail, possibly the representation of a beaver is intended.

Vessel No. 78.—A little bowl, lenticular in shape, of less than one pint capacity, imperforate, lay with a burial. The decoration consists of two incised designs shown in diagram in Fig. 195. With this vessel was the astragalus of a deer. Such knuckle-bones were used in games.[1]

FIG. 194.—Vessel No. 75. Mound near Porter's Bar. (Half size.)

Vessel No. 82.—A vessel, somewhat globular in shape, of about 1 gallon capacity, having a complicated stamp decoration around the upper part (Fig. 196).

Vessel No. 87.—Imperforate, of red ware, of somewhat less than one-half pint

[1] For details, see "Chess and Playing Cards," by Stewart Culin, pg. 826, *et seq*. Report U. S. National Museum for 1896.

capacity. From the center of the base a small knob protrudes. There are holes for suspension (Fig. 197).

Vessel No. 88.—A small vessel intact as to the base, with perforations for suspension (Fig. 198).

Vessel No. 89.—A vessel of about 1 pint capacity, elliptical in longitudinal section, the major sides incurving toward the margin. There are holes on the same side for purpose of attachment. The only attempt at decoration is on the side shown in Fig. 199. The part to the left is very suggestive of an effort to portray a quadruped whose fore-legs are in line and also the hind-legs. The head and tail are shown. The figure to the right may represent a bird.

FIG. 195.—Vessel No. 78. Decoration. Mound near Porter's Bar. (Half size.)

FIG. 196.—Vessel No. 82. Mound near Porter's Bar. (Two-fifths size.)

FIG. 197.—Vessel No. 87. Mound near Porter's Bar. (Full size.)

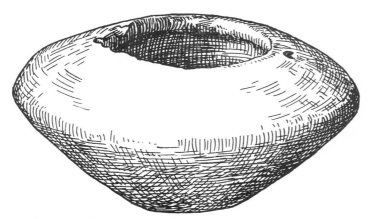

FIG. 198.—Vessel No. 88. Mound near Porter's Bar. (Full size.)

FIG. 199.—Vessel No. 89. Mound near Porter's Bar. (Half size.)

Vessel No. 90.—A compartment vessel consisting of a long division with a a smaller one on either side. A part broken from one end has been filled in (Fig. 200).

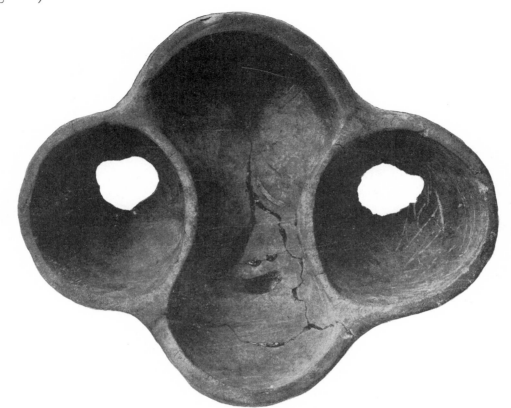

FIG. 200.—Vessel No. 90.   Mound near Porter's Bar.   (Three-fourths size.)

Certain pieces of an effigy-bottle representing the human form, with the head unfortunately absent, were recovered from the mound. The arms and the hands are in relief. Each finger is distinctly shown.

The check stamp was present in the mound but once and, as it lay among the shell, it was probably introduced with it.

Figs. 201, 202, 203, show three sherds with complicated stamp from this mound.

MOUND NEAR GREEN POINT, FRANKLIN COUNTY.

This mound, also on property of Mr. T. J. Branch, was in a field formerly cultivated, a short distance in a SW. direction from the mound just described. There was no sign of previous digging, but members of the family informed us that during cultivation certain relics had been laid bare by the plough. The height of the mound was 2 feet, though on the western side it was necessary to go down 5 feet to reach undisturbed sand. The basal diameter was 62 feet. The mound was completely dug through.

It was composed of sand, light in color as a rule, but blackened with organic matter in certain places.   There were many small deposits of oyster-shells here and there throughout the mound, and scattered shells lay in the sand.   In two or three cases oyster-shells lay with burials, but as there were so many cases where they did

FIG. 202.—Sherd. Mound near Porters Bar.
(Three-fourths size.)

FIG. 201.—Sherd. Mound near Porter's Bar.   (Half size.)

FIG. 203.—Sherd. Mound near Porter's Bar.
(Three-fourths size.)

not and as local deposits of shell were so numerous, it is entirely possible that the proximity of the shells to the burials was accidental.   Burials were in all parts of the mound but were especially numerous in the central portions.

There were in all eighty burials, as a rule closely flexed skeletons, though loosely flexed skeletons, lone skulls, bunches of bones and scattered bones were met with.   No flattening was noticed in the case of any skull whose condition was such as to allow determination.

With burials in different parts of the mound were single vessels of earthenware; also a deposit of thirteen beneath a skeleton in the western part of the mound and a deposit of three vessels, near human remains, a little east of the center.

There were also in the mound, hones, hammer-stones, smoothing-stones, pebble-hammers and kindred objects which it is hardly necessary to describe in detail.

With one burial, among other things, were two rounded ends of "celts" which had no doubt been put in substitutionally, a part for the whole, a most economical method and one widely practised by the aborigines, as we have seen.

There were present also a number of lanceheads and projectile points, all but one or two of which were more or less broken or unfinished.   Three "celts" lay with burials.   Two of these had the cutting edge so badly chipped that prolonged grinding would have been necessary before use.

Forty-four water-worn pebbles, slingstones no doubt, lay together, and a number of burials had with them shell drinking cups mostly having the basal perforation.   Some of these cups were carefully wrought, the whole beak of the shell being ground away, giving the shell a graceful and cup-like appearance.

Fig. 204.—Pendant of shell.   Mound near Green Point.   (Full size.)

Between two burials were: a number of decayed mussel-shells; bits of sandstone; unfinished shell gouges; a rude cutting implement of chert; a bone of a small mammal; fragments of shell; two rectangular pieces of fossilized wood; a number of collumellæ of large marine univalves; sections of columellæ carefully rounded as though for large beads in block; sandstone hones; fragments of various rocks, mostly chert; a small triangular piece of sandstone sharpened as for piercing; a barbed arrowpoint; a small marine shell; an object resembling in shape the tine of a stag horn, a recent formation containing small marine shells; two discs of shell, each about 3.5 inches in diameter, evidently the first stage in the making of gorgets;

two shell discs much smaller; a diamond-shaped section of the body whorl of a large univalve; a pendant made from a marine columella, 5.5 inches in length ; a small gouge of shell; a heavy ornament of shell with two ends grooved for suspension (Fig. 204), 4 inches long and 2 inches thick.   With these objects were many bits of stone and of shell of no particular interest.

Another mortuary deposit consisted of : bits of shell; a large columella worked to a point; another, unworked; one carefully ground to a cutting edge, which, however, is badly chipped; a bit of volcanic rock, a part of an implement;   a chipped pebble; three bits of sandstone; a small mass of hardened clay, seemingly; a small part of a "celt"; three sections of a columella, probably beads in block; a rectangular piece of rock, 7 inches long; parts of two under-jaws of small rodents; a pendant of shell of ordinary demijohn form; a pendant of clam-shell, roughly triangular in shape, grooved at one end for suspension; five triangular gouges with rounded lower corners made from the body whorl of *Fulgur;* forty-three similar implements with undressed sides and unground edges, the first step in the making of a gouge, the nature of this latter deposit showing the aboriginal mind to be fully alive to the fact that the departed would have ample leisure in the life to come.

FIG. 205.—Sherd.   Mound near Green Point.
(Half size.)

FIG. 206.—Sherd.   Mound near Green Point.
(Three-fourths size.)

Contrary to our usual experience, a general deposit of vessels was found on the western side of this mound and another large deposit farther in on the same side, while no other vessels were met with, except immediately with the dead, and these were well in toward the center.

The earthenware of this mound, on an average, was distinctly inferior to any we had met with so far on the coast.   The vessels, when decorated, bore, as a rule, the complicated stamp, often faintly and irregularly impressed.   In Figs. 205, 206,

Fig. 207.—Sherd.   Mound near Green Point.   (Half size.)

207, 208, are shown four fragments of vessels more clearly stamped than the average and with designs new to us.

Incised decoration was met with but three times, on two sherds and on a vessel.

A feature of the mound was the presence of four feet on a considerable percentage of the vessels and scalloped margins on a large number.   Curiously enough, neither of these characteristics was especially noted in the neighboring mound.   In all, about forty vessels were met with, nearly all of which were in pieces or fell apart upon removal.   Of the deposit of thirteen vessels of which we have spoken, but one was taken out entire.   It was apparent that the commonest kitchen ware had been placed with the dead.

We give in detail a description of the more interesting among the vessels.   All are perforated as to the base unless otherwise described.

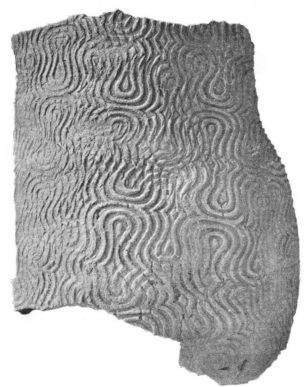

Fig. 208.—Sherd.   Mound near Green Point.   (Half size.)

FIG. 209.—Vessel No. 9. Mound near Green Point. (Nine-elevenths size.)

Vessel No. 1.—A globular bowl with faint complicated stamp and notches on the rim, small and near together, presenting almost a serrated appearance.

Vessel No. 2.—A pot with scalloped rim, having four rudimentary feet.   The basal perforation is made carefully to one side of the feet, a practice to which the aborigines were not given, as a rule, in this mound, as a number of bases with feet upon them, which had been knocked from vessels, were found scattered through the mound.

Vessel No. 3.—Undecorated, of eccentric form.   The lowest part is almost cylindrical but expands somewhat from the base which is flat.   The upper part has been hemispherical, probably.   A part of it is missing.

Vessel No. 4.—An oval jar of about 3 gallons capacity, with scalloped rim and zigzag complicated stamp.

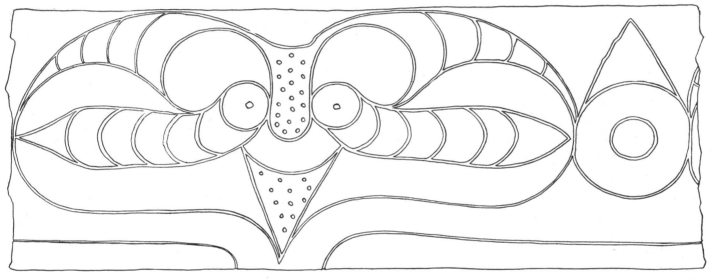

FIG. 210.—Vessel No. 9.   Decoration.   Mound near Green Point.   (Half size.)

Vessel No. 5.—A pot of about 5 gallons capacity, with scalloped rim and complicated stamp decoration.   It fell into bits upon removal.   With it was a knuckle-bone of a deer.   A similar bone lay with another vessel in this mound.

Vessel No. 6.—A large vessel found in pieces.   The decoration was seemingly the impression of basket-work.

Vessel No. 7.—Small, imperforate, undecorated, with flaring rim and four rudimentary feet.

Vessel No. 9.—This vessel (Fig. 209), consists of an undecorated cylinder supporting a much flattened sphere, from which is a flaring neck with scalloped margin. The decoration, which is incised and painted, consists of two similar designs, one of which is shown in diagram (Fig. 210).   Height, 8.8 inches; maximum diameter of body, 8.7 inches.

Vessel No. 10.—A vase of inferior ware, of about 1 quart capacity, with ovoid body, flaring neck and scalloped rim, undecorated (Fig. 211).

Vessel No. 12.—A frail vessel of about 1 pint capacity, elliptical in horizontal section, with rim slightly flaring, having on one side an impression resembling the foot of a bird. On the opposite side the circular portion of the foot is given without the claws (Fig. 212).

FIG. 211.—Vessel No. 10. Mound near Green Point. (One-third size.)

Part of an earthenware smoking pipe lay unassociated in the sand.

From caved sand came part of a smoking pipe of the "platform," or "Monitor," type. A part of one end has been broken off and the endeavor to cut off the rough projecting portion to leave an even surface to join the two parts has been begun but not completed.

In addition to the customary perforation extending through one end of the platform to the bowl, there is another running from the base of the bowl to the base of the platform below (Fig. 213). We wrote to Mr. Warren K. Moorehead as to this curious feature, who most obligingly addressed twelve prominent collectors of this country and forwarded the replies to us.

Smoking pipes with holes accidentally made by the slipping of drills are well known, as are some instances of this carefully made basal perforation. Mr. H. P. Hamilton, of Two Rivers, Wis., kindly forwarded for our inspection two smoking pipes, one showing the accidental perforation, the other the intentional one in the base.

FIG. 212.—Vessel No. 12. Mound near Green Point. (Half size.)

General Gates P. Thruston suggests that this hole in pipes was made to facilitate the cleaning of the bowl and that the hole was plugged during smoking. This seems a probable solution of the question. We are unable to say whether this pipe is stone or earthenware thoroughly baked, and experts, consulted on the subject, have not been able to decide without mutilating the specimen.

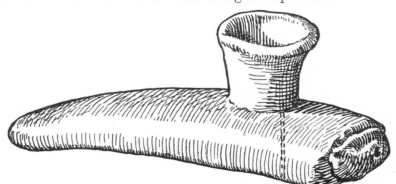

FIG 213.—Smoking pipe. Mound near Green Point. (Full size.)

Mound near Carrabelle, Franklin County.

Within sight of the water, on the right hand side going down the Carrabelle river, about 1.5 miles by land in NW. direction from Carrabelle, is a mound 45 feet across and about 1.5 feet high, which had been much dug into before our visit. On the surface were small fragments of human bones. Considerable trenching yielded nothing of interest.

Tucker Mound, Franklin County.

In sight of the water, which was about 200 yards distant, about one mile from the lower end of Alligator Harbor, on the north side, on property, the ownership of which is uncertain, was a mound about 80 feet in diameter N. and S. and 86 feet E. and W. The slope on the eastern side was much more gentle than elsewhere, forming a graded way. The height of the mound from the general level on the west side was 8.5 feet. A measurement taken near the center, from the surface to the base, showed 9.5 feet.

At various points around the mound were excavations whence the sand came for the building. The mound was entirely demolished by us.

The discovery of burials began at the very margin and continued in, being strictly confined to the eastern and southern sides included between the compass points NE. and SW. In the other parts of the mound were neither burials nor artifacts, with the exception of one undecorated vessel partly broken, probably an accidental introduction. Here we have a striking example of the great quantity of sand piled in certain mounds simply to round out a part used for interments.

Burials, which were mainly in the eastern part of the mound, decreased in number as the digging continued and disappeared entirely 9 feet from the center. Especial care was taken by us as to method and position of interments, since this mound, which was of considerable size, was almost intact at our coming, having in it but two or three holes and these were less than one yard in each of their three dimensions.

Seventy-nine burials were noted by us, including the flexed; the bunched, which sometimes had several skulls; the lone skull; and scattering bones.

Many skulls were past determination as to flattening. The majority of those whose condition permitted a decision distinctly showed flattening but certain others just as distinctly did not.

Burial No. 2, consisting of two decayed fragments of bone, had with it two barrel-shaped beads of galena (lead sulphide) each about .9 of an inch in length and .85 of an inch in maximum diameter. Though cubes of galena are often present in mounds as are masses of the material showing use as hammers, we have but once before, to our recollection, met with an ornament of galena, namely, a bead in the great mound at Mt. Royal, Putnam Co., Fla. With the two beads was a "celt." Incidentally, we may say seven of these implements came from the Tucker mound, all directly with burials except two in whose neighborhood, possibly, bones had disappeared through decay. All these "celts" but one were in marginal parts of the mound, though on or near the base with the original burials, the one exception being under the slope and no wise near the center.

Burial No. 6.—Fragments of bones with which were many conch-shells, not drinking cups, simply the shells (*Fulgur perversum*).

Burial No. 22.—Three skulls with a bit of tibia. With these were a number of large clam-shells and parts of clam-shells showing wear, which probably had been used as tools for cutting and scraping.

With a number of burials in this mound were similar implements of clam-shell.

Burial No. 26.—A closely flexed skeleton lying at the bottom of a grave at the base of the mound which at this point was 5 feet in height. Above the skeleton, which was one of those having a "celt" in association, were 2.5 feet of yellow sand totally differing in color from the gray sand of that part of the mound where the grave was. It would seem as though this grave had been made and filled with sand of another color in a part of the mound but 2.5 feet in height when the grave was made and that later, an additional 2.5 feet had been added to the mound.

Burial No. 28.—A lone skull with charcoal nearby.

Burial No. 30.—A lone skull with a few small shell beads.

Burial No. 33.—A flexed skeleton with two perforated shell drinking cups. A number of such cups were found in the mound but as a rule lying with deposits of earthenware, unassociated with burials.

Burial No. 36.—A lone skull had shell beads and a rude implement of chert.

Burial No. 48.—A flexed skeleton had oyster-shells above it as did Burial No. 57, a flexed skeleton in a shallow grave. These two burials were exceptional in this respect in this mound.

Unassociated with bones were: two small masses of galena; a stone chisel, somewhat broken; mica.

In caved sand was a small fragment of thin sheet copper bearing small *repoussé* designs.

Although there was no marginal deposit of earthenware vessels in the mound, yet the aboriginal custom to place pottery for the dead in general in the eastern portion of mounds, obtained also in this one. Though a number of sherds were found at the start, no vessel was met with until the digging had reached a point 26 feet ESE. from the center where lay together a number of interesting vessels. The deposit of ware continued in between NE. by N. and SE. by S., sometimes single vessels, sometimes a number together. There was no deposit at the center, the last vessel found being 8 feet from it, and but few were met with for some feet farther back.

The vessels, sixty-two in all, whole, nearly so or in a condition to permit reconstruction, all show the basal perforation. As a rule, the ware was inferior and decoration, when present, was usually the complicated stamp, often carelessly applied.

The feature of the mound in respect to earthenware was the presence of many flat bases, even on pots and bowls, where the bases are usually rounded. As usual, numbers of fragments of parts of vessels and whole vessels, crushed together in inextricable masses, lay with whole vessels or with those broken but keeping their form until removed.

We give a detailed description of the most interesting ware.

Vessel No. 1.—This boat-shaped vessel, of about 1 quart capacity, parts of which were found some distance from each other, has since been cemented together, with a certain amount of restoration.   At either end is the head of a duck in relief (Fig. 214).

Vessel No. 2.—This interesting bird-effigy, entire, save for a small basal perforation, has incised decoration on the wings and back, the well-known bird symbol. The aperture is at the base of the neck (Fig. 215).   Height, 8 inches; breadth, 5.5 inches.

Fig. 214.—Vessel No. 1. Tucker mound. (Seven-eighths size.)

Vessel No. 3.—Is of about 1 quart capacity and is without decoration save for the protruding head, probably intended to represent that of a wild cat or of a panther (Fig. 216).

Vessel No. 4.—A bowl in fragments, having the check-stamp decoration.   This instance, with a single sherd in addition, was the only example of this style of decoration noted by us in the mound.

Vessel No. 6.—Of about 2 quarts capacity, with *repoussé* ridges around the body which has been painted crimson (Fig. 217).

Vessel No. 15.—A quadrilateral vessel with circular upright rim, having in each corner an oblong space, *repoussé*, upon which has been a complicated stamp, now very indistinct.

Vessel No. 19.—An undecorated vase of red ware, hemispherical body with long cylindrical neck ending in four pointed corners.

Vessel No. 20.—A small bowl of inferior ware, with a rude dentate design surrounding the upper part, enclosing punctate impressions (Fig. 218).

Vessel No. 21.—A vase of hemispherical body, with constricted neck decorated with upright parallel ridges, ending in a square rim having incised symbols of the bird (Fig. 219).

FIG. 215.—Vessel No. 2. Tucker mound. (Two-thirds size.)

Vessel No. 22.—This vessel, shown in Fig. 220, is undecorated save for the effigy of the head of a horned owl overlooking the aperture. Length, 8.4 inches; breadth, 6.6 inches.

Vessel No. 25.—Shown in Fig. 221, has a spherical body surmounted by a long, flaring rim. The decoration, incised and punctate, is given in diagram (Fig. 222). Height, 7.2 inches; maximum diameter, 5.4 inches.

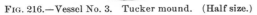

FIG. 216.—Vessel No. 3. Tucker mound. (Half size.)

FIG. 217.—Vessel No. 6. Tucker mound. (Half size.)

Vessel No. 28.—A vessel of about 1 pint capacity, with complicated stamp decoration around the neck.

Vessel No. 29.—Somewhat similar in style to the preceding, with a deeper band of complicated stamp decoration around the upper part (Fig. 223).

Vessel No. 31.—A jar with globular body and long neck slightly flaring, surrounded by a complicated stamp decoration (Fig. 224). Height, 8.7 inches; maximum diameter, 5.9 inches.

FIG. 218.—Vessel No. 20. Decoration. Tucker mound. (Half size.)

Vessel No. 36.—This vessel, crimson in color, found crushed to pieces, has been cemented together with slight restorations. It is particularly interesting as belonging to the

FIG. 219.—Vessel No. 21. Tucker mound. (Half size.)

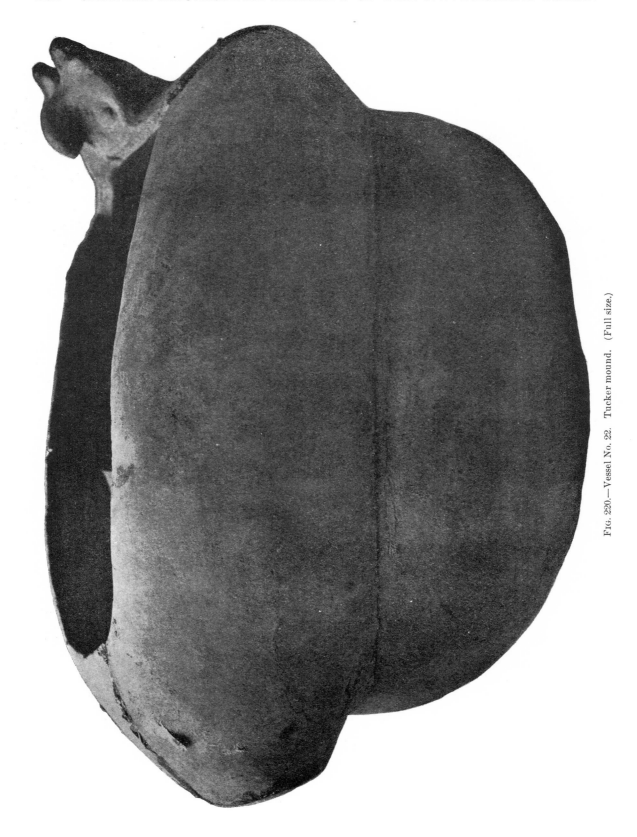

FIG. 220.—Vessel No. 22. Tucker mound. (Full size.)

ready-made mortuary class and has a hole in the base made before baking, as are those in the body and neck of the vessel. This vessel is notable as not being a life-form, to which class ceremonial vessels in this district usually belong.   The

FIG. 221.—Vessel No. 25. Tucker mound. (Full size.)

FIG. 222.—Vessel No. 25. Decoration. Tucker mound. (Half size.)

decoration is incised scrolls with punctate and other markings (Fig. 225).   Height, 7.3 inches; maximum diameter, 8 inches.

Vessel No. 37.—This vessel, crimson inside and out, was found badly crushed and with parts missing.   Cemented together and somewhat restored it seems to be a representation of a shell.   On the opposite sides are convolutions similar to those shown in Fig. 226.   There have been two perforations for suspension, on one side. Height, 4.2 inches; transverse diameter, 4.8 inches.

FIG. 223.—Vessel No. 29. Tucker mound. (Full size.)

FIG. 224.—Vessel No. 31. Tucker mound. (Half size.)

Vessel No. 38.—Part of a compartment vessel which had originally four circular divisions surrounding a fifth placed on a level above.

Vessel No. 44.—A bowl of excellent ware. The decoration, incised, is shown in diagram in Fig. 227. Maximum diameter, 9.5 inches; height, 6.5 inches.

Vessel No. 57.—A pot almost cylindrical, with flat, square base (Fig. 228). The incised decoration showing the bird symbol often repeated, is given diagrammatically in Fig. 229.

FIG. 225.—Vessel No. 36. Tucker mound. (Five-sevenths size.)

YENT MOUND, FRANKLIN COUNTY.

This mound, belonging to the Yent estate, Mrs. James Pickett, of Carrabelle, executrix, was in an old field, now overgrown, about one half mile in a southeasterly direction from the Tucker mound.

The mound, beginning SSW. sloped gently upward in a NNE. direction, a dis-

FIG. 226.—Vessel No. 37. Tucker mound. (Full size.)

tance of 68 feet and, continuing at a level 13 feet, had a descent of 25 feet before reaching the flat ground at the NNE., thus having a major axis of 106 feet along the base. At its broadest part, beneath the level portion, the mound was 74 feet across. There were deep excavations at several places along the border of the mound, whence sand had been taken to build it. The height, above what seemed to be the general level, was 7.5 feet.

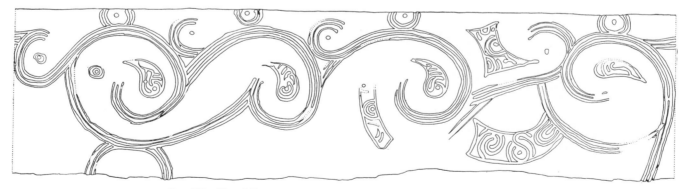

FIG. 227.—Vessel No. 44. Decoration. Tucker mound. (One-quarter size.)

Fig. 228.—Vessel No. 57.   Tucker mound.   (About full size.)

The mound, which had sustained almost no previous digging, was totally demolished by us.

Human remains were met with in seventy-four places, lying throughout the mound from the very margin, sometimes below the base in graves, along the base, and in the body of the mound, but seldom superficially.   There were present

FIG. 229.—Vessel No. 57. Decoration. Tucker mound. (Half size.)

the closely flexed skeleton, the bunch, the lone skull, scattered bones, and skeletons forced into small graves, showing partial flexion at times and, again, disarranged bones with the skull above. There were also bones in caved sand, whose form of burial was not determined, in two or three cases. Though no skulls were saved from this mound, a number were in a condition to allow determination as to cranial flattening. There was no evidence that it had been practised.

Around the great majority of burials were large clam-shells with sometimes a mingling of conchs (*Fulgur perversum*):

Proportionately, the greatest number of burials were marginal, in graves, and with these burials were the most interesting objects in the mound.

With Burial No. 2, a bunch, was a "celt" with a cutting edge 3.5 inches across, while the opposite end tapered gracefully to a blunt point scarcely 1 inch in diameter.

Three other "celts" lay with burials and a small one with a pendant came from a grave where no bones were found though, presumably, lapse of time in wet sand below the base of the mound may account for their absence.

With Burial No. 3, a bunch, were: a canine of a large carnivore; two sheets of mica, roughly shaped to resemble lanceheads; a clam-shell showing wear. A number of such clam-shells with part of the side removed, some with a cutting edge, were met with in this mound.

Burial No. 5, a bunch, had a triangular pebble about 5 inches long, with the greater end showing much use as a hammer.

With Burial No. 8, a mixture of bones, some belonging to an adult, some to a child, near the skull of each was a graceful pendant probably of slate, each about 4.5 inches in length, of the type of a larger one from this mound, to be figured later.

Burial No. 13, a flexed skeleton, had with it four pebbles.

Burial No. 15, a bunch, had with it a rattle made of a turtle-shell holding a number of rather carefully flattened bits of chert.

Burial No. 19, a skull with a single femur, lying in a grave, had a rude earthenware pot some distance above. Probably this association was accidental, as in no other case in this mound was earthenware found with a burial.

With Burial No. 27, a flexed skeleton, were 33 pebbles.

Burial No. 39 consisted of a pit of considerable size, below the base, in which were the flexed skeletons of three adults and parts of skulls and other bones of three infants or children, the remaining bones of these skeletons having doubtless disappeared through decay. At the wrist of one of the adult skeletons were twenty-nine perforated bits of shell, some neatly shaped ; seventy-six teeth of the large porpoise (*Turriops turrio*), kindly identified by Prof. F. A. Lucas, of the National Museum, all perforated, some through the enamel, but nearly all through the base of the tooth ; and eight pieces of bone, all perforated and more or less rudely made to resemble teeth. With these was a small imperforate tooth of a shark of the present geological period. A selection of these ornaments is given in Fig. 230, the shell being to the left, the bone to the right.

As is so often the case with children in mounds, those in this grave had been especially favored. With one was a pendant, probably of slate, about 5 inches long, of the same pattern as the one next to be described, having bitumen still adhering to the groove. With another was the most interesting pendant it has been our fortune to take from a mound. The material is probably slate. The length is 8.75 inches (Fig. 231). The remaining skull had beside it a gorget of shell cut in the shape of a fish. There are two holes for suspension (Fig. 232). In this grave were also a few shell beads.

Burial No. 42, near Burial No. 39, resembled it in being a large grave below the base, but while No. 39 had a few clam-shells only, scattered here and there above it, this grave was filled in with almost a solid mass of them. The grave contained the flexed skeletons of two adults and the bones of an infant or child, badly crushed, with which was the tooth of a fossil shark, 2 inches long, perforated for use as a pendant.

Burial No. 54, a bunch of bones belonging to an adolescent, had inverted over the skull a perforated shell drinking cup.

With Burial No. 72, bones which fell in caving sand, were fragments of a sheet copper ornament corroded through and through.

With other burials were hammer-stones, hones, pebbles, masses of chert and five or six arrowheads or knives, one of chalcedony, one of quartzite, the remainder of chert.

Also in the mound, in caving sand, so that the proximity to bones could not be

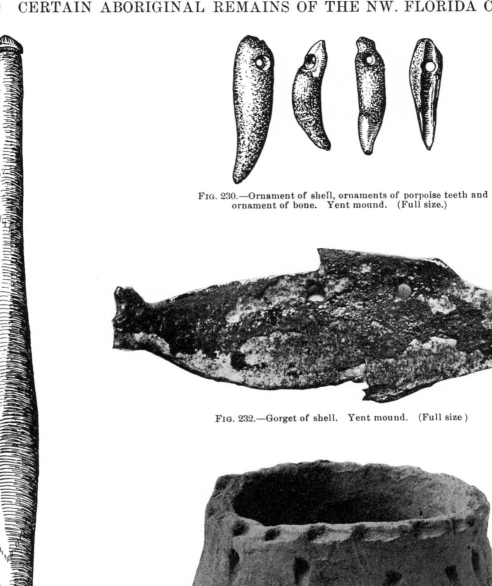

FIG. 230.—Ornament of shell, ornaments of porpoise teeth and ornament of bone.   Yent mound.   (Full size.)

FIG. 232.—Gorget of shell.   Yent mound.   (Full size)

FIG. 231.—Pendent ornament of stone.   Yent mound. (Full size.)

FIG. 233.—Vessel No. 22.   Yent mound.   (About full size.)

determined, or in undisturbed sand with no bones present, though they may have gone through decay, were, singly or associated in considerable numbers: masses of chert; rounded hammer-stones of chert; hones of sand-stone; pebbles; pebble-hammers; smoothing stones; a mass of quartz, roughly chipped; several arrowheads or knives; a handsome pendant 4.5 inches long, similar to the others we have described; part of a "Monitor" pipe of soapstone, highly polished; a pendant chipped from a quartz pebble; a demijohn-shaped pendant made of ferruginous claystone; a globular pendant with an arm for suspension projecting from either end; a rude globular pendant of hematite from which the grooved portion has broken; a globular pendant of decomposed material; a barbed lancepoint of brown chert, somewhat over 4 inches in length; a knife of light-brown chert, with curved cutting edge, nearly 9 inches long, from which about 1 inch of the point is missing; shell drinking cups; an ornament of ferruginous sandstone, about 2.5 inches long and 1.5 inches broad, flat on one side, convex on the other, with an unfinished perforation on either face below the middle of one of the longer sides; rude discs of shell; three shark's teeth of the present geological period, two with perforations; double pointed instruments made from axes of marine univalves; three small fossil shark's teeth without perforations; a sheet of mica, rudely given the outline of a lancepoint; rectangular masses of silicified fossil wood, 7 or 8 inches in length, determined by Mr. Lewis Woolman of The Academy of Natural Sciences of Philadelphia, to have belonged to a coniferous tree. One of these was roughly sharpened to a cutting edge; the others had seen service as pestles or hammers.

The earthenware in this mound, of which sixty-seven specimens were noted by us, discarding parts of vessels and heaps of sherds, consisted of common types and of inferior ware. The vessels lay, as a rule, near the base, often numbers together. The first deposit was found at the very margin of the ENE. part of the mound. Later, a considerable deposit lay somewhat in from the margin in the SW. side, while here and there single vessels were encountered throughout the mound. Numbers of vessels lay near the center, short distances apart.

The majority of vessels, undecorated, or with a complicated stamp applied in a faint and slovenly manner, were dropping to pieces when removed. Incised decoration was met with in but five instances and of these but one showed earnestness of endeavor. The features of the earthenware of the mound were the presence of four feet on a large percentage of the vessels and the number of toy pots and bowls found singly, here and there, in the sand, one of which had a diameter of but 1.5 inches.

With but few exceptions all vessels had the basal perforation.

Vessel No. 19.—Small, undecorated, imperforate.

Vessel No. 20.—A toy vessel of very coarse ware, with four feet and rude incised decoration.

Vessel No. 21.—An undecorated vessel of common type, with four feet and notches around the rim, imperforate.

Vessel No. 22.—A cup of heavy ware, with flat, circular base and inward slope to the sides. The decoration consists of punctate impressions around the rim and, a short distance apart, series of upright parallel rows of punctate markings (Fig. 233.)

Vessel No. 28.—A bowl of ware more solid than that of the majority from this mound. The incised decoration is shown in diagram in Fig. 234.

Vessel No. 31.—A vase of rough inferior material, with four feet. The body consists of four *repoussé* lobes. The neck, upright, flares slightly near the margin. There is no decoration.

Vessel No. 37.—A toy bowl having below the rim an encircling incised line with parallel incised perpendicular lines between it and the rim.

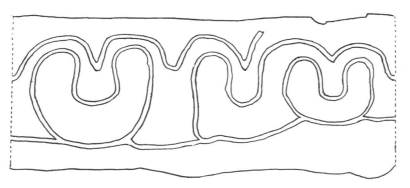

FIG. 234.—Vessel No. 28. Decoration. Yent mound. (Half size.)

FIG. 235.—Vessel No. 40. Yent mound. (Half size.)

Vessel No. 40.—Cylindrical with flat base, and rim .4 of an inch wide extending horizontally. There are perforations on opposite sides for suspension (Fig. 235).

FIG. 236.—Vessel No. 45. Yent mound. (About full size.)

Vessel No. 45.—A graceful vase of yellow ware, whose basal perforation has removed one of its four feet. The rim is crimped. The decoration consists of perpendicular parallel bands made up of incised crescentic markings (Fig. 236).

FIG. 237.—Vessel No. 55. Yent mound. (Half size.)   FIG. 238.—Vessel No. 62. Yent mound. (Half size.)

Vessel No. 55.—A vessel of ware so solid that three heavy blows of a spade chipped but did not shatter. The form is nearly globular with a certain elongation at one side. The aperture, near which are two holes for suspension on opposite

FIG. 240.—Sherd. Yent mound. (Three-fourths size.)

FIG. 239.—Vessel No. 67. Yent mound. (Full size.)

35 JOURN. A. N. S. PHILA., VOL. XII.

sides, is but .8 of an inch in diameter. The decoration, incised and punctate, with light-colored material inset, consists of a rudely executed design, evidently symbolical, four times repeated (Fig. 237). Height, 4.2 inches; maximum diameter, 4.5 inches.

Vessel No. 62.—A vessel of inferior ware, with four feet. The decoration seemingly is cord-marked (Fig. 238).

Vessel No. 67.—The most carefully decorated vessel in the mound, with flat base on which the decoration on the body is continued. A part of the body and neck, missing when found, has been restored (Fig. 239).

A sherd from this mound is shown in Fig. 240.

MOUND ON MARSH ISLAND, WAKULLA COUNTY.

Marsh Island is the northeastern boundary of Ocklockonee bay. The mound was in full sight of the water about 100 yards distant, on property of the Rayker family of Crawfordville, Fla. The usual deep excavations near the mound were present and extensive shell deposits were in the neighborhood.

The mound, which gave little evidence of previous digging, oblong with rounded corners, was 96 feet through the base in an easterly and westerly direction, 68 feet in a northerly and southerly, and had a height of 7 feet. The mound was entirely demolished by us.

Human remains were present at 106 points and their discovery began at the very margin of different parts of the mound. Many burials lay in the eastern portion, but interments in graves below the base were much more numerous on the western side. But few burials were met with in the northern and southern parts of the mound.

There were twenty-five lone skulls, some in little graves of their own below the base, and, in two instances, two skulls lay together without other bones. The flexed burial was met with in twenty-eight instances and the bunch was present forty-four times, counting under this heading masses of bones indiscriminately mixed, including numbers of skulls. There were also several disturbances of remains, probably aboriginal, and cases where bones fell in caved sand before the form of burial was determined. There was also one urn burial.

The question of cranial flattening in this mound will be discussed later.

Thirteen burials lay under oyster-shells sometimes few in number, sometimes in a solid mass. Noteworthy burials, including all associated with artifacts, were as follows:

Burial No. 20—A lone skull had with it a graceful "celt."

Burial No. 24 had a bit of chert in association.

Burial No. 37, a flexed skeleton, lay in a grave below the base. With it was a mass of plumbago, deeply pitted.

Burial No. 38.—A lone skull lay with a "celt."

Burial No. 51, in a grave beneath oyster-shells, consisted of three flexed skeletons, two on the same level, one somewhat above. With them was the knucklebone of a deer.

Burial No. 59, a mass of bones including fourteen femurs and four skulls.

Burial No. 66, a flexed skeleton, had with it a bit of plumbago.

Burial No. 70, four skulls and a lot of long-bones, 2.5 feet below the surface. With them were a pair of scissors and other articles, of iron or steel, badly rusted, glass beads, one large shell bead, one copper or brass sleigh-bell, eleven tubular beads of sheet brass, with overlapping edges. Dr. Harry F. Keller, who made a qualitative analysis of one of these beads, writes: "The tube surrounding the cord is brass. Beside a large proportion of zinc, it contains considerable quantities of lead, silver and iron."

Burial No. 85, about 2.5 feet down, had seven skulls and eighteen femurs with other bones. One small glass bead lay with them and doubtless others were in the sand.

Burial No. 92, had seven skulls with other bones. Articles of iron and of steel were in association.

Burial No. 93, a bunch, had a stone implement with a rude cutting edge, two pebbles and two pebble hammers.

Burial No. 104 had certain burnt and calcined human bones mixed with others unaffected by fire. Above, in the sand, extending a considerable distance upward were masses of charcoal. This may have been a case of cremation or of proximity to ceremonial flames.

Burial No. 105, near the surface, had eleven skulls and many other bones. With them were three copper or brass sleigh-bells, articles of rusted iron or steel and three shell hair-pins.

Burial No. 91, a true urn-burial, was of much interest to us, in that it carried the occurence of the custom so much farther east in Florida.

About 3 feet from the surface, that is to say 3 feet to where the base of the under vessel rested, was an imperforate bowl of solid, but rather coarse ware, 6.75 inches high and 10.75 inches in maximum diameter. The decoration, incised, is carelessly executed. Within the bowl were the bones of an infant. Around each humerus was a bracelet of sheet brass, about 2.25 inches in diameter and 2 inches wide, having two perforations on either side to regulate the diameter by aid of a cord or sinew. Over the bowl, inverted, was another bowl of similar ware and with decoration as carelessly done, imperforate, with two projections at either side. Maximum diameter, 12 inches; height, 4.7 inches (Fig. 241).

In the Marsh Island mound was shown in an interesting way, in our opinion, the use often made of a mound for intrusive burial. In this mound nearly all burials. lay below the base in graves or on the base, or not far above it but no burial of this class had with it a single object of European provenance.

Five burials came from near the surface and one from a pit whose base was 4 feet below the surface, but whose filling in from the surface down was clearly marked by admixture of masses of charcoal.

Of these six burials (we are omitting the urn-burial) four had with them various articles unmistakably obtained from the whites, and glass beads, which undoubtedly belonged to another of them, were found in the sand near where it had lain.   The sixth burial came from near the surface in much caved sand and associated objects could not be definitely located.

The 106 burials in the mound represented a great number of skulls.   Of these skulls a large percentage were so crushed that no determination as to flattening could be arrived at, but on no skull coming from on or near the base was any sign of flattening noticed, while the skulls belonging to the six burials to which we have already referred were as follows:

FIG. 241.—Urn-burial (Burial No. 91.)   Mound at Marsh Island.   (Half size.)

Burial No. 61.—One skull, flattened.

Burial No. 70.—Four skulls, all badly crushed.

Burial No. 85.—Seven skulls.   In the evening of the day when this burial was removed, while writing our amplified notes, we found no reference to cranial flattening in connection with this burial, in the note book used by us at the mound, but it was the strong impression of the one who removed the bones and of ourselves, who saw the bones removed, that such skulls as were not badly crushed, showed flattening and that our failure so to state in our notes was an omission, simply.

Burial No. 92.—Seven skulls, six of which showed flattening; the other was badly crushed.

Burial No. 104.—Three skulls, one flattened, two crushed.

Burial No. 105.—Six skulls flattened; five hopelessly crushed.

Here, then, we have clearly enough, superficial burials with flattened skulls and European artifacts on one hand, and on the other, original burials whose skulls showed no flattening and with which were no articles giving evidence of European contact.

Two "celts" fell in caved sand, doubtless from the neighborhood of human remains.

There were also in the mound, unassociated when found: a few fragments of chert; a small bit of plumbago; mica; scattered pebbles; a deposit of twenty-four pebbles, sling-stones, no doubt; pebble-hammers; hones; a bit of shell; a rude cutting implement; a handsomely made disc of quartzite, cup-shaped on either side, 3 inches in diameter, .85 of an inch in thickness. Each concavity has a depth of .25 of an inch. While objects of this sort are not uncommon in other parts of the country, this is the first found by us during our mound work.

Sand, pink from admixture of hematite, was in the mound in one or two places, unassociated with burials.

At the eastern margin of the mound were a few sherds, one of excellent ware, showing incised decoration. There were also parts of four vessels with practically similar ornamentation consisting of rude animal heads upright around the rim with incised lines and punctate markings below.

Four or five undecorated pots and bowls were found here and there in the mound, unassociated with human remains.

On the eastern side, 24 feet in from the margin, began a deposit of earthenware which, spreading a little to either side, continued in a distance of about 13 feet. These vessels, lying along the base in masses of black sand, as a rule away from human remains, had the basal perforation with three exceptions.

FIG. 242.—Vessel No. 1. Mound at Marsh Island. (Half size.)

Forty-four vessels were noted by us, accompanied by the usual sherds. The ware was most inferior, so porous in cases that water actually could be pressed from it.   The majority of vessels, entirely undecorated or bearing a faint complicated stamp, fell into bits on removal.   Incised decoration was most infrequently met with.

Vessel No. 1.—A bowl, with inverted rim, is of exceptionally good ware for this

FIG. 243.—Vessel No. 2.   Mound at Marsh Island.   (About two-thirds size.)

mound.   The decoration, incised, consists of six rude diamonds enclosing four formed by single incised lines and two by double ones.   Upright and central in each diamond, in a field of horizontal parallel straight lines is the emblem of the bird

Between the lower parts of the diamonds are triangles, sometimes of one line, sometimes of two, containing horizontal parallel lines.   Capacity about 1 quart (Fig. 242).

Vessel No. 2.—A ceremonial vessel of inferior ware, representing the head, body and tail of a bird.   In addition to the basal perforation made before the hardening of the clay, there are similarly constructed holes in the body of the vessel. The exterior surface has been covered with crimson paint (Fig. 243).   Height, 10.2 inches; maximum diameter, 6.5 inches.

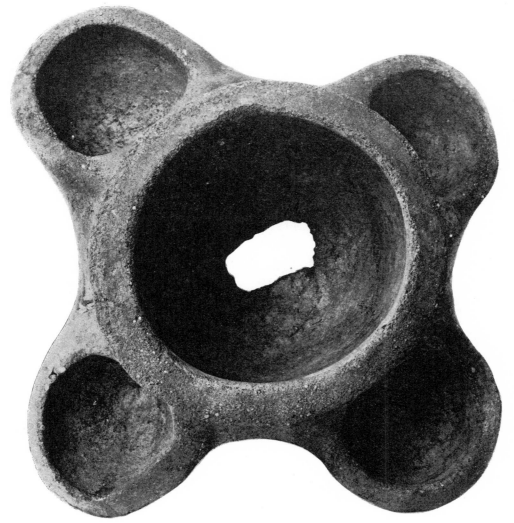

FIG. 244.—Vessel No. 20.   Mound at Marsh Island.   (Five-eighths size.)

Vessel No. 7.—A compartment vessel or part of one, found almost in a pulpy condition.

Vessel No. 8.—A large flattened sphere of red ware, undecorated, which crumbled to bits on removal.

Vessel No. 20.—A compartment vessel having a large central compartment rising above four smaller ones (Fig. 244).   A cross-section is shown in Fig. 245.

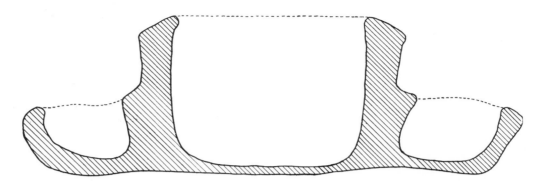

FIG. 245.—Vessel No. 20.   Vertical section.   Mound at Marsh Island.   (Half size.)

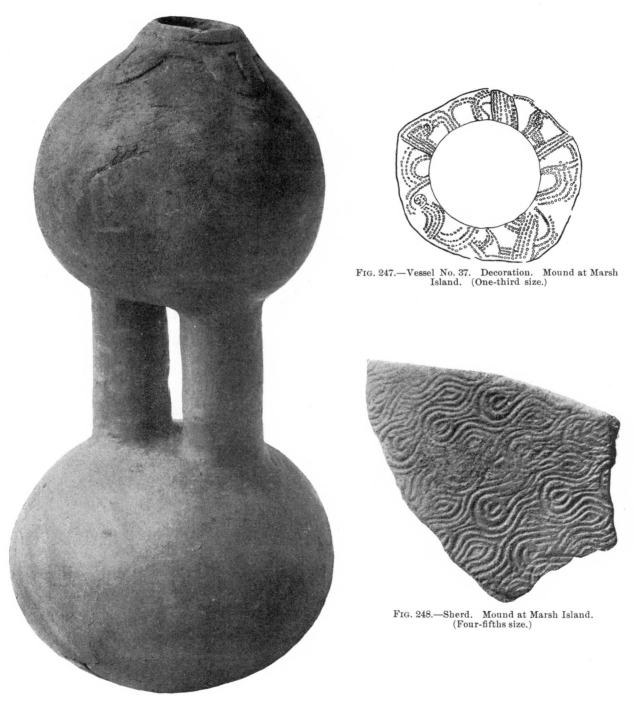

FIG. 247.—Vessel No. 37.   Decoration.   Mound at Marsh Island.   (One-third size.)

FIG. 248.—Sherd.   Mound at Marsh Island. (Four-fifths size.)

FIG. 246.—Vessel No. 34.   Mound at Marsh Island.   (About three-fourths size.)

Vessel No. 33.—A pot of yellow ware, of about 1 pint capacity with four encircling lines of oblong impressions below the rim.

Vessel No. 34.—Two parts of this vessel, having no surface indicating the former junction, were found some distance apart. The restoration is an arbitrary one as the length of the cylinders which joined the globular extremities could be estimated only (Fig. 246).

Vessel No. 36.—A large pot 15 inches across the mouth, which fell into bits before farther measurement could be obtained.

Vessel No. 37.—A vessel of ordinary form, with rude punctate markings below the rim, shown diagrammatically in Fig. 247.

A sherd from this mound with complicated stamp is shown in Fig. 248.

NICHOLS' MOUND, WAKULLA COUNTY.

The estate of Mr. Eli Nichols is situate on the north side of Ocklockonee bay near where the Sopchoppy river unites with the bay.

The principal mound, in a cultivated field not far from Mr. Nichols' residence, is about one-half mile from the landing, in a northerly direction.

The mound, which had suffered no digging except from insignificant efforts of children on the place, was 5.5 feet in height and had a basal diameter of 100 feet save to the SW. where a graded way 12 feet long and about 22 feet across, joined it.

It was our belief from the start that this mound, which covered an area disproportionate to its height and which had a great level summit plateau, had been made for domiciliary purposes. To assure ourselves of the fact, however, and to learn, it our surmise proved true, whether or not a dwelling site had been used for burial purposes, as we have sometimes found to be the case, twenty men on an average worked for two days on the mound, trenching in every direction.

The mound, of dark brown sand, had a thin layer of small clam-shells (*Rangia cuneata*) along the base and, beginning at a certain distance in, another layer of the same kind of shells, about 1 foot in thickness which, at the starting point, was about 1 foot below the surface but three times that depth at the center of the mound.

Burials were all superficial. In the slope and in the outer part of the summit plateau they lay just below the upper shell layer and in each case the layer had been cut through to bury them. In the more central part of the mound the burials lay above the shell layer.

Thirty-three burials were met with during the trenching. Twenty-two were closely flexed. One lay on the back with the knees flexed upward. Six were not exactly determined as to form of burial owing to disturbance either aboriginal in making another grave or by recent digging or by caving sand. Four lay at full length on the back, in each case the feet pointing toward the margin of the mound. Whenever skulls were in a condition to be examined artificial flattening was noted.

Burial No. 7.—A flexed skeleton had a femur the neck of which had formerly sustained a fracture. This bone was sent to the United States Army Medical Museum, Washington, D. C.

Three burials had each a "celt;" one had shell beads while with several were pebble-hammers and flakes of chert.

Unassociated and near the surface, as were all artifacts found in this mound, were three "celts," two together; a bit of chert, with a cutting edge; a mass of galena, considerably larger than a closed hand; a bit of chert, roughly rounded; an interesting finger-ring which seemed to us made from the vertebra of a large fish, as a small groove or band surrounded it. This ring was sent to Prof. F. A. Lucas of the National Museum who kindly devoted considerable time to it. Professor Lucas reports the ring to be a veritable puzzle. It is not bone or shell or vegetable ivory. "It is very likely some large palm seed like the so-called 'sea beans' that come to the Florida coast, and this would account for the curious band, almost continuous, that runs around the rim."

Several sherds were present in the mound, coming probably from midden refuse. The complicated stamp and the small check stamp were represented and there was also a handsome fragment of excellent ware decorated with a circular band of crimson, in which was a circle of punctate markings. One sherd bore a loop-shaped handle.

In sight of Mr. Nichols' house, in an easterly direction from it, was a low ridge in pine woods, seemingly of artificial origin. A few human bones and the base of an undecorated pot were the sole results of careful trenching.

In a field bordering the water, also belonging to Mr. Nichols, near the landing was a mound 34 feet across the base and 4 feet high, through which a small and shallow trench had been dug previous to our visit. In the neighborhood of the mound, both in the field and along the shore, are numerous deposits of shell, some of the oyster but mainly of a small clam (*Rangia cuneata*). All remaining parts of the mound were demolished by us without discovery of artifacts or burials.

This mound was made of mud, probably from the river, with a small admixture of sand and was so solid that picks and axes were employed in its demolition.

MOUND NEAR OCKLOCKONEE BAY, WAKULLA COUNTY.

At the southwestern extremity of Ocklockonee bay are ridges of sand unusually high for this level district. On one of these, at the top, is a mound about 18 inches high and 35 feet across approximately. It had been thoroughly dug into from all sides. Fragments of human bones and bits of aboriginal ware lay on the surface. No investigation was attempted by us.

HALL MOUND, PANACEA SPRINGS, WAKULLA COUNTY.

Panacea Springs, a health resort with many mineral springs, is at the head of King's bay, a part of Apalachee bay.

In pine woods and scrub, about 1 mile in a northeasterly direction from the landing at the Springs, near a large shell-heap, is a mound on property of Mr. Thomas H. Hall, the owner of the Springs, who resides on the place.

The mound, of circular outline, had a basal diameter of about 60 feet. A former excavation in the center of the summit plateau, though filled, seemingly had lessened the original altitude. At the time of our visit the mound was eight feet high. The excavation, the only one previous to our own, was circular with a diameter at the top of from 10 to 12 feet. At a depth of 4 feet it was 8 feet across. It had a diameter of 2 feet 5.5 feet down, where it ended. Joining the mound on the western side was a causeway 60 feet long, 24 feet of which was a graded ascent at the western end. The remainder of the causeway was level until its union with the mound. The causeway, about 5 feet in height, was 47 feet wide at the start, diminishing about 10 feet later, owing to great excavations on either side, whence sand for the causeway or mound had been taken.

The mound was totally demolished by us as was the causeway with the exception of the 24 feet of slope, which were trenched by six men without result save the discovery of a recent burial with parts of a coffin and nails.

We shall first take up the causeway. No burials were found in the marginal parts or in the sides. In the southwestern part, at the union of the slope with the flat surface, was a bunched burial near the base. About 30 feet in from the end of the causeway and about 5 feet from the surface, was a small bunch of bones including a skull. Near these lay two pendants, one of igneous rock, the other made from a quartz pebble, each about 2 inches in length. Their shape is roughly ellipsoidal, each with an extended end around which is a groove for suspension. Near the base, at different points, were two lone skulls.

Under the sloping sides of the causeway were several vessels from which considerable parts were missing. Had it not been that the basal perforation was present in them there would have been grounds to consider them broken and cast aside during the making of the mound.

A number of vessels, none equalling in excellence of ware or decoration the better vessels of the mound proper, were found in the main, or flat portion of the causeway. Some of these will be particularly described with the vessels from the mound proper.

There were also in the causeway one shell drinking cup and two masses of plumbago, deeply pitted.

In the mound proper, beginning at the very margin of the eastern side and confined almost exclusively to that side, were thirty-one burials, including, as to form, the flexed, the bunch, the lone skull. Several were too badly decayed to allow determination and several others came down in caved sand. So badly decayed were the bones that no whole skull or considerable part of a skull was met with, but careful examination of such fragments as were found, discovered no sign of flattening.

The custom to put oyster-shells over burials was chiefly honored in the breach in the Hall mound. Several burials had a few shells lying with them, but two or three only had masses of oyster-shells above them, such as we have found elsewhere.

Practically no artifacts lay with burials. It would seem as though friends of the departed, in placing the general tribute of earthenware, which we shall speak of later, considered themselves released from farther duties in the matter.

Near Burial No. 1, a small bunch with a few oyster-shells, were two "celts."

Burial No. 2, a few bones, had a small number of shell beads and beads were with Burial No. 12, a bunch.

Burial No. 3 had two earthenware vessels nearby but, as a general deposit of earthenware was in that part of the mound where the burial lay, the proximity may have been accidental.

A feature in the mound was the comparative absence of material ordinarily met with. The usual hones, masses of chert and the like were absent. There were found : one "celt" in caved sand ; two small masses of lead sulphide ; two pebble-hammers ; one smoothing stone ; one hammer-stone ; one bit of plumbago ; one perforated shell drinking cup. In a quantity of sand dyed with hematite, the only occurrence in the mound of the red oxide of iron noted by us, was a sheet of mica, shaped to resemble a lancehead.

Beginning at the very edge of the mound, almost due E., and extending slightly toward the N. and toward the S. as the digging advanced, was a deposit of earthenware unassociated with burials, on or near the base, in masses of dark sand sometimes almost of inky blackness. The result of the analysis of this sand is given elsewhere in this report.

This earthenware, as usual, was made up of vessels badly broken of which all parts were present; of single portions of vessels; and of fragments which, when put together, formed only part of a vessel. Here and there with these were specimens of unbroken ware.

Sixty-eight vessels or large parts of vessels, whole and broken, were noted by us in the mound and in the causeway. Had the average of excellence of ware and of workmanship of all vessels in the mound equalled that of the first twenty found by us and of the sherds among which they lay, the record of the mound would have been unique, since many pieces fully held their own with the best ware of the Gulf. As it is, the Hall mound may be considered to hold its own with any opened by us.

The occurrence of this excellent ware was during the digging of the first few feet and the entire deposit of earthenware, which had degenerated into ordinary types, undecorated or with the complicated stamp, practically ended at a point about 22 feet in from the margin, though a few vessels were met with later. All this deposit, so far as noted, had the basal perforation made before or after baking of the clay. There were present, however, here and there in various parts of the mound and of the causeway vessels near the surface or at all events much higher than the general deposit which, as we have stated, lay along the base. A few of these scattered vessels had the basal perforation, but the majority had not, ten having been found without it.

Among the sherds, near the margin of the mound, were many birdhead handles, and fragments of ceremonial vases through the bases and bodies of which perforations had been made before baking.

We shall now describe in detail the most noteworthy vessels from the Hall mound.

Vessel No. 1.—A bowl of excellent heavy yellow ware of about 3 pints capacity (Fig. 249), with complicated incised and punctate decoration consisting of two series, one on either side, separated by undecorated spaces (diagram, Fig. 250).

FIG. 249.—Vessel No. 1.   Hall mound.   (Full size.)

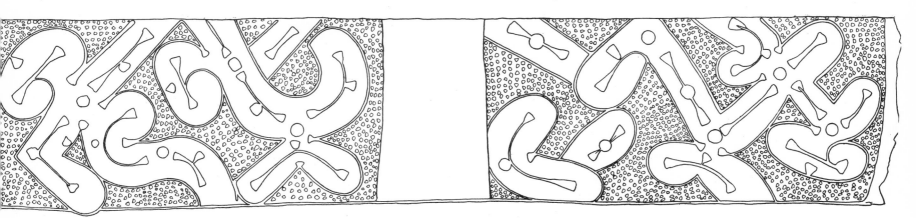

FIG. 250.—Vessel No. 1.   Decoration.   Hall mound.   (Half size.)

Vessel No. 3.—A vase of interesting shape having three lobes joined by a cylinder to a much flattened sphere (Fig. 251). The decoration, incised and punctate, is practically the same on two of the lobes, with a certain variation on the third.

FIG. 251.—Vessel No. 3. Hall mound. (About full size.)

On the upper part of the vessel the design is repeated on the opposite side. There have been two holes for suspension. Height, 6.5 inches; maximum diameter, 5 inches.

Vessel No. 5.—A bowl of about 2 gallons capacity, found crushed but since put

together.   There is incised decoration on the upper part of the body as shown in
Fig. 252.

Vessel No. 6.—Near the surface was a vessel of thick ware, made up of two circular compartments, one higher and broader than the other.   Both are perforated
(Fig. 253).

FIG. 252.—Vessel No. 5. Hall mound. (One-third size.)

Vessel No. 7.—A cylindrical body surmounted by a bird-effigy.   The wings,
repoussé, are decorated with the symbol of the bird.   The head, that of a duck, is
rather rudely done.   The tail projects.   This vessel belongs to the class made
expressly for burial with the dead, having a hole in the base and four triangular

FIG. 253. Vessel No. 6. Hall mound. (Full size.)

holes in the body made when the clay was soft (Fig. 254).   Height, 9 inches; maximum diameter of body, 7.7 inches.

Vessel No. 8.—A much flattened sphere of yellow ware with circular aperture originally about 1 inch in diameter, but now elongated on two sides owing to the breaking away of the margin on either side by a cord or sinew used for suspension.

FIG. 254.—Vessel No. 7.   Hall mound.   (About three-fourths size.)

The decoration, shown in Fig. 255, is rudely executed. A material, probably yellow clay, has been inset in the line and punctate markings.

Vessel No. 10.—A bird-effigy vessel with the upper part of the body and head missing, when found. The body has since been restored and a head found not far distant in the mound, and seemingly belonging to the vessel, has been added. The ware is inferior. The outside has a covering of crimson paint. Throughout the body are triangular holes made before baking, as was the small triangular one in the base (Fig. 256).

FIG. 255.—Vessel No. 8. Hall mound. (About five-sixths size.)

Vessel No. 11.—A bowl of about 2 gallons capacity has four incised designs, those on opposite sides being similar. The two different designs are shown diagrammatically in Fig. 257.

Vessel No. 12.—An oblate-spheroidal body with upright neck (Fig. 258). The decoration, incised to an unusual depth, complicated and interesting, is shown diagrammatically in Fig. 259. It will be remarked that seven groupings running downward resemble each other, with minor points of difference only, and that three groupings extending upward are also much alike, though not entirely so. There are four blank spaces which the aboriginal artist, presumably, did not take time to fill. The vessel, found crushed into many fragments, has been carefully cemented together.

Vessel No. 13.—This vessel, a bird-effigy, belonging to the ready-made mortuary variety, had, when found, a considerable part of the body and tail broken and

absent.   These portions have since been restored (Fig. 260).   Around the lower part
of the vessel is a rattlesnake in relief, given diagrammatically in Fig. 261, with
head, rattles and button distinctly shown.   On the head and tail of the reptile are
symbols of the bird.   While these may be intended to designate the plumed serpent,

Fig. 256.—Vessel No. 10. Hall mound. (About two-thirds size.)

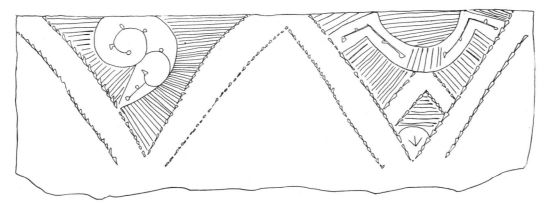

FIG. 257.—Vessel No. 11.   Decoration.   Hall mound.   (One-third size.)

FIG. 258.—Vessel No. 12.   Hall mound.   (Half size.)

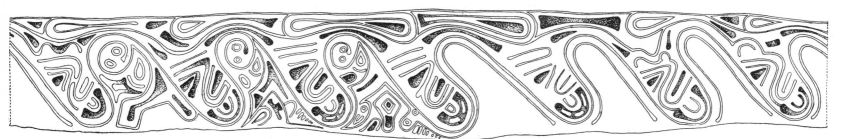

FIG. 259.—Vessel No. 12.   Decoration.   Hall mound.   (One-third size.)

FIG. 260.—Vessel No. 13.   Hall mound.   (About three-fifths size.)

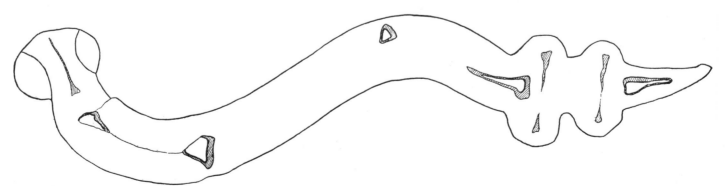

FIG. 261.—Vessel No. 13.   Decoration.   Hall mound.   (Half size.)

which is sometimes depicted in aboriginal art,[1] yet, as we have stated, Professor Holmes has shown that the aborigines were not always consistent in their decorations. Hence the bird symbol in this case may have been used as an ornament solely. In the former part of this report, we spoke of the reverence shown the rattlesnake by Florida Indians, as recounted by William Bartram, and cited the statement by Captain Romans, when writing on Florida, that he had never seen a savage wittingly injure a snake. Adair speaks of the veneration of southern Indians for the serpent and we are told how the aborigines of the St. Johns river, Florida, treated with every mark of respect the head of a serpent cut off by a soldier of de Gourgues.[2]

FIG. 263.—Vessel No. 16.   Decoration. Hall mound.   (Half size.)

FIG. 262.—Vessel No. 16.   Hall mound.   (Half size.)

Vessel No. 16.—A quadrilateral cup with rounded corners and curved rim. Part of the base, which has been flat, is missing (Fig. 262). The decoration shown in the half-tone is uniform throughout, save at one place, where a species of trefoil occurs (diagram, Fig. 263).

Vessel No. 17.—A vase of about six quarts capacity, of excellent yellow ware, having a carefully executed incised decoration as shown in Fig. 264. On the rim are four projections, perhaps rudimentary effigy-handles.

Vessel No. 20.—Another example of ready-made mortuary ware of the usual half-baked clay. In form the vessel is an inverted truncated cone having above it an effigy of a horned owl. The wings, broken in parts, when found, have been. cemented, with missing portions restored. There are a ready-made perforation of base and triangular openings at various places in the body of the vessel (Figs. 265, 266).

Vessel No. 26.—This vessel, with imperforate flat base, fell with caving sand. In form the vessel is a truncated pyramid inverted. The rim, which has slight incised

[1] Two superb examples of the highly conventionalized plumed serpent were found by us engraved on vessels in a mound in Cooper's field, not far from Darien, Ga., and are described in our "Certain Aboriginal Mounds of the Georgia Coast."

[2] "La Reprinse de la Floride," par le Capitaine Gourgues. Cited by Brinton.

decoration, projects somewhat inside and out. The decoration, incised, consists of series of parallel lines, three such series on one side, four on the side shown in Fig. 267. There are two perforations below the rim on the same side.

Vessel No. 27.—An imperforate compartment vessel which fell with caving sand, presumably from a superficial part of the mound. A central compartment rises above four surrounding ones (Fig. 268).

Vessel No. 28.—A vessel of 6 quarts capacity, quadrilateral with rounded corners and square imperforate base, slightly concave. The decoration consists of an incised encircling line below the rim. This vessel fell with Vessel No. 27.

FIG. 264.—Vessel No. 17. Hall mound. (Six-sevenths size.)

FIG. 265.—Vessel No. 20.   Front view.   Hall mound.   (Six-sevenths size.)

Vessel No. 30.—Of eccentric form, undecorated (Fig. 269).   Height, 8.8 inches; maximum diameter, 5 inches.

Vessel No. 32.—From near the surface came an interesting imperforate vessel having a large circular compartment raised above three others with a fourth com-

FIG. 266.—Vessel No. 20. Side view. Hall mound. (About seven-tenths size.)

partment missing.   This vessel, we believe, has been a life-form, a semi-circular compartment at either side of the main one standing for wings, while a more pointed one behind indicates the tail.   Unfortunately, the compartment representing the head is the missing one.

FIG. 267.—Vessel No. 26.   Hall mound.   (Half size.)

Vessel No. 35.—A cylindrical vessel of yellow ware of about 2 quarts capacity, the decoration consisting of an arrangement of zigzag bands and diamond-shaped figures (Fig. 270).   Certain bands and the larger diamonds are the yellow color of the ware, while other bands and the smaller diamonds are colored crimson.   This vessel somewhat recalls many others of the same shape recently found in southwestern United States.

Vessel No. 39.—A hemispherical body and constricted neck around which runs a band of complicated stamp decoration (Fig. 271).

Vessel No. 42.—A pot of about 3 quarts capacity, having a complicated stamp decoration as shown in Fig. 272.

Vessel No. 50.—Quadrilateral with square, imperforate base and constricted neck.   Around the upper part of the body is a band of complicated stamp decoration about 1.5 inches broad.   This vessel fell from near the surface in caving sand.

Vessel No. 53.—A vessel of solid yellow ware with flat imperforate base, with decoration consisting of designs each composed of three concentric triangles, the inner one in each case being deeply cut.   There are two holes on opposite sides for suspension (Fig. 273).

Vessel No. 57.—A vessel of about 3 pints capacity, undecorated save for a graceful scallop around the rim.

Vessel No. 63.—Has three compartments as shown in Fig. 274.   The ware is unusually heavy.   This vessel, which is imperforate, came from caving sand in the causeway.   Length, 8.5 inches; height, 1.7 inches.

Vessel No. 64.—An effigy of the human figure from the waist down, parts of which were missing when found, the remainder having been restored.   This may have been an entire figure which, broken later, has had the irregular margin of the fracture smoothed down to allow the remainder of the vessel still to be of use (Fig. 275).

Vessel No. 65.—This bowl, of inferior ware, found badly broken in the causeway, is of interest in that it presents a combination consisting of a decoration in relief beneath the rim and a faint complicated stamp extending 2 inches farther below (Fig. 276).

With Burial No. 23, in a pit below the base, were two skulls at opposite sides of the grave.   With them was a large effigy of the head of a horned owl, colored crimson, broken from a vessel, no parts of which were present in the grave.   The pointed horns have the inner portion excised (Fig. 277).

In Figs. 278, 279, 280 are shown three bird-head handles found unassociated in the mound.

In Fig. 281 is given part of a vessel from this mound which has had beautifully incised decoration, in part representing wings with the symbol of the bird.   Side by side on the fragment, are two heads probably modelled after that of a vulture.   The

FIG. 268.—Vessel No. 27.   Hall mound.   (About five-sixths size.)

bill of one, missing when found, has been restored.   In the heads, which are hollow, are small objects which rattle when shaken.

FIG. 269.—Vessel No. 30.   Hall mound.   (Five-sixths size.)

The lower part of a vessel, from which certain parts were missing, badly broken, has been cemented together and proves to have belonged to a vessel in all probability similar to No. 13 from this mound.   Around this fragment winds a rattlesnake in relief whose body twists twice upon itself. Restored portions of the serpent are shown in broken lines (diagram, Fig. 282).

An effigy of the human head, in relief, covered with crimson paint, which has projected from the rim of a vessel, was found alone in the mound in the sand near the surface. No fragments were in association nor was any part of a vessel found later, from which it seemed that this head might have come. This fact is much to be regretted as the modelling of the head is excellent (Fig. 283). A part of one cheek and a portion of the nose received blows from a spade.

FIG. 271.—Vessel No. 39. Hall mound. (Half size.)

FIG. 270.—Vessel No. 35. Hall mound. (Four-fifths size.)

FIG. 272.—Vessel No. 42. Hall mound. (Half size.)

FIG. 273.—Vessel No. 53. Hall mound. (Half size.)

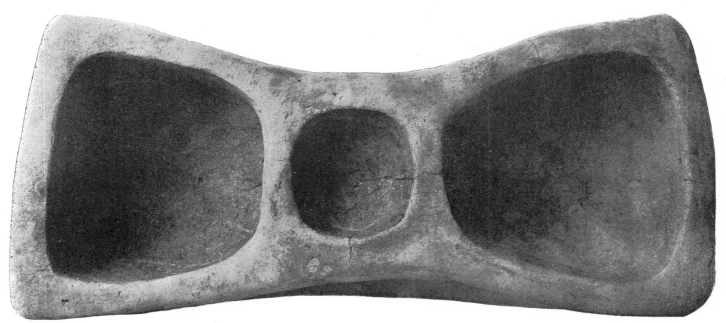

FIG. 274.—Vessel No. 63. Hall mound. (Five-sixths size.)

FIG. 275.—Vessel No. 64. Hall mound. (Half size.)

FIG. 276.—Vessel No. 65. Hall mound. (Two-fifths size.)

FIG. 277.—Handle of vessel. Hall mound. (About full size.)

FIG. 278.—Handle of vessel. Hall mound.
(About two-thirds size.)

FIG. 279.—Handle of vessel. Hall mound.
(About two-thirds size.)

FIG. 280.—Handle of vessel. Hall
mound. (Three-fourths size.)

FIG. 281.—Sherd. Hall mound. (Half size.)

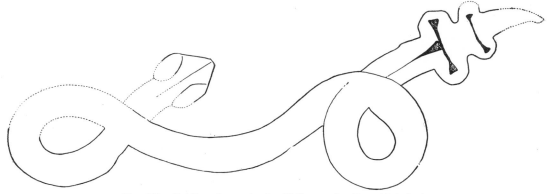

FIG. 282.—Rattlesnake on sherd. Hall mound. (One-third size.)

FIG. 283.—Handle of vessel. Hall mound. (Full size.)

MOUND AT PANACEA SPRINGS, WAKULLA COUNTY.

This mound, in full view of the landing at the Springs, has a height of 4 feet and a basal diameter of 75 feet, approximately.   It had been badly dug into before our visit.

It was examined by us with permission of Mr. Hall, owner of the large mound in the neighborhood.

Many trenches showed the mound to have been domiciliary in character. Except at one place, where, for a considerable area and depth, it was red from the action of a large and long-continued fire, the material of the mound was black, but not of the same character as the dark sand found with mortuary deposits in other mounds, this material being probably from low-lying ground nearby.

MOUND NEAR SPRING CREEK, WAKULLA COUNTY.

Spring creek runs into Oyster bay, a part of Apalachee bay.   The landing on Spring creek is where the great springs, which give the creek its name, pour into it.

This mound, in hammock, on property of Mr. N. R. Walker of Crawfordville, Fla., is somewhat over one mile in a northeasterly direction from the landing at the springs in Spring creek.

The mound, in the form of a ridge, slopes gently upward from E. to W., attaining its greatest height, 8 feet, near the western end, after which the ascent is comparatively abrupt.   The diameter of base, longitudinally, is 104 feet; transversely it is 68 feet.   The mound, which was seemingly intact, had various deep depressions along its margin, whence sand had come for use in its construction.

Twenty-five men digging two days, first went through marginal parts without result of interest, and then gridironed the mound with trenches in all directions.

No general deposit of earthenware was met with and only nine burials were encountered.   It was clear to us that many interments must have disappeared from the mound through decay since so few were met with, and also because a number of objects were found unassociated with human remains, but lying in pockets of dark-colored sand where presumably bones had been.   Such objects included: an elongated, pear-shaped pendant; mica in a number of places, some sheets rudely given the outline of lanceheads; half of a gorget; two pendants and part of one, lying together; a slab of fossilized wood; and the usual quota of bits of chert, hammer-stones, pebble-hammers and the like.

Near the margin was a rude, undecorated pot with the basal perforation. Parts of the rim were missing.

Near the surface, at different points, were two undecorated bowls, badly broken.

About 4 feet from the surface, at the western end, where the mound was highest, were two oblate spheroids of earthenware, evidently parts of the same vessel.   The lower one, imperforate, is undecorated.   The upper one has a neat, uniform design, the incised lines and punctate markings of which are filled with a yellow material as shown in Fig. 284.   We cannot say to a certainty that the vessel was originally as shown in the figure as the margins of the fracture had been carefully smoothed and offered no surface into which the parts could be fitted.

We shall give the burials in detail.

Burial No. 1.—A few crowns of human teeth, with two rude arrowheads; three bits of sandstone; one pebble, flat, oblong, with corners evidently artificially rounded; a rude smoking pipe of clay, of ordinary type.

Burial No. 2.—A few human teeth.

Burial No. 3.—Two small fragments of bone with two sheet-copper earplugs having central bosses in concave spaces. The reader will recall that with earplugs found by us in the mound at Huckleberry Landing were discs of pottery which,

going back of the lobes of the ears, held the copper discs in place. Presumably discs answering the same purpose as the pottery ones, in this case, had been made of wood.

Burial No. 4.—Fragments of bone, with crowns of human teeth. With these were: a pebble; a bit of sandstone; an arrowhead or knife, of chert; a small fragment of some implement or ornament.

Burial No. 5.—A few fragments of human bones, with a chip of chert; an arrowhead or knife, of chert; a small curved knife and a lancehead, of the same material; and one pebble.

Burial No. 6.—Traces of bone, with two decayed bits of shell, a pebble and part of a shell drinking cup.

Burial No. 7.—Fragments of bone, with a coarsely-made

FIG. 234.—Vessel of earthenware. Mound near Spring Creek. (Full size.)

smoking pipe; the lower half of a "celt"; a fragment of shell; a much decayed shell gouge; a double-pointed implement made from the columella of a marine univalve.

Burial No. 8.—Traces of bones, with an unevenly made pendant of ordinary type.

Burial No. 9.—A few bits of bone, with a soapstone smoking pipe of the usual shape; a pebble; a shark's tooth of the present geological period.

Mound near the Mound Field, Wakulla County.

The mound, very symmetrical, was in hammock land on the border of cultivated ground known throughout the region as the Mound Field. The mound was about two miles in NE. direction from the landing on Spring creek, on property belonging to Mr. N. R. Walker, the owner of the Spring creek mound.

The mound had a height of about 9 feet above the surrounding level, though a measurement taken when the mound was in process of demolition, from the summit plateau to undisturbed sand at the base, gave an altitude of about 11 feet.

The outline of the base was circular, with a diameter of 61 feet. Across the the summit plateau was 15 feet. A graded way about 15 feet wide joined the mound on the west, making the slope less steep on that side than on the others. The length of the causeway before union with the margin of the mound was 18 feet.

There had been but little previous digging in the mound which, with the exception of a small portion under two great trees, was thoroughly leveled by us.

Burials were found in twenty one places only, all in the eastern half of the mound, and included the bunch, the single skull, and, on several occasions, two skulls lying side by side. All these burials but two were near the surface, and all were so badly decayed that no determination as to cranial flattening was possible. Two, from near the base, consisted of a bit of femur in one place and two decaying long-bones in another. As the mound throughout was composed of dark, rich, loamy sand and the undisturbed sand beneath was dark brown, we feared, in the early stages of the digging, that we might have passed over graves beneath the base, so few burials were met with. The comparative absence of burials in the body of the mound, however, and the fragmentary condition of those which were found, added to the fact that a great area of the base was dug through to sand unmistakably undisturbed, convinced us that burials were not being passed over. We believe that such burials as may not have been found in the mound and in graves below it, had disappeared through decay.

With the exception of a bit of femur which lay near a vessel of earthenware, perhaps belonging to a pottery deposit, no artifacts were found with the dead.

Four "celts" lay near the surface, singly, as did a lancehead of chert. There were also in the mound : a large, flat pebble used for smoothing ; another flat pebble roughly chipped on two sides ; mica in several places ; and, together, a smoothing stone, a bit of sandstone and two rough chert arrowheads or knives.

Beginning in the eastern margin and extending to the center of the mound, along the base and just above it, was the usual deposit of earthenware.

In this deposit, fifty-eight vessels, all perforate but two or three, were noted, though many others, broken and scattered, must have escaped us. These vessels may be divided into five classes.

1.—Pots and bowls of ordinary form, mostly of moderate size or small, undecorated, the majority found broken or falling into bits on removal. This class outnumbered all the rest.

2.—Vessels of ordinary shape, with incised or punctate decoration, a small class with roughly executed work of simple pattern. A sherd, however, of most excellent ware, equalling anything we have found to the westward, was met with by us, as was part of a bowl, bearing a duck's head in relief and a carefully executed symbolical design (Fig. 285).

3.—Vessels of fairly good ware, small, as a rule, with encircling bands of com-

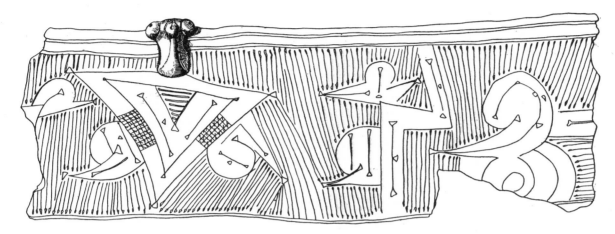

FIG. 285.—Sherd. Decoration. Mound near Mound Field. (Half size.)

FIG. 286.—Vessel No. 2. Mound near Mound Field. (Eight-ninths size.)

plicated stamp decoration below the rims.   None of this class, ten in all, was found until that part of the base was reached which lay beneath the summit plateau.   The decoration on most of these vessels had been executed with much greater care than was the case with the majority of those bearing this sort of decoration found by us

Fig. 287.—Vessel No. 7.   Mound near Mound Field.   (About two-thirds size.)

in other mounds and hence was more deeply impressed and lacked the confusion of design which arises from a double impression on parts of the decorated surface.

4.—This class was made up of vessels coated with crimson pigment, as a rule effigy-vessels, often of birds, and was of the ceremonial, or "freak," variety with basal holes made before the baking of the clay and with perforations of various shapes made at the same time through the body of the vessel.   This ware, whose destination was understood at the time of manufacture, and consequently was but half baked and most inferior, was recovered by us in masses of fragments only, some past restoration.

FIG. 288.—Vessel No. 27.   Mound near Mound Field.   (Two-thirds size.)

5.—Two effigy-vessels, of better ware than that of which the ceremonial vessels were made, did not belong to that class, as holes knocked through the bases after baking and absence of perforations in the bodies, clearly testified.   The aborigines had devoted more care to ware destined for their own use than to that turned out for the service of others in the "happy hunting grounds."   Human nature is ever the same.

The following vessels merit particular description.

FIG. 289.—Vessel No. 29.   Mound near Mound Field.   (Five-sixths size.)

Vessel No. 2.—A vessel of about 2 quarts capacity, of solid ware, with decoration of lines of punctate markings, starting from the rim and converging around an undecorated, elliptical space at the base (Fig. 286). There are perforations for suspension, one at either side of the rim.

Vessel No. 7.—An interesting vessel of the ceremonial variety, covered with crimson pigment, found crushed to fragments. It has been cemented together, with restoration of the tail and a small part of the body (Fig. 287). Maximum diameter, 8.3 inches; height, 9.4 inches.

FIG. 290.—Vessel No. 31. Mound near Mound Field. (Five-sixths size.)

Vessel No. 10.—A bowl of about 1 quart capacity, a part of the rim missing, with decoration much resembling that on Vessel No. 5 from the Hall mound.

Vessel No. 16.—A pot having below the rim two parallel, encircling lines containing parallel, perpendicular lines, all very rudely executed.

Vessel No. 22.—Parts of a ceremonial vessel past restoration, as were a number of others in this mound.

Vessel No. 23.—A bowl of about 1 pint capacity covered with crimson paint inside and out.

Vessel No. 27.—A trilateral bowl with rounded corners, of about 6 quarts capacity, having a small bird-head looking inward. The decoration, which includes the bird-symbol, consists of the two designs shown in the half-tone (Fig. 288) thrice repeated, with but slight modifications.

Vessel No. 29.—A ceremonial vessel with rounded base in the center of which is the usual ready-made perforation. There are also openings around the body. Vertically from the rim rises the head of an owl, from which the beak and part of an ear have scaled away (Fig. 289).

Fig. 291.—Vessel No. 33. Mound near Mound Field. (Half size.)

Fig. 292.—Vessel No. 36. Mound near Mound Field. (About two-thirds size.)

Fig. 293.—Vessel No. 36. Decoration. Mound near Mound Field. (One-third size.)

FIG. 294.—Vessel No. 37. Mound near Mound Field. (About two-thirds size.)

Fig. 295.—Vessel No. 39.   Mound near Mound Field.   (About four-fifths size.)

Fig. 296.—Vessel No. 42.   Mound near Mound Field.   (About five-sixths size.)

Vessel No. 30.—A bowl of about 1 quart capacity, decorated with crimson pigment, with bird-head at one end and conventional tail at the other. The wings are somewhat in relief and are farther indicated by incised lines and certain portions left free from the coloring of the rest of the vessel, showing the yellow ware. Part of the bill is missing. A hole has been knocked through the base.

Vessel No. 31.—Of about 2 quarts capacity, of solid ware but rather carelessly made, having eight *repoussé* ridges of irregular shapes and sizes around the body. The outside is covered with crimson pigment. A hole has been knocked through the base (Fig. 290).

FIG. 297.—Vessel No. 44. Mound near Mound Field. (Five-sixths size.)

Vessel No. 33.—Is of rather coarse ware, with a small bird seated on one side. There has been a certain amount of restoration (Fig. 291).

Vessel No. 36.—The upper part of a vessel of superior ware, shown in Fig. 292, heart-shaped in section, showing traces of crimson pigment, on the outside. The lower part of the vessel was vainly sought by us. The incised decoration is shown diagrammatically in Fig. 293.

FIG. 298.—Vessel No. 45. Mound near Mound Field. (Four-fifths size.)

Vessel No. 37.—This interesting vessel consists of a sphere flattened on one side, on which is placed an effigy of a horned owl. There is a perforation in the base, made before baking (Fig. 294). Height, 11.4 inches; maximum diameter, 10 inches.

Vessel No. 39.—A vessel of about 2 quarts capacity, with complicated stamp decoration around the neck (Fig. 295).

Vessel No. 42.—A vessel of good, solid ware, with complicated stamp decoration on the neck (Fig. 296).

Vessel No. 44.—An effigy-vessel of about 2 quarts capacity, representing an animal, probably a deer, judging from the horns, the cloven hoofs and the short tail. The hind-legs are *repoussé*, while the fore-legs, slightly *repoussé*, were made by the addition of material pressed upon the surface.   There is crimson pigment inside and out.   There are two holes for suspension and one knocked through the base. There has been a certain amount of restoration (Fig. 297).

Vessel No. 45.—An effigy-vessel representing a horned owl with head and tail protruding, and *repoussé* wings.   The vessel has been decorated with crimson pigment, while on the wings are perpendicular, incised lines filled with light-colored

FIG. 299.—Vessel No. 45.   Mound near Mound Field.   (Four-fifths size.)

material (Figs. 298, 299).   This vessel does not belong to the ready-made mortuary class as a hole has been broken through the base after completion of the vessel. Height, 8 inches ; maximum width, 10.5 inches.

Vessel No. 47.—A bird-effigy vessel with incised decoration on wings, tail and back.   The head is missing through an early fracture.   This vessel was made with open base (Fig. 300).

Vessel No. 50-—A cup of about 1 pint capacity with clearly defined complicated stamp decoration (Fig. 301).

Fig. 300.--Vessel No. 47.   Mound near Mound Field.   (Eight-ninths size.)

FIG. 301.—Vessel No. 50.   Mound near
Mound Field.   (Half size.)

FIG. 302.—Vessel No. 55.   Mound near Mound Field.   (One-third size.)

FIG. 303.—Vessel No. 56.   Mound near Mound Field.   (About eight-ninths size.)

Vessel No. 55.—A handsome bowl of excellent yellow ware, of about 3 gallons capacity, with encircling band of complicated stamp decoration, below the rim, which, of unusual shape, bears incised decoration (Fig. 302).

Vessel No. 56.—Has a distinct complicated stamp below the rim (Fig. 303).

There was in this mound part of a vessel of excellent ware carefully smoothed,

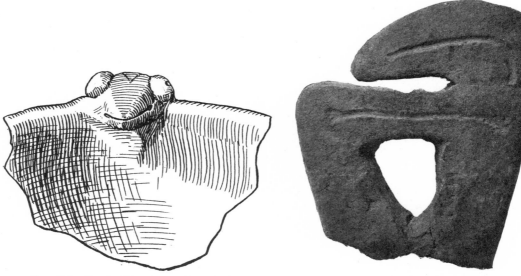

FIG. 304.—Sherd. Mound near Mound Field.
(Full size.)

FIG. 305.—Sherd. Mound near Mound Field.
(Three-fourths size.)

which, on the outside, has well executed incised decoration and the head of a duck in relief.   A curious feature of this head is that a part of it, projecting inward, has been given a mouth, which, taken in conjunction with the rear portion of the eyes belonging to the head in front, gives the appearance of the head of an animal (Fig. 304).

A part of a ceremonial vessel, found alone, has a highly conventionalized bird's head (Fig. 305).

MOUND NEAR ST. MARKS, WAKULLA COUNTY.

This mound is about 2 miles in a northeasterly direction from the light-house at the mouth of the St. Marks river, on ground formerly cultivated, the property of Mr. William Harrell, of St. Marks, Fla.

The mound is on an extensive ridge erroneously believed by many to be artificial.   There are considerable shell deposits in the neighborhood.   The mound, circular in outline, 3 feet high and 40 feet across the base, had been subjected to but little previous digging.   It was totally demolished by us.

Though the sand was dryer than that usually met with in mounds of this section, yet human remains were found by us in the mound but once, a bunch in the eastern margin.   Presumably a number of others had disappeared through decay.

In two places was much sand dyed with hematite.

Unassociated were two "celts" found separately, several sheets of mica, and a few pebbles. Three shell drinking cups, all perforate, lay with the earthenware deposit.

At the eastern edge of the mound began a deposit of earthenware, the usual sherds, large fragments and whole vessels, placed here and there in black sand along the base, through an area about 8 feet across, and continuing well in toward the center. Among the sherds the check stamp was represented, and various forms of punctate impressions as well as carefully incised work. Neither on sherd nor on vessel did the complicated stamp appear, which probably accounts for the considerable number of interesting vessels present in so small a mound.

FIG. 306.—Vessel No. 2. Mound near St. Marks. (Half size.)

Vessel No. 2.—A quadrilateral vessel of about 1 quart capacity, with rounded corners. The decoration is made up of punctate lines, and incised lines on the rim. On each of two opposite sides of the opening is a hole for suspension (Fig. 306).

Vessel No. 3.—A bowl with incised and punctate decoration included in four designs around the upper part of the vessel, with undecorated spaces between. The larger are almost identical, as are the smaller. One of each is shown diagrammatically in Fig. 307. Maximum diameter, 11.5 inches; height, 8.4 inches.

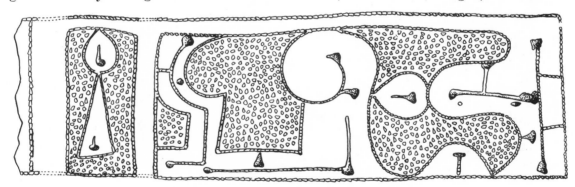

FIG. 307.—Vessel No. 3. Decoration. Mound near St. Marks. (Half size.)

Vessel No. 4.—A bowl of about 1 gallon capacity, of yellow ware, badly discolored, as were all vessels from this mound, with incised and punctate decoration almost identical on opposite sides (Fig. 308).

Vessel No. 6.—A four-lobed vessel with square aperture, shown in Fig. 309, having incised and punctate decoration almost identical on two opposite lobes, the remaining two being undecorated. There are holes for suspension.

FIG. 308.—Vessel No. 4. Mound near St. Marks. (Nine-tenths size.)

Vessel No. 7.—A bowl of about 3 quarts capacity, with inverted rim on which are two small protuberances probably indicating heads.   There are two designs, almost similar, with a smaller one between.   One of the larger and the small one are shown diagrammatically in Fig. 310.

Vessel No. 8.—A large undecorated bowl of heavy ware, with considerable thickening at the rim.

Vessel No. 9.—A vessel originally with five circular compartments, the central one above the rest.   One compartment is missing.   This vessel came from the western part of the mound, alone.

FIG. 309.—Vessel No. 6.   Mound near St. Marks.   (Eight-ninths size.)

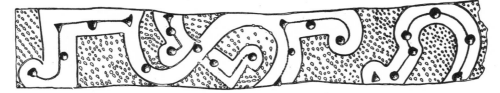

FIG. 310.—Vessel No. 7.   Decoration.   Mound near St. Marks.   (One-third size.)

Vessel No. 10.—This four-sided vessel of about 3 pints capacity, of yellow ware, deeply stained, has incised and punctate decoration consisting of four designs, all alike, on the corners and, on two sides, similar designs, one of which is shown in the half-tone (Fig. 311). The decoration is deeply stained and obscured. On two sides are heads of birds in relief, presumably of the ibis. Formerly the pink ibis, now

FIG. 311.—Vessel No. 10. Mound near St. Marks. (About full size.)

almost exterminated in Florida, was well known there and must have contributed largely to the head-dress of the warriors. At Stowe island, where the Sisters' creek enters the St. Johns, near the mouth of the river, were found, in the spring of 1895, in

the great shell-heap which was then being removed, human bones with large pink feathers in association, which probably belonged to the pink ibis. We inspected this discovery in person.

Vessel No. 11.—A four-lobed vessel of red ware, of about 2 quarts capacity. Two of these lobes have each three semicircular, parallel lines, while one has four. Under these lines, on one lobe, is additional decoration (Fig. 312).

Vessel No. 12.—A small undecorated bowl which came from the northern part of the mound, apart from the pottery deposit.

FIG. 312.—Vessel No. 11. Mound near St. Marks.
(One-third size.)

Vessel No. 13.—A quadrilateral bowl holding somewhat over 1 quart, having crimson pigment inside and out. The four corners of the rim project upward nearly one inch.

Vessel No. 14.—A four-lobed vessel found in fragments.

Vessels from this mound had the basal perforation.

Mound near the Aucilla River, Taylor County.

This mound, on property of Mr. B. F. Lewis, of Monticello, Florida, is in sight of the river, on the right hand side going up, about 2.5 miles from the mouth. A small stable of logs, with an enclosure in front, covers a part of the mound, beginning at the margin on the north side and extending well in to the summit plateau. The mound had been much worn by the trampling of animals, and probably by wash of water, as in time of freshet it is said to be the only place of refuge for stock in the vicinity. The height of the mound, at present, is 6.5 feet, though at one time it must have been considerably greater. The diameter of the base, 64 feet, has been

Fig. 313.—Handle. Mound near the Aucilla river. (Three-fourths size.)   Fig. 314. Vessel No. 1. Mound near the Aucilla river. (Full size.)

increased at the expense of the height. Over the surface of the mound, lying loose or half imbedded in it, are masses of lime rock, varying in size from that of a human head to irregular masses perhaps 1 foot by 2 feet by 1 foot. This lime rock is found off the shallow Florida coast, beginning east of St. Marks and in the small rivers which enter the Gulf, in that district.

As it was not our purpose to injure this place of refuge, our investigation was chiefly devoted to the eastern part of the mound, though other parts were accorded due attention.

The mound was curiously constructed, being made in the upper parts of clayey sand, black and tenacious, probably from adjacent swamps. Below this, varying from 1 to 2 feet in thickness, was a stratum of clay more densely packed as it approached the center, until, under the summit plateau, the removal necessitated the use of a mattock or of a grubbing-hoe.

Throughout that part of the mound investigated by us, sometimes near the base, but usually not far from the surface, were scattered masses of lime rock similar to those we have described. These masses, as we shall see, often accompanied burials, but sometimes they lay unassociated with human remains.

During our work, seventeen burials, much decayed, were met with in various parts of the mound. Of these, fourteen burials were near the present surface of the mound and three flexed burials, unaccompanied by rocks, lay almost on the base. Of the superficial burials, eight were bunched, lying under masses of rock, and four were of the same class of burial, without rocks. One flexed burial lay beneath rocks, while two skulls, together, were surrounded by them.

FIG. 315.—Vessel No. 3. Mound near the Aucilla river. (Nine-tenths size.)

With the exception of several bits of chert, no artifacts lay directly with the dead. Somewhat apart from them, separately, were: one chert arrowhead or knife; a lancehead or dagger, of chert, 4.5 inches long; many chips of chert, scatterd here and there; several perforated shell drinking cups. These cups lay with the pottery deposit and probably were considered mortuary vessels.

At a short distance from the margin of the mound, in the eastern part as usual, began a small deposit of earthenware with the usual sherds and portions of vessels. The sherds, in the main, were of excellent quality. The check stamp was represented but once or twice. There were also the effigy-head of a dog (Fig. 313) and one of an owl. Two large loop-shaped handles also were present. There was basal perforation in each entire vessel found by us.

The deposit lay along the base and numbered fourteen vessels or large parts of vessels. When our work was discontinued the deposit seemed to be ending and the fact that such vessels as might be found would lie in solid clay on which a mattock was used of necessity, rendered the ending of our work less of a disappointment.

FIG. 316.—Vessel No. 7. Mound near the Aucilla river. (About full size.)

Vessel No. 1.—A neat little cup with octagonal rim and carefully executed incised and punctate decoration, one-half of which, shown in Fig. 314, is duplicated on the opposite side.

Vessel No. 2.—Has a band of complicated stamp decoration below the rim.

Vessel No. 3.—A bird-effigy vessel of excellent ware, showing traces of decoration with crimson paint. There is also an incised and punctate design representing a wing, on either side, and markings on the tail. The head represents that of a

FIG. 317.—Vessel No. 8.   Mound near the Aucilla river.   (Four-fifths size.)

turkey or a turkey-buzzard.   In it are objects which rattle when shaken.   There are two holes for suspension (Fig. 315).   Diameter of body, 4.5 inches; height, 3.3 inches; length, 8.2 inches.

Vessel No. 5.—An undecorated bowl of yellow ware, of about 1 quart capacity. The base is flat.

Vessel No. 7.—A compartment vessel of inferior ware, with a small circular compartment near the center, surrounded by three others, two of which are oval in outline, the other, crescentic (Fig. 316).   This vessel may represent a face with eyes, nose and mouth.

Vessel No. 8.—This impressive looking bird-effigy vessel, with head disproportionately small, and extended wings (Fig. 317) has incised and punctate decoration on the tail, shown diagrammatically in Fig. 318.   Length, 11 inches; breadth, 12 inches; height, 8 inches;

Vessel No. 10.—This asymmetrical vessel of four compartments, has had three compartments in line, the central one square and raised somewhat above the other two, one of which has a curved margin. The other has a large portion missing (Fig. 319). The fourth compartment has the outline of a spread wing and would lead us to suppose that this was a compartment effigy-vessel, were a similar wing on the opposite side, but none is, or has been, there. Nevertheless, the vessel may be of the class we speak of, since the aborigines were not always consistent. In a low mound near Jacksonville, Florida,[1] we found a vessel with five compartments, which unquestionably represents a bird. The head, body, tail and wings are clearly outlined, yet the open wings point in opposite directions.

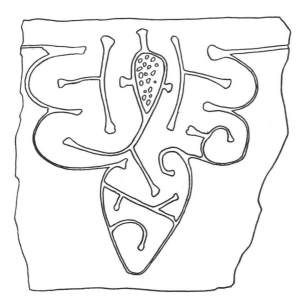

FIG. 318.—Vessel No. 8. Decoration of tail. Mound near the Aucilla river. (Half size.)

Vessel No. 11.—Somewhat over one-half of a vessel which had been made up of two hemispherical cups of solid ware, each of nearly one pint capacity.   The part found by us was imperforate.

Vessel No. 14.—A large pot with complicated stamp decoration, badly broken. Immediately above it lay a mass of lime rock.   We carefully examined the interior of this vessel for human remains, but found none.   As a similar mass of rock lay beside the pot it is probable that the presence of the two masses was accidental.

[1] "Additional Mounds of Duval and of Clay Counties, Florida."   Privately printed, Phila., 1896, pg. 13, Plates I and II.

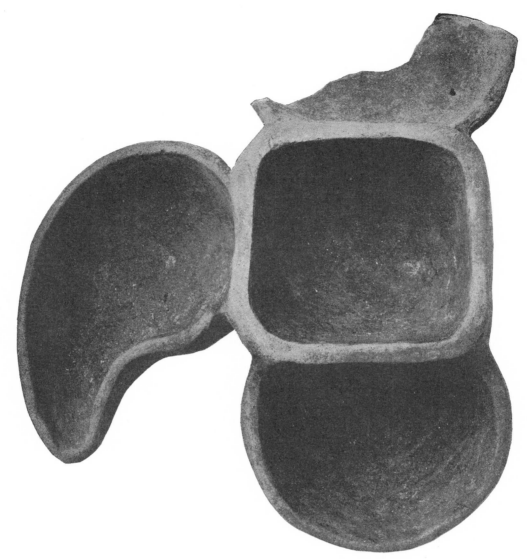

FIG. 319.—Vessel No. 10.   Mound near the Aucilla river.   (Three-fourths size.)

MOUNDS NEAR THE ECONFENEE RIVER, TAYLOR COUNTY.

About 200 yards in the hammock, in a northerly direction from the "fish-camp," which is about 3 miles up the Econfenee river, on the left hand side, going up, is a mound 3.5 feet high and 50 feet across the base. This mound, the only place of refuge for stock, from the water of storm tides, was occupied by a family who had erected a small house on a portion of the western part and an out-door kitchen on part of the eastern side.

The mound was carefully trenched, with the exception of the part on which the house stood, digging being carried on within the kitchen.

The mound, of white sand, yielded nothing in the way of artifacts with the exception of a pebble-hammer, an arrowhead or knife and several bits of chert.

In the western slope was a burial consisting of a skull and, at a short distance, the lower part of a skeleton with the feet, however, turned toward the skull. As the skull was small and the other bones were small and delicate, it is likely all belonged to the same individual.

About 1 mile farther up the river and 50 yards in, from the left bank going up, approximately, on the edge of hammock land was a mound 2 feet high and 32 feet across the base. Thorough trenching yielded nothing beyond a few masses of lime rock in the center of the mound.

MOUNDS NEAR THE WARRIOR RIVER, TAYLOR COUNTY. MOUND A.

These mounds, on property belonging to the East Coast Lumber Co., Watertown, Fla., John Paul, Esq., President, were in dense undergrowth near a tract formerly under cultivation, known as the Pope Field. This field is about 2.5 miles in an easterly direction from the mouth of the Warrior river and 300 yards distant, approximately, from the south side of the stream.

FIG. 320.—Vessel No. 2. Mound A, Warrior river. (About three-fourths size.)

Mound A, the more northerly, with a circular basal outline, had a diameter of 65 feet. Its height above the general level was 9.5 feet, though deep excavations along the margin, gave an appearance of considerably greater altitude.

On the surface of the mound, especially on the eastern and southern parts, beneath which most of the earthenware and burials lay, were slabs and thick masses of lime rock, water-worn, doubtless brought from the neighboring stream. Subsequently, when the mound was completely demolished, similar masses were found

FIG. 321.—Vessel No. 3.   Mound A, Warrior river.   (Eight-ninths size.)

here and there somewhat below the surface.   These masses were often much larger than those described as being in the mound near the Aucilla river.

Mound A was of yellow sand except where pottery deposits lay, where it was much darker in color.

Human remains were found twenty-nine times and, as some of the burials were badly decayed, it is possible that others had entirely disappeared.   As usual, there were present the bunch, the flexed burial and the lone skull.   A few burials, falling in caved sand, did not afford data as to their form.

FIG. 322.—Vessel No. 4.   Mound A, Warrior river.   (About five-ninths size.)

Of the twenty-nine burials, many of which were on or near the base, nine lay immediately beneath the rocks, but in each case these burials were superficial, the least so being an interment 3.5 feet deep, almost in the middle of the summit plateau, around which had been many masses of rock, instead of the customary two or three.   This burial had been disturbed by the only previous digging in the mound, a hole 4 by 2 by 6 feet deep, which had cut away part of the skeleton.   In addition to this case, those under rocks, in this mound, were two bunched burials; two flexed burials; two skulls together; two skulls with long-bones, together; a lone skull; and bones which fell in caved sand.

No skulls were saved from this mound, but certain ones permitted determination as to the existence of cranial compression.   None was evident.

With one burial was a " celt; " with another, a flat rectangular gorget, probably of fine-grained, garnetiferous schist, 1.1 inches broad by 3 inches in length, having two perforations. An arrowhead or knife, of chert lay with a vessel of earthenware, and three perforated shell drinking cups were found in the line of the earthenware deposit. These, exclusive of earthenware, were the only artifacts noted by us in the mound, the usual hones, hammers and the like, not being met with.

Near the margin, on the north side, a vessel covered with crimson paint was found, crushed to bits.

Soon after the digging was begun, S. by E. in the mound were found a number of sherds, all of excellent ware and some with interesting and carefully executed incised decoration. No vessels, however, were found until a point had been reached about 10 feet in from the margin, where the sherds had been, when four vessels were found together. About 2.5 feet distant was a burial, which, however, we do not connect directly with the earthenware, since these vessels, as we have said, presumably belonged to the general deposit. This deposit lay on, or near, the base.

After these four vessels, for a period, none was met with, but later, as the digging progressed, others were encountered in ones and twos until the central portion of the mound was reached where were a considerable number, singly, here and there.

While the vessels in this mound were all of superior ware, with the exception, of course, of the ceremonial or ready-made mortuary ones, where excellence of material is not looked for, a point was markedly noticeable in this mound, as it had been in nearly all others of this district, namely, that the best and most interesting vessels are found among the first, and, therefore, must have been placed on the outskirts of the general deposit. Almost invariably, undecorated vessels or vessels bearing the complicated stamp, lie thickest toward the center, while interesting pieces, which called for care and individuality in execution, are found among the first when the pottery deposit is reached.

Twenty-four vessels came from this mound, of which the following offer features of interest. All not otherwise described have the basal perforation.

Vessel No. 1.—A flattened hemispherical vessel, badly crushed, with crimson paint for its only decoration.

Vessel No. 2—An interesting bowl having the extended head of a vulture with a conventional tail, opposite it and, on either side, a wing in relief. Curiously enough, this vessel, which is of the ready-made mortuary variety, is imperforate as to the base, but has three round holes on either side of the body (Fig. 320). Maximum diameter, 12.5 inches; height, 5.5 inches.

Vessel No. 3.—A human-effigy vessel, found broken into fragments, with portions missing. There are two small holes front and two back for suspension and a hole knocked through the bottom of one leg. Part of the face, with the nose, has been restored (Fig. 321). Height, 11 inches; width, 6.7 inches; thickness, 4.3 inches.

Vessel No. 4.—A bird-effigy vessel of the ceremonial variety, with head thrust forward, and a conventional tail. The wings, which are in relief, have three perforations made before baking and there is also a basal perforation made at the same time.

A portion of the beak is missing owing to the scaling off of small fragments, a frequent occurrence in vessels of this inferior, mortuary ware (Fig. 322).   Diameter of body, 8 inches; height, 6.5 inches.

FIG. 323.—Vessel No. 8.   Mound A, Warrior river.   (Two-thirds size.)

Vessel No. 5.—A vase with pinched decoration around the neck.

Vessel No. 7.—A vessel of yellow ware, somewhat stained, so exactly resembling a gourd that a countryman visiting the mound, believed it to be one containing water for the men.

Vessel No. 8.—A vessel of thick ware, decorated with crimson paint on the upper portion, is surrounded by seven projections.   Above these are four designs, all similar, each including a vertical bird symbol.   These designs are connected by

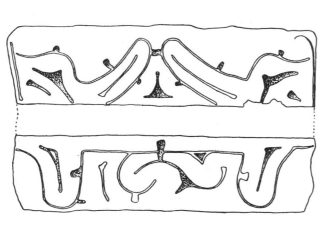

FIG. 324.—Vessel No. 13.   Decoration.   Mound A, Warrior river. (Half size.)

FIG. 325.—Vessel No. 20.   Mound A, Warrior river. (Two-fifths size.)

FIG. 326. — Vessel No. 22.   Mound A, Warrior river.   (Full size.)

FIG. 327.—Vessel No. 23   Mound A, Warrior river.
(Half size.)

FIG. 328.—Handle.   Mound A, Warrior river.
(About two-thirds size.)

punctate markings (Fig. 323). This vessel, whose capacity is about 1 quart, is a highly conventionalized life-form, the knobs representing projecting organs.

Vessel No. 9.—A large pot with complicated stamp decoration, in fragments.

Vessel No. 10.—A small imperforate vessel with quadrilateral body, flat base and round upright neck encircled by a complicated stamp decoration.

FIG. 329.—Sherd. Mound A, Warrior river. (Two-thirds size.)

Vessel No. 11.—An undecorated gourd-shaped vessel of yellow ware, with a small perforation in the side in addition to the usual one in the base. This vessel, of unusual size to find intact, was recovered by us from the mound without injury. Maximum diameter, 14.8 inches; height, 14.3 inches.

Vessel No. 12.—A large pot bearing the complicated stamp, found in fragments.

Vessel No. 13.—A bowl of about 1 quart capacity, with a rim turned inward and upward, bearing incised animal symbols, including the fore-legs and hind-legs, as shown diagrammatically in Fig. 324, where the distance between the two designs on the vessel is ignored.

Vessel No. 14.—A small undecorated vessel, lenticular in longitudinal section.

Vessel No. 18.—A much flattened sphere with high neck, slightly flaring, around which is complicated stamp decoration.

Vessel No. 20.—A pot bearing a clearly impressed complicated stamp (Fig. 325).

Vessel No. 22.—A handsome vessel of excellent ware, highly polished, of somewhat less than 1 quart capacity. The decoration, raised and incised, may be highly conventionalized fore-legs and hind-legs (Fig. 326).

Vessel No. 23.—Is undecorated, imperforate, of about 1 quart capacity (Fig. 327).

Fig. 328 shows an animal head which has served as a handle for a vessel.

A complicated stamp decoration is given in Fig. 329.

MOUNDS NEAR THE WARRIOR RIVER, TAYLOR COUNTY. MOUND B.

This mound, in thick hammock, about 200 yards in a southerly direction from Mound A, was of irregular outline, with major and minor diameters of 76 feet and 54 feet, respectively. Its height was about 7 feet. There were great excavations in places around the margin, whence sand for the erection of the mound had come.

There had been no previous digging.

Owing to the marginal excavations to which we have referred, it was impossible to determine, from its appearance, just where the mound began, therefore twenty men were placed around it in a circle whose diameter exceeded that of the mound, and trenches, each about 3 feet across, were continued in the direction of the center until the exact margin of the mound was located.

Contrary to the usual course of events in our work in this district, when the trenches had gone 2 or 3 feet into the mound, earthenware vessels were met with in the western and southern parts. These vessels were not accompanied by sherds and did not lie together in a deposit, but had been placed here and there, singly.

After this discovery, the trenches in the western half of the mound were joined and the total demolition of that part of the mound began.

Shortly after this junction of the trenches on the western side, the trenches in two-thirds of the eastern side were joined and continued until the mound was dug down.

Not until the trenches had gone a distance of 22 feet into the remaining third of the eastern part, was anything of interest met with, when the discovery of a vessel of earthenware, caused the union of the remaining trenches.

Soon after the first junction of the trenches, that is 2 or 3 feet in from the margin, burials were met with in the W., NW. and SW. outskirts of the mound and, later, in part of the eastern portion. While burials were met with here and there in the parts of the mound we have referred to, none was found in the remaining portion of the eastern part until the center of the mound had almost been reached.

In all, thirty-five burials were counted by us, the majority in small bunches, though solitary skulls were present and, rarely, two skulls together.

The flexed burial was not noted.

Neither in our field notes, where the burials are described one by one, nor in our amplified notes, always written immediately at the end of the investigation of the mound, do we find any reference to cranial compression in connection with the burials in this mound. Neither do we recall the discovery of any cranial flattening, and it is our belief that none was met with.

The sand in this mound was not discolored in any way. It was remarkably dry and caved readily. On the surface lay a single mass of lime rock, and in the mound were a few similar masses unassociated with burials, while twice only, burials lay beneath them. A few oyster-shells were with two other burials, but not in the way we have noted in places to the westward where masses of shells lay over bones.

With one burial was sand colored with hematite. Another burial lay near three vessels of earthenware, while mica and a pebble lay together with human remains.

Unassociated with human bones, together, were: four pebble-hammers; two flat pebbles; eight chips of chert; seven very rude arrowheads or knives, of the same material, three with points missing.

In another place where no bones were met with, though they may have disappeared through decay, were: a long flake, intended for a knife; an arrowhead or knife; another with the point missing; a small knife with curved edge. All these were of chert.

There were also in the mound: a large tooth of a fossil shark, showing no mark of use in a handle; a large slab of ferruginous sand-stone; a lancehead of chert, 4 inches long and nearly 3 inches in maximum diameter, so rudely made that it would seem that mortuary deposits of inferior quality, made expressly for the dead, were not confined to vessels of earthenware.

FIG. 330.—Object of kaolin. Mound B, Warrior river. (About five-sevenths size.)

We have referred to a curious object of impure kaolin, found by us in the mound near Porter's bar. An object exactly similar in shape, carefully smoothed and enlarged at either end, about 9.5 inches long, was present in this mound. It, also, has suffered through the chipping off of portions, but not to the same extent as had the other (Fig. 330). As is the case with the other, traces of decoration in low relief are visible in places. This curious object, the second found, would seem to belong to a class perhaps of ceremonial batons. It is certain that a material so soft could not have been chosen for any practical use. Dr. H. F. Keller, to whom a part of the object was submitted for analysis, writes: " It consists of an intimate mixture of kaolin and finely-divided silica. The constituents are silica, alumina, oxide of iron, moisture, and traces of magnesia. A rough determination of the silica yielded 75%, which is 27% in excess over the amount present in pure kaolinite. The proportion of iron, too, is considerable. Under the lens the powdered substance appears quite homogeneous, but under higher powers it shows crystalline particles of two kinds, as well as dark specks."

There was also in the mound a rectangular mass, seemingly of clayey material, with rounded corners and a small groove at either end, about 6 inches long.

The earthenware in this mound did not lie in black sand, nor was there any general mortuary deposit, four vessels together in the southern margin being the nearest approach to one.

The ware, in marked contrast to that of the neighboring mound, was of poor quality and undecorated or bore the complicated stamp, as a rule. Incised decoration was encountered in three instances only, among the forty vessels noted by us, and in each case the work was unambitious and careless in execution.

The features of the earthenware in this mound were the large number of vessels with inturned rims and, consequently, comparatively small openings; and the unusual percentage of imperforate bases present, no less than 22 of these being included among the 42 vessels met with, and others badly broken, may have been imperforate also. Marginal vessels, as a rule, were perforate; of the first twelve vessels found, but one had the base intact. Most of these vessels came from the south and southeastern margins and perhaps were in place of a general deposit.

In this mound were no ceremonial vessels and, consequently, no basal perforation made previous to baking.

Fig. 331.—Vessel No. 4.   Mound B, Warrior river.   (Nine-tenths size.)

The following vessels are worthy of particular notice, those omitted being, as a rule, undecorated or bearing the complicated stamp in well known patterns.

Vessel No. 4.—Of about 1 pint capacity, with horizontal ears extending one from either side, beneath the rim. There is roughly incised decoration (Fig. 331). There is a basal perforation.

Vessel No. 5.—Of red ware, undecorated, with cylindrical body, rounded base and upper end constricted to form a small opening. This vessel, of about 1 quart capacity, fell into many pieces on removal.

Vessel No. 7.—Has the base and lower part of the body knocked out, in performance of the customary mutilation. This vessel, of about 3 pints capacity, has the upper part turning inward and upward, about 1.5 inches, forming an aperture of about 2.5 inches (Fig. 332). The decoration, incised, the only example in the mound not subsidiary, is shown diagrammatically in Fig. 333.

Vessel No. 11.—A small bowl with flat base and clearly defined complicated stamp decoration (Fig. 334).

Vessel No. 14.—Considerable parts of a bowl of yellow ware, in fragments,

FIG. 332.—Vessel No. 7.   Mound B, Warrior river.   (Five-sixths size.)

having as decoration lines, triangles and circular markings, all in black pigment. This is the first example, we believe, of the use of black paint on earthenware found during our mound work, though, as the reader is doubtless aware, this form of decoration was in vogue among the aborigines in various parts of the country. Portions of this vessel were found scattered over an area of about 4 feet by 12 feet, showing that the individual having in charge the immolation of the vessel, went at the work with a will.

Vessel No. 16.—Of about 1 gallon capacity, undecorated and rounded at either end (Fig. 335).

Vessel No. 17.— A most interesting vessel of heavy red ware, with five compartments, consisting of a circular, central compartment raised above the level of the rest, with two truncated, triangular ones on opposite sides and two triangular ones on the remaining sides. Projecting from the end of one compartment is the head of a bird, decorated on the upper side only. The opposite end, the tail, unfortunately, is

missing. On the body of the vessel the bird-symbol appears in many places (Fig. 336). This vessel, the central part of which was filled with charcoal, and a compartment on either side, with sand blackened by fire, would seem to be a connecting link between the com-

FIG. 333.—Vessel No. 7. Decoration. Mound B, Warrior river. (Half size.)

FIG. 334.—Vessel No. 11. Mound B, Warrior river. (Half size.)

partment vessel and the bird-effigy vessel, the other being where the bird is given in outline of the compartments only. Diameter across wings, 10.2 inches; height, 2.5 inches.

Vessel No. 20.—A neat, imperforate, undecorated bowl of less than 1 pint capacity, greatly thickened at the rim.

Vessel No. 21.—Red ware, imperforate, with the rim inturned somewhat. On the upper part are three encircling lines made up of upright punctate impressions. The capacity is about 1 quart.

Vessel No. 24.—A small pot, imperforate, with rude complicated stamp, and three feet on the base instead of four, the usual number in this part of Florida.

Vessel No. 26.—A small, undecorated, imperforate bowl, elliptical in longitudinal section.

FIG. 335.—Vessel No. 16. Mound B, Warrior river. (One-third size.)

FIG. 336.—Vessel No. 17.   Mound B, Warrior river.   (About seven-tenths size.)

Vessel No. 31.—An imitation of a gourd, which is made complete by the yellow color of the ware and a rusty appearance imparted by age, seen in places on the vessel and often met with on the natural gourd. The capacity is about 2 quarts (Fig. 337).

Vessel No. 38.—An imperforate, undecorated vessel of about 2 quarts capacity, scaphoid in shape. There are traces of crimson pigment exteriorly.

FIG. 337.—Vessel No. 31. Mound B, Warrior river. (Four-fifths size.)

A point of interest impressing itself on us in connection with Mounds A and B, near the Warrior river, is that here, at Alligator Harbor and near Spring creek, two mounds of considerable size are at each of these places in close proximity one to the other. In each of these pairs of mounds one was symmetrical, while the other was in the form of a ridge. From the symmetrical mound, in each case, came ware much superior to that found in the asymmetrical ridge.

MOUND NEAR STEINHATCHEE RIVER, LAFAYETTE COUNTY.

The mound, in thick scrub, is about one-quarter of a mile in a SE. direction from Rock Landing, which is about 4 miles above the mouth of the river. The height is 4.5 feet; the diameter of base, 62 feet.

Extensive digging was first done around the margin, showing the sand to be bright yellow with no trace of discoloration. One sherd only was met with.

Next the mound was dug centrally, with four large trenches radiating to the margin.   One sherd was found and sand discolored by hematite, in one place.   In three places, rather superficially, were bits of badly decayed bones.

MOUND NEAR GOODSON'S FISHCAMP, LAFAYETTE COUNTY.

The site of the fishcamp is on a small water-way extending in from the Gulf, about 2 miles in a SE. direction from the mouth of the Steinhatchee river.

The mound, in pine woods, on the edge of the sawgrass marsh, on property of the East Coast Lumber Company, was much spread by trampling of cattle.   A few fragments of human bone lay on the surface.   Its height was 4 feet; its basal diameter, 66 feet.   Apparently, there had been no previous digging.

The mound was trenched in every direction by us and dug marginally and centrally.   The sand was bright yellow with no sign of that darkening which so often accompanies an earthenware deposit.   A single skull was found 1 foot below the surface, and a small bunched burial elsewhere at about the same depth.

A large stone hatchet lay 6 inches beneath the surface.

A globular vessel of inferior ware, with a perforation knocked through the base, having faint punctate decoration below the rim, lay alone about 6 inches down.

A carefully made discoidal stone of quartzite, with a small concavity in the base which is somewhat broader than the upper part, lay unassociated.   This discoidal stone is of interest, in that it is the first found by us in peninsular Florida, in which this mound is, though we have met with the type in abundance in Georgia to the eastward, and in Alabama to the westward.

MOUND NEAR BEAR HAMMOCK, LAFAYETTE COUNTY.

This mound, in pine woods, on the eastern edge of Bear Hammock, about 3 miles in a SE. direction from the mouth of the Steinhatchee river, on the property of the East Coast Lumber Company, was intact at the time of our visit.   Its height was 4.5 feet; its basal diameter, 52 feet.

Thorough trenching showed the mound to be of bright yellow sand.   No burial or artifact was met with.

MOUND NEAR MURPHY LANDING, LAFAYETTE COUNTY.

Murphy Landing is on the coast about 2 miles above Horseshoe Point.

The mound, in a field formerly under cultivation, the property of the East Coast Lumber Company, about one-quarter mile from the Gulf, had a height of 4 feet 3 inches; a basal diameter of 52 feet.   The outline was circular.   We heard of previous digging in the mound, but as we saw no trace of it, presumably, it was insignificant.

The mound, which was of light sand with a dark streak at the base, was completely demolished by us.

Human remains were met with at thirty-six places, and included the lone skull, the bunch and the flexed burial.   No skull was in a condition to keep, but a number showed that no cranial compression had been practised. Burials were first met with in the eastern margin, but, later, were encountered throughout the mound. In the eastern part of the mound, after a number of single burials had been met with, a layer of bones was encountered extending in, toward the center, a considerable distance. This deposit, which was counted as a single burial, had with it much sand dyed with hematite.

In the western part of the mound, about midway between the margin and the center, began a thin layer of oyster-shells on which lay several burials. Two burials lay with oyster-shells, locally. Two others had "celts" nearby, while with two more were a few small shell beads.

Unassociated, was a nodule of chert, the shape of a finger slightly bent and about its length, with double its diameter. At one end is a certain amount of chipping, seemingly preliminary to making a cutting tool. There were also in the mound an arrowhead of chert and a ball of lime rock about 1 inch in diameter.

Earthenware was represented in the mound by a few sherds of markedly inferior ware, some having a slight admixture of sand in the clay. In the way of decoration sherds bore the small check stamp, a rude punctate marking and, in one case, a pinched design. A small, undecorated bowl, with a hole knocked through the bottom, fell with caved sand.

Mounds near Horseshoe Point, Lafayette County.

These mounds, in thick hammock, on property of the East Coast Lumber Company, lie near the edge of the marsh, somewhat to the north of Horseshoe Point. A visitor would find it to his advantage to follow a road about two miles in a northeasterly direction from the landing.

The principal mounds, three in number, lie in sight of one another and are near considerable shell deposits. A large fresh-water pond is nearby and a natural waterway to the Gulf, doubtless available for canoes, ends in sight of the mounds, which are surrounded now, as no doubt they were in former times, by hammock-trees, including tall palmettoes and magnolias.

The mound nearest the Gulf was built on the end of a shell-heap, a part of the mound extending over to the general level beyond. Its outline was circular; its diameter, 40 feet; its height above the shell-heap, 6 feet. A great trench had been dug from the SE. margin to the center. The remainder of the mound was practically demolished by us.

A number of burials were met with at various points in the mound. No flattening was apparent on the skulls, which, however, were not in a condition to save.

Mainly from the western side and from near the center, comparatively near the surface, were ten vessels of inferior ware, all found singly. None of these bore incised decoration, save one, which had two encircling lines. One sherd, however, of the few found in the mound, was of excellent ware and bore a carefully incised conventionalized bird's wing.

Vessel No. 1.—A vessel of about 3 quarts capacity, shown in Fig. 338, with four projections, perhaps indicating a highly conventionalized life-form.   The upper part of the body is painted crimson; the lower has the natural yellow color of the ware.   Part of the base has been knocked out.

Vessel No. 2.—A bowl of about 2 quarts capacity, with three encircling lines of triangular punctate markings.   There is a basal perforation.

Vessel No. 3.—A large undecorated vessel of yellow ware, modelled after a gourd, with a portion missing.

Vessel No. 4.—A vessel with oblate spherical body and high upright neck bear-

FIG. 338.—Vessel No. 1. Mound near Horseshoe Point.
(One-third size.)

FIG. 339.—Vessel No. 4. Mound near Horseshoe
Point. (Half size.)

ing a distinct complicated stamp (Fig. 339).   The base is missing through mortuary mutilation.

FIG. 340.—Vessel No. 6. Mound near Horseshoe Point. (Half size.)

Vessel No. 5.—Another large vessel modelled after a gourd, found in fragments.

Vessel No. 6.—A double vessel of yellow ware, also of the gourd pattern (Fig. 340). There is a basal perforation.

FIG. 341.—Vessel No. 10. Mound near Horseshoe Point. (Two-fifths size.)

Vessel No. 7.—A small, imperforate vessel, with rude, punctate decoration.

Vessel No. 8.—An undecorated, perforate bowl of about 6 quarts capacity, scaphoid in shape, with red paint inside and out.

Vessel No. 9.—Small, undecorated, with four-lobed body. There are two holes for suspension; also a basal perforation.

Vessel No. 10.—Of heavy ware, undecorated, of about 1 pint capacity. In form this vessel resembles an inverted acorn. There are two holes for suspension and a perforation in the base (Fig. 341).

The next mound was a ridge 80 feet long by 58 feet across. The maximum height was 6 feet. The highest portion was carefully trenched by us, yielding beside a number of burials, three " celts," two of which are of a chisel-form, and a small undecorated bowl with basal perforation.

The third mound, circular in outline, 3 feet 4 inches high, 54 feet across the base, furnished one broken arrowhead as the result of careful trenching. This mound was probably domiciliary.

MOUND ON HOG ISLAND, LEVY COUNTY.

Hog Island is a small key between the eastern and western passes into the Suwanee river.

The mound, but a short distance from the marsh, is in a dense mass of trees, bushes, and palmetto scrub. Its height is 9 feet 3 inches; its basal diameter, about 50 feet.

This mound seemed to be a shell-heap covered with from 12 to 18 inches of sand. A hole put in by a former digger, showed only shell, as did a large cavity caused by the fall of a great tree. Trenches put in by us reached shell almost immediately, and, after considerable digging in this material, the investigation of the mound was abandoned.

MOUND ON PINE KEY, LEVY COUNTY.

Pine Key, a small island, lies about one-quarter of a mile from a great shell-heap on the mainland. This shell-heap, visible at a long distance from the Gulf, the northernmost of the great shell-heaps of the west coast, lies about 5 miles in a northerly direction from Cedar Keys.

Pine Key, largely marsh, has a certain amount of solid ground rising from 2 to 3 feet above the general level.   About one-quarter acre of this higher ground had been used as a sort of burial place, or cemetery.   There had been considerable previous digging, and fragments of human bones and bits of earthenware of the most inferior quality lay scattered over the surface.

The cemetery was trenched in all directions.

In places, bones lay in profusion, while again burials were met with singly, the flexed burial, the bunch and the lone skull being represented.   No cranial flattening was noticed.   The remains, as a rule, were about 1 foot below the surface, though several burials were met with at a depth of 3 feet.

A "celt" was found not far from the surface, as were a shell drinking cup with a basal perforation, and many sherds, all of poor ware, undecorated in the main, though the check stamp and the complicated stamp were represented.

Also near the surface was the lower part of a ceremonial, mortuary vessel having a basal perforation made before baking.   The portion found resembled an inverted cone.   Just above the base were two deep, encircling grooves made when the clay was soft.   The ware and workmanship were of the coarsest description.

MOUND NEAR THE SHELL-HEAP, LEVY COUNTY.

This mound is in thick scrub, about 300 yards from the homestead of Mr. W. R. Young, who lives on the great shell-heap, to which we have referred, and is the owner of the mound in the rear.   This mound, 6.5 feet high, 64 feet through its circular base, had been dug into from the NE. margin previous to our coming, a trench 6 feet wide having been carried to the center where it broadened to include a space about 10 feet in diameter.   A few fragments of human bones and two or three bits of rude earthenware lay on the surface.

Seven large trenches made by us, not all of which were entirely carried to the base, some having been abandoned when results of others were noted, showed the mound to be mainly of oyster shells irregularly placed.

At the center a measurement from the top showed 18 inches of sand, 22 inches of shell, 14 inches of sand, 1 foot of shell, in order, going down.   Beneath, was undisturbed sand.   The mound probably was built on rising ground, as its height, taken from the margin, is not accounted for by these measurements.

On the south side of the mound trenching showed 18 inches of sand on top, with a solid mass of shells below, and other trenches gave but slightly varying results.

No human remains or artifacts were met with in our digging, though one bit of human bone, just below the surface, projected from the side of the former trench.

At Cedar Keys our mound investigation for the season was brought to an end.

A continuation of our work farther south hardly would have been consistent with the title of this report.   Moreover, Mr. J. S. Raybon, captain of our steamer, who had worked so successfully for us to the northward and to the westward, had been unable to locate any new mounds of importance between Cedar Keys and

Tampa bay. It is only fair to say, however, that owing to the lack of inhabitants along that part of the coast, from whom inquiry could be made, certain mounds may have escaped him. Besides, several years before, we had covered the territory from Tampa almost to Clearwater Harbor (see outline map) with but negative results, while two men in our employ, one of whom was very familiar with the coast, had searched from Tampa to Anclote Key, finding only mounds previously located and dug into by Mr. S. T. Walker,[1] whose researches were continued still farther north without discovery of importance.

Mr. Cushing,[2] it is true, opened a mound at Tarpon Springs, in which he found fragments of interesting ware, but we believe this mound to have been an exception to the general run of mounds from Cedar Keys southward. Just north of Cedar Keys the great shell-heaps of the west coast begin, and neither on the east coast, where large shell-heaps are throughout, nor in the territory of the great shell-heaps on the west coast have we found the contents of mounds to be of much interest.

As we have stated, our work of last season ended at the eastern extremity of Choctawhatchee bay and began this year at the western end of St. Andrews bay, in direct continuation (see map).

During our season's work certain points were brought to our attention.

Going eastward along the coast, we saw the waning influence of Alabama and of the middle Mississippi district as to composition of ware, the admixture of shell[3] entirely disappearing, none having been met with by us east of Choctawhatchee bay, which marks also the easternmost limit of the polished, black ware of Mississippi, as found by us.

[1] Smithsonian Report, 1879.

[2] Proceedings American Philosophical Society, Vol. XXV, No. 153.

[3] In a thoughtful article in the "American Antiquarian," May and June, 1902, entitled "Primitive Keramic Art in Wisconsin", the author of that paper is inclined to believe that a mineral substance, and not pounded shell, is used to temper earthenware through parts of the mound region, where hitherto we have been led to believe pounded shell was used.

To determine this matter, we submitted to Prof. Harry F. Keller, Ph. D., a fragment of thick, porous earthenware found by us in Alabama, which contained a considerable amount of what we have always considered broken shell used for tempering.

Dr. Keller's report is as follows :

June 24, 1902.

"The analysis of the carefully picked material (shell) from the specimen of earthenware from Alabama gave the following results :

Insoluble in dilute acid,	3.09%
(Silica and ferruginous clay)	
CaO (Lime)	54.07
MgO (Magnesia)	.19
MnO (Manganous oxide)	.09
Fe_2O_3 (Ferric oxide)	.11
CO_2 (Carbonic anhydride)	41.58
P_2O_5 (Phosphoric anhydride)	.62
Moisture	.11
	99.86

"The small amounts of the oxides of iron and maganese may be derived from adhering matrix. The insoluble residue contains traces of carbonaceous matter."

Here we have almost pure carbonate of lime, showing the scaly fragments in the earthenware to be shell.

The growing influence of Georgia in decoration became noticeable also, the complicated stamp, the specialty of that State and of territory to the northward, coming more and more into use.   Such being the case, we should look for the clay tempered with coarse gravel, the well-known "gritty ware" of Georgia, but it is not present.

The earthenware of the northwest Florida coast is purely aboriginal in style. Probably most of the mounds there ante-dated the coming of the whites, and where they did not, their builders saw too little of the strangers to suffer modification in their art.   It is true that some writers have cited the presence of feet on aboriginal vessels as an indication of European influence, and such vessels are often met with in the mounds of the northwest coast, but we have seen vessels with feet, in various localities, in too many mounds in which no European artifacts were found, to coincide with this idea.

In material and decoration the pottery of the Florida northwest coast averages far above that of such mounds of peninsular Florida, in which earthenware is met with.

For one reason or another, the occurrence of earthenware vessels is infrequent in the burial mounds of the coast of peninsular Florida.   We have searched almost the entire east coast between the Georgia boundary and Lake Worth without finding a single vessel, and our good friend, the late Andrew E. Douglass, devoted many seasons to mound work along the east coast, going even as far as Miami, with a like result.

On the west coast, Mr. Cushing found fragments of important vessels in the mound opened by him at Tarpon Springs, but from near that point southward, almost to the end of the peninsula, we saw not a single vessel of earthenware, though there are a few fragments in the shell-heaps.

It is true Mr. Cushing found several vessels of earthenware in the muck at Marco, with his great discovery of objects of wood, but the vessels were few in number and unimportant as to shape and decoration.

Presumably, then, the custom to inter earthenware vessels with the dead obtained but little, if at all, along the Florida east coast, and the lower half of the west coast of peninsular Florida.   If, in these districts, vessels to any extent were put into the mounds, these vessels were of wood and perishable.

Superior as is the earthenware of the northwest Florida coast to most of that of the peninsula, it does not excel a few of the finest specimens met with by us in the mounds of the St. Johns river.   A duck-vessel [1] from near the mouth of the St. Johns ; sherds of excellent paste and superior decoration, from near Dunn's creek [2] (see outline map) ; still more beautiful ones from a neighboring mound ; part of a vessel and a handle representing a vulture's head, beautifully incised and showing the fine yellow of the paste, alternating with crimson pigment, from a mound near Lake Monroe, hold their own with the finest earthenware of the northwest coast of Florida.

[1] "Certain Sand Mounds of Duval County, Florida." Plate LXXXIII.
[2] "Certain Sand Mounds of the St. Johns River."   Part I, Pl. II, Fig. 1.   Incidentally, at this mound was the southernmost occurrence of ware bearing the complicated stamp decoration.

We have two hypotheses to offer to account for this:

1.—That the aborigines of the peninsula possessed fine ware, but did not, as a rule, inter it with the dead.

It must be borne in mind that the natives of the peninsula did not make great mortuary deposits of earthenware as did those of the Florida mainland, the vessel of earthenware being simply one of a great number of objects from which selection was made. Fewer vessels were put into the mounds, and as earthenware was not so exclusively a mortuary selection, perhaps less attention was paid to the quality of that taken for burial. Besides, the interment of "freak," or ceremonial, ware, which is always inferior to the other ware of the district where it was used, was more largely practised in the peninsula than it was on the northwest coast and, therefore, the pottery of the peninsular mounds may not be representative.

2.—That the finest vessels of the peninsula were importations.

From the island of Marco, southwest Florida, we got two large bird head handles, of excellent design, found alone, one representing the head of a turkey, the other that of a predatory bird. Around one of these heads a groove had been made to permit use as a pendant. The other head had doubtless served a similar purpose, as circular spaces, through which a cord could pass, had been left, at the time of manufacture, through the neck and through the bill. Not only was the workmanship of the heads markedly that of the middle Mississippi district or of the Gulf, but the ware was what is known as shell-tempered, which ware was in use in the districts we have named, but not in peninsular Florida. These heads were doubtless importations, and other fine specimens of ware may have been importations also.

On the whole we are inclined to believe that the best ware found in the peninsula was exceptional and perhaps got there through barter. The lower average of excellence of sherds in the peninsula argues a supply of inferior vessels, and the fact that the "freak," or ceremonial, ware is so much below the standard of that of the northwest coast might indicate a lower quality for vessels of other classes also. Had the natives of the peninsula possessed vessels of the highest grade in great numbers, we believe, in one way or another, more indication of it would have come to light.

In the first part of this report we spoke of a mortuary custom prevailing in peninsular Florida [1] to knock a hole through the base of a vessel, presumably to "kill" the pot, that its soul might accompany that of the dead man. We spoke of a refinement of this custom, and described vessels of fantastic form and flimsy material made expressly for interment with the dead, in the bases of which holes

---

[1] In the "American Antiquarian," Sept.–Oct., 1902, is a paper by Mr. Francis U. Duff, on the antiquities of the Mimbres valley, New Mexico, describing, among other things, the finding of "large bowls inverted over the crania of the departed. Each of these bowls, before being deposited in the grave, had a small hole broken in its bottom." It is interesting to note the occurrence of the mortuary perforation of the base of vessels in this remote region so far removed from where this mortuary custom flourished at its fullest. In the Mimbres valley, however, bowls were not inverted over lone skulls or skulls with a few scattered bones, as they were in the graves of the Florida northwest coast, but were placed over skulls interred with their skeletons.

had been made previous to the baking of the clay. Incidentally, we found this "freak," or ceremonial, ware in the peninsula, from the mouth of the St. Johns river to Lake Beresford (see outline map), going southward, and in the lake district at the head of the Ocklawaha river.

A few examples of this ready-made "freak" ware were met with by us east of Pensacola bay during our work last season. During this year's investigation, as our readers may recall, examples of this form were found in increasing numbers, and individual vessels were often of much greater size than anything of the kind we had met with to the westward on the coast, or, incidentally, in peninsular Florida, save in the mounds of Volusia, south of Lake George.

As our work progressed more to the east, a new feature in "freak" ware was encountered. In the mounds of St. Andrew's bay two vessels of a new type, and fragments of similar ones, were found, while farther to the east vessels of this kind were encountered in considerable numbers. These vessels were life-forms, usually, but differed from other life-forms of the same district, in that they were inferior to them as to ware and workmanship, and that they had various perforations made previous to baking, in the body of the vessel as well as the customary one in the base. [1]

An interesting custom noted with but few exceptions along the northwest coast was the placing in the mounds of general deposits of earthenware, nearly always in the eastern part of the mound. These deposits were found in darkened sand, often at the very edge of the mound, and continued with the blackened sand, a few vessels together, in toward the center or to it. Sometimes the deposits were met with at some little distance in from the margin, but nearly always in the eastern side of the mound.

These masses of blackened sand in which the general deposits of earthenware lay were noticed by us in the mounds during our former season's work and were referred to by us in Part I of our report. So almost universal was the juxtaposition of darkened sand and general deposits of ware in the mounds, during our work this season, that considerable thought was devoted by us to the matter. Sand of this

---

[1] Among numbers of small "freak" vessels found by us in the Grant mound, near the mouth of the St. Johns river, was part of a vessel filled with perforations, like a sieve. We are uncertain whether or not this vessel should be included in the same class as those having occasional perforations in the body.

The incense-cups of Mexico and of Central America, though they have perforations of the body, made before baking, do not seem to us to be of the same class as these large vessels from northwest Florida, which have basal perforations in addition to those in the body. These latter vessels with their ready-made body-perforations would seem to be intimately connected with the ceremonial vessels of peninsular Florida, since both classes possess the perforation of the base, made before the baking of the clay, though the vessels of peninsular Florida do not show the body-perforations which are probably only an amplification of the mortuary perforation of the base. Therefore, as the ceremonial vessels of peninsular Florida, being without body-perforations, could not have served as incense-burners, it is not likely that the ceremonial vessels of northwest Florida, which are so nearly related to the others, though possessed of body-perforations, were intended for the burning of incense.

The Twentieth Annual Report of the Bureau of American Ethnology will consist of Prof. W. H. Holmes', "The Pottery of the Eastern United States," a most admirable memoir, part of which it has been our good fortune to see in manuscript.

We earnestly advise those interested in the subject of aboriginal ware carefully to study this memoir, on its appearance.

45 JOURN. A. N. S. PHILA., VOL. XII.

kind was often carefully examined by us for charcoal, but none was found, nor was adjacent sand burnt or discolored as by fire. In our account of the mound at West Bay post-office, in the early part of this volume, we have stated that a sample of this blackened sand, examined chemically and microscopically, showed its color to be due to carbonaceous matter, very probably of animal origin, and that the material, in all probability, could not have come from anything in the vegetable line. As this report is not intended for popular reading, in all probability our readers are as able to draw conclusions as we are. It would seem to us, however, that masses of animal matter, incinerated in a way to escape mixture with charcoal, have been mingled with sand which was placed in that part of the mound devoted to deposits of earthenware, put in for the dead in common. What these masses of flesh consisted of we are unable to decide. If the flesh belonged to lower animals and the bones were not removed before burning, and it seems unlikely that they should have been, the incineration must have been complete, as particles of half-burnt bone are not present in the sand.

If we suppose, on the other hand, that the flesh which we know was sometimes stripped from human skeletons when taken from the dead-house, was cremated, the absence of particles of bone can be accounted for. We think this latter supposition the more probable since aboriginal cremation did not seem to reduce bones in a thorough way, judging from our rather extensive experience of the matter in the mounds of Georgia.

Burials of human remains, also, were in greater numbers in the eastern portions of the mounds, sometimes being there and in the central parts, exclusively. In other cases, however, human remains were met with throughout the entire mound.

No new feature as to form of burial was noted during this season's work. The lone skull, the bunch, the flexed burial, the burial at length were met with; also loose bones scattered here and there. The urn-burial, also, was found in two localities.

The question of urn-burial in Florida is an interesting one since we know the custom to have been largely in vogue in Alabama and in Georgia, and yet there is no evidence [1] of the extension of the custom into peninsular Florida.

We have seen how large bowls were put over skulls at Perdido bay, the boundary between Alabama and Florida, and how the custom, continuing eastward into Florida, was noted along Santa Rosa sound and at the eastern extremity of Choctawhatchee bay, where, also, in one instance, an inverted bowl was found covering another bowl containing human remains.

This season we have remarked the existence of a cemetery with urn-burials still farther east, at the town of St. Andrews, and have found a single urn-burial in a mound on Ocklockonee bay farther yet to the eastward, though still on the mainland.

Beyond this point, in all Florida, we have met with no example of urn-burial, nor is there one on record.

[1] With the exception of a statement made in a newspaper by an investigator of a single mound and omitted from his official report.

Cremation, which we met with so frequently in Georgia, but saw but once during our work on the Alabama and Tombigbee rivers, was not noted by us during our first year's work along the northwest Florida coast, and but twice, unmistakably, during this, our second year's work.   In the peninsula of Florida we have not met with true cremation where it was evidently the purpose to burn the body as a form of burial, such cremation as is found there apparently being where single bones or parts of skeletons have lain in close proximity to ceremonial fires.   These fragments of burnt bone are often found lying with bones unaffected by fire, while, at times, a skeleton is seen to have the bones of one arm burnt or calcined, or sometimes a portion of the skull, and the like.

Cremation, then, as a form of burial, cannot be said to have obtained in peninsular Florida and was practised but occasionally in the mainland, or northwestern portion.

There seems to be a possible explanation for this occasional occurrence of cremation in a district where inhumation was so generally practised.   Cabeça de Vaca, who, as the reader is aware, spent some years among the aborigines of the northwest Florida coast, tells us that persons there in general were buried, but that doctors were cremated.   In our work on the mounds of the Georgia coast we pointed out that this statement could not apply to that part of the country, since cremation was very widely practised there, and, moreover, often included the bodies of infants. But along the northwest Florida coast, the district of which Cabeça de Vaca's statement was made, the result of our investigations seems to bear out the assertion.

It was our intention, another season, to carry our investigation from Mobile bay westward along the coast, in the endeavor to trace connection between that district and the region we have covered to the east.

Since our return, this spring and summer (1902), Mr. J. S. Raybon, captain of our steamer, who has in previous years so successfully located mounds for us, went over part of Mobile bay and most of the Mississippi coast.

A few mounds rewarded his search on the eastern shore of Mobile bay, but along the coast of Mississippi, apart from shell-heaps, almost nothing was met with.

Certain Aboriginal Mounds of the Apalachicola River

BY

CLARENCE B. MOORE

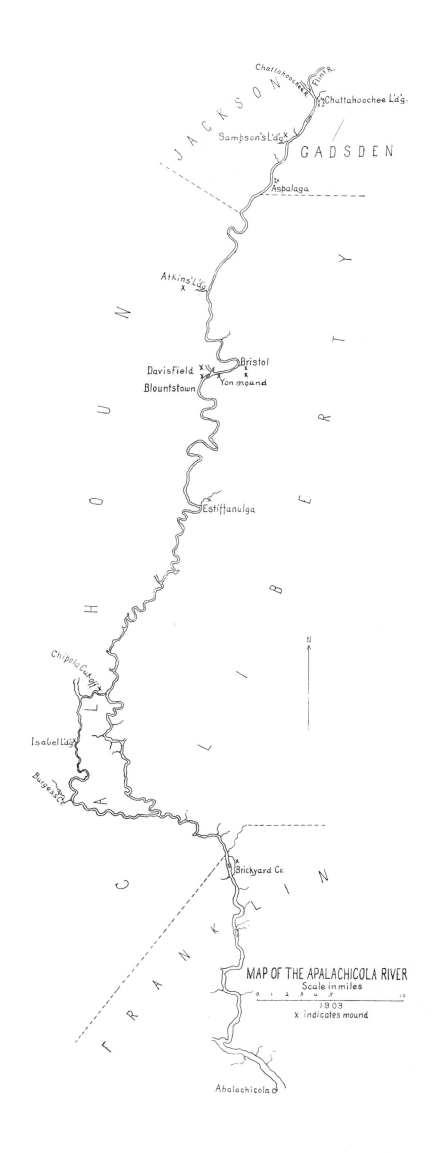

Chattahoochee
Flint R.
Chattahoochee L'd'g.

J A C K S O N

Sampson's L'd'g.

G A D S D E N

Aspalaga

C A L H O U N

L I B E R T Y

Atkins' L'd'g.

Bristol
Davis Field
Yon mound
Blountstown

Estiffanulga

Chipola Cut-off

Isabel L'd'g.

Burgess Cr.

N

Brickyard Cr.

F R A N K L I N

MAP OF THE APALACHICOLA RIVER
Scale in miles
0 1 2 3 4 5   10
1903
x indicates mound

Abalachicola

CERTAIN ABORIGINAL MOUNDS OF THE APALACHICOLA RIVER.

By Clarence B. Moore.

The Apalachicola river, formed by the union of the Chattahoochee and the Flint, at the boundary between Georgia and Florida, keeps a southward course through the Florida mainland and empties into Apalachicola bay, a part of the Gulf of Mexico. The length of the river is about 70 miles in a straight line, and about 105 miles, following the course of the stream.

What we have said as to the reproduction of vessels and as to the preparation of the report, at the beginning of the paper on the mounds of the Florida west-coast, applies equally to this report.

Mounds Investigated.

Mound on Brickyard creek, Apalachicola river.
Mound near Burgess creek, Chipola river.
Mound near Isabel Landing, Chipola river.
Mound near Chipola Cut-off, Chipola river.
Mound near Estiffanulga, Apalachicola river.
Mound near Blountstown, Apalachicola river.
Mound in Davis Field, Apalachicola river.
Yon mound, Apalachicola river.
Mound below Bristol, Apalachicola river.
Mound at Bristol, Apalachicola river.
Mound near Atkins' Landing, Apalachicola river.
Mounds near Aspalaga, Apalachicola river (3).
Mound near Sampson's Landing, Apalachicola river.
Mounds at Chattahoochee Landing, Apalachicola river (7).

In addition to these mounds, we investigated, the previous season, at and near the town of Apalachicola, eleven mounds, full accounts of which are given in our "Certain Aboriginal Remains of the Northwest Florida Coast," Part II.

Mound on Brickyard Creek, Franklin County.

This mound, immediately on the eastern bank of Brickyard creek, about one mile from its junction with the Apalachicola river (see map), on property of Mr. Frank Massina, of Apalachicola, had been dug through and through, previous to our visit.

The mound, probably, had been about 4 feet in height and 35 feet across the circular base, approximately. What was left of the mound was completely demolished by us.

One human femur, badly decayed, one molar and some fragments of bone too small for identification were the only signs of burial met with by us in the mound, though fragmentary human bones lay upon the surface.

There were present, here and there in the mound : two arrow-heads or knives, of chert; two piercing implements of bone; three columellæ of marine univalves, pointed as for use, found together; two pebble-hammers; flakes of chert; a triangular bit of chert, chipped to a cutting edge on one side; a fragment of ferruginous sandstone; mica; an oblong piece of silicified wood, which had seen use as a hone.

Owing to the great amount of previous digging, data as to position of objects in the mound were hard to obtain. However, sherds and piles of fragments of different vessels, placed together, were noted in undisturbed

FIG. 91.—Sherd. Mound on Brickyard creek. (Half size.)

FIG. 92.—Earthenware handle of vessel. Mound on Brickyard creek. (Full size.)

sand in the eastern part of the mound, as we had so often found to be the case in mounds of the northwest Florida coast.

There were also in the eastern part of the mound nine vessels of inferior ware, some badly broken, all showing the basal perforation where their condition allowed determination.

Vessel No. 2.—In a sort of pit, in the SE. margin, was an unassociated bowl of about one quart capacity, having an incised scroll-decoration, with punctate markings, in addition.

Vessel No. 4.—A quadrilateral vessel undecorated save for an incised line around the rim.

Vessel No. 5.—A vessel probably representing a section of a gourd cut longitudinally.

Vessel No. 6.—A bowl in fragments, with notches around the rim and four very rude animal heads.

Vessel No. 7.—A vessel badly crushed, having a broad band of complicated stamp-decoration around the neck.

Vessel No. 8.—A bowl of heavy ware, badly broken, covered with crimson pigment, inside and out.

Vessel No. 9.—A quadrilateral vessel with rounded corners and convex base, having for decoration beneath the rim a broken line with an incised line below it.

Among the sherds, the check-stamp was represented as was the complicated stamp, one pattern of which is shown in Fig 91.

Much ware bore incised and punctate decoration of familiar patterns. There were found also a handle representing the head of a duck (Fig. 92) and a small handle, a bird head in profile, having a perforation in place of eyes.

MOUND NEAR BURGESS LANDING, BURGESS CREEK, CALHOUN COUNTY.

Chipola river is a tributary of the Apalachicola.

Burgess creek enters the Chipola river on the west side, about eight miles up. Burgess landing, on the west side of the creek, is about one mile above the junction of the creek with the river. The mound, on property of Mr. S. S. Alderman, of Wewahitchka, Florida, was about 100 yards from the landing, in full view from the road.

The mound, much spread by previous digging here and there, had also a narrow trench entirely through it in an eastwardly and westwardly direction. The height of the mound at the time of our investigation, was 4 feet 9 inches; its diameter, 48 feet. Trenches were run in from all sides, a distance of about 3 feet when it became evident that the mound proper, with a diameter of 42 feet, had been reached. The mound, of clayey sand, very tenacious in places, was entirely demolished by us, with the exception of small portions around several trees.

Human remains were not met with until the digging had advanced well into the body of the mound, when, at different points, and especially, near the center, fragments of single skulls and bits of long-bones were found. Once, fragments of a skull lay with the remains of one radius and of one femur. In all, human remains lay in twelve places, but so near together, at times, that some of these may have belonged to the same burial.

No artifacts lay with the bones, but scattered through the mound were: two small "celts" of polished rock, at one place and one at another; four hones of ferruginous sandstone; mica, in two places; a rude arrowhead of chert.

All in the eastern side of the mound, beginning a certain distance in from the margin, were deposits of sherds, often parts of a number of vessels together, and entire vessels, broken and whole. Altogether about two dozen vessels were met with, all of inferior ware, none showing any novelty as to form or decoration. The majority were undecorated, several had a faint check-stamp. The complicated stamp, faintly impressed, was on one sherd and on one vessel. Rude, punctate decoration was shown on two or three vessels, and a somewhat better executed line and punctate design was on part of a vessel found in three pieces.

FIG. 93.—Vessel No. 5. Mound near Burgess Landing. (Three-quarters size.)

Thirteen or fourteen vessels, mostly pots, some badly crushed, lay in contact one with another.

In cases where the condition of the vessel allowed determination, the hole knocked in the base to "kill" the pot was found to be present.

But two vessels merit particular description.

Vessel No. 2.—A vessel of about three pints' capacity, of elliptical section, with a projection on two opposite sides, perhaps a conventional head and tail, undecorated, save for crimson pigment on the exterior.

Vessel No. 5.—This vessel, found in fragments and since cemented together, with restoration of certain missing parts, including where the tail should be, has for handle the head of a wood-duck (Fig. 93). Upon the vessel is a certain amount of crimson pigment. The base has the usual mortuary mutilation made after the baking of the clay.

Mound near Isabel Landing, Chipola River, Calhoun County.

This mound, about 100 yards west of the landing, on property of Mr. L. M. Ware, of St. Andrews, Florida, had been literally honey-combed by holes and trenches. At the time it was dug down by us, with the exception of parts around certain trees, it had a height of 4 feet 7 inches; a basal diameter of 48 feet.

Though much of the mound still remained intact, especially the lower portion, human remains were found by us but twice: a single skull badly decayed, 3 feet down in the SE. part of the mound; a few bones, probably disturbed by a former trench.

In the eastern part of the mound, near the margin, were a few undecorated sherds and several with the small check-stamp. Farther, in the same direction, here and there, stopping short of the center, were five or six vessels of ordinary type and inferior ware, undecorated, several with parts missing. Among these was a pot with a complicated stamp decoration consisting of squares made up of parallel lines, a pattern found by us on the northwest coast. This vessel had two perforations, one on either side of an early fracture, to permit a cord or sinew to bind the parts together.

All vessels in this mound, of which sufficient remained to allow a determination, had the mortuary perforation knocked through after baking.

There were also in the mound: a sherd with the complicated stamp; one with rude punctate decoration; mica; a flake of chert; a quartz pebble.

Mound near Chipola Cut-off, Calhoun County.

The Apalachicola and Chipola rivers, some miles above their junction, are united by a sort of canal which is called the Chipola Cut-off.

In a swamp, about 40 yards from the bank, on the northern side, near the eastern end of the cut-off, was a mound on property under control of Mr. F. B. Bell, of Wewahitchka, Florida. Between the mound and the water is a considerable excavation whence the material for the mound was taken.

The mound, which had been dug into in almost every direction, had, at the time of our visit, a height of 5 feet 3 inches. The base, circular in outline, was 45 feet in diameter.

The mound, which was totally dug down by us, was composed of brown sand with a certain admixture of clay. The sand in the eastern and southern parts of the mound, where most of the pottery was found, was of a deeper brown than elsewhere. Below the mound was sand seemingly undisturbed, yellow, rather coarse, without admixture of clay.

Burials were noted at forty-two points, and were met with marginally, and throughout the mound to the center, the greater number being in the southeastern, southern and southwestern parts, where the principal deposit of pottery was found, though the pottery was seldom directly associated with burials.

The forms of burial were similar to the majority of those found along the northwest Florida coast, consisting of the flexed skeleton, the bunched burial and the lone skull. The condition of the bones was fragmentary through decay, crania being represented by one calvarium. Upon this no artificial flattening was apparent.

With the burials were a number of artifacts, including several vessels of earthenware, one immediately over a skull; chisels wrought from lips of marine univalves; shell beads, large and small; fifty small shells (*Marginella*) perforated for use as beads; many small, round masses of hematite, perhaps used in a rattle; a number of "celts" of various rocks; two hones of ferruginous sandstone; a number of small, sharp flakes of chert, together; one glass bead from the body of the mound; several columellæ of marine univalves, with pointed ends.

With Burial No. 15, a bunch, were: two large columellæ, each pointed at one end and each having a portion of the shell remaining on the upper part, doubtless to serve as a handle; two shell hair-pins; mussel-shells; one stone "celt;" shells used as beads (*Marginella*); two shell chisels made from lips of marine univalves; two fine shell gouges wrought from the body whorl of *Fulgur*; two bones of a lower animal, probably ulnæ of deer, badly decayed, with the proximal articular parts present, and the distal ends, which, seemingly, had been worked to a point, missing; two tibiæ of the deer, with both ends cut off, doubtless handles; a number of fragmentary implements of bone. With these was a fish-hook of bone (Fig. 94), 3.2 inches in length, having two features not before met with by us in our mound work. The lower end has a part of the articular surface of the bone remaining, and the hook has a well-defined barb. Barbed fish-hooks of aboriginal make are met with infrequently enough anywhere, but in the southern United States this barbed hook must be almost unique.

Another fish-hook, probably similar to this one, came from elsewhere in the mound. Unfortunately, the point of the hook was broken in removal, and the most careful search failed to recover it.

FIG. 95.—Object of bone, probably fish-hook. Mound near Chipola Cut-off. (Full size.)

In Fig. 95 is shown an implement of bone, probably a fish-hook of another variety, found with the fish-hook first described.

This swamp-mound, under water in times of freshet, was somewhat above water-level at the period of our visit. Burial No. 19, consisting of a few fragments of badly decayed bone, lay in a distinctly marked pit, below the base, where the dark-brown, clayey sand of that part of the mound extended into the coarse, yellow sand considerably below the water level. With the bones, and extracted with great difficulty, owing to the rapid filling of the pit with water, were : two vessels of earthenware, one badly broken ; a disc of sheet-brass, about 4.5 inches in diameter, without decoration, having two holes for suspension, about .75 of an inch apart, near the margin ; a disc of sheet-brass, nearly 8 inches in diameter, also undecorated, having a small hole in the center for attachment.

This disc, which was somewhat broken in removal, still showed traces of fiber in which it had been wrapped, as did the other disc. Also with these objects were three glass beads ; doubtless many others were left at the bottom of the pit, since the removal of objects so small, when one is working at arm's-length under water, is a difficult matter.

Burial No. 25, a few bones, lay also in a pit, under water, below the base of the mound. With them were shell beads and a stone " celt."

Burial No. 30, two skulls, had with it a *Fulgur perversum*, 15.2 inches in length, the largest shell of this variety of which we have been able to learn.

With Burial No. 32, bones which fell with caved sand, was a circular ornament of sheet-brass, 4.5 inches in diameter, slightly concavo-convex, without decoration, with a central perforation, somewhat broken, bearing traces of fiber, like the others.

Burial No. 41, a bunch, lay in a pit with Vessels Nos. 48 and 49.

Burial No. 42, the skull of a child, had with it fragments of an undecorated disc of sheet-brass.

Unassociated were : three pebbles ; one sandstone hone ; several flakes of chert, with cutting edge on one side. There were also many objects of shell, such as we have described as present with burials. These objects, in all probability, though not found with bones, had been with them before disturbance by recent diggers.

Twenty-four " celts " of various rocks, from 2.6 inches to 9.8 inches in length, many with ends gracefully tapering opposite the cutting edge, were present in the mound, some with burials as we have stated, many alone. Certain of these lay in the very margin of the mound and evidently had been placed there ceremonially, since burials were not met with until farther in.

While sounding with an iron rod in and around the burial pits of which we have spoken, a member of the party, with no particular reason, drove the rod through the bright yellow sand which, as we have said, was seemingly undisturbed and underlay the base of the mound. Greatly to our surprise, about 2.5 feet below the level uncovered by our men, which was supposed to be the base of the mound, a solid object was encountered. After much labor, including repeated use of a portable pump, this object was found to be a beautiful chisel or hatchet, of trap rock, 9 inches long and about 3.5 inches in maximum breadth with a maximum thickness of .8 of an inch. This implement, flat on one side, slightly convex on the other, had a well-made cutting edge at the broad end. With this implement were two ordinary " celts." We are at a loss to explain the presence of these objects where they were found. We are loth to believe in the presence of burials beneath the base, unnoticed by us, as a careful lookout was kept by the diggers who had been with us mostly for long periods, and by those having the work in charge. The regular burial-pits found by us, as we have said, were filled with a material differing from the sand into which they extended. Possibly this deposit was a ceremonial one, or a cache made before the building of the mound.

At the very start, all around the margin, but mainly in the S. and SE. parts of the mound, sherds were met with, followed by considerable deposits of various parts of broken vessels, in masses, in no case, however, having a full complement of any one vessel. Near these, occasionally, were single vessels, and later, numbers of vessels together, extending in to the center of the mound—in fact, the same ceremonial deposit of earthenware with which those who have looked over our reports of the mounds of the northwest Florida coast, must be familiar. In this case, however, vessels, to a certain extent, were found with burials, and the ceremonial deposit, in a certain degree, was met with in parts of the mound other than those we have named.

The ware from this mound is, as a rule, inferior, though some is of excellent quality, including certain bowls of black, polished ware, the specialty of Mississippi, which ware we had found before no farther eastward than Choctawhatchee bay (see outline map) where it was, as in the Chipola mound, represented by a few examples, perhaps importations.

Curiously enough, also, other ware from the mound, besides that we have mentioned, recalls ware belonging to more western districts in composition and in finish, while the decoration, largely made up of the scroll, resembles that described in the first part of our report on the mounds of the northwest Florida coast, rather than that of the second part, in which the Apalachicola coast-region is included.

There fell to our portion as gleaners, after the wide-spread, previous digging in this mound, fifty-one vessels, including whole vessels, vessels with but small parts missing, and others, in fragments, where the full complement or almost the complement of the vessel is present.

We shall describe in detail the most notable of these vessels. All, unless otherwise described, have the usual basal mutilation made before the baking of the clay.

Vessel No. 6.—A small bowl notched around the margin, with incised and punctate decoration, as shown in Fig. 96.

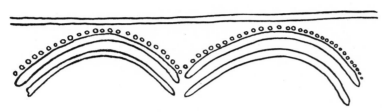

FIG. 96.—Vessel No. 6. Decoration. Mound near Chipola Cut-off. (Full size.)

Vessel No. 7.—A bowl of about one quart capacity, with incised and punctate decoration on the sides and base, shown diagrammatically in Fig. 97.

Vessel No. 8.—A small bowl of inferior ware, oval in section, with a rudely executed bird-head on one side and a rudimentary, conventional tail on the other (Fig. 98). The decoration, incised and punctate, representing wings in part, is shown diagrammatically in Fig. 99, where it has been found impossible to follow an exact scale, owing to the curvature of the base.

Vessel No. 10.—A five-pointed dish of yellow ware, with incised and punctate decoration (Fig. 100).

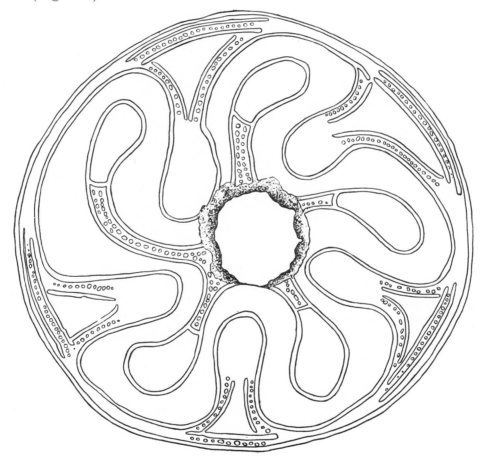

FIG. 97.—Vessel No. 7. Decoration. Mound near Chipola Cut-off. (Half size.)

57 JOURN. A. N. S. PHILA., VOL. XII.

FIG. 98.—Vessel No. 8.   Mound near Chipola Cut-off.   (Full size.)

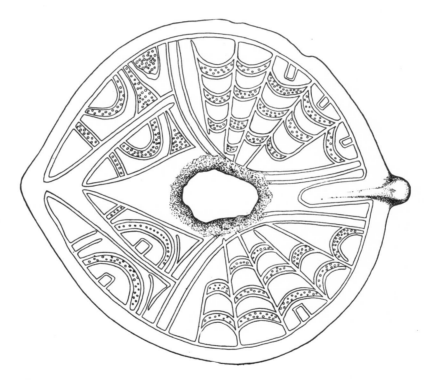

FIG. 99.—Vessel No. 8.   Decoration.   Mound near Chipola Cut-off.   (Not exactly on scale.)

Vessel No. 12.—A bowl of about four quarts' capacity, with notches around the margin, having an incised and punctate design six times repeated (Fig. 101).

Vessel No. 13.—Has for decoration upright, parallel lines between two encircling, parallel lines.

Vessel No. 14.—A bowl of about five pints' capacity, of inferior ware, having a

FIG. 100.—Vessel No. 10.   Mound near Chipola Cut-off.   (Half size.)

FIG. 101.—Vessel No. 12.   Mound near Chipola Cut-off.   (About three-quarters size.)

scalloped margin.   On the seven apices of the scallops have been an equal number of small, rude animal-heads, all but one of which are missing.

Vessel No. 15.—A vase of yellow ware (Fig. 102), with incised and punctate decoration shown in diagram (Fig. 103).

Vessel No. 16.—A dipper representing a section of a gourd.   There is rude, incised decoration in which the scroll figures.

Vessel No. 20.—This interesting, mortuary vessel, 13.25 inches in height, 8.75 inches in maximum diameter (Fig. 104), with upright bird head handle, was not represented in the mound by its full complement of parts.   Such portions as were missing have been restored, but in no case has any opening been introduced, unless

FIG. 102.—Vessel No. 15.   Mound near Chipola Cut-off.   (About five-sixths size.)

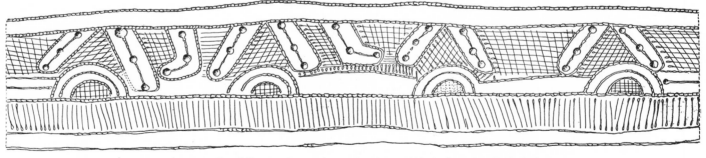

FIG. 103.—Vessel No. 15.   Decoration.   Mound near Chipola Cut-off.   (Half size.)

its former presence was clearly indicated by marginal parts.   Nearly the entire base has been broken out.

Vessel No. 21.—A water bottle of coarse ware, with uniform incised and punctate decoration, in which the partly interlocked scroll is prominent (Fig. 105).

Vessel No. 22.—A handsome dipper, modelled after a section of a gourd, of

FIG. 104.—Vessel No. 20.   Mound near Chipola Cut-off.   (Half size.)

FIG. 105.—Vessel No. 21.   Mound near Chipola Cut-off.   (About four-fifths size.)

FIG. 106.—Vessel No. 22.   Mound near Chipola Cut-off.   (Five-sixths size.)

FIG. 107.—Vessel No. 22.   Decoration.   Mound near Chipola Cut-off.   (Not exactly on scale.)

FIG. 108.—Vessel No. 24.   Mound near Chipola Cut-off.   (About two-fifths size.)

black, polished ware, recalling that of Mississippi (Fig. 106), with the entire body and base covered with incised decoration in which the scroll is prominent, shown diagrammatically in Fig. 107. At the end of the handle is a small hole for suspension. The basal perforation is absent.

Vessel No. 24.—A bowl 7.5 inches high and 12.8 inches in maximum diameter, with a uniform decoration (Fig. 108).

FIG. 109.—Vessel No. 26. Mound near Chipola Cut-off. (Four-sevenths size.)

Vessel No. 26.—This vessel, of heavy but coarse ware (Fig. 109), notched around the rim, has for decoration incised crosses on two opposite sides and incised, partly interlocked scrolls on the other two. Other decoration, seemingly punctate, proves, on examination, to have been done with a stamp. One-half the decoration, almost a repetition of the other half, is shown diagrammatically in Fig. 110.

Vessel No. 28.—A compartment vessel originally consisting of a square com-

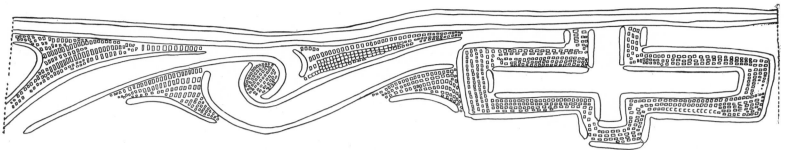

FIG. 110.—Vessel No. 26. Decoration. Mound near Chipola Cut-off. (Half size.)

FIG. 111.—Vessel No. 28. Mound near Chipola Cut-off. (About three-fourths size.)

FIG. 112.—Vessel No. 29. Mound near Chipola Cut-off. (Full size.)

partment with round ones on three sides. One of these, missing when the vessel was found, has been restored (Fig. 111).

Vessel No. 29.—This diminutive, imperforate vessel, with semi-globular body and upright neck slightly expanding, having small holes on opposite sides for suspension, is but 2.2 inches in height (Fig. 112). The incised decoration, shown diagrammatically in Fig. 113, evidently represents two eyes and a nose on one side and probably hair on the other. The decoration around the neck of the vessel is not so readily determined.

Vessel No. 32.—An imperforate vessel of about two quarts' capacity, notched around the

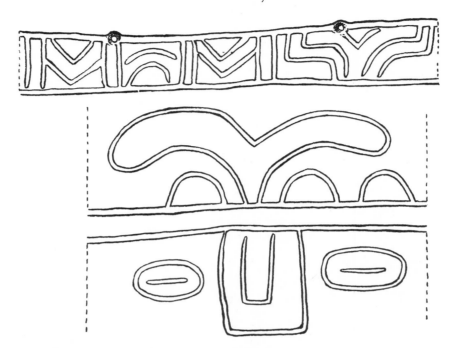

FIG. 113.—Vessel No. 29.   Decoration.   Mound near Chipola Cut-off.   (Full size.)

FIG 114.—Vessel No. 32.   Mound near Chipola Cut-off.   (About three-fourths size.)

rim, which has, in addition, four upright protuberances, probably rudimentary animal heads (Fig. 114).

Vessel No. 33.—This vessel has notches around the rim and an incised decoration of animal paws and partly interlocked scrolls below (Fig. 115).

Vessel No. 34.—A bowl with incised decoration shown in Fig. 116.

Vessel No. 35.—This vessel, with rather rudely incised decoration, is shown in Fig. 117.

Vessel No. 36.—An imperforate bowl of polished, black ware, with a small bird-head at one side and the conventional tail at the other (Fig. 118). The incised decoration is shown diagrammatically in Fig. 119.

Vessel No. 37.—A broad-mouthed, imperforate water-bottle of dark ware seem-

Fig. 115.—Vessel No. 33.   Mound near Chipola Cut-off.   (About five-sixths size.)

FIG. 116.—Vessel No. 34. Mound near Chipola Cut-off. (About two-thirds size.)

FIG. 117.—Vessel No. 35. Mound near Chipola Cut-off. (About two-thirds size.)

Fig. 118.—Vessel No. 36.   Mound near Chipola Cut-off.   (Full size.)

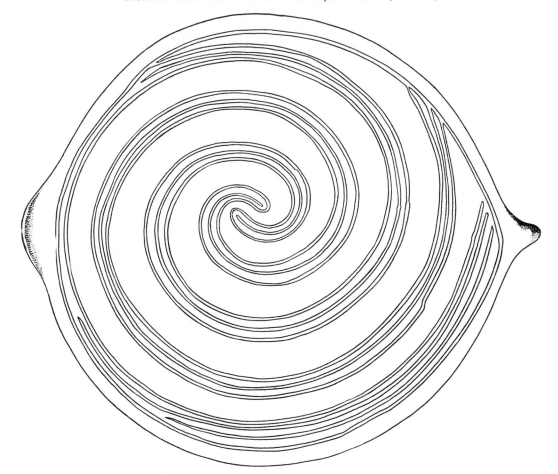

Fig. 119.—Vessel No. 36.   Decoration.   Mound near Chipola Cut-off.   (Not exactly on scale.)

ingly tempered with pounded shell, in every way resembling a type found much farther to the westward.

Vessel No. 38.—A vessel of heavy ware, lenticular in section, undecorated save for one encircling, incised line below the rim.

Vessel No. 41.—A pot with complicated stamp-decoration (Fig. 120).

Vessel No. 42.—A small bowl with a complicated stamp faintly impressed.

Vessel No. 47.—A jar with a complicated stamp-decoration around the neck.

Vessel No. 49.—A vessel with incised decoration of a pattern frequently encountered in this mound (Fig. 121).

FIG. 120.—Vessel No. 41. Mound near Chipola Cut-off. (Five-sixths size.)

Among the masses of fragments in the margin of the mound were many large portions of bowls, four of which are shown in Figs. 122, 123, 124, 125.

In Fig. 126 is shown part of a bowl with the head of a fish in profile.

In Fig. 127 is shown a part of a vessel with the neck divided into two parts before joining the body, a type not met with by us before in Florida, but well-known elsewhere, including Missouri, Tennessee and Peru.

Many loop-shaped handles were present in the mound and a considerable number of handles representing heads of quadrupeds and of birds.   A selection of these is shown in Fig. 128.

Three stopper-shaped objects of earthenware came from this mound, one with a central depression in the top, and an encircling line of impressions made by a triangular point, around the margin (Fig. 129).

Fig. 121.—Vessel No. 49. Mound near Chipola Cut-off. (Five-sixths size.)

Fig. 122.—Sherd. Mound near Chipola Cut-off. (Half size.)

Fig. 123.—Sherd.   Mound near Chipola Cut-off.   (Half size.)

Fig. 124.—Sherd.   Mound near Chipola Cut-off.
(One-third size.)

Fig. 125.—Sherd.   Mound near Chipola Cut-off.   (Half size.)

Fig. 126.—Mound near Chipola Cut-off.   (Full size.)

Fig. 127.—Sherd.   Mound near Chipola Cut-off.   (Full size.)

FIG. 128.—Handles of earthenware vessels.   Mound near Chipola Cut-off.   (Full size.)

This mound was distinctly a post-Columbian one. Glass came from below the base, and brass was met with in it in three different places. Presumably, previous diggers had removed other objects of European provenance. The reader is urged to contrast this mound with that near the great shell-heap on Crystal river, described in the paper preceding this, where, among hundreds of objects, nothing indicating a European origin was found. In that mound the copper found was native copper, which, by analysis, can readily be distinguished from the impure results of the smelting processes formerly in vogue in Europe, by which copper was recovered from arsenical, sulphide ores. Much of the so-called sheet-copper traded with aborigines by Europeans is in reality brass. If any repoussé or open-work designs, such as are found on native copper in many of the larger mounds which contain no objects admittedly of European provenance, have been found on either sheet-brass or on sheet-copper of the impure kind furnished by Europeans, it has eluded our most careful inquiries.

FIG. 129.—Stopper-shaped object of earthenware. Mound near Chipola Cut-off. (Full size.)

MOUND NEAR ESTIFFANULGA, APALACHICOLA RIVER, LIBERTY COUNTY.

This mound, in pine woods, about one mile in a NE. direction from Estiffanulga, on property of Hon. Thomas Johnson, resident near that place, had been dug into in but a very superficial way prior to our visit. Its height was 3 feet; its basal diameter, 38 feet. The mound, composed of yellow, clayey sand, was totally demolished by us, with the exception of small portions around certain trees.

Human remains were met with but once, 4 feet down, in the center of the mound, in white sand with intermingling of bits of charcoal. The burial consisted of decaying remnants of a lower jaw, two femurs, one tibia.

In the southwestern slope was a rather graceful, spheroidal vessel of fairly good ware, undecorated, with a thickening of rim which projects slightly outward. The usual basal perforation is present.

In the eastern margin was a bowl with perforate base, bearing a small check-stamp.

There were several fragments of undecorated vessels and undecorated vessels in fragments, about the mound, also one sherd with a complicated stamp-decoration.

Separately, here and there in the mound, were three graceful "celts" of various rocks, and another "celt" which, seemingly, had been used to smooth or to polish with, as a surface about .75 of an inch in breadth was present where the cutting edge had been.

There were also in the mound three arrowheads or knives, of chert, one somewhat broken, and one large, round pebble.

MOUND NEAR BLOUNTSTOWN, APALACHICOLA RIVER, CALHOUN COUNTY.

About one mile in a NE. direction from Blountstown Landing, a short distance in from the river, is a mound whose southeastern side, facing the water, is on the edge of a terrace along which the river runs in time of flood (see plan, Fig. 130). Much of this side of the mound has been eaten away by freshets, leaving it almost perpendicular.

The mound, on property of Mr. George W. I. Landau, of Patterson, N. J., does not owe its irregularity of shape entirely to the action of the river. The summit plateau slopes gently down from the side bordering the water, and has a maximum height of 19.5 feet, or 2 feet more than the opposite side. On the plateau are the remains of a live-oak, part of which has fallen through decay. The upright portion, 5 feet from the ground, is 16 feet in circumference.

On the side farthest from the water is a small, graded way reaching from the level ground to the summit plateau.

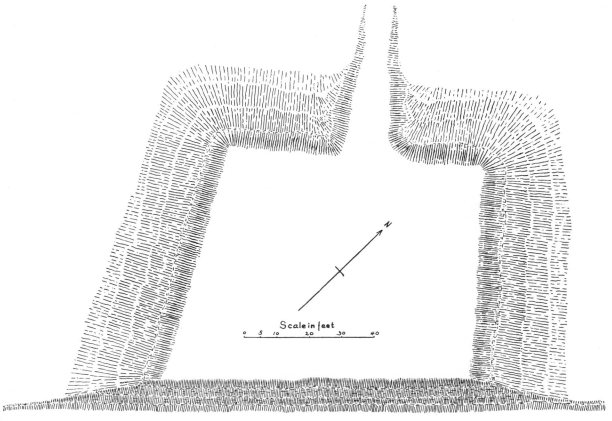

FIG. 130.—Plan of mound near Blountstown.

When our representative located this mound, previous to our visit, through some error the name of the rightful owner was not obtained, and, at the time of our visit, on account of the owner, in his absence, having a watchful representative on the spot, we were unable to investigate. Full permission to dig reached us after our departure. However, the mound was doubtless domiciliary, as indicated by its shape and by the section laid bare by the river, which showed neither bone nor artifact.

Mound in Davis' Field, Apalachicola River, Calhoun County.

About one mile in a northeasterly direction from Blountstown is Davis' Field, long under cultivation in time gone by, but now covered with a sprinkling of pine and other trees, on property of Hon. F. M. Yon, of Blountstown.

The mound, which had been much ploughed over and considerably spread, bore trace of but little previous digging. Its height was 4.5 feet; its basal diameter, considerable of which, however, was due to former cultivation, was 70 feet.

Fourteen trenches were dug inward by us from the margin of the mound, as found by us, until the original margin, presumably, was reached, when what remained of the mound, with a diameter of about 50 feet, was completely dug down, with the exception of small parts around several large pine trees.

The mound, circular in outline, was made of clay having a small admixture of sand, with here and there, small layers and pockets where clayey sand predominated. Throughout, at various points, were more or less charcoal and several fireplaces of considerable size. In the northern part of the mound, extending inward ten feet along the base, with a maximum width of 6 feet and a maximum height of 3 feet, was a mass of fire-hardened clay, red from the effect of heat. Curiously enough, while, here and there, a bit of charcoal lay near this mass, the amount present seemed disproportionately small considering the extent and duration of fire necessary to produce such an effect.

The burials in this mound, which were hardly of more consistency than would be damp sawdust compressed, were met with in twenty-six places. Many of these were found on or near a central space showing marks of fire, and probably belonged to a general interment made at the same time. We shall refer to this matter, later.

The first burial, a few small bits of bone, was met with in the eastern part of the mound at what probably was the original margin. This burial lay near a deposit of earthenware but may have had no connection with it.

The next burial, fragments of a femur, lay in the NW. part of the mound, much farther in than the first burial. After this, burials consisting of the bunch, single skulls, fragments of long-bones, etc., continued to be met with until well in toward the center of the mound, after which flexed skeletons alone were found, beginning with Burial No. 15. Several lay in shallow pits below the base of the mound.

With no burial was an artifact immediately associated, with the exception of a shell drinking-cup found with the skeleton of a child.   Certain sheets of mica, one with a small circular hole in the center, were found near earthenware vessels, and were probably put into the mound ceremonially, as were the vessels.

Toward the center of the mound, somewhat above the base, was an area perhaps about twelve feet square, consisting of masses of charcoal, over and under burials, and in one place bark seemingly with no mark of fire, two thicknesses in one place, three, in another.   This layer of bark, 40 inches long and about 2 feet wide, had at one end, at right angles to it, the remains of a log about 6 inches in diameter and about 3 feet in length.   Both bark and log were little more than dust. This bark layer lay above a skeleton.   The burials under charcoal and under bark were not contiguous, but being on the same plane and near each other, it is probable this area, with its flexed burials, was created at one time and served as a nucleus for the mound.

FIG. 131.—Vessel No. 1. Mound in Davis' Field. (About three-quarters size.)

Vessel No. 1.—Almost due east, probably where the original margin of the mound was, lay a vessel in fragments, with traces of red pigment, inside and out, and a space where a bird-head handle had been (Fig. 131). In the base is a circular hole made before the baking of the clay and, in the body of the vessel, are open-

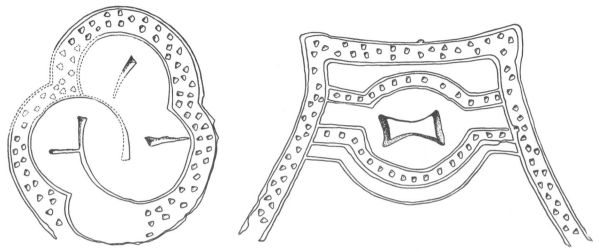

FIG. 132.—Vessel No. 1. Decoration. Mound in Davis' Field. (Half size.)

ings made at the same time. In Fig. 132 is shown diagrammatically the incised and punctate decoration on the wings and on the tail, that on each wing to the left, on the tail to the right. Here we have a ceremonial vessel such as was frequently

FIG. 133.—Vessel No. 2. Mound in Davis' Field. (One-third size.)

met with by us along the northwest coast of Florida between St. Andrew's bay and the Warrior river (see outline map).

Vessel No. 2.—Near Vessel No. 1 lay a mass of fragments, a mixture of sherds and parts of vessels, also several undecorated vessels badly crushed. Several feet on either side of this deposit were parts of vessels or possibly whole ones which had been broken and scattered. Certain fragments from this material, cemented together, with slight restoration at places, are shown in Fig. 133. With these fragments was a small, earthenware head of an owl which, like the vessel, which is colored with red pigment inside and out, bore traces of crimson paint. We have tried in vain to find a connection between the head and the vessel. This vessel belongs strictly to the ceremonial class, having body perforations and a basal hole, made before the clay was "fired."

Vessel No. 3.—This vessel, of graceful form, but of inferior ware, as are practically all vessels in Florida, especially made for interment with the dead, is a bird-effigy of the ceremonial class, with a perforation in the base and others in the body, all made before the baking of the clay (Fig. 134).   In the body of the bird, but not shown in the figure, is a triangular hole above the tail and a small circular one below

FIG. 134.—Vessel No. 3. Mound in Davis' Field. (About half size.)

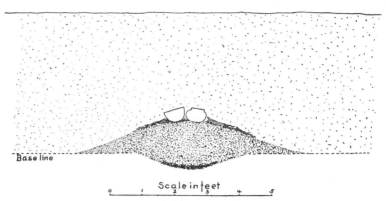

FIG. 135.—Section of ceremonial mound. Mound in Davis' Field.

FIG. 136.—Vessel No. 15. Mound in Davis' Field.
(About half size.)

it. This vessel, found in fragments, has been cemented together. The bill, unfortunately, is missing. An incised decoration on the body of the bird has become faint through the inferiority of the ware.

Seven feet farther in, in the same direction, was a most interesting ceremonial deposit. A pit 6 inches in depth and 3 feet 6 inches in diameter had been dug below the base of the mound. On the bottom of this pit lay charcoal where, evidently, a fire had been. Rising above this pit 1.5 feet from its base was a mound composed of clay blackened with fragments of charcoal. This mound was much spread at its base, where it was 7 feet in diameter (see section, Fig. 135). The main body of the mound rose from the center of the basal portion. From the top of this mound of blackened clay to the surface of the mound proper was 3 feet 6 inches. On the apex of this small, ceremonial mound were three vessels, two being visible when the mound was come upon from the eastward, as is shown in the section. These vessels, which fell into fragments when removed, were bowls with thickened rims, covered with crimson pigment, inside and out. One had, for a handle, a rude representation of a head of a quadruped; another, a place where a head of some sort had been.   One had had a hole knocked through the base; the others were too fragmentary to allow determination.

One of these vessels, in addition to the crimson pigment of which we have spoken, bore a complicated stamp-decoration, the first example of this combination in all our mound work, we believe.

On the sides of the small, ceremonial mound were large fragments of earthenware and two shell drinking-cups, badly broken.

Considerably nearer the center, but in the same line with the rest of the earthenware, were twelve jars, pots and bowls, all of ordinary type and all showing the basal perforation, when not too badly broken.   Some were undecorated; some had bands of complicated stamp-decoration; one or two were covered with it.   All but two were badly broken, some being crushed into minute fragments.

One vessel (No. 15), of eccentric form (Fig. 136), originally covered with red pigment, inside and out, had about one-third, which included almost the entire upper portion, missing.   Certain fragments from this portion served as a sure indication for restoration.   The usual hole knocked through the base is present.

With the exception of the mortuary deposit running in from the eastern part of the mound, not a sherd was met with, to our knowledge, in the entire mound.

YON MOUND, APALACHICOLA RIVER, LIBERTY COUNTY.

This fine mound, about two miles below Bristol, in full view from the river, on property belonging to Hon. F. M. Yon, of Blountstown, Florida, is square in outline, with rounded corners at the present time.   The basal diameter of the mound is 157 feet.   The height depends much upon the side from which the mound is examined, as the surrounding country is irregular, probably 29 feet may be considered the most accurate measurement.   There is no graded way and the slope of the sides is steep, as the mound, of hard clay, seems to have washed but little since its making.   Two determinations, not especially selected, gave angles of ascent of 38 degrees and 43 degrees, respectively.   The diameter of the summit plateau is 68 feet.

This mound gave every evidence of being domiciliary but, as we have sometimes found burials in the summit plateaux of domiciliary mounds,[1] many trenches were dug in the plateau of the Yon mound, resulting in the discovery of one small bunch of human remains, some fragments showing marks of fire.

MOUND BELOW BRISTOL, APALACHICOLA RIVER, LIBERTY COUNTY.

This mound, in an old field, about one mile in a WSW. direction from Bristol, on property belonging to Mr. Robert Shuler, of that place, was of sand, circular in outline, with a basal diameter of 50 feet.   Its height was 3 feet 5 inches.   No previous digging was noticeable in this mound.

[1] For example: the Shields' mound, near the mouth of the St. John's river, Florida; the mound at Matthews' Landing, Alabama river; the mound on Perdido bay and the one on Santa Rosa sound, Florida.

Fifteen trenches dug in from beyond the apparent margin indicated the advisability of joining these trenches to include an area of 50 feet in diameter E. and W. and 46 feet N. and S. This portion of the mound was completely demolished by us, with the exception of certain parts around three trees of considerable size.

Almost at the western margin of the mound, in a pit below the base, were a fragment of a cannon bone of a deer and an earthenware smoking-pipe of ordinary shape. With these were three gouges wrought from the body whorl of *Fulgur*. No human remains lay with these relics, though, no doubt, a burial had been there. In the entire mound human remains were found but once and were represented by a fragment of cranium, which lay with a bit of deer bone in what seemed to be the run-way of a small rodent.

Unassociated in the mound were: a rude arrowhead or knife, of chert; one pebble; a pitted stone about 6 inches square.

Almost at the outset, several sherds having the small check-stamp were met with in the SE. part of the mound. Soon after, three vessels were found, and about 3 feet farther south, on line with the others, twenty-one vessels were grouped together. Near these, a little farther in, were four additional vessels. After these, still continuing toward the center, the area of deposit, widening by a few feet, yielded eighteen vessels, singly and in pairs, until the central part of the mound was reached, making forty-six in all. With these was one shell drinking-cup. There were no masses of sherds such as are usually found in ceremonial deposits of this sort.

Never has it been our fortune to open a mound where a number of vessels presented so low an average of excellence. The ware was of the poorest quality. In form, the vessels, mostly pots, offered not a single departure from ordinary varieties. Incised decoration was unrepresented, the sole ornamentation being notches and scallops, and faint and carelessly-applied complicated stamps on three or four vessels and on one sherd. Not a vessel was recovered whole, though the sand was comparatively dry and almost free from roots, where the vessels were. Some were crushed through inferiority of ware, others had been put into the mound with portions missing. All, where determination was possible, showed the basal perforation made after baking.

MOUND AT BRISTOL, APALACHICOLA RIVER, LIBERTY COUNTY.

This mound, in woods, about 300 yards in a NW. direction from the town of Bristol, on property of Mr. J. E. Roberts, of that place, was on the slope of a ridge of sand. The mound rose about 2.5 feet above the level of the ridge and extending down the slope, gained several additional feet in depth. The mound, which was of sand and circular in outline, had a basal diameter of 56 feet. A trench, 10 feet across, dug prior to our visit, extended from the NE. margin 30 feet into the mound. Trenches beginning in the level ground were dug into the mound from all sides a distance of 3 feet, when, it having become apparent that the original mound had been reached, the trenches were joined and the remainder of the mound, with a diameter of 50 feet, was entirely dug down.

Fourteen burials were met with by us, the majority deep in the mound, one being 5 feet 4 inches from the surface. These burials lay throughout the mound, and were characterized by the paucity of bones constituting a burial, the upper half of a skeleton being the largest interment met with. Ten burials consisted of single skulls or skulls associated with a few minor bones. Other burials were : the upper half of a skeleton ; part of a thigh bone ; two skulls with a tibia and a femur ; a femur and a tibia.

Burials Nos. 1 and 2, a skull with cervical vertebræ and clavicle, and the upper half of a body, respectively, each had neatly rounded shell beads of moderate size, at the neck. These were the only artifacts present with burials. Unassociated, 4 feet down, was a small, waterworn boulder about 8 inches long by 9 inches wide, shaped somewhat like a " celt," which, possibly, had seen service as a maul. A sheet of mica, rudely given the shape of a spearpoint, fell in caved sand.

FIG. 137.—Vessel No. 1.   Mound at Bristol.   (About three-fifths size.)

Almost due east, beginning about 3 feet from the margin of the mound, a point probably marking the original margin, was the usual deposit of earthenware, which continued in to the center, extending but little to either side. The deposit began with a considerable number of sherds and fragments of large vessels, also complete vessels in fragments, nearly all bearing the small check-stamp. Farther in, this decoration was entirely supplanted by other varieties. Here and there, throughout the earthenware deposit, were shell drinking-cups in fragments.

Seventeen vessels were noted by us as complete or nearly so, with the exception of the basal perforation. Many of the vessels, broken and scattered throughout the mound, a custom which was widely practised along the northwest Florida coast, have not been included in our list. These vessels, however, presented no feature of particular interest.

FIG. 138.—Vessel No. 2.   Mound at Bristol.   (Half size.)

FIG. 139.—Vessel No. 3.   Mound at Bristol.   (Half size.)

We shall now describe in detail the most interesting vessels from this mound.

Vessel No. 1.—Has a semiglobular body with a long, upright neck, first contracting, then flaring. The decoration is the small check-stamp. A hole has been knocked through the base (Fig. 137).

Vessel No. 2.—A bowl of excellent ware, 11.25 inches in diameter, 7 inches

Fig. 140.—Vessel No. 8. Mound at Bristol. (About four-fifths size.)

Fig. 141.—Vessel No. 10.   Mound at Bristol.   (About three-fifths size.)

high, in fragments when found, has been cemented together, with a certain amount of restoration (Fig. 138).   Below the rim is a series of designs, probably representing the eye.

Vessel No. 3.—An urn of graceful outline, bearing a small check-stamp, found in bits and since put together, with slight restoration (Fig. 139). Two holes below the rim show where a former fracture has been held together by the aid of a cord or sinew. There is the usual hole broken through the base.

Fig. 142.—Vessel No. 13.   Mound at Bristol.   (Half size.)

Vessel No. 6.—This vessel, found in fragments, had a rude decoration below the neck made up of diagonal lines.

Vessel No. 8.—An interesting ceremonial vessel having red pigment inside and out, and for handle a head representing that of a turkey-buzzard (Fig. 140).   Perforations surround the body of the vessel, all of which, including one through the base, were made before the clay was baked.   Height of body, 6.5 inches; maximum diameter, 6.25 inches.   There has been a certain amount of restoration on the body, but none unless adjacent parts clearly authorized it.

FIG. 143.—Vessel No. 14.   Mound at Bristol.   (About four-fifths size.)

Vessel No. 9.—A graceful, undecorated, globular bowl with a small perpendicular rim.

Vessel No. 10.—A ceremonial vessel partly covered with red pigment, 11 inches maximum diameter of body; height, 8.75 inches (Fig. 141).   There are two bird-head handles, on one of which a central portion of the bill has been restored, and an entire bill, added to the other.   There are two encircling rows of circular holes, made before the clay was "fired." Curiously enough, this ready-made mortuary vessel has no basal perforation.

Vessel No. 11.—A globular bowl of thick ware, decorated on the inside with crimson pigment. The only part of the outer surface showing decoration is an upright rim about 1 inch in height.

Vessel No. 13.—A bowl of yellow ware, shown in Fig. 142. A perforation has been broken through the base.

Vessel No. 14.—Has a complicated stamp decoration around the neck (Fig. 143). The usual hole has been knocked through the bottom.

Vessel No. 16.—An ordinary shape having for decoration two incised, encir-

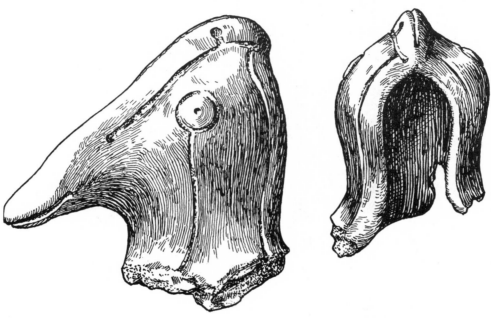

FIG. 144.—Handle of earthenware vessel. Two positions. Mound at Bristol. (Full size.)

cling lines just below the rim. This vessel, which has the ordinary basal perforation, was broken when placed in the mound, as one-half was found within the other half, in a reversed position.

Unassociated, was a bird-head handle decorated with crimson paint, having a feature not before met with by us, consisting of an opening at the back of the head. This head is shown, side view and back view, in Fig. 144.

MOUND NEAR ATKINS' LANDING, APALACHICOLA RIVER, CALHOUN COUNTY.

This mound, on the edge of the swamp, about one mile in a SE. direction from the landing, on property of Mr. W. R. Shields, living nearby, had been riddled with holes and seamed with trenches previous to our visit. Its height is 3 feet, its basal diameter, 40 feet.

Such parts of the mound as had been left intact yielded nothing to our investigation.

MOUNDS NEAR ASPALAGA, APALACHICOLA RIVER, GADSDEN COUNTY (3).

About one mile in a NE. direction from Aspalaga Landing, on high ground, is a large field, long under cultivation, property of the late Mr. John L. Smith and now under management of Mr. William Smith, living nearby. Over this field, and especially over spaces, dwelling sites, having a sprinkling of broken mussel-shells and of *Georgiana vivipara* and *Campeloma lima*, were bits of pottery, undecorated, with small check-stamp, with complicated stamp, with rude punctate decoration, and, in one or two instances, of good ware with superior, incised decoration. There were also, scattered here and there over these sites, pebbles, hammer-stones, hones, fragments and flakes, of chert, partially-made arrowheads, a few complete ones.

In this field were three mounds, all of sand, two of which, low and much spread, were shown by thorough digging to have been domiciliary in character.

The third and largest had a somewhat irregular outline caused, or, at all events, increased, by the use of the plough. As the mound stood on a gentle slope, the height of the artificial portion was hard to determine. Measurements from the west side gave an altitude of 6 feet 8 inches. On the east side, where the foot of the slope was, the mound was 9 feet 5 inches high. According to members of the family, the height of the mound had been reduced at least 5 feet by continued cultivation. East and west the basal diameter of the mound was 98 feet, and 90 feet, north and south.

While there had been a certain amount of previous digging, it was small considering the area of the mound. The mound, including certain additional territory surrounding it, was completely dug through by us.

Human remains were found at fifty-four points, mainly in the eastern and western sides, though burials extended around somewhat as the body of the mound was reached, certain ones being in the central portion. The forms of burial were: the lone skull, the bunch, the flexed burial, and bones scattered here and there. In addition to these there was, on the base of the southwestern portion of the mound, a small pocket of calcined fragments of human bones. Such deposits are met with occasionally in mounds along the northwest Florida coast.

The condition of human remains was fragmentary in the extreme, and such parts as remained were in the last stage of decay. Burial No. 29 consisted of a dark stain in the sand, and several teeth crumbling into dust. Burial No. 34 was made up of a few minute fragments of bone. Presumably, certain burials in this mound had entirely disappeared.

But one calvarium was recovered. It showed no artificial flattening.

Considering the extent of the mound, remarkably few objects had been placed with the dead.

Burial No. 2, near the surface, a skeleton from which the ribs and one arm were missing, had seven shell beads of fair size, at the neck, and a polished "celt" under the arm.

Burial No. 18 was represented by one bit of bone. With this burial was charcoal and what remained of a shell drinking-cup.

Burial No. 26, remnants of a skull, had in direct association, about one-third of a large pot.

Burial No. 28, indications of a flexed burial, had a few shell beads.

Burial No. 39, the remains of a skull, had nearby: a polished "celt;" a discoidal stone of quartzite, 3 inches in diameter on top, with sides slightly converging toward the base, and a shallow pit in the center of the upper part, rough in appearance, possibly used for the cracking of nuts; a lance-head of chert, 4.5 inches in length; two arrow-points or knives, of the same material; part of a lance-head, a flake, two irregular bits, all of chert; one smoothing pebble; one pebble-hammer; one triangular gouge of shell, with unground edge; two cutting implements wrought from columellæ; certain shells (*Murex flavescens*, *Rangia cuneata*, *Dosinia discus*).

With several burials was more or less charcoal. In one place, where bones probably had disappeared through decay, was sand tinged with hematite. Just above the base, at the center of the mound, was a local layer of red clay, on part of which lay a few scattered bones.

Unassociated objects, except earthenware, were: several pebbles; one arrow-head or knife, of chert; a thick sheet of mica, roughly rounded; another with the

Fig. 145.—Pebble-hammer.   Mound near Aspalaga.   (Full size.)

outline of a spear-point; several shell drinking-cups found with the pottery deposit; a pebble-hammer of sedimentary rock, about 4 inches long, showing an encircling band at the middle, consisting of the original surface, the remainder being worked down and rounded as to the ends, one of which is somewhat chipped by use (Fig. 145).

In the eastern part of the mound, under the slope, with a sherd deposit, were a number of masses of lime-rock, each from 1 foot to 18 inches in diameter. Rock of this sort is found along the northernmost parts of the Apalachicola river, near which this mound was.

At the extreme eastern margin of the mound, the advance guard of the pottery deposit, was a number of sherds scattered here and there, some undecorated, some bearing a complicated stamp, also several bases of vessels with four feet. These sherds were followed by portions of vessels in fragments, and by vessels from which considerable parts were missing. All these were of inferior ware and decoration.

The first whole vessel, a small bowl with in-turned rim, undecorated, was met with 8 feet from the margin, somewhat north of east in the mound. This vessel was followed by single ones, mostly pots, here and there, some a little more to the eastward. Some of these were undecorated or had a faint complicated stamp; several had feet; and some, notches around the rim. Among these vessels were fragments of others, also of inferior ware, showing the ready made basal perforation.

Still farther in were a few vessels, or large parts of vessels, all badly crushed, some of which, cemented together and restored in part, are included among vessels particularly described.

All these vessels and sherds lay in sand much darker than that of the remainder of the mound, a feature so frequently noted among the mounds of the northwest Florida coast.

The more noteworthy vessels will now be described in detail. But one is without the usual mortuary perforation.

Vessel No. 2.—Part of a vase of yellow ware, with the upper portion missing (Fig. 146).

Fig. 146.—Vessel No. 2. Mound near Aspalaga. (Full size.)

Vessel No. 4.—A diminutive pot, undecorated save for notches around the rim.

Vessel No. 5.—Certain parts of a large, globular vessel of porous, inferior ware, decorated on the outside with red pigment. The body has numerous perforations made before the "firing" of the clay. The base is missing. A large, red, bird-head handle was found with this vessel, but the parts uniting it to the vessel were not met with.

Vessel No. 7.—A vase 10.5 inches high and 8.25 inches in maximum diameter of body which is heart-shaped in longitudinal section. The neck is upright and flaring, and has incised and punctate decoration with crimson pigment in places.

The base is somewhat flattened to allow the vessel to maintain an upright position (Fig. 147).

Vessel No. 8.—A vessel of about 4 quarts' capacity, of inferior, yellow ware, found in fragments, and restored in places (Fig. 148). The interesting, incised and punctate decoration, shown diagrammatically in Fig. 149, is repeated on the opposite side of the vessel.

FIG. 147.—Vessel No. 7. Mound near Aspalaga. (Half size.)

Vessel No. 9.—Certain parts of a large human effigy-vessel were met with at different levels in the mound and often many feet distant one from another. Part of the base, some of the body, and the face, with the exception of a fragment of the lower left-hand part, were recovered and have been cemented together, with considerable restoration which, however, was clearly indicated by portions present. An interesting and novel feature is perforations in the eyes and ears (Fig. 150). A number of other vessels, broken and scattered in the way this figure was, were present in the mound.

FIG. 148.—Vessel No. 8.   Mound near Aspalaga.   (Three-fifths size.)

FIG. 149.—Vessel No. 8.   Decoration.   Mound near Aspalaga.   (Two-thirds size.)

FIG. 150.—Vessel No. 9.   Mound near Aspalaga.   (About half size.)

Vessel No. 10.—Ovoid, with circular depressions covering the entire body, much like a vessel found by us in the smaller mound near Hare Hammock, northwest Florida coast,[1] though that vessel is more carefully made, and has, also, a narrower opening.   The impressions on that vessel have a comparatively smooth sur-

[1] *Op. cit.*, Part II, Fig. 138.

face, while those on the vessel from this mound seem to owe their origin to a circular object with a slight, rough projection at the center.

Vessel No. 11.—Twenty-one feet in from the eastern margin of the mound the black sand ended and no earthenware of any sort was met with in the mound afterward, with the exception of an unassociated vessel in the southern portion, having an ovoid body with upright rim flaring, then constricted. There is a rather rough, complicated stamp-decoration. This vessel has no basal perforation (Fig. 151).

Several bird-head handles lay unassociated in the sand. One has a perforation apparently cut after the baking of the clay (Fig. 152). Another (Fig. 153), large and hollow, has red pigment around the eyes.

In Fig. 154 is given a selection of sherds from this mound. As might be expected, since the territory in which the mound was is near Georgia, the complicated stamp is largely represented. One, on the left of the second row, did not come from the mound, but from the surface nearby.

FIG. 151.—Vessel No. 11.   Mound near Aspalaga.   (About four-fifths size.)

FIG. 152.—Earthenware handle of
vessel. Mound near Aspalaga.
(Full size.)

FIG. 153.—Earthenware handle of vessel. Mound near Aspalaga. (About full size.)

FIG. 154.—Selection of sherds. Mound near Aspalaga. (Half size.)

MOUND NEAR SAMPSON'S LANDING, APALACHICOLA RIVER, JACKSON COUNTY.

This mound, within sight of the road, about one-half mile in a W. direction from the landing, on property belonging to Mr. D. L. McKinnon, Marianna, Florida,

FIG. 155.—Vessel of earthenware. Mound near Sampson's Landing. (About four-fifths size.)

had been dug into superficially in the center, in addition to which a hole about 2.5 feet square had been sunk to the base.   The mound, sand with a certain admixture of clay and gravel, had a height of 4.5 feet; a basal diameter of 45 feet.   It was totally dug down by us, with the exception of parts left around two trees.

Human remains were encountered forty-seven times, the bones being badly decayed, enough only remaining to indicate the form of burial.   Several calvaria, recovered uncrushed, gave no evidence of artificial flattening.

The burials, found in all parts of the mound, from the margin in, were as follows as to form: scattered bones, 1; lone skulls, 13; bunched burials, 11; flexed skeletons, 22.   Of the flexed skeletons, none of which was met with until the digging approached the body of the mound, all were flexed on one side or on the other, except one which lay on the back with the knees raised.   Three flexed burials lay under masses of lime-rock.   One lone skull was in dark sand, with charcoal nearby.

FIG. 156.—Vessel of earthenware.   Mound near Sampson's Landing.   (Five-sixths size.)

There were in the mound, in addition to several pebbles, two " celts " which lay separately, unassociated, and seemed to have been put in in a general way. Near certain earthenware were mica and part of a shell drinking-cup.

Soon after the digging began a few scattered sherds were found, plain, with the small check-stamp, and with a complicated stamp.   Later, part of a pot with a complicated stamp, and with a hole knocked through the base, came from the southwestern part of the mound, and a large fragment with rude, incised decoration and basal perforation lay near the southern margin.

When the digging had progressed a number of feet into the eastern side of the mound, a number of parts of vessels, of inferior ware, as were all the vessels in this mound, bearing the small check-stamp, were encountered. Just behind these were six vessels together, one, undecorated, of rather graceful, elliptical section, with a hole knocked through the base, in common with all vessels from this mound. Four vessels of this deposit are undecorated; the sixth has a series of roughly incised, diagonal, parallel lines, around the neck which, long and flaring, rises from a globular body.

Just to one side of these was a mass of sherds from various vessels, and a little farther in, were two pots with portions missing, one having a faint complicated

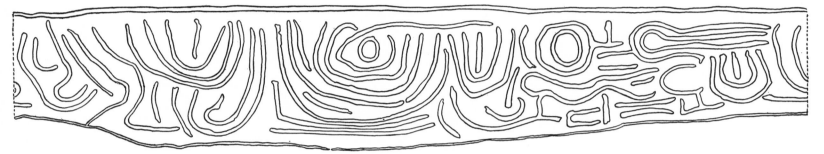

FIG. 157.—Decoration on vessel shown in Fig. 156. Mound near Sampson's Landing. (Half size.)

stamp, the other undecorated. With these was a graceful jar of about three quarts capacity, shown in Fig. 155, having a flat, square base. Around the neck is a complicated stamp-decoration. Near this jar was a vessel in fragments, having a complicated stamp, and a rude pot also with a stamped decoration around the neck.

Somewhat farther in the same direction, well toward the center of the mound, were four pots and bowls, three broken and undecorated. The fourth vessel (Fig. 156) has a curious, incised design, evidently symbolical, shown diagrammatically in Fig. 157. Part of the rim has been restored. A few feet to one side of this vessel was a pot with parallel lines roughly incised beneath the rim.

This was the last occurrence of earthenware met with by us on the Apalachicola river, and it is interesting to note the persistence of the ceremonial deposit of earthenware in the eastern part of the mounds and the occurrence of the mortuary mutilation of the base.

MOUNDS NEAR CHATTAHOOCHEE LANDING, APALACHICOLA RIVER, GADSDEN COUNTY (7).

On the river's bank, at the landing, half cut away by the wash of freshets, is part of a domiciliary mound of clay, formerly circular in outline. Height, 7 feet; diameter of base, 78 feet; diameter of summit plateau, 38 feet.

A short distance farther up, along the bank, is the wreck of a large mound half washed away by the river. This mound, of clay, has several frame buildings upon it. Its height is 11 feet.

In the swamp, in sight from the river, and but a short distance from the mounds just described, are four others. The southernmost, of circular outline, composed of sand with a certain admixture of clay, is 4 feet in height, 70 feet across the base, and 40 feet across the summit plateau.

About 50 yards farther, in a NW. by N. direction, is a circular mound of clay, covered with a considerable thickness of sand. Basal diameter, 66 feet; diameter of summit plateau, 36 feet; height, 3 feet.

Fifty yards in a NW. direction from the last mound, is a mound of circular outline, 3.5 feet high, 58 feet across the base and 26 feet across the summit plateau.

Continuing 40 yards WSW., we came upon a mound near the road, much spread, 46 feet in diameter of base, and 1.5 feet high.

The two mounds partly cut away by the river were not dug into by us, the cross-section made by the river showing them to have been domiciliary.

The swamp-mounds were thoroughly investigated and found to be domiciliary in character.

The mounds of the Apalachicola river yielded nothing especially novel.

The forms of burial were the same as those prevailing along the northwest coast of Florida, namely, the bunch, the flexed skeleton, the lone skull, scattered bones, and, very rarely, the pocket of calcined remains. The burial of skulls under great bowls, a custom met with in places along the Florida coast as far east as St. Andrew's bay, was not met with on the Apalachicola river; nor was the urn-burial proper, where bones are placed in vessels covered by others, inverted, met with by us on the river, though, last season, we found one example of this form of burial in a mound on Ocklockonee bay, to the eastward of Apalachicola.

The earthenware of the river was found to be inferior in quality. The gritty ware of Georgia was not met with nor was the shell-tempered ware of Alabama, with the exception of certain pieces in a single mound. In this mound, curiously enough, were several vessels of polished, black ware, the specialty of Mississippi, which we had not found east of Choctawhatchee bay, on the coast, and many earthenware vessels which, in material, shape and decoration, recalled the yield of mounds considerably farther to the westward.

Ceremonial vessels, "killed" by a basal perforation and by holes throughout the body, made before the firing of the clay, were found in considerable numbers along the Apalachicola river and, as is the case with similar vessels met with by us along the Florida coast between St. Andrew's bay and the Warrior river, the ware is most inferior in quality, as might be expected of vessels purposely made for interment with the dead.

The custom prevalent along the northwest Florida coast, to place deposits of vessels for the dead in common in the eastern part of mounds, obtained also on the Apalachicola river.

Mounds of the Lower Chattahoochee and Lower Flint Rivers

BY

CLARENCE B. MOORE

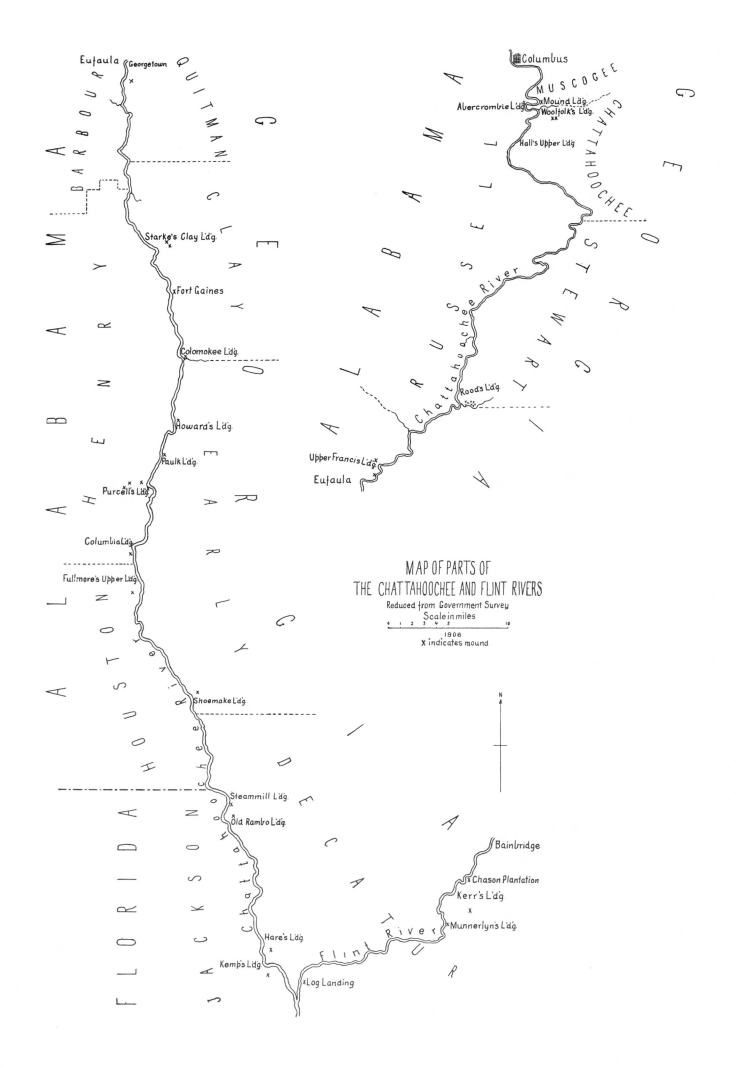

MAP OF PARTS OF
THE CHATTAHOOCHEE AND FLINT RIVERS
Reduced from Government Survey
Scale in miles
0 1 2 3 4 5   10
1906
x indicates mound

Columbus

MUSCOGEE

Abercrombie L'd'g.   x Mound L'd'g.
Woolfolk's L'd'g.

Hall's Upper L'd'g.

RUSSELL

Chattahoochee River

CHATTAHOOCHEE

GEO

STEWART

Rood's L'd'g.

Upper Francis L'd'g. x

Eufaula

GEORGIA

Eufaula   Georgetown

QUITMAN

BARBOUR

CLAY

Starke's Clay L'd'g.

x Fort Gaines

Colomokee L'd'g.

Howard's L'd'g.

Paulk L'd'g.

Purcell's L'd'g.

EARLY

Columbia L'd'g.

Fullmore's Upper L'd'g.

HENRY

HOUSTON

Chattahoochee River

Shoemake L'd'g.

DECATUR

N

Steammill L'd'g.

Old Rambro L'd'g.

Bainbridge

x Chason Plantation

Kerr's L'd'g.
x

x Munnerlyn's L'd'g.

Hare's L'd'g.

Flint River

Kemp's L'd'g.

x Log Landing

FLORIDA

JACKSON

Chattahoochee River

ALABAMA

MOUNDS OF THE LOWER CHATTAHOOCHEE AND LOWER FLINT RIVERS.

By Clarence B. Moore.

Chattahoochee river, having its source in northeastern Georgia, continues in a southwesterly direction until it reaches the middle of the western boundary of the State at Westpoint; thence, flowing in a southerly direction, it forms the boundary between parts of Georgia and of Alabama and, later, between parts of Georgia and of Florida, until its union with the Flint river when, as the Apalachicola river, it continues in a southerly direction to the Gulf of Mexico.

Flint river rises approximately in the central part of Georgia and keeps a southerly and southwesterly course to its junction with the Chattahoochee.

This report treats of the aboriginal remains of part of the Chattahoochee and of part of the Flint rivers, in each case our journey being northward from the junction of the two streams, at which point our investigation of a previous season had come to an end.[1]

The portion of the Chattahoochee covered by us (see map) lies between River Junction, Fla., and the city of Columbus, Ga., a distance of 161 miles by water; and that part of the Flint investigated extends from the Junction to Bainbridge, Ga., 28 miles up the stream,—in each case our work being continued practically to the end of navigation.

As in former years, two agents, one of whom is thoroughly familiar with mound investigation, were sent out in advance of us thoroughly to cover our field of work that the exact situation of mounds and the names of their owners might be known to us, previous to our coming, thus saving a great expenditure of time.

On the Chattahoochee the presence of burial mounds was noted by us as far up as Columbia, Ala., a distance of 48 miles by water. Thenceforward mounds of a domiciliary character only were met with, having near them, doubtless, cemeteries in level ground. These cemeteries, however, we failed to find, save in one instance.

It is interesting to note, in the burial mounds of the lower Chattahoochee, the continuance of certain customs which have been practised in the mounds of the northwestern Florida coast and of the Apalachicola river, namely, the ceremonial deposit of earthenware in the eastern part of the mound for the dead in common, the use of life-forms in earthenware, excisions in the body of vessels, and the mortuary perforation of the base.

As to the mounds of lower Flint river, so few were found by us that no definite conclusion can be reached.

All measurements of earthenware vessels herein given are approximate only, and reduction of size in the illustrations is linear.

[1] See "Certain Aboriginal Mounds of the Apalachicola River." Journ. Acad. Nat. Sci. of Phila., Vol. XII.

Dr. M. G. Miller, as during all our previous archæological investigations, had charge of the anatomical part of the work of the expedition herein described.

The warm thanks of the Academy are tendered those owners of mounds on the Chattahoochee and on the Flint who kindly placed their mounds at its disposal.

Mounds and Sites Investigated on Chattahoochee River.

Mound near Kemp's Landing, Jackson County, Florida.
Mound below Hare's Landing, Decatur County, Georgia.
Mound near Old Rambo Landing, Decatur County, Georgia.
Mound near Steammill Landing, Decatur County, Georgia.
Mound near Shoemake Landing, Early County, Georgia.
Mound near Fullmore's Upper Landing, Houston County, Alabama.
Mound below Columbia, Henry County, Alabama.
Mounds near Purcell's Landing, Henry County, Alabama (4).
Mound near Paulk's Landing, Early County, Georgia.
Mound near Howard's Landing, Early County, Georgia.
Mound near Colomokee Landing, Clay County, Georgia.
Mound at Fort Gaines, Clay County, Georgia.
Mounds near Starke's Clay Landing, Clay County, Georgia (2).
Mound near Georgetown, Quitman County, Georgia.
Mound above Eufaula, Barbour County, Alabama.
Mound near Upper Francis Landing, Barbour County, Alabama.
Mounds near Rood's Landing, Stewart County, Georgia (8).
Dwelling site near Hall's Upper Landing, Chattahoochee County, Georgia.
Mounds near Woolfolk's Landing, Chattahoochee County, Georgia (2).
Mound and cemetery at Abercrombie Landing, Russell County, Alabama.
Mound at Mound Landing, Muscogee County, Georgia.

Mounds and Sites Investigated on Flint River.

Mound near Log Landing, Decatur County, Georgia.
Mound near Munnerlyn's Landing, Decatur County, Georgia.
Mound near Kerr's Landing, Decatur County, Georgia.
Burial-place on the Chason Plantation, Decatur County, Georgia.

MOUNDS AND SITES INVESTIGATED ON CHATTAHOOCHEE RIVER.

Mound near Kemp's Landing, Jackson County, Fla.

The mound, in high swamp, dry at low stages of the river, on property of **Mr. M. A. Warren** of DeFuniak Springs, Fla., lay about one mile in a SSE. direction from the landing. Its height was about 4.5 feet; its basal diameter, 33 feet. A broad trench had been dug in from the western side through the center of the mound, previous to our visit, leaving, however, the eastern part intact.   What was left of the mound was leveled by us.

Human remains found were confined to a small fragment of a skull.

Almost at the eastern margin, and extending to the northeast, began the usual ceremonial deposit of earthenware, put in for the dead in common, such as we have fully described in our reports on the mounds of the northwestern Florida coast and of the Apalachicola river.   This particular deposit presented no new features.   It began with sherds and parts of vessels and continued inward a number of feet, the latter part of the deposit being made up of groups of two or three vessels placed together, at short distances apart.   Owing to the nature of the mound, which was of clay, no vessel was recovered entire, though a number were represented by a full complement of parts.   There was little variety of form, pots and bowls being met with exclusively.   The ware is inferior.   Gritty tempering is absent. Decoration, when present, consists of the small check-stamp; the complicated stamp, faintly impressed; very rude incised line decoration in two instances in sherds; in one case an incised decoration of wavy lines and punctate markings as shown in Fig. 1.   The rim of this vessel, which has been slightly restored in places, is not even, but rises and is depressed in the manner of the decoration beneath.

FIG. 1.—Vessel of earthenware. Mound near Kemp's Landing. (Diameter 5.7 inches.)

All vessels from this mound are small or of medium size, and all, including those represented by fragments, so far as could be determined, had undergone the mortuary perforation of the base so well known in Florida and in parts of Georgia and of Alabama, which was supposed to "kill" the pot and thus free its soul to accompany the souls of those for whom the mound was built.

MOUND BELOW HARE'S LANDING, DECATUR COUNTY, GA.

This mound, in high swamp, about a mile and a half in a southeasterly direction from Hare's Landing, on property of the Stuart Lumber Company, of Brinson, Ga., had a height of 5 feet, a basal diameter of 48 feet.

The mound, seemingly intact, symmetrical, circular as to its base, was composed of sand in the outer parts and of sand with a considerable admixture of clay farther in.   With the exception of a comparatively small portion of the outer western part, it was completely leveled by us.

Human bones, so badly decayed that at times minute fragments alone remained, were found in forty-three places, from 2 feet below the surface down to the base.

In several instances the bunched burial was indicated, as was the flexed form of burial—parts of one at least showing a close flexion of a skeleton lying on the back.

In a number of cases charcoal lay with the bones, as did occasional masses of phosphate rock. Similar masses lay here and there in the mound, not closely associated with burials, though possibly in some instances accompanying bones had disappeared through decay.

Two feet from the surface, well in from the margin but not occupying a central place in the mound, were the remains of what probably had been a flexed burial, below which was a thin layer of charcoal extending beyond at each end. Immediately above the bones, for the full length of the burial, were masses of phosphate rock. A similar mass lay beside the skull.

With the exception of several bits of earthenware, no artifacts accompanied the bones in this mound.

Separately in the soil were flakes and chips of chert; decayed fragments of conch-shells; several pebbles of fair size, one showing marks of use; a mass of galena (lead sulphide) about the size of a child's fist, showing facets on all sides but one, on which was a slight depression; mica in two places; two handsome "celts" of hard rock not found in Florida, the larger 12.25 inches in length.

In the eastern marginal part of the mound were, here and there, a few fragments of pottery together. Thirteen feet in, in the same line as the deposits of fragments, vessels or large parts of vessels, all badly crushed with but few exceptions, were encountered together in twos and threes. With these were occasional decayed fragments of shell drinking-cups.

FIG. 2.—Vessel No. 2.   Mound below Hare's Landing.   (Diameter 7.1 inches.)

These small deposits of vessels of shell and of earthenware continued almost to the center of the mound. The vessels of earthenware and large parts of vessels, nearly all of inferior ware, and all, so far as could be determined, having the usual basal perforation, numbered twenty-eight in the aggregate. The decoration consists variously of a uniform coat of red paint; incised work on several occasions; the small check-stamp; the complicated stamp faintly and carelessly impressed; punctate markings.

We shall describe in detail vessels showing any features of interest, omitting the great majority which consists of pots and bowls, either plain or bearing commonplace decoration.

Vessel No. 2.—A bowl with punctate decoration shown in Fig. 2.

Vessel No. 3.—This beautiful vase of eccentric form, graceful outline, and excellent ware, bears a coating of red paint (Fig. 3). In addition, there is a well-executed incised decoration shown diagrammatically in Fig. 4. This vessel has a double base—the body proper having one, and the extension below it having another. Both have the usual mortuary perforation.

Vessel No. 4.—An effigy vessel about 12 inches in height, showing the human form, found in many fragments, but since joined together. Unfortunately the nose is missing. The figure is carelessly made and is distinctly inferior to similar vessels from the northwestern Florida coast.

Vessel No. 6.—A vessel of yellow ware, with ovoid body (Fig. 5), bearing a rather carelessly made punctate and incised decoration shown in diagram, Fig. 6.

Vessel No. 7.—This interesting vessel (Fig. 7), belonging to the ceremonial mortuary class, with excisions in the body (a variety first made known by us in our reports of the mounds of the northwestern Florida coast and of the Apalachicola river), was found in fragments which have since been cemented together, with slight restoration involving no important part.

FIG. 3.—Vessel No. 3. Mound below Hare's Landing. (Height 7.5 inches.)

The base is missing. The ware, porous and generally inferior, as is usually the case with vessels made expressly for interment with the dead, is decorated with red paint. On one side is a handle or decoration consisting of the head of a long-billed water-bird.

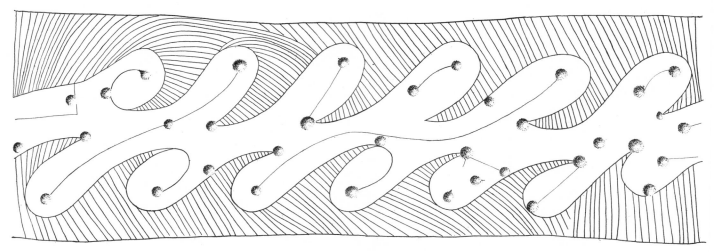

FIG. 4.—Vessel No. 3. Decoration. (About half size.)

The discovery of this type of vessel in this mound marks, we believe, its northernmost occurrence thus far reported.

Vessel No. 8.—Another ceremonial vessel, with open-work decoration, consisting in part of two excised leg-symbols on two opposite sides, bears a projecting head of a quadruped. There are traces of red pigment on the outer surface of this vessel (Fig. 8).

Vessel No. 9.—A ceremonial, mortuary vessel (Fig. 9) bearing slight traces of crimson pigment on the outside. Excised feather-symbols, upright and horizontal, surround the vessel, though no bird-head appears on the rim. A small part of this rim, not recovered by us with the rest of the vessel, may possibly be thought to have supported a plastic model of a bird's head, though we deem this most

FIG. 5.—Vessel No. 6. Mound below Hare's Landing. (Height 6.5 inches.)

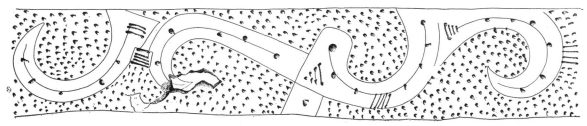

FIG. 6.—Vessel No. 6. Decoration. (About one-third size.)

FIG. 7.—Vessel No. 7.   Mound below Hare's Landing.   (Height 11.9 inches.)

unlikely, as the missing part of the rim is small, and surrounding parts show no thickening for the support of the head as almost certainly they would do had a head been present. Moreover, the feather-symbol (like others) is often used independently in decoration.

FIG. 8.—Vessel No. 8. Mound below Hare's Landing. (Height 10.4 inches.)

Vessel No. 10.—A graceful, mortuary vessel (Fig. 10) of the ceremonial class, with open-work decoration showing the feather-symbol, and having remnants of crimson paint on the outside.   On one side of the opening the neck and head of a bird, from which the bill is missing, project upward.

The four ceremonial vessels from this mound, all of which were found in fragments, have in each case a hole knocked in the base and not made there previous to the firing of the clay, as is often the case with ceremonial vessels of this class.

FIG. 9.—Vessel No. 9.   Mound below Hare's Landing.   (Height 7 inches.)

Vessel No. 15.—Oblate-spheroidal in shape, found in fragments since joined together, having a low, upright rim.   The decoration consists of a coating of red paint, inside and out.

Vessel No. 18.—This perforate vessel, shown in Fig. 11, of excellent yellow ware, has for decoration below the rim a band of punctate markings.

Vessel No. 27.—An imperforate vessel (Fig. 12) of good ware, found in fragments but since repaired.   A deep depression around a central boss on each of the two longer sides is the only decoration.   There are two perforations on one side slightly below the rim.

FIG. 10.—Vessel No. 10.   Mound below Hare's Landing.   (Height 13 inches.)

In one vessel from this mound was a small sheet of mica; in another was part of a cannon-bone of a deer.

MOUND NEAR OLD RAMBO LANDING, DECATUR COUNTY, GA.

In a cultivated field on a plantation of Mr. J. L. Dickenson, of Donalsonville, Ga., is a mound about one-half mile in a NNE. direction from Old Rambo Landing. Correct measurements of this mound were difficult to obtain. Not only is the mound on a decided slope, but its lower parts at least have long been under cultivation and are much spread in consequence. A diameter of 65 feet for the roughly circular base, and a height of 6 feet for the mound are the approximate dimensions. There had been previous digging to a limited extent. Considerable inves-

FIG. 11.—Vessel No. 18. Mound below Hare's Landing. (Height 4.8 inches.)

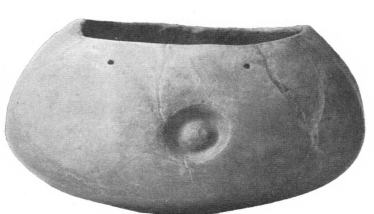

FIG. 12.—Vessel No. 27. Mound below Hare's Landing. (Length 6.4 inches.)

tigation on our part indicated that the mound, which was of sandy clay, had been made for domiciliary purposes.

MOUND NEAR STEAMMILL LANDING, DECATUR COUNTY, GA.

Three-quarters of a mile below Steammill Landing, and about 100 yards from the bank, on another plantation belonging to Mr. Dickenson, is a low and much-spread mound of clay in a cultivated field. No success rewarded our digging in this mound.

MOUND NEAR SHOEMAKE LANDING, EARLY COUNTY, GA.

In a cultivated field, belonging to the plantation of Mrs. Blanche Chancy, of Jakin, Ga., about one mile in a northerly direction from Shoemake Landing, was a mound about 2 feet high and 45 feet across its circular base, at the time of our visit. The mound, of sand, had been long plowed over, and probably considerably reduced in height. It had been dug into to a great extent previous to our visit, including a trench across from west to east and a central excavation more than 15 feet in diameter.

While we were well aware that little but gleanings could await our search, we practically dug the mound through a second time, finding in some small, undisturbed parts a few fragments of decaying human bones.

Evidently there had been in the eastern part of the mound the customary ceremonial deposit made for the dead in common, inasmuch as many sherds, and large fragments of vessels which had been broken presumably by the previous digger, were found in disturbed sand. The ware, which ranges from ordinary to excellent, when decorated, bears: the small check-stamp; the complicated stamp, one variety being shown in Fig. 13; rude punctate decoration; incised parallel lines; incised decoration of complicated design, superior in every way.

FIG. 13.—Sherd. Mound near Shoemake Landing. (Half size.)

Lying on its side, so that previous digging had passed above it, was an interesting vessel about 11 inches in height, and with a maximum diameter of 8.3 inches, representing an owl (Figs. 14, 15). The head, incised and in relief, has the beak missing through former breakage. The wings are incised, as is the tail, on each side of which is the leg-symbol so well known on the western coast of Florida and elsewhere. The feathers are represented by punctate markings as hair sometimes is indicated in early Egyptian art.[1] The entire decoration on this interesting vessel is shown diagrammatically in Fig. 16. It has not been found possible to draw the decoration exactly to scale and to preserve the resemblance to the original at the same time; consequently the periphery of the field has been somewhat enlarged.

The base of this vessel has been knocked out, and many scattered fragments of earthenware from the mound indicated a mutilation of other vessels.

MOUND NEAR FULLMORE'S UPPER LANDING, HOUSTON COUNTY, ALA.

This mound, apparently untouched previous to our investigation, with the exception of a small hole in the center and a certain leveling due to recent cultivation, was in the southern end of a large corn-field, about a mile and a half in a SSW. direction from Fullmore's Upper Landing, on property of Mr. Coy Thompson, of Columbia, Ala.

The mound, which was completely demolished by us, had an average height

[1] Jean Capart, "Primitive Art in Egypt," Figs. 128, 129.

of about 3 feet, but being on the side of a natural slope its height varied decidedly according to the side whence the measurement was taken.

In a number of places in the mound were a few fragments of decaying human bones, but insufficient in form and quantity to indicate the character of burial.   With

FIG. 14.—Vessel of earthenware.   Mound near Shoemake Landing.   (Height 11 inches.)

FIG. 15.—Vessel of earthenware. Side view. Mound near Shoemake Landing. (Height 11 inches.)

FIG. 16.—Decoration on vessel.   Mound near Shoemake Landing.   (About half size.)

56 JOURN. A. N. S. PHILA., VOL. XIII.

the bones were fragments of decomposed chert,[1] some about the size of the human head, some somewhat larger, others smaller. The number of these masses with what had been a single burial ranged from one to four. Numerous other masses of this stone were present in the mound, perhaps marking places where burials had wholly decayed.

FIG. 17.—Vessel No. 1. Mound near Fullmore's Upper Landing. (Height 7.5 inches.)

Beginning at the eastern margin of the mound and continuing well toward the center, was the usual deposit of earthenware consisting of: scattered sherds; fragments of parts of vessels, placed together; vessels in fragments; considerable parts of vessels; and a few entire ones.

The decoration presented no new features. When the incised variety was present it was inferior to the best met with on the Chattahoochee.

Excluding the most ordi-

nary types present in the mound, we shall describe the others in detail.

Vessel No. 1.—A vessel of compact, yellow ware with decoration of incised, encircling lines, cross-hatch, and punctate marking, shown in Fig. 17. A part of the vessel, missing through early breakage, has been restored.

Vessel No. 2.—A vessel of good, yellow ware (Fig. 18). The base, which is missing, was almost flat. The incised and punctate decoration is shown diagrammatically in Fig. 19.

Vessel No. 3.—Almost ovoid in shape, decorated inside and out with a uniform coating of red pigment. In addition, the upper part of the vessel

FIG. 18.—Vessel No. 2. Mound near Fullmore's Upper Landing. (Height 4.3 inches.)

[1] Kindly identified by Dr. George P. Merrill, Head Curator of Geology, United States National Museum, Washington, D. C.

bears evenly distributed, punctate markings.   Parts of this vessel, missing when the rest were found, have been restored.

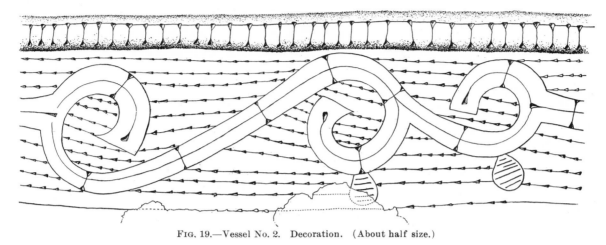

FIG. 19.—Vessel No. 2. Decoration. (About half size.)

Vessel No. 4.—A vessel of rather coarse, yellow ware, having a hemispherical body and a long, upright, cylindrical neck (Fig. 20), around which is an interesting incised and punctate decoration shown diagrammatically in Fig. 21.

Vessel No. 5.—An almost cylindrical vessel found in fragments, with certain parts missing. This vessel, which has been put together with some restoration (Fig. 22), bears an incised and punctate decoration with portions of the field covered with red pigment. This decoration, shown in diagram in Fig. 23, where the red is represented by stipple, is once repeated on the opposite side of the vessel.

Vessel No. 6.—A bowl of yellow ware, bearing incised decoration on a punctate field, the design being five times repeated (Fig. 24).

Vessel No. 7.—An imperforate vessel having five circular compartments, four being on one plane, the fifth rising above them centrally. The decoration consists of red

FIG. 20.—Vessel No. 4. Mound near Fullmore's Upper Landing. (Height 9.3 inches.)

pigment inside and out on the central compartment, and on the inside of the four lower compartments, which are smaller.

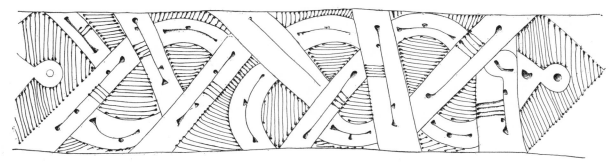

FIG. 21.—Vessel No. 4.   Decoration.   (About one-third size.)

FIG. 22.—Vessel No. 5.   Mound near Fullmore's Upper Landing.   (Height 10 inches.)

Vessels of this class, of course varying in detail, have been found by us in Florida along the northwestern coast from St. Andrews Bay to Cedar Keys; on lower St. Johns river; and on Apalachicola river. We have vainly sought to determine the use to which these vessels have been put. Their form might suggest receptacles for various pigments, but never have we found a deposit of paint remaining in a vessel of this class.[1]

All vessels in the mound, so far as noted, with the exception of the compartment vessel, had the usual mortuary perforation.

With the exception of the earthenware deposit, no artifacts were met with in the mound.

MOUND BELOW COLUMBIA, ALA.

On the same side of the river and in full view from the water, is a mound about a mile and a half below Columbia, on property of Mr. W. L. Crawford, of that place. The mound, evidently built for domiciliary purposes,

[1] Mr. F. W. Hodge, to whom we are indebted also for careful literary revision of these papers, has contributed the following note:

"The Pueblo Indians make and use such as condiment vessels. They generally have two compartments—one for salt and one for chile—but there are cups with several such compartments. Similar vessels are used of course for paints of different colors."

has a height of 8.5 feet above the level of the field behind it. On the river side it rises in line with the bluff. Its general symmetry has been somewhat impaired by wash of water in flood-time, though it still presents an impressive appearance. Its

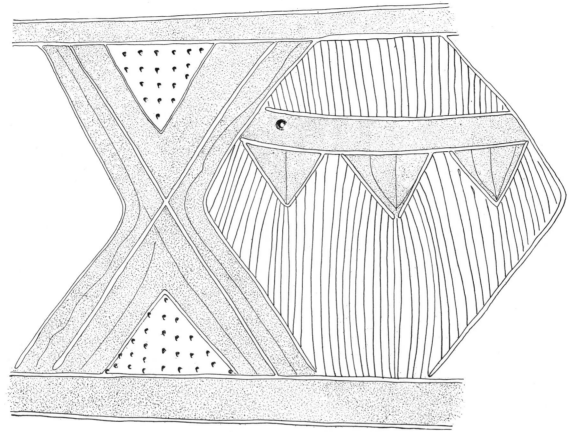

FIG. 23.—Vessel No. 5. Decoration. (About half size.)

length of base, N. by W. and S. by E., parallel with the river, is 138 feet. Its present width varies owing to wash of water in the past. Its base is 57 feet across at the northern end; 68 feet at the center; and 88 feet across the southern end. The summit plateau is 93 feet in length. Its width at the northern end, the middle, and the southern end, is, respectively, 23 feet, 34 feet, and 54 feet.

FIG. 24.—Vessel No. 6. Mound near Fullmore's Upper Landing. (Diameter 4.9 inches.)

As domiciliary mounds (of which class we judge this mound to have been) at times contain superficial burials, a number of trial-holes were dug in the summit plateau of this mound, with but negative results.

MOUNDS NEAR PURCELL'S LANDING, HENRY COUNTY, ALA. (4).

On the river bank, about one-half mile N. by W. from Purcell's Landing, on the plantation of Mr. Harrison Purcell, of Columbia, on which also are the three mounds subsequently to be described, is a remnant of a mound, parts of the mound having been washed away in time of freshet. Considerable digging showed this remnant to be partly of clay and partly of sandy clay, in which were numerous masses of rock. No artifacts or bones were discovered.

About one mile westwardly from Purcell's Landing, in a corn-field, is what is left of a mound which has almost disappeared under cultivation. Trial-holes produced no material result.

In a field which has been under cultivation, but now lies fallow, about one-quarter mile NNE. from the preceding mound, is another, much spread by the plow in former times. Its present height is about 2 feet. Trial-holes gave only negative result.

In woods, about one-half mile eastwardly from the mound just described is a rise in the ground hardly distinguishable above the general level, which was mostly dug away by us. No bones were encountered, but in the eastern margin where, doubtless, a burial had been, were several large fragments of pottery and two bowls of moderate size, one having a decoration of red paint, the other, punctate marking below the rim. Each had the customary mortuary perforation of the base.

MOUND NEAR PAULK'S LANDING, EARLY COUNTY, GA.

This mound was reported to us by our agent as being 200 yards from the river's bank and one-quarter mile in a NE. direction from the landing. The diameter was given as 80 feet; the height, as 5 feet.

The mound was not visited by us, as the owner put a high price on the privilege to dig it—a proceeding in marked contrast to that of most mound-owners with whom we have had to deal.

MOUND NEAR HOWARD'S LANDING, EARLY COUNTY, GA.

This mound, in a cultivated field, about one-quarter mile NE. from Howard's Landing, seems to be largely of clay. Its height is about 3 feet; its basal diameter, 75 feet approximately. In appearance, the mound greatly resembles a class of flat, circular, domiciliary mounds found on the Chattahoochee river and elsewhere. We did not deem it worth our while to offer any inducement to the owner, who seemed to be courting a pecuniary offer before permitting investigation.

Mound near Colomokee Creek, Clay County, Ga.

This mound, on the river bank, about 150 yards above Colomokee creek, had been greatly spread by cultivation. Its height is about 4 feet; its diameter, about 80 feet. The mound, which had been courteously placed at our disposal by its owner, Mr. J. C. Neves, of Fort Gaines, Ga., had many trial-holes dug into it by us, showing it to be mainly of red clay, and apparently a former dwelling site.

Mound at Fort Gaines, Ga.

This mound, about 3.5 feet high and 90 feet across its circular base, is in the modern cemetery belonging to the town of Fort Gaines. Permission to dig it was granted us in a former season by Mr. J. Eugene Peterson, Acting Mayor of Fort Gaines, but the river at that time not being suitable for our steamer, our plans did not materialize. At the time of our visit, the permission given by Mr. Peterson was renewed by Mr. W. A. McAllister, Mayor of Fort Gaines, and by Mr. J. E. Paullin, President of the Cemetery Committee, all of whom expressed their willingness to permit the removal of a summer-house situated on the mound, should we find it necessary to do so.

A number of trial-holes, however, in many parts of the mound, showed it to be domiciliary in character.

Mounds near Stark's Clay Landing, Clay County, Ga. (2).

About one mile in an easterly direction from Stark's Clay Landing, in a cotton-field forming part of the plantation of Dr. J. T. Mandeville, of Fort Gaines, is a conical mound of sandy clay, the symmetry of which has been but little impaired by the spiral furrows left by cultivation. Rising from the level field, the mound, 126 feet in basal diameter and 18 feet in height, is a conspicuous object.

Previous to our visit a trench 12 feet wide, beginning part way up on the western side of the mound, had been carried in 23 feet, where it broadened into an oblong excavation 18 feet long by 15 feet wide. As much of the material had been thrown back by the diggers, the original depth of the trench could not be determined, but it must have been considerable.

Many trial-holes made by us, and considerable work in the former excavation, yielded neither bone nor artifact. No history was forthcoming as to any discovery made by former diggers. Presumably the mound was made for purposes other than that of burial.

A short quarter of a mile in a southeasterly direction from the mound just described is another, evidently domiciliary. This mound, on a slope, varies as to height. Probably 9.5 feet, the measurement as taken from the south, would be a fair average. The length of base is 230 feet, almost east and west; the width is 110 feet. The summit plateau is 146 feet by 74 feet. A number of trial-holes produced no material result.

MOUND NEAR GEORGETOWN, QUITMAN COUNTY, GA.

This mound, about a mile and a half in a southerly direction from George-town, in a cotton-field on the plantation of Mr. W. W. Green, of Gay, Fla., has been under cultivation for years and is greatly reduced in height. Its present altitude is 5 feet 4 inches; the diameter of its circular base, 100 feet. The surface is covered with camp-site debris, consisting of bits of pottery, flakes of chert, and the like. Although the mound had been long under cultivation, and, in addition, an upper portion had been carted away, it is said, we could learn from those in charge of no discovery of artifacts or bones. Trial-holes sunk by us were without result.

MOUND ABOVE EUFAULA, BARBOUR COUNTY, ALA.

About two miles above Eufaula, in view from the river, remains about half of what had been an oblong mound of red clay, with a flat summit plateau, the other part having been washed away during periods of high water. This mound, on property of Mr. H. Lampley, of Eufaula, was evidently domiciliary, as is indicated by its shape and by the negative result of a number of trial-holes dug by us.

MOUND NEAR UPPER FRANCIS LANDING, BARBOUR COUNTY, ALA.

This mound, near the northern side of Williams Lake, about one-half mile from Upper Francis Landing, was visited by our agent in advance of our coming. Its height is reported to be 13 feet; its basal diameter, about 100 feet. The mound was not investigated by us as the owner refused permission, though much influence was brought to bear.

MOUNDS NEAR ROOD'S LANDING, STEWART COUNTY, GA.

On the Rood plantation, about a mile and a half in from Rood's Landing, is a group of eight mounds, to some extent calling to mind the great earthworks at Moundville, Ala., though the mounds at Rood's Landing are much smaller, as a rule, and the circle around a central mound is incomplete, there being no mounds on the southern side, where a creek passes through the property.

These mounds, of the ordinary domiciliary variety, oblong, with summit plateaus, ranged between estimated heights of 7 feet and 20 feet, which latter is believed to be the altitude of the central mound.

Though the place has long been under cultivation, there is no history of the finding of artifacts, in which respect it greatly differs from the territory around Moundville, where for years objects of interest have been unearthed.

The owners of this plantation not only refused permission to dig even to the smallest extent, but practically declined to allow a survey, by prohibiting the cutting of branches of trees, without which proceeding lines could not be run; consequently we were unable to make an investigation of this interesting locality.

Dwelling Site near Hall's Upper Landing, Chattahoochee County, Ga.

About one-eighth of a mile in an easterly direction from Hall's Upper Landing, on the property of Mr. W. C. Bradley, of Columbus, Ga., is a large, cultivated field, thickly strewn with signs of aboriginal occupancy, including very many pebbles and parts of pebbles; occasional chips of chert; fragments of pottery of excellent ware, as a rule, but undecorated, with the exception of the use of green paint in one instance and of red pigment in another; bits of glass; many parts of clay trade-pipes made for barter with later Indians; part of what had been a well-made pipe of soapstone; strips of brass; a triangular object of sheet-brass, probably an arrowhead; a silver button, etc.

Although no doubt a cemetery is present in some part of this property, careful sounding with iron rods failed to locate it.

Mounds near Woolfolk's Landing, Chattahoochee County, Ga. (2).

About one mile ESE. from Woolfolk's Landing, on the plantation of Mr. B. T. Hatcher, of Fort Mitchell, Ala., are two small mounds closely associated, almost leveled by long-continued cultivation. Many trial-holes were without result.

Mound and Cemetery at Abercrombie Landing, Russell County, Ala.

About 50 yards from the river's bank, at Abercrombie Landing, on the plantation of Mrs. Mary D. Hall, of Atlanta, Ga., is a mound 14 feet high, irregular in basal outline, presumably owing to cultivation of the surrounding area. Its diameters of base are 85 feet and 95 feet. Considerable digging failed to show the mound to be other than what it seemed to be, namely, a domiciliary mound.

Over the surface of the field surrounding the mound, debris from aboriginal occupancy was more thickly scattered than we recall having seen in any former experience. In addition to the usual pebbles and fragments of pebbles, we gathered a neatly-made little "celt;" part of a small stone pendant; bits of brass; a knuckle-bone of a deer; several discoidal stones shaped from pebbles; discs made from fragments of earthenware, etc. There were almost innumerable fragments of pottery, many of excellent shell-tempered ware, some of which was black. Some of the sherds bear incised decoration wrought with a rather broad point, but the designs are neither new nor especially striking.

In the level ground around the mound is a cemetery in which we found, from 1 to 2 feet in depth, skeletons, some loosely flexed, some lying at full length on the back. There were also aboriginal disturbances where the bones of a skeleton had been disarranged by a burial made at a later period.

The individuals whose skeletons were found by us evidently had experienced the advantage, or disadvantage, of contact with Europeans, as many of the artifacts buried with them clearly proved.

One skeleton had glass beads at the neck, and a bit of sheet-brass and a lump of hematite nearby; a steel or iron blade of a large knife on the body; a broad chisel of iron or of steel on the pelvis; and an iron or steel axe a little to one side of the body.

Another skeleton at full length on the back had shell beads around the neck, which, probably, when strung, supported a disc of sheet-copper, 4 inches in diameter, having a central hole, and two perforations for suspension near the rim, which lay nearby. At an ankle and a wrist of this skeleton were a few shell beads. In the clay thrown out from the grave were two triangular sheet-brass pendants, and an annular ornament of the same material, 2 inches in diameter, and having an intervening space where the metal had broken between two perforations for suspension.

Another skeleton had a large number of small sea-shells (*Marginella apicina*)[1] pierced for suspension as beads.

Above the skull of a skeleton was a small slab of stone,[2] rounded to some extent, and four piercing implements of bone, three of which had the articular processes remaining. Below the skull was a triangular slab of stone and a large mussel-shell.

Near a skeleton was an earthenware pipe of ordinary form, undecorated and of most inferior ware.

Realizing that we had to do with burials of comparatively late Indians, we did not push the investigation of this place to the extent we would have done had the cemetery been of an earlier period. The mound we believe to antedate the post-Columbian burials near it.

MOUND AT MOUND LANDING, MUSCOGEE COUNTY, GA.

On property of Mr. J. Kyle, of Willet, Ga., in full view from the river, is the remnant of a mound which repeated floods have largely washed away. No investigation was attempted by us at this place, though the mound was courteously put at our disposal by the owner.

MOUNDS AND SITES INVESTIGATED ON FLINT RIVER.
MOUND NEAR LOG LANDING, DECATUR COUNTY, GA.

In high swamp, dry in low stages of the river, about one mile in a N. by E. direction from a log landing on the east side of Flint river, one mile approximately above its union with the Chattahoochee, is a mound on property of Mr. L. B. Edwards, of Chattahoochee, Fla.

---

[1] Kindly identified by Dr. H. A. Pilsbry, of the Academy of Natural Sciences of Philadelphia.

[2] As this object seems to be of small importance, we have not had the stone exactly determined. Incidentally, we may say that exact determination of many rocks demands chemical analysis and the making of slides for microscopic examination. Even then, exact determination is not always arrived at. Determination by inspection alone is a snare. We once submitted to a well-known expert dealer twelve "celts," each marked with a number, and carefully registered the determinations, all which were based on inspection only. Later, the identical twelve "celts" were resubmitted to the same expert who believed them to be a different lot. The determinations of but four coincided with those previously given.

The mound, of sandy clay, about 3.5 feet in height and 50 feet across its circular base, was dug by us to a width of from 3 to 4 feet around its marginal part. In addition, thirteen trial-holes were sunk into the remaining portion. No bones were encountered.

In the soil was the upper part of a so-called hoe-shaped implement which had been broken transversely in a line with the perforation.

Just below the surface of the mound was an undecorated bowl of inferior ware, having a flat, imperforate base. Within the bowl were fragments of shells and a soapstone pipe, undecorated, of a common type, which has a bowl about equaling in size the part intended to hold a stem, both parts being about square in transverse section.

We regarded this bowl and its contents as a cache in a domiciliary mound.

Mound near Munnerlyn's Landing, Decatur County, Ga.

This mound, of sand, 2 feet 9 inches in height and 50 feet across its circular base, on property controlled by Mr. H. C. Allen, of Bainbridge, Ga., was in an old field about one-quarter mile in a southerly course from Munnerlyn's Landing.

The mound, which was completely dug away by us, with the exception of a portion around a small fruit tree, had sustained practically no digging previous to our visit, but evidently had been spread somewhat by cultivation. However, as none of the sixteen burials met with by us in the mound was less than one foot from the surface, it is not likely that any material damage had been wrought by the plow. Some of the skeletons were too badly decayed to enable determination of the form of burial; some indicated a close flexion.

Near a burial was a fragment of a soapstone vessel, worked into an ellipsoidal form, 4.25 inches in length. Below the skull of another burial was the lower part of an earthenware vessel; otherwise, the burials, two of which lay near deposits of charcoal, were not associated with artifacts. Apart from human remains lay: a "celt;" a rude cutting implement of chert; several chips of chert, singly; and a deposit of small masses of chert.

A few feet in from the eastern margin of the mound began a deposit of earthenware, including many small fragments of various vessels, some large parts of vessels, and several entire ones. The ware of all is inferior. Tempering with gravel or with shell is not present. Parts of one vessel show an exterior coating of red paint; the small check-stamp was encountered once; incised or punctate decoration is unrepresented. Several vessels and parts of vessels bear faint, complicated-stamp decoration. Two large fragments have this form of decoration more distinctly marked, one bearing a design showing the human eye (Figs. 25, 26).

Two vessels, the only ones presenting any divergence from ordinary forms, have flat, square bases with pronounced corners serving as feet.

Two small, undecorated vessels were found together, apart from the ceremonial deposit of earthenware and, like all vessels and large parts of vessels from this mound, bear the basal, mortuary perforation.

MOUND NEAR KERR'S LANDING, DECATUR COUNTY, GA.

This mound, circular in outline, almost entirely of sand, with a height of 5 feet 2 inches, a basal diameter of about 62 feet, in a field formerly under cultiva-

FIG. 25.—Sherd. Mound near Munnerlyn's Landing. (Half size.)

tion, forming part of the plantation of Judge B. B. Bower, of Bainbridge, is about 2 miles in a southeasterly direction from Kerr's Landing, and about 5 miles below

FIG. 26.—Sherd. Mound near Munnerlyn's Landing. (Height 8.4 inches.)

Bainbridge. A deep excavation about 30 yards west of the mound showed whence its material had come.

The mound, which had been considerably dug into before our visit, was entirely leveled by us with the exception of parts around four trees. Near the center of the base was a former fireplace with considerable charcoal remaining.

Human remains, encountered in twenty-five places, were all so badly decayed that the form of burial was evident in but few instances. The closely-flexed form, however, was represented in some cases, as also probably were bunched burials.

With one burial was a "celt" of volcanic rock, 6 inches in length—the only artifact found in direct association with the dead. With another burial was a mass of material, 8 by 8 by 5 inches, determined by Dr. Harry F. Keller to be "clay mixed with a few per cent. of carbon in the graphitic form, as well as some coarser and finer grains of quartz sand." "The particles of carbon," says Doctor Keller, "are very fine and pretty thoroughly disseminated through the mass."

With some burials was sand colored with hematite; with others, charcoal.

Not found directly with burials were: two arrowheads or knives, of chert; several flakes of the same material; two masses of galena (lead sulphide) from the carbonate deposit occurring on which the aborigines made white-lead paint; a few scattered sherds; a large deposit of earthenware.

This deposit, beginning near the eastern margin of the mound, as usual, covered a considerable area and extended a number of feet toward the center. It consisted mainly of a great number of fragments of vessels, several hundred at least, and represented parts of many vessels, none of which, so far as we could determine, had a full complement of fragments present. Of course, the determination of the number of fragments of a vessel which may be in a mound is more difficult when a vessel is undecorated or bears a check-stamp decoration, as identifications of adjacent parts is less readily made in such cases than when distinctive decoration aids the investigator. However, it is entirely possible that parts of decorated vessels even escaped our vigilance by being thrown back by shovels with sand, for when sherds are widely scattered, one lying here and one there, the whole area in which they lie cannot be passed through a sieve as can be done and is done by us when fragments of vessels lie more closely together.

Beside the small check-stamp, which greatly predominated, the forms of decoration present on the ware were: a few examples of the complicated stamp, faintly impressed; the cord-marked; several designs with red paint; a few interesting patterns, sometimes incised, sometimes neatly made with the impress of a point or, in some instances perhaps, of a roulette.[1]

Gritty ware was sparingly represented; no shell-tempered ware was found. Here and there in the deposit, farther in than were most of the fragments, were several whole vessels and large parts of vessels. All these had mortuary perforation of base, which was apparent also on many fragments.

Certain sherds had belonged to vessels bearing feet.

Entire vessels and large parts of vessels from this mound will be described in detail:

Vessel No. 1.—The greater part of a bowl which had been surrounded below the rim by a band of rather rudely-executed, incised decoration.

Vessel No. 2.—A pot of inferior ware having a rather faintly-impressed, small check-stamp.

Vessel No. 3.—A bowl of yellow ware, undecorated save for a single, incised line immediately below the rim.

Vessel No. 4.—A bowl of inferior material, rudely decorated with incised, parallel lines below the margin.

[1] "Aboriginal Pottery of Eastern United States," W. H. Holmes, Fig. 43. Twentieth Ann. Rep. Bur. Am. Ethnol., 1898–99.

Vessel No. 5.—A large part of a bowl which has since been somewhat restored, though no part of this restoration shows in the reproduction (Fig. 27). The punctate design, beautifully executed, which is shown in the illustration, appears four times on the vessel. In the base are two carefully-made, circular, mortuary perforations, side by side. Such duplication of the mortuary mutilation is unusual.

Vessel No. 6.—A vessel of excellent, yellow ware, graceful in form (Fig. 28), having an interesting, incised decoration shown diagrammatically in Fig. 29.

FIG. 27.—Vessel No. 5. Mound near Kerr's Landing. (Diameter 10.6 inches.)

Vessel No. 7.—Similar to Vessel No. 6 as to ware and shape, but without decoration. With this were the decaying remains of a large conch (*Fulgur perversum*). Vessels Nos. 6 and 7 were found together somewhat farther toward the center of the mound than the general deposit of earthenware.

Certain vessels have been made up with partial restoration, from fragments present in the mound, as follows:

Vessel No. 8.—A pot of inferior ware having for decoration on the upper part rudely-incised, parallel lines crossed by parallel, diagonal ones.

Fig. 28.—Vessel No. 6. Mound near Kerr's Landing. (Height 7.7 inches.)

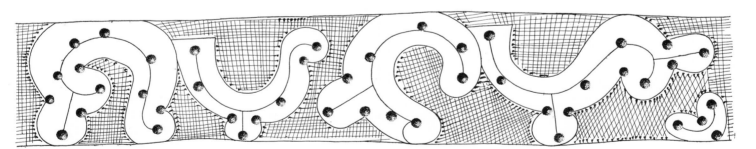

Fig. 29.—Vessel No. 6. Decoration. (About one-third size.)

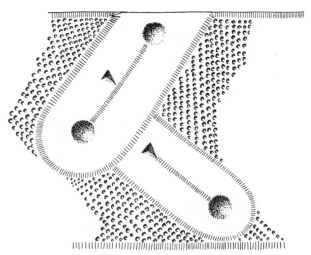

FIG. 30.—Vessel No. 10.   Decoration.   (About two-thirds size.)

Vessel No. 9.—A dish or platter, 8 inches square, having a slightly concave base, and two knobs on opposite sides, rising above the rim. There has been a decoration consisting of broad bands of red pigment, which we have been unable to restore owing to the absence of the central part of the dish.

Vessel No. 10.—A bowl of excellent ware having a carefully-executed, punctate design, shown in Fig. 30, a number of times repeated.

Two sherds from this mound are shown in Figs. 31, 32.

BURIAL PLACE ON THE CHASON PLANTATION, DECATUR COUNTY, GA.

The Chason Plantation, belonging to Dr. Jefferson D. Chason, of Bainbridge, is on the eastern side of Flint river, about 3.5 miles below the city named. A slight rise in the ground in a cotton-field forming part of the plantation was reported

FIG. 31.—Fragment of vessel.   Mound near Kerr's Landing.   (Half size.)

FIG. 32.—Sherd.   Mound near Kerr's Landing.   (Half size.)

to be the spot where two earthenware vessels on exhibition at Bainbridge had been found.

Trenching and careful sounding with iron rods over the whole surface of the higher ground resulted in the discovery of two decaying skeletons and part of an earthenware vessel.

The Northwestern Florida Coast
Revisited

BY

CLARENCE B. MOORE

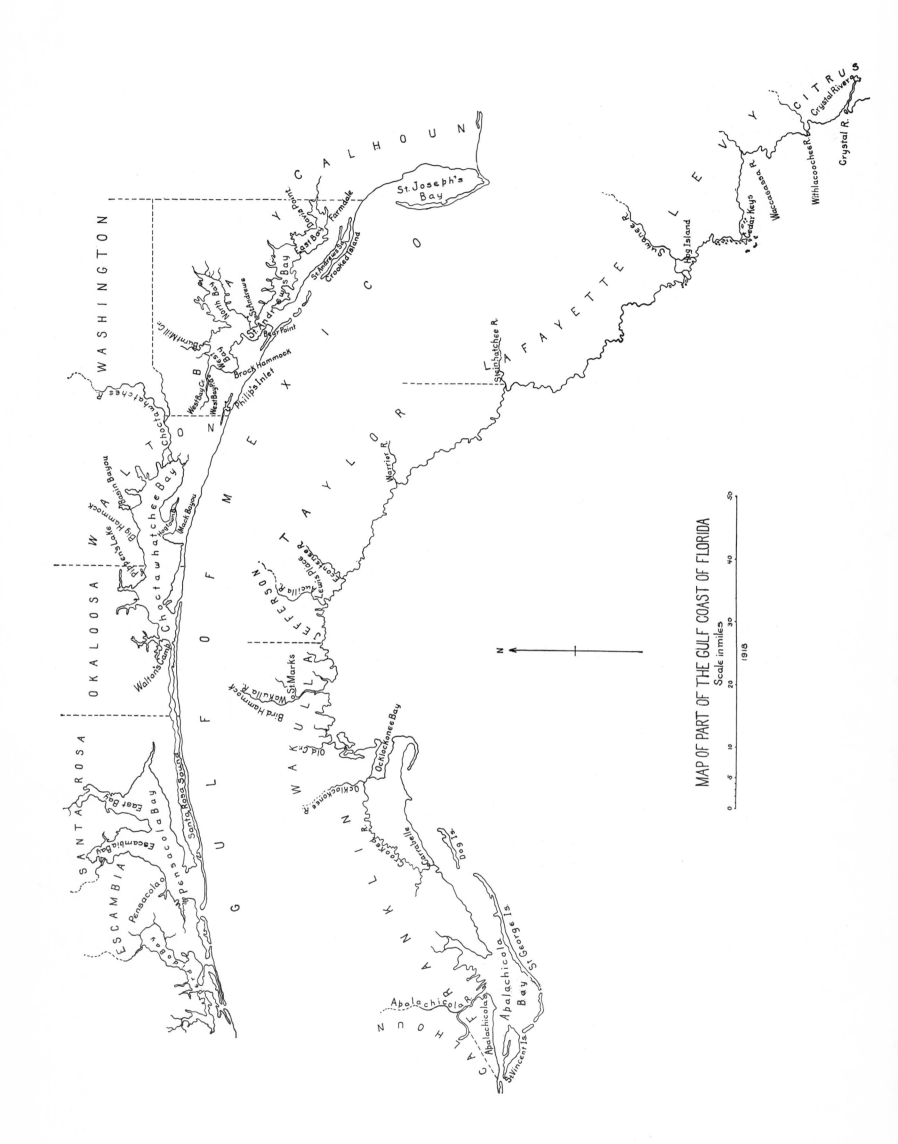

MAP OF PART OF THE GULF COAST OF FLORIDA

Scale in miles

0   5   10   20   30   40   50

1918

N

THE NORTHWESTERN FLORIDA COAST REVISITED.

BY CLARENCE B. MOORE.

INTRODUCTION.

The end of our work along Green river, Kentucky, in 1916, virtually completed for us the list of all rivers navigable by our steamer, and at the same time not likely to be affected by ice in winter (in summer cultivation bars effective search), to be found in southeastern United States. In addition, all the coast of the same region, navigable to us, had been carefully investigated by our expeditions extending over a period of about twenty-seven seasons.[1]

One river, the Choctawhatchee, in Alabama and northwestern Florida, opened to navigation since our latest visit to the region drained by it, by the removal of a bar at its mouth and by the uprooting of a multitude of snags from its bed, remained uninvestigated, and this stream we determined to search, and, in addition, for the second[2] time carefully to cover the northwestern Florida coast, impelled thereto by reasons which we shall proceed to explain.

It may be well to say here, to any not familiar with the archæology of Florida, that it was an aboriginal custom there often practised, to "kill" a vessel to be interred with the dead, by breaking a hole in its base, thus freeing its soul[3] to accompany that of its owner to the life beyond.

Doubtless some of the more thrifty among the aborigines regretted this

[1] Two additional seasons of exploration detailed in this report bring the total to twenty-nine.

[2] As to our first visit (1901 and 1902) consult "Certain Aboriginal Remains of the Northwest Florida Coast, Parts I and II." JOURN. ACAD. NAT. SCI. PHILA., vols. XI and XII.

[3] We are indebted to Col. G. E. Laidlaw for the following references as to the Eskimo, which are interesting for comparison.

Geological Survey, Ottawa, Canada, Memoir 91, Number 14, Anthropological Series. "The Labrador Eskimo," by E. W. Hawkes.

"The small specimen [a stone kettle], which came from an old grave, has two holes bored in the bottom. All lamps and kettles placed on graves were treated in like manner, to liberate the *inua* of the utensil and allow its use by the shade of the owner, in the other world." Page 90.

"On top of the grave are laid the effects of the deceased, . . . All the effects of the deceased are broken to liberate the spirit residing there, so that it may be useful to the shade of the owner. The clothes are torn; the dishes split; and holes bored in the soapstone lamps and kettles." Page 120.

"The Eskimo believe that not only all animals but also any prominent physiographical feature, such as a rock, point, cove, or mountain, is inhabited by a spiritual counterpart, the *inua*, the genius or thinking spirit of the object or spot. This is the third person possessive form of *inuk*, man, and means literally 'its man,' which perhaps expresses the idea as well as it can be explained." Page 127.

It may be worth while also to cite here one of the many accounts of mortuary mutilation of objects placed with the dead in Africa.

The Ekoi of Western Africa erect little funeral shrines over the graves of persons of distinction. "Round these are scattered various pieces of property, such as plates, dishes, etc., all broken. . . .

"The things scattered round are broken so that their astral forms may be set free, to be borne by the shade of their owner into the spirit world." "In the Shadow of the Bush," P. Amaury Talbot, London, 1912, page 6 *et seq.*

expenditure of serviceable pottery and hence arose a refinement of the custom, widespread in Florida and met with by us at one place even in western Louisiana,[1] namely, the manufacture of mortuary vessels otherwise useless, of inferior ware as a rule and having a basal perforation made previous to the firing of the clay.

Probably through this class a further evolution is found (along part[2] of the northwestern Florida coast and its hinterland, including some mounds on the Apalachicola,[3] Chattahoochee and Flint rivers[3]), namely, the "openwork" vessel, having ready-made excisions in the body of the vessel, which often formed parts of the decoration.   Vessels of this class, first discovered by the expeditions of the Academy of Natural Sciences and described in the Journal of the Academy, are to be seen, at the present writing (1917), in no other institution, we believe.

The desire to obtain other examples of this class of ware and the added hope to discover more of another class, namely, those superb bowls forming a part of the urn-burials found mostly to the westward[4] of the locale of the openwork ware, were the motives suggesting to us a second visit to the northwestern Florida coast.   In this purpose we were encouraged by the knowledge that the population there had greatly increased in number since the period of our first visit, and that the consequent spread of cultivation in places hitherto unreclaimed, must have brought to the attention of inhabitants mounds, even though small (for we were convinced we had investigated all the large ones), as to which we could learn by inquiry.

A feature in the archæology of the northwestern coast of Florida, in addition to that of the ceremonial "killing" of pottery, is that almost without exception a deposit of earthenware is found in the eastern part of the mounds, and that little else was put by the aborigines in the way of a ceremonial deposit, elsewhere in the mound or individually with the dead.

This custom inured to our benefit, for treasure-seekers and diggers from the neighborhood of the mounds usually contented themselves with a hole in the central part and presumably rarely obtained more than the physical benefit derived from outdoor exercise.

Mr. F. W. Hodge, on the eve of his departure for field work in New Mexico, has sent the following note: "Cushing in his paper on the work of the Hemenway Expedition, published in the Proceedings of the VII International Congress of Americanists held at Berlin in 1888 and published in 1890 [page 172], refers to the 'killing' of pottery vessels by the ancient inhabitants of the Salt River Valley, Arizona.

"The same custom was practised also by the ancients of the Mimbres Valley in New Mexico, as described by Fewkes in a paper published by the Smithsonian Institution three or four years ago.

"The mortuary vessels unearthed by me at the ruins of the pueblo of Hawikuh, near Zuñi, last summer were killed by being thrown into the graves and thus broken to pieces."

[1] Lake Larto, Catahoula Parish. "Some Aboriginal Sites in Louisiana and in Arkansas." JOURN. ACAD. NAT. SCI. PHILA., vol. XVI.

[2] From the western extremity of St. Andrews Bay to the Warrior River, inclusive.

[3] "Certain Aboriginal Mounds of the Central Florida West-Coast; Certain Aboriginal Mounds of the Apalachicola River." JOURN. ACAD. NAT. SCI. PHILA., vol. XII.

"Moundville Revisited; Crystal River Revisited; Mounds of the lower Chattahoochee and lower Flint Rivers." JOURN. ACAD. NAT. SCI. PHILA., vol. XIII.

[4] Choctawhatchee Bay, Santa Rosa Sound, Perdido Bay. "Certain Aboriginal Remains of the Northwest Florida Coast, Part I."

Of our season of 1916–1917, some days of November and December, 1916, and of January, 1917, we devoted to archæological research among sites near Golden Lake, Ark., about thirty-five miles above Memphis, Tenn. The remainder of January and part of February, 1917, were consumed in reaching Florida and in visiting *en route* down Mississippi river certain sites that we hoped might prove of interest. Notes as to this work on Mississippi river form the concluding part of this report.

The remainder of the season (more than two months) was spent in the investigation of Choctawhatchee Bay, Florida, and Choctawhatchee river and tributary streams, Florida and Alabama.

In the autumn of 1917 and the winter and part of the spring of 1918 the expedition investigated, for the second time, the Apalachicola river and Flint river to Bainbridge, Georgia, and continued its work down the Florida coast, from St. Andrews bay to Crystal river, somewhat below Cedar Keys, inclusive.

In advance of our coming, as usual, search was made by Mr. J. S. Raybon, for many years captain of our steamer, with a companion, along Choctawhatchee river from Pate Landing, Alabama, to Choctawhatchee bay, Florida, into which the river empties, a distance of 122 measured miles by water, and in addition 27 miles along Holmes river to the end of navigation on it. Captain Raybon also covered for the second time (a search by him having preceded our first visit) the northwestern coast of Florida from Pensacola to Cedar Keys. In this way knowledge as to additional sites and permission to investigate them were obtained by us prior to our visit, a great saving in time.

Choctawhatchee river has its source in southeastern Alabama, pursues a southerly course into northwestern Florida, and continuing southerly and southwesterly about 94 miles enters the eastern end of Choctawhatchee bay, as stated.

This stream was investigated by us as far up as Pate Landing, Ala. In addition, Holmes river, an affluent, was searched about 20 miles up by us.

Choctawhatchee river, as it had been reported to us as likely to be, proved unproductive from an archæological point of view. The banks, mostly lowlying, are wooded, habitations being rarely visible from the water, all of which tended to make it extremely difficult to obtain information as to the whereabouts of the few small mounds that seem to be the only kind along the stream.

All mounds visited by us along Choctawhatchee river and on the northwestern Florida coast were of sand, unless otherwise described.

Our thanks are tendered Dr. M. G. Miller, who accompanied the expedition as anatomist during the past two seasons, as he has done throughout all our archæological work in the South, and has aided in preparing this report and in putting it through the press.

Also we wish to return thanks to Mr. L. B. Smiley, who lent efficient aid as general assistant during part of our investigation.

The warmest thanks of the Academy are extended to the numerous owners of mounds and sites along our line of work, who so courteously placed them at its disposal.

The Academy also desires to express its obligation to Dr. H. F. Keller for chemical determinations, to Mr. F. W. Hodge for literary revision of this report, and to Miss H. Newell Wardle for assistance with the index.

Measurements in this report are approximate; reductions are linear.

All objects of any importance found by us between St. Andrews bay and Crystal river, inclusive, have been presented to the Museum of the American Indian, Heye Foundation, New York, our Academy having a very comprehensive collection from this region.

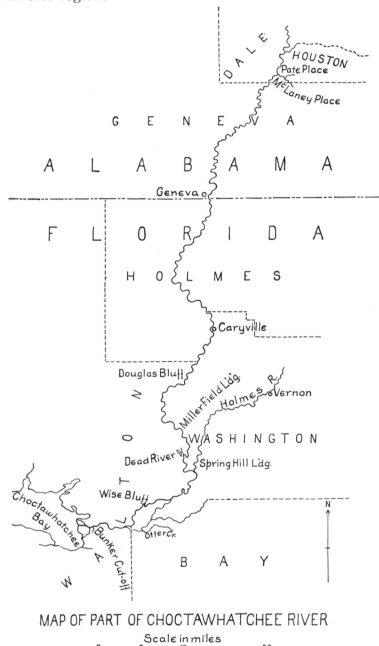

MAP OF PART OF CHOCTAWHATCHEE RIVER

Scale in miles

SOME ABORIGINAL MOUNDS ON CHOCTAWHATCHEE RIVER.

MOUNDS INVESTIGATED.[1]

(The mounds are given in order going up-stream.)
Mound near Bunker Cut-off, Walton County, Florida.
Mound near Otter Creek, Bay County, Florida.
Mound near Wise Bluff, Walton County, Florida.
Mound near Spring Hill Landing, Washington County, Florida.
Mounds near Dead River, Walton County, Florida.
Mound near Miller Field Landing, Washington County, Florida.
Mound near Douglas Bluff, Walton County, Florida.
Mound on the McLaney Place, Houston County, Alabama
Mounds on the Pate Place, Houston County, Alabama.

MOUND NEAR BUNKER CUT-OFF, WALTON COUNTY, FLORIDA.

The property of Mr. J. W. Windsor, resident on it formerly belonging to Mr. G. W. Lee, may be reached by going up Choctawhatchee river about three miles to Bunker cut-off, another mouth of the river, and continuing one-quarter mile, approximately, down the cut-off. On this property, in pine woods, was a mound of circular outline, 43 feet in diameter of base and 3 feet 8 inches high. The mound probably had been considerably spread by wear and by wash of rain, and doubtless in the past had a greater height and a less extended base.

The mound was entirely dug down by us, great care being taken closely to observe the base which, no doubt the original surface, was one foot in thickness and much darker than the sand of the mound. It overlay undisturbed yellow sand having a slight admixture of clay.

An excavation about 6 feet in diameter had been put down centrally in the mound by digging previous to ours, the sand filling the hole containing fragments of human bones.

In the sand thrown back by our men in the demolition of the mound were: fragments of flint; a pitted hammer-stone; a large iron spike; a rude arrowhead or knife, of flint; an object of limestone, perhaps a knife, nearly semilunar in outline but having one end sharpened as for insertion in a handle; a number of sherds. These sherds, some from vessels of considerable size, show in one instance the small check-stamp, and in others incised designs similar to those figured[2] by us as on earthenware coming from cemeteries along the Florida coast between Perdido bay and Choctawhatchee river. One sherd with a graceful line decoration is shown in Fig. 1.

[1] Between Douglas Bluff and the town of Caryville, 13 miles following the course of the stream, high water prevailing at the time of our visit prevented investigation of several low mounds and rises.

Between Caryville and Geneva, Ala., 29 miles by water, no mounds were seen or heard of by our agents or by ourselves.

[2] See "Certain Aboriginal Remains of the Northwest Florida Coast, Part I." JOURN. ACAD. NAT. SCI. PHILA., vol. XI.

55 JOURN. A. N. S. PHILA., VOL. XVI.

No burials were encountered by us until the central part of the mound had been reached, where, from the upper surface of the basal layer to the surface of the mound, the depth was 3 feet. Twenty-six inches down were the decayed remains of a small, bunched burial represented by fragments of a skull, of a femur, and of a humerus.   Near them was a discoidal stone of silicious rock, 3 inches in diameter.   This stone is of the truncated-cone variety and could not have been used to roll in the game of chungkee.

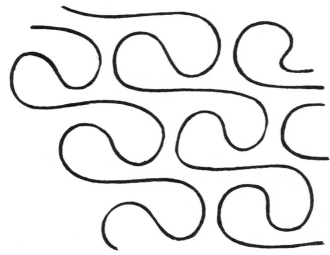

FIG. 1.—Decoration on sherd.   (Full size.)

About 3 feet distant from the preceding burial, at the same level, was a more extensive bunch, decayed remains of one skeleton including skull, ribs, vertebræ, humeri, bones of the forearms, pelvis, femora.

At depths of 10 inches and 18 inches, respectively, were decaying remains of small bunched burials, and 28 inches and 30 inches down were traces of single skulls, with one being a biconical pipe of earthenware, having a small part missing. On the bowl still remain traces of a uniform coating of red paint.

Approaching the central part of the base was a group of three grave-pits near together, probably all that had been in the mound, as the previous digging did not extend to the depth reached by the pits in question.

One of these pits, 34 inches by 40 inches where it cut through the basal layer, extended 3 feet into the undisturbed, yellow sand, having a slight admixture of clay, which underlay the mound.   This pit became somewhat conical and ended in a base roughly circular with a diameter of about 22 inches.   The grave had been filled with a mixture of the sand of the basal layer and of the underlying sand from the grave, and was readily distinguishable.

Thirteen inches down in the pit were the remains of a skull, with fragments of pottery, mostly undecorated, scattered below it, and continuing to the bottom of the pit.   No complete vessel was represented by these sherds.

The second grave-pit, 3 feet by 4 feet, and extending 32 inches below the base of the mound, maintained its oblong shape to the bottom with great regularity, though slanting inward somewhat, its basal dimensions being 22 inches by 45 inches. No trace of bone was discovered in this grave, but as the material filling it was decidedly moist, a burial formerly in it unquestionably had decayed away.

The third grave, 34 inches by 55 inches, extending 27 inches below the base of the mound, resembled the second one in the regularity of its shape; the dimensions of its base were 23 inches by 4 feet. No trace of bones was present in it.

Mound near Otter Creek, Bay County, Florida.

This mound, in pine woods, on property belonging to Miss Minnie Anderson, of High Point, N. C., was reached by going about 4 miles up East river (a division of the Choctawhatchee) to its union with Otter creek, and then continuing about three miles up the creek to a landing on the south side and walking inland about one-half mile, in an easterly direction.

The mound, much spread apparently, 4 feet in height and 75 feet in diameter, had centrally a hole about 6 feet by 10 feet which had been put down between the time of the visit of our agent and our own. Residents in the neighborhood who said they had been present when the hole was dug, asserted that nothing had been found.

The mound had all the appearance of being a domiciliary one. It was trenched and dug into in a number of places by us without encountering bone or artifact.

Mound near Wise Bluff, Walton County, Florida.

In a cultivated field, on the property of Mr. Robert Bozeman, at Wise Bluff, resident on the place, was the remainder of a mound much spread by cultivation, which, we were told, had been considerably dug into without success. Fragments of human bones, however, were on the surface.

This remainder, 2.5 feet in height and 38 feet in diameter, was entirely dug down by us. The remains of a skull and a few long-bones together, traces of skulls in three places, one in a hole made and refilled by previous digging, were encountered in different parts of the mound.

With one of the skulls had been most of an undecorated pot in fragments, 1.5 foot from which was another pot having a part missing, bearing a complicated stamp carelessly applied.

Almost exactly in the eastern part of the mound, 6 to 8 inches below the surface when dug by us, was the ceremonial deposit of pottery usually encountered in mounds in this region. This deposit consisted of fragments of various vessels, some plain, some with pinched decoration, one having a punctate and line design, and one a complicated stamp.

With these were two vessels, one diminutive, decorated on the upper half of the body with diagonal, parallel, incised lines; the other carefully made, having the same kind of decoration and a rim effective in appearance, somewhat flaring and sloping upward gradually at three equidistant points.   At one of these a missing part has since been restored.   This vessel, shown in Fig. 2, has a basal

Fig. 2.—Vessel of earthenware.   Mound at Wise Bluff.   (Height 4.8 inches.)

perforation, as have all but one found at this place which were sufficiently whole for determination.

Through the side of the vessel in question is an even, round hole equaling a lead pencil in diameter and resembling a perforation made by a sounding-rod, though it can hardly be such, as these rods are not known to have been used on this river, and the vessel, when found, was upright and could not, when in the mound, have been evenly pierced through the side by such an appliance.

MOUND NEAR SPRING HILL LANDING, WASHINGTON COUNTY, FLORIDA.

About one-half mile southeast by east from Spring Hill Landing, on Holmes river, an affluent of the Choctawhatchee, on the property either of the J. P. Williams Land Co. of Tallahassee, Fla., or of the R. E. L. McCaskill Co. of De Funiak Springs, in the same state, is a mound about 5 feet high and 33 feet in diameter.   Persons living near the mound informed us that the land of these companies adjoined and that residents there were unable to say on which side of the line the mound stood.

The mound, in an old field, though plainly the eminence never had been plowed over, was a truncated cone and symmetrical, though previous diggers had put down a hole centrally in it 4.5 feet by 12 feet—probably getting a few fragments of bones for their pains.   The mound was completely dug through by us.

Six burials, all single skulls save in one instance where probably two had been interred together, as they were but 4 inches apart, lay in the eastern side of the mound, but not with the mortuary deposit of pottery, all being away from it and at higher levels.   With some of the skulls were a few fragments of other bones.

Several bits of mica lay apart in the mound, as did the remains of a large marine shell that probably had been a drinking-cup.

About due east, in the margin of the mound, the usual mortuary deposit began and extended in, on or near the base, a total distance of about 13 feet.   Its width at first was approximately 4 feet, and it was composed of mingled fragments of different vessels of ordinary form and commonplace decoration, evidently intentionally spread to occupy space.   With these, here and there, were a few vessels, probably whole or nearly whole when interred, but in fragments lying together in place when found.

Following this part of the deposit, which extended in 4.5 feet, was a gap of about one foot and then the deposit commenced again, having about the same width, with eight vessels, some fairly large, all upright originally and but short distances apart.   Most of these vessels were badly crushed.

Following these came vessels entire or nearly so, vessels in fragments and numerous sherds, the deposit continuing to the end in diminishing width.

In this latter part of the deposit were some fragments of large marine shells and considerable charcoal.

The pottery found at this place presents little of interest, most of the vessels being of ordinary form and without decoration.   Some bear imprints of a thumbnail or of the section of a reed (perhaps both in different instances), some have incised line decoration of a simple pattern.   All the vessels were found to have the mortuary perforation when sufficient parts were obtained for determination.

A small bowl is decorated with crimson pigment interiorly.   Another bowl, 13.8 inches in diameter, found entire, has an incised decoration, shown in diagram in Fig. 3, appearing twice in the circumference of the vessel.

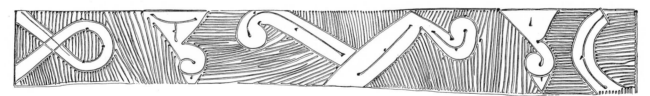

Fig. 3.—Decoration.   (One-third size.)

A bowl of excellent ware, broken when found but now having the parts cemented together, is shown in Fig. 4.

Mounds near Dead River, Walton County, Florida.

Dead river, a former course of the Choctawhatchee, joins it 33 miles above the mouth of that stream.   Going up Dead river about one mile one comes to a landing on the left-hand side, near which is the property of the R. E. L. McCaskill Co. of DeFuniak Springs, Fla., to which we are indebted for permission to explore its numerous properties. About one-eighth mile in a southwesterly direction from the landing, on fallow ground belonging to the company, was a mound 28 feet in diameter, evidently much spread by cultivation. Its height was about 14 inches. This mound was completely dug through by us.

Fig. 4.—Vessel of earthenware. Mound near Spring Hill Landing. (Diameter 6.75 inches.)

In the margin, exactly in the eastern part, was a ceremonial deposit of pottery, the vessels all small or of moderate size, some undecorated, some bearing the check stamp or a scanty, incised, line decoration. Three vessels were entire, while a number of others were more or less largely represented by broken parts. With this deposit was the crown of a human tooth, an indication of a burial.

In two other instances in this mound burials were found consisting of traces of a skull and other bones. With one of the burials were fragments of charcoal.

About 6 feet from the deposit of pottery was an undecorated bowl somewhat crushed.

About three-quarters of a mile southerly from the first mound, also on fallow land and belonging to the same owner, was another mound, evidently much affected by the plow, 30 feet in diameter and 16 inches in height. This mound was entirely demolished by us. In the margin and almost due east in the mound was a small, undecorated pot.

Northeasterly in the mound were a skull and parts of other bones, 1.5 foot distant from which were four pots together, the largest 7 inches in height and 5.5 inches in maximum diameter. These are of rather inferior ware, one undecorated, one having incised lines below the opening, two with encircling bands of decoration—one a complicated stamp, the other lines of pinched markings near the aperture.   Five feet from this deposit were two pots, one decorated with two parallel, encircling lines, the other having a simple punctate design.   These had suffered the usual ceremonial breaking of the base, as had all the vessels from this place of which sufficient parts were recovered to permit determination.

Still in the eastern part of the mound, but farther in, perhaps a continuation of the deposit, were three vessels some distance apart, two undecorated, one having below the opening a band filled in with a complicated stamp.   Two of these vessels, like most of the others from this place, were found to have parts missing, probably breakage sustained in household use which impaired the value of the vessels and made them especially fitted for mortuary deposit.   With these receptacles was a small mass of galena, largely oxidized into sulphate and carbonate of lead.

Three burials were encountered, all in the eastern part of the mound, each consisting of fragments of a single skull and of various other bones.   With one burial were three undecorated pots and the lower part of a toy vessel, also undecorated.

A large fragment belonging to the skull of this burial had an elliptical perforation, evidently old, that might well have been made by a spike-shaped arrowhead, which, however, if such were the case, presumably had been withdrawn before the interment, as nothing of the kind was found in the mound.

Mound near Miller Field Landing, Washington County, Florida.

In pine woods, about one mile southerly from Miller Field Landing, on property of Mr. Fleming Yan, living nearby, was a mound 30 feet in diameter and 2 feet in height, having at the time of our visit an excavation in the central part, 6 feet square, and a trench about 4 feet wide, from the western margin to the center.   This remainder of the mound was practically demolished by us.

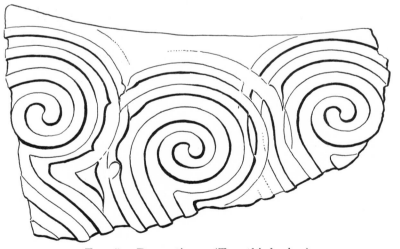

Fig. 5.—Decoration.   (Two-thirds size.)

Almost due east in the marginal part of the mound began a deposit of pottery, broadening to a width of about 3 feet and continuing well toward the center. This deposit, not continuous, strictly speaking, included only one vessel that could be said to have been buried entire, and in many instances it was certain that parts only had been put into the mound.

So inferior is the ware that nearly all the deposit was in small fragments. In addition to considerable undecorated ware is one piece having a scanty design composed of incised parallel lines, and a number of others bearing complicated stamp decoration.   One of these is shown in Fig. 5.

On the opposite side of the mound, alone, were fragments of most of an undecorated pot.

In the northern part of the mound, somewhat in from the margin but by no means central, was a grave of rather indefinite outline, about 6 feet long and 3 feet 3 inches wide, extending about 3 feet below what we considered to be the base of the mound.   This grave contained traces of a considerable quantity of bones, including a skeleton almost at full length, three additional skulls, a small pile of long-bones, and other bones here and there.

MOUND NEAR DOUGLAS BLUFF, WALTON COUNTY, FLORIDA.

Douglas Bluff is 54 miles up Choctawhatchee river.   About three-eighths mile north from the upper end of Douglas Bluff, in pine woods, partly on property of the R. E. L. McCaskill Co. of DeFuniak Springs, Florida, whose courtesy to

FIG. 6.—Vessel of earthenware.   Mound near Douglas Bluff.   (Height 5.1 inches.)

the Academy we have had occasion to acknowledge before, and in part on that of a person whose name we did not learn, was a mound through which a trench about 4 feet wide had been dug north and south.   The eastern half of this mound, which was 3.5 feet in height and 42 feet in diameter, was dug away by us.

In five places human bones were encountered, three skulls separately, a skull with fragments of other bones, and traces of bones.

The usual mortuary deposit of earthenware, in this instance composed of vessels and parts of vessels, in fragments, a few whole vessels and several entire with the exception of a part, lay away from the burials.   With them were the remains of what had been a shell drinking-cup, and in another part of the deposit some small sheets of mica.   The deposit was first encountered in the northeastern part of the mound, about 3.5 feet inward from the margin, and, considerably spread and scattered, continued in about 14 feet.

More attempt at decoration on the earthenware (gritty ware in one instance) was present in this mound than we usually found along the Choctawhatchee. This decoration, punctate and incised as a rule, includes the complicated stamp and the small check-stamp only to the extent of several small sherds.   In form also a few of the vessels are somewhat out of the ordinary.   All determinable are seen to have the mortuary hole knocked through the base.

The following ware is worthy of especial description.

A pot (Fig. 6) having an interesting line and punctate decoration, shown in diagram in Fig. 7.   Red pigment, which at one time had considerable part in the decoration of the vessel, is present on much of the surface.

FIG. 7.—Decoration.   (Two-thirds size.)

An undecorated, lenticular vessel of good, hard yellow ware is 3.5 inches high and 8 inches in length.

One vessel, of which only part was present in the mound, and this part in many fragments, has had a flattened spherical body and an upright, circular neck, the rim of which projects somewhat at four equidistant points (Fig. 8). The decoration is a line and punctate design.

Part of another vessel, also of excellent yellow ware, found in many fragments, is shown in Fig. 9.   The decoration, deeply marked, includes a variety of crosses surrounding the neck.

A decoration on part of another vessel is shown in diagram in Fig. 10.

Fig. 8.—Vessel of earthenware.   Mound near Douglas Bluff.   (Height 8.5 inches.)

MOUND ON THE McLANEY PLACE, HOUSTON COUNTY, ALABAMA.

One mile below Pate Landing is a bluff on the east side of the river.   One-half mile east, approximately, from this bluff, on hammock land, is a mound on the property of Mr. H. C. McLaney, living nearby.   This mound, symmetrical and having sustained but little previous digging, was 4 feet 10 inches in height and 33 feet in diameter of base.   It was completely dug away by us with the exception of a marginal part on one side, mostly surrounding a tree.

About 3 feet in from the margin, in the east northeastern part of the mound, was seemingly the ceremonial deposit of pottery, though the makers of the mound had not imposed on themselves any great sacrifice of earthenware vessels.   To-

FIG. 9.—Vessel of earthenware.   Mound near Douglas Bluff.   (Height 6 inches.)

gether were an undecorated vessel, badly broken; some fragments of another vessel having a rude decoration; and what had been an imitation of a gourd, with line decoration and red paint, in places.   Unfortunately this last vessel, which originally must have been very attractive in appearance, has lost a part of what

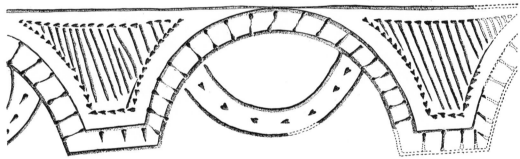

FIG. 10.—Decoration.   (One-half size.)

represented the stem end of the gourd, and this part presumably was missing before the interment of the vessel; in fact its imperfect condition may have suggested its ceremonial use with the dead.   The ware is excellent, the decoration carefully done.   This vessel, whose imperfect condition was a great disappointment to us, is shown in Plate XIII, Fig. 1; its decoration, in diagram, Fig. 11, in which the red pigment (except on the stem portion, which is not shown) is indicated by diagonal lines.

A short distance farther into the mound fragments of other decorated vessels were found.

No bones lay with any of the earthenware.   Apart from human remains was a mass of flint, rudely chipped into the form of an axe.

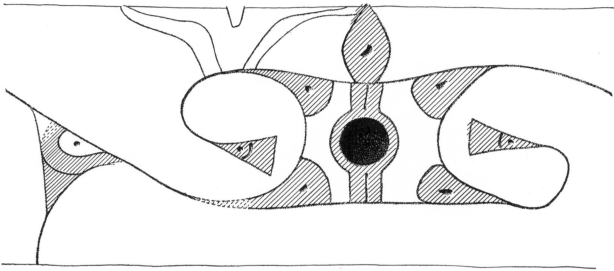

Fig. 11.—Decoration.   (Two-thirds size.)

The burials, five in number, with one exception were near what seemed to be the base, which consisted of yellow, undisturbed sand differing from the gray of the mound.

Mounds on the Pate Place, Houston County, Alabama.

Pate Landing is slightly more than 123 miles up Choctawhatchee river.   The mound, a short distance from Pate Landing, though not noteworthy as to size, is a veritable landmark on the Choctawhatchee.   Persons more than fifty miles away told us of visits to it and described their digging.

The height of the mound is about 8 feet at present; it has been so dug into, having a great excavation centrally, and others all over it, including large trenches from the margin inward, that it no longer possesses any regularity of outline, so that it would be impossible to indicate its original diameter.

We learned that the mound had changed ownership since our permission to dig it had been obtained, and we made no effort to procure the consent of the present owner after having observed the condition of the mound.

Mounds and Sites Investigated on the Northwestern Florida Coast and Rivers.[1]

Mound near Pippen's Lake, Choctawhatchee Bay, Walton County.
Mounds in Big Hammock, Choctawhatchee Bay, Walton County.

[1] The Flint, a river of Georgia, is included in this list.

Mound near Basin Bayou, Choctawhatchee Bay, Walton County.

Aboriginal Cemetery on Hogtown Bayou, Choctawhatchee Bay, Walton County.

Mound near Mack Bayou, Choctawhatchee Bay, Walton County.

Mound near Philip's Inlet, Gulf Coast, Bay County.

Mound near West Bay Creek, St. Andrews Bay, Bay County.

Mounds in Brock Hammock (2), St. Andrews Bay, Bay County.

Mound west of Burnt Mill Creek, St. Andrews Bay, Bay County.

Site near Bear Point, St. Andrews Bay, Bay County.

Mound near Davis Point, St. Andrews Bay, Bay County.

Mound near Farmdale, St. Andrews Bay, Bay County.

Mounds near Crooked Island, St. Andrews Sound, Bay County.

Mound near Michaux Log Landing, Apalachicola River, Liberty County.

Mound near O. K. Landing, Apalachicola River, Calhoun County.

Mound near Rock Bluff Landing, Apalachicola River, Liberty County.

Mound near Hardnut Landing, Flint River, Decatur County, Georgia.

Aboriginal Cemetery near Carrabelle, Gulf Coast, Franklin County, Florida.

Mound near Old Creek, Gulf Coast, Wakulla County.

Mounds in Bird Hammock, Wakulla River, Wakulla County.

Site on the Lewis Place, Aucilla River, Taylor County.

Mound near the Warrior River, Taylor County.

Mounds on Hog Island, Gulf Coast, Levy County.

Mound in Cedar Keys, Gulf Coast, Levy County.

Aboriginal Cemetery in Cedar Keys, Gulf Coast, Levy County.

Aboriginal Site on Crystal River, Citrus County.

Mound on the Greenleaf Place, Crystal River, Citrus County.

MOUND NEAR PIPPEN'S LAKE, WALTON COUNTY.

On open hammock land bordering a small sheet of water known as Pippen's Lake and between it and the beach of Choctawhatchee bay, about midway between White and Stake points on the bay, was the remainder of a mound said to be on land belonging to the state. Previous diggers had made a circular hole centrally in the mound, having a diameter at the top of 10.5 feet. The mound, 35 feet in diameter, was 2.5 feet in height as to the part remaining. This was completely dug down by us.

No bones were found, but beginning about 3 feet in from the margin in that part of the mound included between east and northeast, lying near together, was the regular ceremonial deposit of earthenware to be expected in mounds along the Florida coast in this region, and continuing a considerable distance to the southward.

So far as we could determine, there were fifteen vessels or considerable parts of vessels, some badly broken, and, in addition, a quantity of fragments of various vessels, including the neck of a wide-mouthed water-bottle. These vessels, whole and fragmentary, lay in sand tinged slightly pink by admixture of iron ore and had with them two small sheets of mica. They are all of yellow ware, all small or of moderate size and each, so far as determinable, has the mortuary perforation of the base. A number of commonplace forms are undecorated or bear slight pinched, punctate, or line decoration.

Vessel No. 7 (Plate XIII, Fig. 2) has on two opposite sides birds' heads modeled without detail, and on the other two sides incised decoration representing tails and wings, the designs being practically the same.

Vessel No. 9, shown in Fig. 12.

FIG. 12.—Vessel No. 9.   Mound near Pippen's Lake.   (Height 6.25 inches.)

Vessel No. 13.   This bowl, otherwise undecorated, has, around the opening, a novel and artistic arrangement in relief consisting of two fillets, the ends of each placed one above and one below that of the fillet opposed to it (Fig. 13).

MOUNDS IN BIG HAMMOCK, WALTON COUNTY.

In Big Hammock, which is about midway on the northern side of Choctawhatchee bay, all on property of Mr. Lee H. Jernigan, of Freeport, Florida, were three small rises in woods, some distance apart, most difficult to find without the services of a guide.

MOUND A.   Near the west side of Mullet creek, about 400 yards from the beach, was a rise about circular, 18 inches in height, having a diameter of 25 feet. It was dug completely away by us, nothing being met beyond a few sherds.

FIG. 13.—Vessel No. 13.   Mound near Pippen's Lake.   (Length 6.75 inches.)

MOUND B.   A rise about one foot in height, circular, having a diameter of about 36 feet.   The rise was entirely dug away, yielding nothing except a few sherds, a very rude arrowhead or knife, and a small deposit of oyster shells, perhaps the debris of a meal eaten while the mound was building.

MOUND C.   About 18 inches in height, with diameters 22 feet and 35 feet. The mound was completely demolished.   In several places were fragments of skulls and of long-bones badly decayed.   About one foot below fragments belonging to a skull, was a celt probably of igneous rock, 7.8 inches in length.

In a pile near the center of the mound were parts of four vessels, but not nearly the complement of any one.   Three had borne the small check stamp and one had been undecorated.

MOUND D.   This rise, on property belonging to Mr. D. S. Sellars, of Bolton, Fla., also in Big Hammock, was at the terminus of a low ridge, making the dimensions of the artificial part of the rise somewhat hard to determine.   Probably a height of 2 feet and diameters of 42 feet and 60 feet would be approximately correct.

The eastern, and as it happened, the higher part of the mound, was entirely dug down by us, care being taken to keep the digging along undisturbed yellow sand where graves below the base could be detected, if present.   A single, small sherd was the only object encountered.

Mound near Basin Bayou, Walton County.

The mound near this bayou described in a previous report[1] was on the western side of the bayou, while the one in question lay to the eastern side in pine woods, the property of the R. E. L. McCaskill Co. of DeFuniak Springs, Fla.

Fig. 14.—Vessel of earthenware. Mound near Basin Bayou.   (Height 5.25 inches.)

This mound, 47 feet by 38 feet in diameter, had centrally an excavation 11 feet by 13 feet made previous to our visit.   The height of the mound, 2 feet 10 inches, no doubt had been affected to some extent by the excavation.

On the surface was a fragment of bone, apparently human, and other fragments, seemingly thrown out from the central hole, were found in our digging, which practically included the entire mound.   No undisturbed burials were encountered.

Fourteen feet in from the margin, on the base of the eastern part of the mound, were seven vessels, two in fragments, the others having portions missing.   Two are undecorated, three bear a rude complicated-stamp decoration encircling the rim, while two have interesting incised designs.   The decoration of one, a kind of jar (Fig. 14), is shown in diagram in Fig. 15.   The other vessel, of yellow ware, approaches in shape an inverted, truncated pyramid with

Fig. 15.—Decoration.   (One-half size.)

[1] "Certain Aboriginal Remains of the Northwest Florida Coast, Part I." Journ. Acad. Nat. Sci. Phila., vol. XI.

rounded corners, though the opening of the vessel representing the base of the pyramid is somewhat constricted.   There are four interesting designs, one on each side.   In spite of considerable ceremonial breakage, in one instance from

Fig. 16.—Vessel of earthenware.   Mound near Basin Bayou.   (Height 5.9 inches.)

the inside out, and the absence of some of the fragments, the designs on each pair of opposite sides being the same save for minor details, we are able to form a clear idea of the ornamentation.   One of the designs is shown on the vessel (Fig. 16), and the other in diagram (Fig. 17).   The square, flat base of this vessel was intact when found, as was that of the vessel previously described.

Near this ceremonial deposit was a small bowl, and in the southern part of the mound, together, were a small undecorated bowl and a vessel in many fragments, bearing a complicated stamp.

ABORIGINAL CEMETERY ON HOGTOWN BAYOU, WALTON COUNTY.[1]

In 1901, as we have stated, we carefully investigated the region bordering Perdido bay (the coast-boundary between Alabama and Florida), Pensacola

[1] Since our first visit to Hogtown bayou, that part of Washington county which then included the bayou has been added to Walton county.

57 JOURN. A. N. S. PHILA., VOL. XVI.

bay, Santa Rosa sound, Choctawhatchee bay, on the northwestern Florida[1] coast, publishing a report[2] of our work the same year, with full descriptions and numerous illustrations.

In our report (p. 496) we wrote as follows, describing certain shell deposits on Hogtown bayou,[3] Choctawhatchee bay:

"At Hogtown bayou are the principal shell deposits of Choctawhatchee bay, which are extensive, but in no wise comparable with those of the St. Johns river [Florida], or with many on the Florida east coast, or on parts of the west coast, farther south.

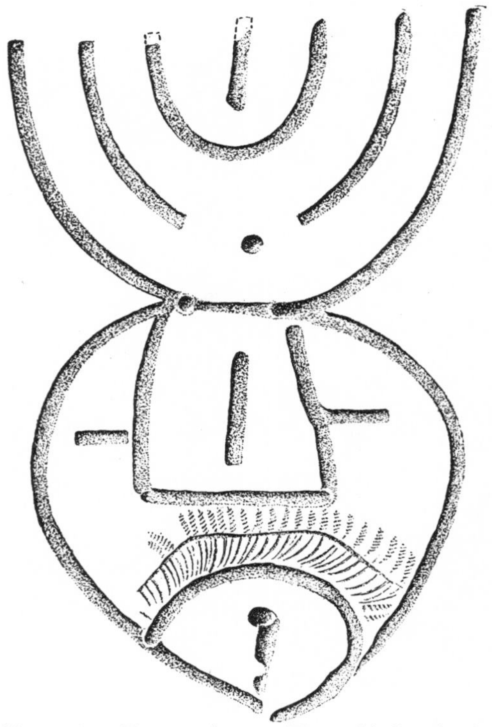

"It is our belief that a cemetery lies undiscovered at this place, as previous search by others has failed to locate a mound there, and careful investigation on our part availed only to find a small mound near the water's edge, about one mile up the bayou, on the south side."

At that time the region was comparatively wild, and information derived from inhabitants was difficult to obtain, while obviously an individual or members of an expedition could not spare unlimited time forcing a way through a wide extent of undergrowth in the hope of coming upon surface indications of an aboriginal cemetery.

FIG. 17.—Decoration.   (Two-thirds size.)

Since our first visit, however, there has been a considerable influx of settlers around the bayou, and on thick hammock[4] land, near Mack Bayou, a part of Hogtown bayou, on property the ownership of which we did not exactly determine, near but not immediately with the shell deposits, an aboriginal cemetery has been discovered and considerably dug into in a desultory way by residents and others.

The cemetery, consisting of various low rises of sand, near together, was first noted, we were told, through the presence of aboriginal pottery projecting above the surface.   The aboriginal cemetery near Point Washington, which we

[1] Except part of Perdido bay.

[2] "Certain Aboriginal Remains of the Northwest Florida Coast, Part I."   JOURN. ACAD. NAT. SCI. PHILA., vol. XI.

[3] Some now call it Santa Rosa bayou.

[4] Hammock land on which grow palmetto, oak, and other non-resinous woods, the term being used in contradistinction to pine woods, the prairie, the swamp, or the marsh.   The word is used by Captain Bernard Romans writing in the eighteenth century in his "A Concise Natural History of East and West Florida," New York, 1775.

dug out on our previous visit to this region, on Choctawhatchee bay, to the east-ward of this cemetery, originally had been come upon in this way.[1]   On our visit this season to the Hogtown bayou site we devoted seven working days, with six men to dig, to the investigation of the place.   The rises, as a rule riddled with small excavations and covered with fragments of pottery, were surrounded by us and completely dug through where indications from trial-holes and the use of the sounding rod justified it, yielding excellent results, though in addition to the previous wreckage we had to contend with adverse natural conditions.   The sand was very damp, water being reached at a depth of less than three feet during part of our visit, and at considerably less than that throughout the remaining part when high tides prevailed in the bay.   Consequently the earthenware, saturated with moisture, presented but little resistance to the roots with which the whole area was replete, including the permeating ones of the scrub palmetto found filling many of the vessels in solid masses.   These roots not only were direct agents in the wrecking[2] of much pottery, but were the cause of extensive breakage when our men were forced to cut through them with spades or with axes.

Although this site, as we shall see later, was post-Columbian all the pottery found by us in fragments on the surface or in the course of our investigation is purely aboriginal in every detail, and of the same class as is that found by us in our former investigation in the aboriginal cemeteries between Perdido and Choc-tawhatchee bays, inclusive.   The abundant decoration consists largely of com-binations of straight lines, of the scroll, and of animal elements (limbs, mouth, eyes, etc.), incised or trailed, and sometimes heads modeled in relief or in the round.   Considerable of the incised decoration, mainly from one of the rises, at the Hogtown bayou site, contains kaolin in the lines, the white clay presenting a pleasing contrast to the dark background of the ware.

As this ware is so extensively shown in our earlier report, it has not seemed necessary to illustrate it here.   Practically all of it has been presented by us to the Museum of the American Indian, Heye Foundation, New York City.

The ceremonial "killing" of the vessel, varying between a carefully drilled hole about the diameter of that of a lead pencil, and the knocking out of the entire base, was practised at this site, though some vessels, including several found over burials, had bases intact.   The mortuary perforation made in the base of vessels previous to the firing of the clay was not found.

That form of urn-burial,[3] namely, a bowl turned over a skull alone, or a skull having a few bones or fragments of bones with it (sometimes mere traces at this place, where moisture speeded decay), first described by us as occurring in this region, was abundantly represented here.   The proportion of such, however, among the unenclosed burials varied greatly in the different rises.

[1] "Certain Aboriginal Remains of the Northwest Florida Coast, Part I," page 472.

[2] A large bowl from this site, found by us in forty-nine fragments and subsequently put together, retains its pristine symmetry.   It has been presented by us to the U. S. National Museum.

[3] See our "Urn Burial," Handbook of American Indians.   Bul. 30, Part 2, Bur. Amer. Ethn.

The covering bowls ranged in diameter between 18 and 6.5 inches, the latter fitting the skull like a cap, though such small bowls were exceptional. However, a few even smaller were found inverted over traces of bones presumably of infants whose remains had almost decayed away. In fact no bones from this place were in a condition to permit their preservation entire.

The unenclosed burials at this site usually were only parts of the skeleton, decaying and broken, most often including what had been the skull. Some of these burials are described in detail in connection with the artifacts accompanying them.

The interments, at various depths, were surrounded by gray sand and sometimes extended into yellow sand which was the color of the undisturbed material of the site, except on the surface where the gray sand was found. Individual burials, however, were not distinctly marked, and it is likely the burials were made in groups, at times, at all events.

This cemetery distinctly had not been a dwelling-site in which interments had been made, as we sometimes see elsewhere, no midden debris being on the surface or in the sand, and the shells of the oyster denoting the use of this bivalve for food were, as we have said, at some distance from the burials.

With the unenclosed interments sometimes were artifacts, and also, occasionally with the urn-burials, in some cases under the bowls, and in other instances just outside the vessels. These accompanying artifacts included: glass beads with a number of burials; objects of iron or of steel, among which, in one instance, was a pair of scissors; shell beads; columellæ of marine univalves; rude shell implements; one shell ear ornament of the pin variety; thirteen celts, all wrought from imported rocks, between 2 inches and 8.5 inches in length; a graceful discoidal also of material foreign to Florida, 2.7 inches in diameter, slightly convex on each side, and having an even circumference permitting the object to roll in a direct course—doubtless a chungkee stone; four wrought stones in diameter from 1.6 inch to 2.6 inches, shaped like much truncated cones (save in three instances the upper side was somewhat convex), presenting, owing to the slanting surface of the periphery, a difficulty in keeping a straight line in rolling. Henry Timberlake in his "Memoirs" (p. 77) speaks of a game played with stones having beveled sides. One of these stones had on the upper side a pit in which perhaps nuts had been placed for cracking.

There was also a rude disc made from silicious material, most likely a pebble pecked into shape.

With the burials as a rule, were twenty-four lancepoints and arrowheads or knives, nearly all very rudely made, owing perhaps to the inferiority of the flint. In only one instance among them, we believe, can a projectile point be differentiated from an implement for incision.

With a burial lay a disc about 2.25 inches in diameter and 4 inches in thickness, approximately, which Doctor Keller has determined to be almost pure tin interiorly, having a sharply defined brownish-gray crust on the outside.[1] Also

---

[1] Curiously enough, this object has led to the discovery of a new salt of tin. Consult "A new

with bones was the object of earthenware shown in Fig. 18. This object cannot be a trowel used in the smoothing of earthenware, the presence of the knob precluding the idea. It most resembles a stopper for a bottle, but bottles in this region, when occasionally found, have wide mouths, so the question of identity remains an open one.

The following burials are worthy of description in detail, giving as they do a fair conception of the interments in general and showing how accompanying artifacts lay in relation to them.

Burial No. 2, fragments of bone, crowns of teeth of an adult. With these were two spearheads of flint, a celt, and the stopper-shaped object of earthen-ware already described.

Burial No. 3, a few fragments of long-bone and crowns of teeth, having a large bowl inverted over them. Also inverted, on the base of the larger vessel and covering the ceremonial hole in it, was a small bowl, crushed when found.

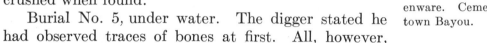

FIG. 18.—Object of earthenware. Cemetery on Hogtown Bayou. (Full size.)

Burial No. 5, under water. The digger stated he had observed traces of bones at first. All, however, had disappeared in the mingling of water and sand. With this presumable burial was a deposit of eight spearheads or arrowheads and knives, some broken; a small, quartz discoidal; nodules and chips of flint; bits of sandstone for hones.

Burial No. 10, fragments of a skull covered by an inverted bowl on which was another bowl inverted. An ear-plug of shell was with the fragments of bone.

Burial No. 17, part of a large, inverted bowl, under which no bones were found, though doubtless, as no sign of disturbance was present, some had been there. This substitution of a part for the whole, in this connection, was repeatedly noted by us here under conditions precluding any idea of previous disturbance, which might account for the fragmentary condition of the bowl.

On and over the basal perforation of the large fragment was a small, undecorated pot, erect. Beneath the fragment were two inverted vessels of medium size in which no trace of bones remained. Outside the large fragment, together, were an inverted vessel containing only clear sand, and a six-pointed platter, a form, we believe, not found outside this Florida coast region.

Burial No. 19, small fragments of bone from a femur, pelvis, etc., not covered by a bowl but accompanied by a small, undecorated pot containing two large shell beads. Near this pot were a small bowl and another small pot.

Burial No. 33, fragments of bone, some having belonged to a skull, covered by a large part of a vessel inverted and by a number of other fragments not belonging to the vessel of which the principal fragment was a part. Surmounting this deposit of broken pottery was an entire bowl inverted.

Oxychloride of Tin," by Harry F. Keller. *Journal of the American Chemical Society*, vol. XXXIX, No. 11, November, 1917, p. 2354 *et seq.*

Burial No. 36, an inverted bowl only 5.5 inches in diameter, covering a single remaining fragment of bone.

Burial No. 39, immediately below another urn-burial and probably interred at the same time with it, was a large, inverted fragment of a bowl covering parts of a skull and of a clavicle. Partly under the large fragment and extending beyond it were a number of parts of other vessels, together.

Burial No. 45, remains of a bunched burial, having fragments of three skulls and other bones. Associated with these were a quantity of discoidal shell beads, a pair of shears greatly rusted, and a bell of brass, resembling our sleigh-bells, possibly a hawk-bell, though seemingly large for such a purpose.

Burial No. 47, a bowl inverted over a skull. In contact with this bowl on one side, also inverted and apparently an additional contribution, was a six-pointed platter.

Burial No. 63, fragments of a vessel over a skull with which were two lance-points of sheet-copper, each 4.5 inches in length, lying evenly one upon the other. The points of these objects are so rounded that they hardly can have served for use in war, and may have been ceremonial. Moreover, the length of one side of each has, near the margin, a row of small indentations, and the stems, one of which is rounded, the other rectangular, have, respectively, one and two per-forations, indicating that the objects may have served as pendants. With them was a tubular bead of glass. Near, and probably with, this burial were a small celt, and three arrowheads or knives, of flint.

Burial No. 67, traces of bone having near them a vessel only 2 inches in diame-ter, and in a little pile: a tubular bead of silicious material, 1.7 inch in length; a similarly shaped one of red claystone, 1.4 inch in length; and two shell beads.

Burial No. 69, indications of a skull and long-bones, having with them two bottles, two small bowls, and another vessel, the bowls inverted, the others up-right.

Burial No. 91, a bowl inverted and having leaning against it two vessels, each on edge. Beneath the bowl was a jar also inverted, covering traces of bones and three shell beads.

Burial No. 97, a large bowl inverted over another, along side which was part of a bowl. These deposits below rested on a skull and fragments of other bones.

Burial No. 99 was about 3 feet from Burial No. 97. It consisted of a bowl inverted over fragments of bone not including a skull, and the remainder of the bowl of which part was found with Burial No. 97. This half with Burial No. 99, however, covered no human remains, so far as we could determine. We con-sider this discovery of two parts of the bowl, each placed with a different burial, to be a very interesting feature.

Burial No. 111, an inverted bowl, imperforate, covering a skull.

Burial No. 112, a bowl, imperforate and inverted immediately below Burial No. 111. Resting on its upturned base was the skull belonging to that burial. Beneath this bowl (Burial No. 112) were traces of a skull. These two burials presumably had been made at the same time.

Below Burial No. 112 was still another bowl, crushed (as were so many at this cemetery, though we have not felt it necessary to specify each case), probably covering a third burial, but this bowl being under water, the question could not be determined where bones were so decayed.

MOUND NEAR MACK BAYOU, WALTON COUNTY.

About one-eighth mile east of Mack bayou, on the shore of Hogtown bayou, was a mound of yellow sand, on property belonging to Dr. Charles E. Cessna, of Oak Park, Ill.

This mound, about 2.5 feet in height and 28 feet in diameter, in which a hole about 3 feet square had been dug centrally previous to our coming, was practically demolished by us.

Thirty-two inches down, somewhat in from the margin, in sand considerably darker than that of the mound, forming a kind of deposit 18 inches by 3 feet and from 2 to 3 inches in thickness, was a pendant of ferruginous claystone, about 3.5 inches in length, flat on three sides, convex on one of the major sides. The hole for suspension shows signs of wear on one side, as by a cord. No bones were with this object, though presumably a burial had caused the discoloration of the sand.

On the center of the base of the mound (not reached by the previous digging) was a bar-amulet of chloritic schist, also in dark sand in which no bones remained.

An imperfect arrowhead or knife, of flint, and a hone of sandstone, apart, lay in the yellow sand of the mound.

MOUND NEAR PHILIP'S INLET, BAY COUNTY.

On hammock land, the property of Judge Ira A. Hutchinson, of Chipley, Fla., was a mound about 300 yards in from the Gulf beach and about one-half mile northwest from Philip's Inlet. This mound, circular as to base, had a diameter of 45 feet. The height was difficult to determine, as the mound had been dug into centrally to a considerable extent, and the sand thrown out, covered with growth, resembled a part of the mound. Probably originally the altitude was between 4 and 4.5 feet. While several small trenches had been dug into the mound prior to our coming, the eastern part of it was intact. All this eastern part, all the central part including much surrounding the previous excavation, and most of the rest of the mound were dug down by us.

Two burials only were encountered, 8 feet and 7 feet in from the margin, respectively, both near the pottery deposit to be described later. One burial consisted of a few decaying fragments of bones; the other was a small bunched burial badly decayed, having with it two celts which, like two other hatchets found apart from burials in this mound, are seemingly of eruptive rock. These varied between 5.5 and 8 inches in length.

Also two arrowheads of flint and some bits of mica were found separately.

On the base, near together, in the central part of the mound, were two deposits of clamshells (*Rangia cuneata nasuta*), each consisting of about a quart.

The pottery deposit commenced at the margin of the east northeastern to the east southeastern part of the mound, and continued in about to its center, though in greatly diminishing quantity.   A few whole vessels had been put in (all having the mutilation of the base), but parts of vessels and deposits of fragments of various vessels mixed together predominated.   In decoration the small check stamp and the complicated stamp are represented, while one small vessel has a rather faint, incised design.   Two sherds of the same vessel, which had borne an interesting incised decoration, were found a considerable distance apart.   A small bowl has a kind of meander design incised and punctate.

Fig. 19.—Vessel of earthenware.   Mound near West Bay Creek.   (Height 5.25 inches.)

MOUND NEAR WEST BAY CREEK, BAY COUNTY.

On hammock land belonging to Mr. Linzey Buchanan, living on the place, was a mound about one-half mile east northeast from the union of West Bay creek with the extremity of West bay, a part of St. Andrews bay, and about one hundred yards in from the shore of the bay.

The mound, about 2 feet high and 25 feet in diameter, was dug out by us except some marginal parts, no burials being found, though doubtless some formerly there had decayed away.

Beginning near the margin of the eastern part of the mound and extending about 8 feet in, near the surface, was a deposit of pottery consisting of two whole vessels, small and undecorated, one being without the basal perforation, and fragments belonging to various other vessels, a mixture in which, in no instance, were found materials for a complete reconstruction.

Among the fragments were represented the small check stamp and the complicated stamp.

A number of parts of a vessel, found considerably separated, when put together proved to have belonged to a most interesting vessel on which, in relief, had been representations of four duck heads (Fig. 19). Unfortunately not sufficient of this vessel was found to furnish a basis for a complete restoration of the extreme upper part. The base is intact, the breaking and scattering presumably fulfilling the ceremony.

Several low mounds in pine woods in this region were explored without discovery of bones or of artifacts.

MOUNDS IN BROCK HAMMOCK, BAY[1] COUNTY.

A small mound in Brock Hammock, about 3 miles southerly from West Bay P. O., is described by us in a former report.[2] Near this mound, on hammock land belonging to the West Bay Naval Stores and Lumber Co., St. Andrews, Fla., were two low rises, a short distance apart.

Careful search with trial-holes unearthed dwelling-site debris, shells, fish-bones, sherds, etc. In one was a skeleton partly flexed to the right.

MOUND WEST OF BURNT MILL CREEK,[3] BAY COUNTY.

In pine woods belonging to the Sale-Davis Co., Southport, Fla., was a mound about one-quarter mile west of Burnt Mill creek and one mile from its mouth, approximately. This mound, about 2.5 feet in height from the outside and 3 feet from base to summit, had a basal diameter of 45 feet.

All the eastern part of the mound and also considerable on each side of it (in which latter digging nothing was found), as well as all the central portion, were dug out.

On the base near the center was an inconsiderable deposit of human bones

[1] That part of St. Andrews bay in which these mounds are was included in Washington county at the time of our visit in 1902.

[2] *Op. cit.*, p. 140.

[3] In our 1902 report two mounds on the opposite side of this creek are described, *op. cit.*, p. 140, *et seq.*

58 JOURN. A. N. S. PHILA., VOL. XVI.

cremated into small fragments.   Centrally were two bunched burials of limited size, and part of a skull alone.

Also near the center of the mound were bits of an ornament of sheet-copper and a fragment of human skull which the copper salt had preserved.   No other bones were near.   This affords an example of how skeletal remains may disappear, since but for the presence of the copper salt no trace of this burial would have remained.

Apart from burials were: a small celt of sedimentary rock; a thick sheet of mica; a mass of graphite, dark and soft, somewhat worked out, perhaps for paint.

Beginning at the eastern part of the mound, at the very margin, and continuing in about 8 feet was the ceremonial deposit of pottery, made up almost entirely of vessels that had been put in whole (though some were crushed when found) or having only minor parts missing through former breakage.   All these had the usual perforation knocked through the base.

Comparatively few fragments were with this deposit, which consisted of twenty-one vessels, without any deposits made up of miscellaneous bits of earthenware from various vessels, such as one often finds in this region.

A few thin sheets of mica, and at one place a deposit of charcoal about 1.5 foot by 2 feet, lay with the earthenware.

The following vessels from this mound merit special description:

Vessel No. 1.   A vessel of excellent ware bearing in relief an effigy of the head of a horned owl from which a small part of the beak is missing (Plate XIV). Deeply incised decoration is about the head; the wings, in relief, also have an incised design, while another, shown in diagram in Fig. 20, represents the tail.

Fig. 20.—Vessel No. 1.   Decoration.   (Two-thirds size.)

Vessel No. 2, in fragments, of which a number are missing, has been of the open-work variety, small portions having been excised in places around the upper part of its body.   In addition it has had an incised conventionalized representation of a rattlesnake, a most interesting design, from which, however, so much is missing that restoration is impossible.

Vessel No. 3, found broken but with all parts present, bears five deeply incised designs, three apparently representing the wings, and two the tails, of birds (Fig. 21).

FIG. 21.—Vessel No. 3.   Mound west of Burnt Mill Creek.   (Height 8 inches.)

SITE NEAR BEAR POINT, BAY COUNTY.

In our former report on this region[1] we describe a mound near Bear Point (then included in Washington county) which was dug by us, and speak, in addition, of a neighboring circular enclosure of shell.

Later, in the town of St. Andrew, not far from Bear Point, we found an aboriginal cemetery which was enclosed by a similar wall.[2]

In the hope that the Bear Point enclosure might also contain a cemetery, we visited the place again and carefully prodded all the area within the circular wall, but without success.   In addition, the three flat mounds at Bear Point,[3] pronounced domiciliary by us, were prodded over with the utmost care, without any tangible result, however.

[1] *Op. cit.*, p. 174, *et seq.*
[2] *Op. cit.*, p. 175.
[3] *Op. cit.*, p. 175.

Mound near Davis Point, Bay County.

About one mile northerly from Davis Point, on East bay, a part of St. Andrews bay, on property of Mrs. A. W. Kirven living nearby, was a mound on the verge of hammock[1] land, about 3 feet in height and 45 feet in diameter of its circular base.   Evidence of but little previous digging was apparent.

Fig. 22.—Vessel No. 1.   Mound near Davis Point.   (Height 6.25 inches.)

Having found with the aid of steel rods the pottery deposit where we expected it would be, we dug a trench at the eastern margin of the mound, carrying it some distance beyond the center.   This trench, 28 feet wide at the beginning, narrowed to a width of 12 feet at the end, its length being 30 feet.

The pottery deposit commenced almost due east in the margin of the mound, and continued in about 13 feet.   It was not a layer, being somewhat scattered, and, beginning with a number of miscellaneous sherds, continued composed of vessels sometimes in groups, sometimes separately, with numerous fragments associated   Seven feet from the margin of the mound the deposit was an equal

[1] It may be well to repeat that the hammock in southern United States bears the palmetto, the oak, and other woods, and the term is used in contradistinction to pine woods, the prairie, the marsh, and the swamp.

number of feet in width, at which it continued to the end, where it broadened about 2.5 feet additionally, apparently to join Burial No. 1, the first to be encountered in the digging.

The vessels, complete or nearly so as a rule, though some lay crushed to fragments, all, where it was determined, had the mortuary mutilation of the base.

About thirty-two nearly complete vessels were represented. On these but little decoration is apparent. With one exception, that on a large fragment, practically no incised design was encountered in the pottery of the mound. Two vessels have lines of punctate markings near the openings, and the small check-stamp, poorly done, is on several sherds.

Some vessels bear in places a complicated stamp decoration, faintly impressed, and, as a rule, not covering the entire body. Some clearer designs, however, appear on a few of the pottery fragments.

In form the vessels are generally commonplace and the workmanship displayed in their making leaves much to be desired.

In this eastern arm of St. Andrews bay, however, some fine examples of aboriginal earthenware were found at the time of our previous visit.

The following vessels from this place are worthy of special note:

Vessel No. 1, an effigy vessel of a rude description, having a human head in relief (Fig. 22).

Fig. 23.—Vessel No. 3.   Mound near Davis Point.   (Height 5.1 inches.)

Vessel No. 3 has a body composed of four lobes, above which is an upright neck about one inch in height (Fig. 23).   Traces of red pigment are apparent on two of the lobes and around the neck.

Vessel No. 4 has a body composed of two lobes.   Above the low neck appears a rude head of a bird, with prominent eyes.   Height 5.5 inches.

Vessel No. 5 has been a compartment vessel having three divisions in line, one of which unfortunately is absent.   Throughout our first visit to the northwest Florida coast numerous compartment vessels of various forms were found.

Seven burials, all badly decayed, were encountered in the digging, only one having an artifact in association.   Five were small bunched burials; each having a single skull; one consisted of a skull alone, and Burial No. 1, found 30 inches from the surface, at the northern limit of the pottery deposit, was a small, bunched burial having two skulls.   With it were a few oyster shells and a celt of volcanic rock, 8 inches in length.

Burial No. 2, the isolated skull, was at the end of the pottery deposit, nearer the center of the mound.   The remaining five burials lay apart from the deposit at some distance from it laterally, or beyond it in the mound.

About on the base of the mound was a small deposit of charcoal.   Two flat pebbles, one of which had been used as a hammer, and several fragments of marine shells, were included in the pottery deposit.

MOUND NEAR FARMDALE, BAY COUNTY.

About 2 miles due east from Farmdale, in pine woods bordering a small hammock just back of the bay shore, on property of Mr. S. M. Smith, of Auburn, Fla., was a mound about 2 feet high and 35 feet across the base.   A small excavation had been made in it prior to our coming.

A trench along the base, 35 feet wide at its beginning in the eastern margin of the mound, was carried by us 31 feet, passing through its center, gradually diminishing in width until at the end it was but 10 feet across.

About 6.5 feet east from the center commenced a deposit of charcoal of considerable size, the original limits of which, unfortunately, we could not determine, as the central digging, before referred to, had disturbed it.   Though the sand below the charcoal showed evidence of heat, there was not sufficient to induce us to believe that a fire had been maintained there, but rather to suppose that burning wood had been placed on the sand and covered.   Moreover, the charcoal was in large masses and no ashes accompanied it.

With the charcoal were a few fragments of calcined human bones.   Probably the greater part of the deposit had been removed by the early digging.

Near the charcoal and cremated remains were two lanceheads of flint, near together, one 3.9 inches in length, having lost a barb; the other a handsome piece 6.2 inches long.

About 18 inches down, 8 feet northwest from the center of the mound, were traces of bones, probably human.   No other burials were met by us in the mound, though fragments of bones thrown out by the previous digging were encountered.

At the margin of the mound was a small pot.   The deposit of earthenware scattered here and there, including eleven vessels, many whole or nearly so, and a number of unrelated sherds, continued to about the beginning of the charcoal deposit.

With the vessels were three shell drinking-cups, one in fragments, two sufficiently preserved, though much decayed, to show the basal perforation which also is present in all the vessels, one having even two holes knocked from the inside outward.

Six of the vessels are plain, while five have line or punctate decoration in simple designs. One, a rather striking piece, bears a modified scroll of parallel lines, carefully executed. The rim, rising obliquely, presents four equidistant corners (Fig. 24).

Fig. 24.—Vessel No. 1.   Mound near Farmdale.   (Height 5.25 inches.)

One sherd, part of a broken bowl, bears a decoration which, while not artistic, undoubtedly would be striking if entire. A kneeling male figure, 1.5 inch in height as it appears at present, has been modeled in high relief, the part including the belly standing out about 1.2 inch from the bowl. Unfortunately the head of the figure is missing.

A hone of fine-grained sandstone was found apart from burials.

MOUNDS NEAR CROOKED ISLAND, BAY COUNTY.

A mound included in Calhoun county at that time was dug into to a small extent by us in 1902, and is described in our report as the "Smaller Mound in

Hare Hammock."[1]   This mound, 3 feet in height and about 45 feet in diameter, was in an abandoned field, the property of Mr. E. E. Harrison, of Farmdale, Fla., and had been under cultivation.   It was about 400 yards north from the head of St. Andrews sound.   On one side of the mound was a depression caused by the removal of material for its making.   Numerous low shell deposits were nearby in the hammock.   It was completely dug down by us.

Thirteen burials, one a disturbance by recent digging, were encountered throughout the mound, the deepest 3 feet down, all very badly decayed.   Of the twelve burials found in place, two were of the flexed variety, the rest being small bunches of bones, parts of skeletons, or mere fragments of them.

Four burials, including one of the flexed kind, had no shells in association. Of the remaining eight, six lay with deposits of shells (*Busycon perversum* and *Fasciolaria*, mostly the former), not numerous enough to be called in layers, above and beside them.

Two having regular shell deposits in connection with them will be described in detail.

Burial No. 5, partly flexed on the left, lay beneath a shell deposit of irregular

FIG. 25.—Vessel of earthenware.   Mound near Crooked Island.   (Height 6 inches.)

[1] *Op. cit.*, p. 207, *et seq.*

outline, 5 feet 8 inches long by 3 feet 6 inches in width, and about 20 inches in thickness, approximately.   In line and in contact with the foregoing, extending in toward the center of the mound, was another deposit of shells, 4 feet 8 inches by 2 feet 7 inches, and of the same thickness as the other. From it, extending farther in, was a kind of arm, 2 feet 5 inches in length by 10 inches wide.   Beneath this deposit and the extension only a single fragment of a femur (Burial No. 6) was found, the rest of the skeleton probably having decayed away.

With a few of the burials were fragments of earthenware, some undecorated, some bearing a complicated stamp faintly impressed.

Apart from the burials were an undecorated pot and numerous sherds, mostly undecorated, some in little piles, also a very rude celt of sedimentary rock.

In level ground adjoining the eastern side of the mound, extending out a few feet from it were ten vessels, some having parts missing in addition to the ceremonial hole broken in the base. Three of these merit particular description:

A vessel of yellow ware having a globular body and an upright neck, around which is a decoration made by imprints of some implement (Fig. 25).

A bowl (Fig. 26), some parts of which were not recovered, bears an interesting

FIG. 26.—Vessel of earthenware.   Mound near Crooked Island.   (Diameter 9.1 inches.)

incised decoration including portrayal of a bird's head, inverted, on two opposite sides.   The designs between these heads vary somewhat and are represented in diagram, Fig. 27.

In Fig. 28 is shown a beautiful representation of a gourd in hard, smooth ware, bearing an incised decoration conferred with considerable care.   Unfortunately a small part of the stem end of the gourd is missing through an early fracture.

About 400 yards northwest by west from the mound just referred to was the fine mound in which such interesting earthenware vessels were found by us, described in our 1902 report[1] as the "Larger Mound in Hare Hammock."[2]

A small remainder of the western part of this mound, left by us at the time of our first visit owing to the presence of recent burials, was dug down by us, this season, the burials having been removed.

[1] *Op. cit.*, p. 197, *et seq.*

[2] It seems to be doubtful if the hammock in which this mound was situated ever bore this name, generally at all events.

59 JOURN. A. N. S. PHILA., VOL. XVI.

Six burials, badly decayed, some mere fragments, representing the bunched and the individual burial, were encountered on the base of the mound, all without artifacts and having above them no deposits of the *Busycon*[1] *pugilis*, such as

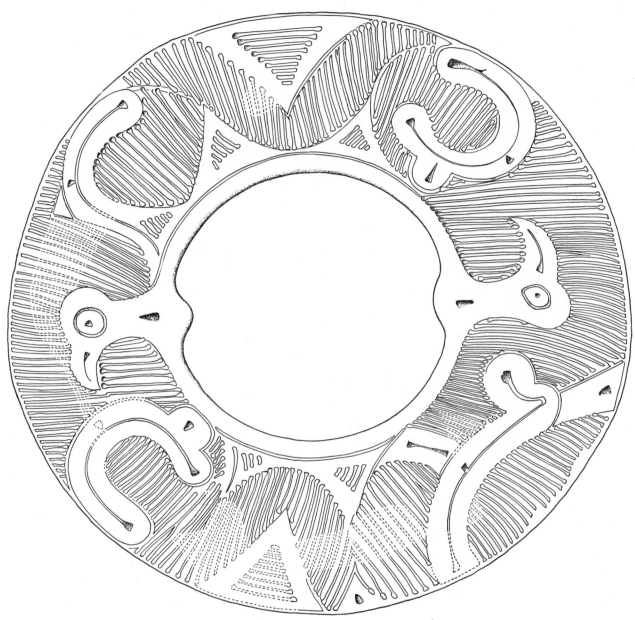

FIG. 27.—Decoration. (One-half size.)

were found with the burials in the other part of the mound at the time of our first visit.

A single undecorated bowl, somewhat broken in addition to the usual basal perforation, lay alone in the sand.

[1] At one time called *Fulgur*.

About 200 yards north by east from the mound is a dwelling-site about 2.5 feet in maximum height and 87 feet by 80 feet in diameter.   This site, largely sand, contained considerable shell deposits here and there and numerous fragments of earthenware, mostly of excellent quality, with other general dwelling-site refuse.   Trial-holes failed to come upon burials.

FIG. 28.—Vessel of earthenware.   Mound near Crooked Island.   (Height 4.1 inches.)

MOUND NEAR MICHAUX LOG LANDING, LIBERTY COUNTY.

This mound, on Apalachicola river, which could not be reached from the stream at the time of our former visit, owing to high water, is in woods on property of Messrs. L. E. and S. W. Michaux, living in the neighborhood, the mound being about a mile in a straight line in an easterly direction from Michaux Log Landing, which is about 8 miles by water and somewhat more than 4 miles by land, above Estiffanulga.

The mound, but little dug into before our coming, was about 3.5 feet in height, with diameters of 37 and 40 feet.   A converging trench 37 feet in width on the chord of the margin was carried through the center of the mound.

Fragments of pottery were found a little north of east, about 2 feet in from the margin, the deposit continuing in about 11 feet and consisting in the main of fifteen vessels having but few intervening sherds.   These vessels, whole or nearly entire as a rule, or if broken, having full or almost complete complement of fragments lying together, and probably accidentally crushed after interment and not broken and the parts ceremonially scattered, are commonplace in form. Some are without decoration; one bears the small check stamp; a number have the complicated stamp faintly impressed in various designs.   Incised decoration of poor quality is on one vessel and also on a single sherd.   All have the basal mortuary mutilation.

One vessel, almost cylindrical, bearing a complicated stamp, lacks the entire rim.   The part remaining has a diameter of 3.5 inches and is 8.5 inches in length.

Part of a quartz pebble, and a large barbed arrowhead of flint, were found apart from burials.

When our trench, which followed the base of the mound, was 18 inches deep, it came upon gray sand along the lower part, very compact and hard to dig, seemingly showing the effect of heat and having throughout particles of charcoal intermingled.   This hard material, throughout covered by about 1.5 foot of ordinary sand, was still present when our digging was discontinued beyond the center of the mound, and was then about 2 feet in thickness.   Presumably the entire nucleus of the mound consisted of this burnt sand.

The pottery latest found lay in this material, as did all the five burials encountered but one, none of these, however, being with the pottery.

Seven feet northeast from the center of the mound was a small deposit of calcined human bones.   The other bones, single skulls in three instances, and once a skull having remnants of long-bones near it, were badly decayed.

Mound near O. K. Landing, Calhoun County.

About one mile in from Apalachicola river, following the road from O. K. Landing, in woods, is a mound about 3.5 feet in height and 35 feet across the circular base.   Its ownership was not ascertained.   Evidence of previous digging in it to a limited extent was apparent.

The eastern part of this mound, dug out by us, yielded two burials represented by fragments of bone.   With one burial was a mass of galena, about the size of a fist of a child, pitted in several places as by use.

The pottery deposit consisted of various fragments showing, when decorated at all, the small check stamp, the complicated stamp, or incised designs of rudimentary character, with one exception, where somewhat better work is apparent.

There are also several undecorated bowls and another with encircling area about 2 inches in width beginning just below the rim, adorned with parallel ridges thrown into relief by trailing a tool with remittent pressure.   The usual mortuary hole knocked through the base has been duplicated through one side in this vessel.

A small lump of galena was found apart from any burial.

Mound near Rock Bluff Landing, Liberty County.

We found at this place but a remnant, a large trench having been put through the mound from east to west by others before our coming, who, in addition, had extended the trench to include all the central part of the mound.

The mound, on the slope of a hill, originally may have been about 4 feet in height and 45 feet in diameter. It was on property of Mr. Richard Lester, living nearby, and was about one mile east northeast in a straight line from Rock Bluff Landing on Apalachicola river.

Considerable of the eastern part of the mound remained beyond the trench, which also was shallow in the outer portions, passing over considerable of the pottery deposit.

Thirteen burials were found by us, all too decayed to give any idea as to form. These burials were exceptional for this region in that a number of them lay in the area of the pottery deposit and with one individually had been placed a pot, while with another was a quantity of shell beads. Evidence of the use of fire was present with several of the burials.

In sand thrown back by the former diggers was a delicately wrought arrowhead of flint, and a beautiful celt seemingly of eruptive rock, 7 inches long, tapering at one end almost to a point.

In the eastern part of the mound such pottery deposit as was found included vessels and parts of vessels bearing the check stamp, the complicated stamp, several with interesting incised designs, and one in fragments with some parts missing, since restored, having two parts roughly globular joined by a cylindrical portion in which are four excisions. Below the rim is a kind of collar, the upper surface of which shows trailed decoration, while beneath it is a series of vertical imprints made with a tool. A mortuary perforation has been knocked through the base (Plate XV).

One bowl from this mound has, instead of the basal perforation knocked out after the baking of the vessel, a hole carefully fashioned previous to the firing of the clay.

Mound near Hardnut Landing, Decatur County, Georgia.

About one-half mile southwest from Hardnut Landing, on the right-hand side of Flint river, going up, now in woods but said to have been in a cultivated field in former times, at present the property of Mr. Samuel White, of Mt. Pleasant, Fla., was a mound 65 feet in diameter and 2 feet 4 inches in height. The diameter no doubt had been increased by the plow at the expense of the height.

The mound was dug throughout by us with the exception of some marginal parts, near which no burial or artifact was found, and which perhaps had been spread by cultivation.

Twenty-one burials were encountered, all, with one exception, apart from the earthenware deposit in the mound, and having with them no object except a sheet of mica in one instance. Badly decayed and only in part remaining, they indicated the flexed burial so far as we could determine, with one exception, a bunch. Evidence of the use of fire was present with some, as, for example, Burial No. 1, which apparently had been on the back, the knees drawn up, a space that might be expected under such circumstances intervening between the remains of the lower extremities and remnants of teeth. Charcoal lay above where the head and trunk had been, but there was no evidence of heat on the surrounding clayey sand, of which the mound was composed.

Fig. 29.—Vessel of earthenware.   Mound near Hardnut Landing.   (Height 6.5 inches.)

Burial No. 8 lay alongside the pottery deposit.   Near this burial were charcoal and a fireplace.

A general mortuary deposit of earthenware began near the east by south part of the margin of the mound, extending in about 14 feet and including fragments of conch shells which probably had been drinking-cups.

Nearly all the vessels, few of which were entire or were even represented by full complements of parts, are of ordinary form, though of fairly good ware. Many are plain. In decoration the complicated stamp largely predominates. Several examples of uniform coating of red pigment were met, while the small check stamp and elementary incised decoration each are once represented. Part of a vessel that had borne a handsome, punctate design, skilfully wrought (recalling ware found by us on this river at the time of our first visit[1]), and a fragment belonging to it, lay many feet apart, thus further illustrating that the well-known ceremonial custom of breaking and scattering earthenware had obtained in this region in aboriginal times.

Two open-work vessels came from this mound, the more interesting having eight excised portions in the upper part of the body, just below the neck, which is somewhat flaring and bears a rather rude line and punctate decoration as shown in Fig. 29. Both receptacles have holes knocked through the base in addition to those excised from the body before the firing of the clay.

Two bowls each having the head of a bird as an ornament above the rim were found, and also part of a vessel that entire would be somewhat unusual, a large representation of the beak of a bird projecting from the body of the vessel, eyes being represented by perforations with countersunk margins.

Where determinable, basal perforations made after firing were noted in all the vessels from this mound.

Aboriginal Cemetery near Carrabelle, Franklin County.

About 1.5 mile north northeast from the town of Carrabelle, on the Gulf coast, is a low ridge (any elongated elevation, however slight, in this level territory is called a ridge) covered with scrub and scattered pine, having its eastern extremity almost enclosed by a small, shallow, fresh-water pond somewhat in the form of a horseshoe. This ridge is of white sand on the surface, darkened by vegetal deposit and the charcoal of fires that have spread over it. Below the white sand, which is from four inches to one foot in depth, is yellow sand of uniform shade.

For some reason not disclosed, a citizen of Carrabelle had selected this barren ridge as a likely spot to dig for treasure, and had prodded it over and put down numerous holes in it, the eastern end, where he came upon many fragments of aboriginal earthenware, being literally covered with his small excavations.

This seeker after buried treasure, not embittered by lack of success, sent us word that if we desired Indian pottery, we should search the ridge, adding how the locality could be reached.

A trench was dug by us longitudinally through that part of the eastern end of this ridge where the fragments of pottery had been thrown out and where many also had been found in place by our sounding rods.

Possibly some sherds were left by us outside of the part dug through, but

[1] "Mounds of the Lower Chattahoochee and Lower Flint Rivers." JOURN. ACAD. NAT. SCI. PHILA., vol. XIII, p. 454.

presumably they were few in number as the central part of this cemetery on the eastern end of the ridge was entirely cleared out, and there alone deposits of earthenware of any size were encountered.

The trench, 2 feet deep, was 85 feet in length and 41 feet across at the beginning, tapering to 12 feet at the end. Also, at the middle part of the northern side of the trench, an offset at right angles was dug 25 feet wide and extending a distance of 14 feet, in order to learn if deposits of any importance had been overlooked. This, however, was found not to be the case.

Deposits of earthenware in the central part of the cemetery, and scattered sherds in the outskirts, lay on the yellow sand or in it, none deeper than 20 inches from the surface.

There was no base-line at this cemetery, nor was there any admixture of white sand with the yellow sand when the deposits of earthenware were enclosed in the yellow sand. Hence one is left in doubt how the ware could have been deposited in holes made through the present surface layer of white sand, or, as an alternative, how yellow sand could have been piled on a surface to receive the pottery, for in that case a base-line of white sand would remain.

Fig. 30.—Vessel of earthenware.   Aboriginal cemetery near Carrabelle.   (Length 7 inches.)

If, however, the aborigines cleared away the surface layer of bleached sand before interring the earthenware, the conditions under which the pottery was found can be understod, though we are by no means sure that this is the correct solution of the question.

The deposits of pottery found centrally in the cemetery varied greatly in size and consisted usually of piles of mingled fragments of various earthenware vessels, among which it was impossible to find nearly the full complement of any. One exception to this rule, however, was a deposit consisting of all the fragments of a vessel having two compartments communicating at the base and resting on four feet. It bears a rude attempt at trailed decoration (Fig. 30). There are three ceremonial holes, one broken through the base and one near the bottom of the outer side of each compartment.

Three small bowls found separately, each having the ceremonial hole knocked through the base, were the only otherwise entire vessels found.

The earthenware from this place is yellow, fairly hard, and tempered with coarse sand. In form nearly all the ware had consisted of bowls and pots, some of the latter fairly large and having four feet.

The decoration is almost exclusively the imprint of the basket in which, evidently, the vessels had been made. A few sherds bear the check stamp, and several have interesting punctate designs applied with considerable symmetry. A selection of sherds from this place is shown in Fig. 31.

Fig. 31.—Fragments of earthenware vessels. Aboriginal cemetery near Carrabelle. (About two-thirds size.)

In the entire cemetery but two burials were found by us, each a small pocket of calcined fragments, probably of a single human skeleton thoroughly cremated. These lay in the pottery area, but not immediately with deposits, at depths respectively of 20 and 25 inches. It is barely possible that deeper burials escaped us since the cremated remains, like some of the pottery, lay in the yellow sand and gave no evidence of being graves, through intermixture of sands of different colors that could be followed down.

None of the pottery, however, as stated, was found at a depth greater than 20 inches, though determined prodding was done which would have discovered it at a considerably greater depth and it seems unlikely that burials would be much deeper than the mortuary offerings of pottery. It is most unlikely that this cemetery, with its very numerous deposits of earthenware fragments and of scattered sherds, was made for so limited a number of interments as were found by us or could have been displaced by the previous digger, whose work in the pottery area was, of course, much less than our own. Presumably many non-cremated skeletons had entirely decayed away, as they often do.

The result of our work at this cemetery was a disappointment, in view of the number of entire vessels and of others which, though broken, were represented by all or by most of their parts, found by us in previous seasons to the westward along the Florida coast.

Mound near Old Creek, Wakulla County.

In piney woods about one mile north northwest from the landing near the mouth of Old creek, on property the ownership of which was not determined, was a rather flat, circular mound about 2.5 feet high and 50 feet in diameter of base, composed of coarse sand.

A trench 39 feet wide was dug in from the eastern margin a distance of 27 feet, tapering at the end to a width of 22 feet.

From the margin scattered fragments of pottery were encountered, and at times three or four bits together, bearing the small check stamp, a complicated stamp, or some interesting line or punctate markings, when decorated. One fragment of a large vessel shows a loop-handle with three small knobs where the loop joins the rim. Most of the fragments are of coarse ware, tempered with sand or with fine gravel.

Eleven feet six inches in, at the southern side of the trench, one foot in depth, were remains of five vessels, half to three-quarters of each being present, all showing the basal perforation. All of these are of poor quality as to ware; four are undecorated.

Near these fragments was a small bunched burial including remains of one skull. This burial and a few fragments of a femur found near the margin were the only human remains met in the mound.

An upright bowl bearing a complicated stamp decoration was the only entire vessel encountered in the digging, which was not discontinued until long after the pottery deposit evidently had been exhausted.

MOUNDS IN BIRD HAMMOCK, WAKULLA COUNTY.

This site on the Nolan estate, under control of Mr. W. H. Walker, of Talla-hassee, Fla., was reached by us by landing on the west bank of Wakulla river, about two miles above the town of St. Marks, and walking inland approximately two miles in a westerly direction to Bird Hammock, over an old road used by turpentine workers.   The site includes two mounds between which are various low humps and ridges, all of artificial origin.

MOUND A.

Mound A, the northernmost of all, dug into superficially before our visit, was 8 feet 6 inches in height and 66 feet across its circular base.   The entire eastern half of the mound, and much in addition, was dug down by us.

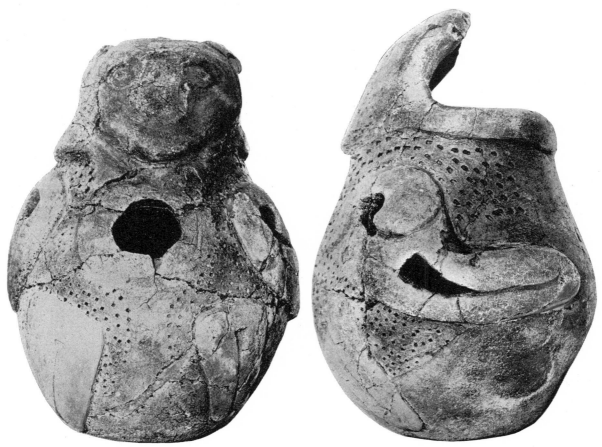

FIG. 32.—Vessel No. 8. Front view. Mound A, Bird Hammock. (Height 10.5 inches.)

FIG. 33.—Vessel No. 8.   Side view.

The pottery deposit, represented by sherds at first, extended almost from the margin to the center of the mound, largely in the eastern and southeastern parts. The deposit was made up mainly of fragments of parts of vessels and of undecorated ones when entire, and included in the way of decoration, the small check stamp, numerous examples of the complicated stamp, and some finely executed incised decoration, though unfortunately vessels thus adorned were not represented by a full complement of parts.

About 21 feet in was a small group of vessels, probably almost entire when interred though badly crushed when unearthed, including Vessels Nos. 8 and 9, of the "open-work" class. These, put together and restored as to missing parts by the Museum of the American Indian, Heye Foundation, New York City, are shown in Figs. 32, 33, 34, 35, 36 from photographs kindly furnished by that institution. The catalogue numbers are respectively $\frac{8}{2455}$ and $\frac{8}{2456}$.

FIG. 34.—Vessel No. 9.   Front view.   Mound A, Bird   FIG. 35.—Vessel No. 9.   Side view.
Hammock.   (Height 9.1 inches.)

While the pottery deposit extended along the base, such burials as were found, fifteen in number, were higher in the mound as a rule, though one burial, found near the margin, lay with the pottery deposit. These burials were mere fragments and traces of bones, save in one instance where not far from the center of the mound was a small deposit of calcined human remains.

In sand, away from burials, found separately, were a small sheet of mica and an oblong quartz pebble showing no sign of use as a hammer, though its shape was adaptable to such a purpose.

Mound B.

About 335 yards south southwest from Mound A was another, 5 feet 9 inches in height, having diameters north and south and east and west of 56 feet and 75 feet, respectively.   Two short ridges or causeways leading to the mound join it at about one-half its height, one on the southeast, one on the southwest, that on the southeast being 23 feet long by 24 feet wide, the other having a length of 38 feet and a width of 30 feet.   De-pressions in the soil around the mound and causeways showed whence the sand for their mak-ing had come.

A trench 75 feet across at the beginning, including the east-ern part of the mound, was car-ried in 21 feet, where it had a width of 38 feet.

There was no deposit of ear-thenware of the usual kind, in this mound, though sherds were fairly numerous at the margin of the excavation.   Here and there, at various depths, a few vessels of inferior ware, plain or coarsely decorated, lay singly, the first being encountered 8 feet in from

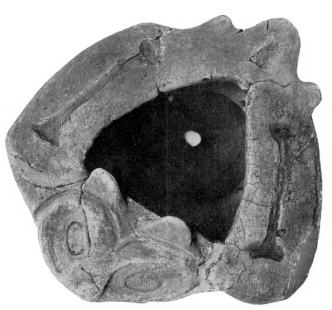

Fig. 36.—Vessel No. 9.   Top view.

the margin.   These vessels showed a basal perforation, as did all from this site where this feature was determinable.

The burials, fifteen in number, very badly decayed, hardly more than traces in some instances, lay at various depths in proximity to the earthenware vessels, but not immediately with them.   In one instance a bunched burial having re-mains of four skulls was indicated.

Contrary to the general rule in this region, some artifacts had been placed with the dead.

Burial No. 4, fragments of a skull, had with it a rude lancepoint of flint, 5.25 inches long; an arrowhead of inferior workmanship; two bits of flint, probably knives; a small sandstone hone.

Burial No. 5, parts of a skull, had in association three hones of sandstone, also three fragments partly worked, twenty-eight flakes and chippings, seven implements shaped in part, three portions of arrowheads and lanceheads, six rude arrowheads and knives, one lancehead 4 inches in length, all of flint.

Dissociated when found, though burials originally with them may have de-cayed away, were: nineteen quartz pebbles, more or less round; a hone of fine-grained ferruginous sandstone.

Curiously enough, though vessels and sherds in this mound were notably of inferior quality, one exception, a large fragment of good ware, bore an interesting design in red and in white pigment.

The humps, rises, and low ridges between the two mounds proved to be places of abode, the sand being black from admixture of organic matter and containing quantities of marine shells, mainly of the oyster, fish-bones, fragments of turtle-shell, bits of earthenware, etc., and being without burials so far as investigated.

SITE ON THE LEWIS PLACE, TAYLOR COUNTY.

In 1902 we visited the Aucilla river, lying anchored in the Gulf outside the river's mouth, not venturing in with our steamer owing to the number of limerocks present near the entrance and in the bed of the stream, but entering with the aid of bateaus.

This season the possession of a motor launch gave us access to sites farther up the stream than we had been able to visit before, our investigation, however including the Lewis Place (the owner, Mr. B. F. Lewis, residing there), described in our earlier report.[1]   At the time of our first visit the mound at this place, then in part occupied by a small stable with an enclosure, yielded very interesting pottery from the eastern part exclusively.   It was also found to contain, where dug into, burials unaccompanied by artifacts, but in many instances interred under masses of limerock of the kind found along the coast, beginning at St. Marks and continuing down a long distance.

This year, finding the stable and its appurtenance had been removed, we dug the mound completely.

Fifty-two burials were encountered, including the flexed, the bunch, skulls apart from the rest of the skeleton, all forms of burial in the main similar to those found at the time of our first visit, though the proportion of flexed burials encountered was much greater in the later investigation.

There were also several burials of parts of skeletons.

As noted before, some of the burials lay under masses of limerock, others being without them.

No burials of children were found at the first investigation, while five were unearthed at our second visit, including one of considerable interest.   In a shallow grave, 7 feet from the surface, about in the center of the beginning of the mound, as was clearly shown by the sharp curve of strata piled over it, but not exactly at the center of the base of the completed mound, was the skeleton of a child of about eight or ten years, lying under masses of limestone.   Apparently we have here the nucleus of an important mound 64 feet in diameter and 6.5 feet in height, containing only the skeleton of a child.

One burial (Number 15) closely flexed face down, knees to the right, had charcoal in association and one side of part of the pelvis colored with red pigment. The skull of this skeleton was the only one to be saved from this place.

[1] *Op. cit.*, p. 323, *et seq.*

At our first investigation no artifacts were found with the dead. At our second visit, however, while the absence of artifacts might still be considered a general rule, there were exceptions to it, as follows:

Burial No. 19, closely flexed to the right, had at the feet an undecorated bowl with the usual mutilation, and the remains of a shell drinking-cup.

Burial No. 35, flexed to the right in a shallow grave 7 feet below the summit-plateau, unaccompanied by masses of rock, had at the right knee a small arrowhead or knife, of flint, whose presence possibly was adventitious.

Burial No. 40, closely flexed to the left, having with it two other skulls and a few other bones, without masses of limestone, had a shell drinking-cup with the mortuary mutilation in the base.

About half a dozen parts of vessels in fragments, and piles of sherds from various vessels, were found singly in different parts of the mound in the second investigation, and a pot (Fig. 37), square in cross section, having a complicated

Fig. 37.—Vessel of earthenware.   Mound on the Lewis Place.   (Height 4.1 inches.)

stamp decoration around the neck, came from about where we discontinued our digging at the time of our first visit.

FIG. 38.—Image of earthenware.   Side view.

Near one side of our former digging and well in the eastern half of the mound, evidently belonging to the general deposit of earthenware found at the time of our first visit, near together, were numerous sherds and a number of vessels, some having parts missing.   These vessels were in the main uninteresting, being undecorated or having only bands of complicated-stamp decoration below the rim.   One, however, is worthy of particular description.

Beneath a mass of limerock lay a vessel in fragments, none of which was missing.   These parts, carefully put together, formed by far the best human effigy-vessel we have seen from the Florida coast, though this is not high praise, the region, as is well known, not furnishing remarkable vessels of this class. The image, shown in Plate XVI, and in profile in Fig. 38, wears a kind of breechclout and seems to be bearing a pack.   In the base is a hole made prior to the baking of the clay.

So far as determined, all vessels from this place, except the effigy, had been "killed" after the baking of the clay.

Eleven arrowheads and knives, of flint, and various parts of others, also numerous flakes of the same material, were found separately in the mound apart from burials.   Also dissociated were found: nearly half a banner-stone of the butterfly type, of quartz so highly polished that it reflects the rays of the sun; an awl of bone; several rude cutting implements or wasters of flint; a sheet of mica.

In all directions near the landing at the Lewis Place, the ground gives evidence of former aboriginal occupancy, and discovery of several objects of interest in it are reported by Mr. Lewis.

In a field near the Lewis home, a short distance from the landing, was a low rise of sand blackened by organic matter, in which trial-holes came upon thirteen closely flexed burials and three disturbances.

The absence of artifacts with the dead, so marked in the mound at this place, was noticeable also in the rise, though there was no general deposit of pottery or of masses of rock with the burials. There were, however, two exceptions. With a skeleton closely flexed to the right was a celt, seemingly of eruptive rock, 8 inches in length, a beautiful specimen carefully ground at the edge and rounded and dressed at the poll. This hatchet lay parallel to the skeleton at the outer side of the right forearm, the left forearm crossing the body to the implement. With another burial was an object of limestone, flat, almost oblong, without perforation, 3.5 inches in length, having a blunt edge.

A bone awl, a sheet of mica, a lancehead of flint, and several unfinished implements of the same material were found apart from human remains.

A number of other places visited by us on the Aucilla river proved to be only aboriginal dwelling-sites, yielding nothing of interest.

Mound near the Warrior River,[1] Taylor County.

About one mile up Warrior river are some frame buildings known as the Fish Camp. Following the road out from this Fish Camp for a mile approximately, one comes to a mound in sight from the road, in scrub growth and pine, about 4 feet high and 48 feet in diameter, said to be on railroad land.

Ten large trial-holes, all greatly extended, ultimately including much of the eastern part of the mound, came upon four burials.

Burial No. 1, fragments of a skull and of a humerus, near the center of the mound.

Burial No. 2, fragments of bones, having about 2 feet distant and perhaps not connected with them: a sheet of mica; three small, undecorated bowls; part of a compartment vessel having had at least four divisions, only two of which, however, remained entire.

Burial No. 3, a skull, femur, tibia, all in fragments and not in order.

Burial No. 4. Centrally, with a sheet of mica, was a skull near a small

[1] In 1902 we visited this river and investigated two fine mounds in its vicinity. *Op. cit.*, p. 331, *et seq.*

The Warrior river we believe to be the southernmost limit of the Florida coast where deposits of earthenware were interred in the eastern part of mounds for the dead in common. Farther down, individual deposits of artifacts, if any, are to be expected.

excavation made by some previous digger, which may have disturbed other parts of the burial.

Apart from human remains, separate, were three sheets of mica and a rude bowl.

No earthenware found in this mound had the basal perforation.

MOUNDS ON HOG ISLAND, LEVY COUNTY.

Hog island lies on the Gulf Coast between mouths of the Suwannee river. That part of the island on which the mounds are is owned jointly by Messrs. B. A. Thrasher, of Gainesville, Fla., and J. L. Robison, residing on the island.

The mounds are on hammock land about three-quarters of a mile northeast from the first high land up Hog Island creek, in connection with a considerable shell deposit.

One, on the shell ridge, having a diameter of 40 feet and a height of about 3 feet, had been dug into to some extent by others. Investigation by us indicated it to be of shell covered with sand to a depth of about one foot in which were burials, the bones badly broken, some by previous disturbance, others probably owing to roots of the scrub palmetto that were thickly interwoven in the mound.

Nearby was a somewhat larger mound that had been considerably dug into centrally. Seemingly it had been similar in construction to the smaller one, with the addition of some masses of limerock.

Another mound on Hog island was visited by us in 1902.[1]

MOUND IN CEDAR KEYS, LEVY COUNTY.

In the town of Cedar Keys, alongside the road bordering the water and near the great shell deposits there, is a mound on the property of Mr. W. H. Hale, of Cedar Keys. This mound, about 7 feet high and having diameters of 73 and 32 feet at present, is largely of sand, though some shell is found in it in places. On the side toward the water, however, Mr. Hale informed us, much shell was hauled away for use on the streets of the town, thus accounting in part, at least, for the difference in diameters. On the water side shell must have predominated in the mound.

Much digging by others before our coming had been done in the mound, and we were shown several celts and told of others and of quantities of shell beads, celts and beads all said to have been found superficially in the mound, or, in the case of some of the beads, to have been washed from it.

Three excavations, 6 by 3.5 feet, 6 by 4 feet, 16.5 by 6 feet, were put down by us centrally in the mound to its base, a depth of 7.5 feet, all passing through sand in the main, though shell was encountered in comparatively small quantities.

About one foot down fragments of human bones having belonged to different individuals were encountered, probably a recent disturbance.

[1] *Op. cit.*, p. 348.

Five feet down a graceful celt, apparently of sedimentary rock, was found, 7.5 inches in length.

About 8 inches below and 1.5 foot away from the celt was a thigh bone and part of the base of the skull of a child, accompanied by a number of shell beads.

Five feet eight inches down, apart from bones, was a fragment of an ornament of sheet-copper.

ABORIGINAL CEMETERY IN CEDAR KEYS, LEVY COUNTY.

In the town of Cedar Keys, in a large vacant lot, about 150 yards in a southerly direction from the principal school-house of the place, a large, brick edifice, is an aboriginal cemetery in ground on property controlled by Mr. W. R. Hodges, of Cedar Keys. This cemetery had been dug into to a considerable extent prior to our visit, though much of it remained intact. Remarkable stories of the discoveries made at the time of the earlier digging were related to us and of various interesting vessels accompanying the burials. So plentiful were the relics, it was said, that objects of interest actually had been dug out with spoons by persons living nearby. On our return to the North we addressed the Buffalo Society of Natural Sciences, of Buffalo, N. Y., for whom the work had been done, and most courteously were forwarded by Mr. W. L. Bryant, Director of the Society, who had participated in the investigation, details of the digging in the cemetery and, in addition, his illustrated catalogue, a very interesting book, and a large number of photographs of objects, mostly pottery, discovered in the cemetery.

FIG. 39.—Vessel of earthenware. Aboriginal cemetery, Cedar Keys. (One-half size.)

The pottery from this place presents no marked novelties though it includes specimens of the interesting incised decoration found in this region, an example of which, selected from the photographs sent by Mr. Bryant, is shown in Fig. 39. The projection of the decoration, also furnished by Mr. Bryant, appears in Fig. 40.

FIG. 40.—Projection of decoration.   Vessel of earthenware.   Cedar Keys.

An interesting pendant[1] of diorite, in the form of a duck's head, also was found by Mr. Bryant in this cemetery.

A portion of the unexplored part of the cemetery was dug through by us. In addition to several disturbances, aboriginal or recent, we came upon eleven skeletons, closely flexed, partly flexed, at full length, none having a skull in condition to save.   Eight of these burials lay in sand, each having above it a deposit of shells, indicating that interments had been made in graves which were then filled with shell almost to the surface.

At one part of the cemetery a general shell deposit was reached, which, however, was not apparent above the level.   Three burials were found in that portion of this shell deposit explored by us, and these lay entirely enclosed in shell.

FIG. 41.—Fragment of earthenware.   Aboriginal cemetery, Cedar Keys.   (About two-thirds size.)

[1] Our Academy possesses a cast of this rare piece, presented to it by the United States National Museum.

No artifacts lay with any of the burials found by us, and but two or three bits of pottery were encountered in all our digging. One of these, however, is of excellent ware, bearing an interesting incised decoration, perhaps including the well-known step design (Fig. 41).

It is evident from the results of the Buffalo Society's digging and from ours that the aborigines had used one part of the cemetery in which to place burials with mortuary deposits and had selected another part to make interments without such deposits.

ABORIGINAL SITE ON CRYSTAL RIVER, CITRUS COUNTY.

In two reports[1] we have described our investigation of the aboriginal site at the great shell mound[2] on the bank of Crystal river, about two miles from its union with the Gulf.

This site, belonging to Mr. and Mrs. Robert J. Knight, of Safety Harbor, Fla., through whose kindness all our investigations in it have been made, included as one of its component parts, as may be seen in our earlier and more complete reports on the subject, some flat ground and a rise culminating in a mound, all surrounded by an irregularly circular embankment of sand having a maximum height of about 6 feet.

The rise and the mound, entirely dug away by us during our former visits, yielded a rich harvest, consisting mainly of ornaments of copper, of shell and of stone, including several beautiful charm-stones of rock-crystal and one of amethystine quartz, a veritable gem.

In the enclosing embankment, dug into but to a very moderate extent at the time of our two previous investigations, a few burials, none accompanied by artifacts, were found.

The contrast between these burials in this respect and many of the burials in the mound and in the rise, was so marked that we determined, this season, to revisit the site in order to make a more thorough examination as to this subject.

In the southern portion of the embankment, which included its highest part, much digging was done, showing that part of the embankment to be constructed, not of white sand such as is found in the neighborhood, but of sand evidently darkened by admixture of organic matter and containing marine shells here and there, bits of pottery, other midden debris, and numerous scattered fragments of human bone, sometimes only a single one lying alone. Evidently the material for the embankment had been gathered from a dwelling-site.

Burials were numerous in the highest part of this southern portion of the embankment, nearly every trial-hole in it coming upon at least one burial (5 feet being the maximum depth), and were found here and there in other parts of it.

[1] "Certain Aboriginal Mounds of the Central Florida West-Coast." JOURN. ACAD. NAT. SCI. PHILA., vol. XII, pages 379–413. "Crystal River Revisited." JOURN. ACAD. NAT. SCI. PHILA., vol. XIII.

[2] Locally known as the Spanish mound, though, of course, Spaniards had no connection with its origin.

In all twenty-four interments were unearthed, and, in addition, many skeletons parts of which had been cut away in making other graves, and bones which seemingly had been gathered up and thrown in when the embankment was made.

The form of burial was either flexed or at full length on the back, some burials being under a layer of shell.

It was impossible to determine whether the interments had been made from the present surface of the embankment or in various stages of its construction, all the material being homogeneous. One burial extended about a foot into pure, white sand underlying the embankment. In this instance, at least, the interment had been made in a grave whose limits, however, we could not trace above the white sand.

With the burials were artifacts as follows:

Burial No. 5, extended on the back, had, at the outer side of the left shoulder, a small charmstone or pendant of shell.

Burial No. 6, partly flexed to the right, was accompanied by a shell tool, probably a chisel.

Burial No. 8, aboriginal disturbance, to some extent put in disorder by another burial. Under the upper part of the thorax was a drinking-cup made from a conch (*Busycon*), having a ceremonial hole knocked through the base. This cup was covered by a large fragment of pottery.

Burial No. 11, partly flexed to the left, had below it and crushed against it a skeleton of a child. Possibly at the neck of the adult, or perhaps belonging to the child, were four pendants of shell and one of limestone. With these was a gorget of shell having a large, central, circular excision and rude, incised, concentric circles on the convex side.

Under the knees of the adult was a mass of sand tinged with hematite, in which were bits of sandstone and two rude pendants, one seemingly of sedimentary rock, the other of limestone.

Burial No. 15, partly flexed to the right. Along the right forearm was an implement of bone.

Burial No. 21, partly flexed to the left, had at the thorax an arrowpoint of flint.

About 6 inches below an aboriginal disturbance were three rude limestone pendants and two of shell, all erect and grouped closely together, the grooved ends uppermost.

Apart from human remains were a number of pointed implements of bone, two shell pendants, a pendant of limestone, a shell drinking-cup having the mortuary mutilation, a gouge made from part of the body whorl of a marine shell, a number of columellæ of the conch wrought into chisels.

Considerable, though not exhaustive, digging in the remainder of the embankment, most of which was decidedly lower than the southern part, failed to come upon burials, as was the case in our previous search.

In consequence of this latest investigation at the Crystal River site it becomes evident that the few objects found, though showing that the burials in the embankment were not absolutely without mortuary deposits, nevertheless emphasize the discrepancy between the burials in the embankment and those found in the rise and in the mound as to abundance and quality of such deposits, and indicate that the embankment, or that part of it containing burials (the increased portion of the southern part), was made at a different time from that of the interments within the enclosure when a much greater liberality as to gifts to the dead prevailed.

About one mile in a northerly direction from the Spanish mound, on hammock land, is a mound of very irregular shape, having a large circumference and a maximum height of 6.5 feet. Extensive digging showed this mound to be of white sand without discoloration and indicated it to have belonged to the domiciliary class.

MOUND ON THE GREENLEAF PLACE, CITRUS COUNTY.

About 3.5 miles in a southerly direction from the town of Crystal River, on hammock land on the Greenleaf Place, now belonging to Mr. J. K. Eubanks, of Crystal River, is a mound that had been greatly dug into before our investigation of it. Human bones lay in many places on its surface. Its diameters were 70 feet and 50 feet. Its original height probably had been about 4 feet, though burials were found at a greater depth than that. Whether these burials lay in graves, however, it was impossible to determine, as there was no definite baseline, and the sand underlying the mound seemed the same as that of which the mound itself was composed.

Trial-holes put down in such parts as seemed to have escaped earlier digging reached eight burials, all of the bunched variety, some representing but a small part of a single skeleton. With one burial, however, were two skulls, while three were found with another.

Burial No. 5, consisting of fragments of two femora, one tibia, and one humerus, parts of a skull lying two feet from the rest of the burial, had with it one sheet of mica and a small quantity of sand tinted a pale pink with admixture of powdered hematite.

Two arrowpoints of flint were found separately apart from burials, and two charmstones, which probably had been together, lay in sand thrown out from one of our trial-holes. These objects are now in the Museum of the American Indian, Heye Foundation, and through the courtesy of Mr. George G. Heye they were submitted to Prof. Charles P. Berkey, of Columbia University, who kindly has determined their material as follows: Museum No. $\frac{8}{2054}$. Igneous, of basic composition, about that of basalt. Probably occurs as a dyke or sill and would be classified as a "trap" or diabase.

Museum No. $\frac{8}{2055}$. Metamorphic sediment. Exact composition obscure, but very complex. May have been associated closely with such rock as the other sample. Would be classified as a "graywacke" (which is a species of metamorphosed, very impure, grayish green sandstone).

Aboriginal Sites near Golden Lake, Mississippi River. Site at Evadale, Mississippi County, Arkansas.

In the village of Evadale, about 2 miles in, following the road from Golden Lake Landing, on property of Mr. Peter Notgrass, Mr. M. J. Blackwell, lessee, both of Evadale, is a site on which is considerable midden debris. This site, a ridge in part covered by dwellings, has been, we were informed, in common with other sites near Golden Lake, prodded and dug by Crowfoot, the Indian, for the last twenty years.

After a careful examination of this place, in which four skeletons at length were found, all badly prodded and two having the skulls (and presumably accompanying earthenware) removed, we discontinued work, convinced that while the reputation of the place lingered, its pottery had departed. Our only discovery with the remains was an imperfect vessel of commonplace form.

Several other sites near Evadale, kindly put at our disposal by Mr. Notgrass, were not investigated by us, as they had shared the attentions of Crowfoot, and doubtless of others, equally with the one visited by us.

Site near Bassett, Mississippi County, Arkansas.

On property belonging to Mr. Charles M. Bell, living nearby at Bassett, Ark., is an aboriginal dwelling-site about 4 miles inland from Golden Lake Landing, reported to have been thoroughly searched by wielders of the prodding iron, including the indefatigable Crowfoot.

We were courteously permitted to dig in a spacious enclosure in front of the dwelling on the property occupied by Mr. A. S. Catching, Mr. Bell's son-in-law, which had been refused to Crowfoot, though some digging had been done in it by members of Mr. Bell's family.

Seven hours' digging with four men yielded six skeletons from this enclosure and one from a field behind the house. These burials consisted of five adults extended on the back, and two children, the deepest 3 feet 8 inches down.

Burial No. 1, a child, having at the left shoulder an undecorated bottle and a bowl with rude animal head and conventional tail on opposite sides.

Burial No. 2, adult. At the right forearm were an undecorated bowl, and a bottle having in relief, surrounding the base of the neck, a symbol so well known on the pottery of this part of Arkansas and figured by Holmes[1] and by us in various publications.

A fine bracket-shaped ear-plug of shell, having a perforation at the end of the shank to aid in attaching it, lay in place at each side of the skull.

Across the lower part of the thorax lay an object of elk antler, about 10 inches

[1] William H. Holmes. 20th Ann. Rep. Bur. Amer. Ethn., Plate XIII f.

in length. This object, which has been carefully smoothed, has a perforation near the proximal end, through which apparently a pin of bone or of antler, has been, a part remaining filling the perforation.   This interesting object, submitted by us to a high authority who, it was hoped, might determine its former use, was lost in transit by the express company.

Burial No. 3, adult, having shell beads at the neck, some as large as the end of a human finger, had near the skull an undecorated bottle and two broken mussel-shells lying near it.

Burial No. 4, adult.   At the left humerus were fragments of mussel-shells and a small sandstone hone; over the left shoulder was an undecorated bottle.

Burial No. 5, adult, had been discovered by prodding previous to our coming, and the skull, presumably with accompanying pottery, had been removed.

Burial No. 6, a child.

Burial No. 7, an adult, the skull of which was saved.   Above the skull was a pile of fragments of a bottle which had borne in relief a symbol similar to the one to which reference has been made in connection with Burial No. 2.   These fragments evidently had been tossed in when the skull, which showed evidence of prodding, had been dug down to by some pot-hunter who, finding the vessel badly broken, had not cared to take it away.   It has been cemented together, with some restoration, and with everything found at this place except the object of antler, has been presented by us to the Royal Ethnographical Museum, Stockholm, Sweden.

Mounds near Transylvania, East Carroll Parish, Louisiana.

About 2 miles in from the Mississippi and in sight from the railroad station at Transylvania, on the extensive property of Messrs. Helgason Brothers (T. A. and E. B. Helgason) of Vicksburg, Mississippi, is a group of four mounds and two humps, of clay, all near together, as shown on the plan (Fig. 42) from a survey made by Dr. M. G. Miller at the time of our visit, the humps doubtless remainders of mounds once somewhat larger.

The mounds, evidently at one time of the usual domiciliary shape found in southern United States (quadrangular with spacious flat tops) are now of very irregular outline through trampling of cattle and mules, wash of rain, and erosion of the basal parts in periods of flood in earlier times, though of late, we were informed, the land on which the mounds are, being somewhat higher than the surrounding terrain, has been but little affected when the levee has given way.

The extensive wash of water to which the mounds have been subjected, while destroying their symmetry, has been an aid to investigation, inner parts formerly now being superficial, and gullies and channels, some as much as 8 feet in depth, having been cut in places along the sides.

A careful search over exposed parts showed a few fragments of human bones on Mound C (see plan), and here and there on the group small bits of earthenware almost invariably undecorated and resembling the somewhat inferior ware of

62 JOURN. A. N. S. PHILA. VOL., XVI.

vessels intended for culinary purposes. Also on Mound C and elsewhere were numerous small masses of burnt clay, some evidently from wattle-and-daub erections destroyed by fire, as they bore imprints of reeds or of twigs.

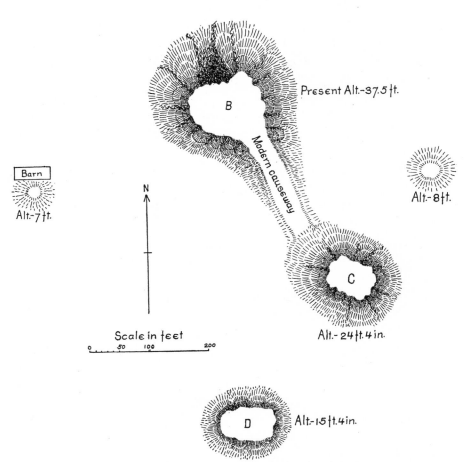

FIG. 42.—Plan of mounds. Transylvania, La.

There is no history of the discovery of any Indian relics in plowing on this place, and boys living on it knew nothing of arrowheads of flint, so numerous on some aboriginal sites. Doubtless, however, fifty years ago prehistoric objects were plentiful enough here on the surface and in the furrows.

In 1911 we visited the Transylvania group of mounds and were much impressed with the height of one (Mound B). On our return (the winter of 1917) to survey the site, the members of the party who had seen the mound before were nonplussed to find it of much more modest proportions than they had supposed it to be, and were far from flattered at their apparent inability to estimate heights.

Later, however, Mr. J. A. Helgason, son of one of the owners of the estate, informed us that in 1912 a force of men and teams ordinarily used in work on the levees, had been transferred to Mound B, whose height had been reduced thereby about 20 feet to supply material to construct a causeway leading from the ground to the present top of the mound, to enable stock to reach the summit in case of serious overflow from the river, the sides of the mound having become almost perpendicular through wash of rain. Incidentally Mr. Helgason said that some pottery in fragments had been found during the work.

In but two of the mounds was there considerable area of summit plateau intact, namely on Mound D, where the clay had an unpromising appearance and where trial-holes were unsuccessful, and on Mound C, where the soil was dark in shade and was interspersed with small masses of clay reddened by fire to a depth ranging between 3 and 4 feet.

Here three burials were found, all reached by one trial-hole, one flexed and two extended on the back, the flexed burial having two vessels in association. One, a bowl of excellent black ware having a small, flat, circular base, bears an incised decoration of fair execution. This bowl lay inverted over another, of inferior ware, having scanty, incised lines by way of ornament.

The upper bowl, only an average example of the excellent pottery of the lower Mississippi valley, which at its best includes specimens excelling in quality of ware, in grace of form, and in beauty of incised decoration, has been presented to the Museum of the American Indian, Heye Foundation, New York City.

2

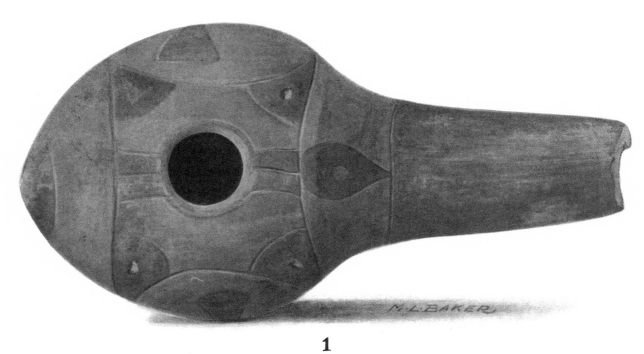

1

1. MOUND ON THE McLANEY PLACE, VESSEL OF EARTHENWARE. (FULL SIZE.)

2. MOUND NEAR PIPPEN'S LAKE, VESSEL NO. 7. (FULL SIZE.)

MOUND WEST OF BURNT MILL CREEK, VESSEL NO. 1.   (FULL SIZE.)

MOUND NEAR ROCK BLUFF LANDING, VESSEL OF EARTHENWARE. (FULL SIZE.)

MOUND ON THE LEWIS PLACE, EFFIGY OF EARTHENWARE.   (FULL SIZE.)

Index

INTRODUCTION: CLARENCE B. MOORE'S WORK IN
NORTHWEST FLORDIA, 1901–1918

(David S. Brose and Nancy Marie White)

shell middens, 6, 13
Shoemake's Landing, 7
site formation processes, noted by C. B. Moore, 9
site names. *See* archaeological sites, names
Smith, Betty A., 11
Smith, Bruce D., 1
Smith, Hale G., 10, 12
Smithsonian Institution, 1, 9; Museum of the American Indian, 11; River Basin Survey Program, 10
South Carolina ceramics, 8
Southeastern Ceremonial Complex, 4
Southern Cult. *See* Southeastern Ceremonial Complex
Sowell mound, 5
Spanish artifacts, 4, 12
St. Andrews Bay, 4, 5, 12
Sterling, Matthew, 8
Sternberg, 4
Stoltman, James B., 3, 8
Strong, Duncan, 9
Swift Creek: archaeological culture, vii, 7; ceramics, 7, 12

Tampa Bay, 5, 8
Tarpon Springs, 3
tax records, used to relocate sites, 8
Texas archaeology, 8
Thomas, Cyrus, 1–2, 4, 9
Thomas, Prentice, 13
Tick Island, 1
treasure hunting, 7, 11

Tucker site, 6
Twelfth Annual Report of the Bureau of Ethnology, 1, 4

United States Army Corps of Engineers, 10
University of Florida, 10
University of South Florida, 6, 11, 13
University of West Florida, 11
urn burial complex, 4, 8

Walker, S. T., 1, 4
Walter F. George Dam and Reservoir, 10
Walthall, John A., 10
Walton's Camp. *See* Fort Walton Temple Mound
Wanamaker's, 3
Wardle, Harriet Newell, 2
Warrior River mounds, 6
Wauchope, Robert, 4
Weeden Island: archaeological culture, vii, 6–8, 12; ceramics, 6, 7, 8, 12
Weeden Island site, 8
West Bay Post Office site, 6
White, Nancy Marie, 10, 11, 12, 14
Willey, Gordon R., 1, 2, 3, 8–9, 11, 12, 13; Smithsonian publication on Florida archaeology, 9, 13
Woodbury, Richard, 9
World War I. *See* Great War for Civilization
World War II, 8

Yale University, 10
Yent site, 6
Yon site, 6, 16

Index

Dwelling-site, near Hall's upper landing, 437

Ear-plugs
    of copper, 238, 307
    of copper and silver, 226; probably of aboriginal make, 226
    of shell, 53, 470, 471, 506
    overlaid with copper, 219
Earthenware, 362, 363, 364, 365, 366, 367, 368, 369, 370, 371, 372, 373, 374, 375, 376, 377, 378, 379, 380, 381, 382, 383, 384, 385, 390, 391, 392, 393, 394, 395, 396, 397, 398, 399, 403, 404, 405, 406, 407, 408, 410, 411
    broken and scattered throughout mounds, 133
    ceremonial deposits of, 415, 417, 418, 426, 430, 439, 441
    character of, 56, 92, 122
    deposits of
        in eastern parts of mounds, 355, 448, 453, 455, 456, 458, 459, 461, 463, 466, 474, 475, 476, 478, 488, 493
        in masses of blackened sand, 355
    of Florida west-coast, purely aboriginal, 353
    pipe, biconical, 452
    platters, six-pointed, 471, 472
    stopper-shaped object, 471
Econfenee river, mounds near, 332
Effigy-vessel, 390, 391, 404, 415, 419, 420, 423, 426
    of human form, 83, 149, 150, 151, 181, 203, 204, 251, 299, 336, 404, 498
    of owl, 476
    with relief of human head, 479
    representing grub-worm, 224
Eleven Mile Point, mound at, 216
Elk-antler, object of, with burial, 506
Enclosed burial, one example of, 113, 122
Engraved decoration on bottle, 87, 88
Eskimo burial customs, 447 (n. 3)
Estiffanulga, mound near, 386
Evadale, Ark., site at, 506
Excised, or "openwork," vessels, 448, 476, 487, 489, 494
Excised ware, northernmost occurrence of, 420
Excisions in pottery vessels, 415, 419, 420, 423
Eye-design on pottery, 439

Fanning's bayou, mound near, 154
Farmdale, mound near, 480
Feather-symbol, 420, 422, 423
Feet on vessels, 441
Fewkes, J. W., on ancient burial customs of Mimbres Valley, N.M., 448 (unnumbered footnote)
Finger-rings

of glass, 99
    made from "seabean," 284
Fireplace near burial in mound, 488
Fish, gorget of shell in shape of, 271
Fish-head, bowl decorated with, 382
Fish hook of bone, 366, 367
Five-pointed dish, 85, 369
Flattening of skulls
    among the Choctaws, 99
    caused by binding on bags of sand, 170
Flint River, its course, 415
Fractured femur, 222, 283
Frog-shaped vessel, 72, 73

Galena, 418, 441, 457, 486
    ball of, 92
    beads of, 259
Glass beads, 367
Glue-pot, aboriginal, 234
Golden Lake, Ark., aboriginal sites near, 506
Goodson's fishcamp, mound near, 347
Gorget
    of bison bone, 227
    of brass, 438
    of ferruginous sand-stone, 200
    of shell, 504; in shape of fish, 271
Gotier Hammock, mound in, 212
Gouge wrought from body whorl of a shell, 504
Gourd, imitation in pottery, 461
Gourd beautifully represented in earthenware, 483
Gourd shaped vessel, 81, 108
Graphite, mass of, perhaps used for paint, 476
Graveyard Point, mound near, 61
Greenleaf Place, mound on, 505
Green Point, mound near, 251
Grub-worm, effigy of, in earthenware, 224

Hair-pins of shell, 277
Hall mound, 284
Hand, open, on earthenware vessel, 224, 225
Handles of vessels, bird-head, which rattle, 183, 301, 329, 331
Hardnut Landing, Ga., mound near, 487
Hare Hammock
    larger mound in, 199
    smaller mound in, 209
Hatchets, double-bladed, 235
Hawkes, E. W., on Eskimo burial customs, 447 (n. 3)
Head, human, finely modeled effigy of, 302, 305
Heads of animals, effigies of, as handles of vessels, 56, 114, 117, 120
Hematite, sand colored with, 152, 227, 232, 241, 279, 286, 322, 340, 348, 402